Jumbos and Jackasses

Jumbos and Jackasses

A Popular History of the Political Wars

By

EDWIN P. HOYT, JR.

Doubleday & Company, Inc.
Garden City, New York
1960

Library of Congress Catalog Card Number 60–9480

To my wife, Olga Gruhzit Hoyt, who did a very great deal of the basic research for this book.

Preface

This is the story of the two major American political parties, their leaders, and the issues over which they fought in twenty-five presidential campaigns. Some of the issues were in the party platforms, some were found in the character of the men who ran. Some of the issues were brave and important. Some were insignificant or even dishonest. Some of the men were heroic, some were statesmen, and some were simpletons or gullible fools. None of the men who ran for President was an outright scoundrel. Every one of them who was elected surpassed his own previous record for statesmanship—even the weakest of the lot, Warren Gamaliel Harding.

Throughout the century under discussion (1860–1960) American elections have been a two-party affair, with the single exception of the 1912 elections in which the Bull Moose, Theodore Roosevelt, polled more votes than his Republican enemy and erstwhile friend, William Howard Taft. Lesser parties, such as the Greenback in 1878, and the Populists in the '90s, played important parts. They are mentioned here as their part was often important, and on balance they brought a succession of new ideas to the body politic—ideas the big parties did not hesitate to pirate.

The story of American politics is the story of the give and take of the Republican and Democratic parties, and it begins in 1860. That is the year in which the two faced each other squarely, uncluttered with the blurry edges of Know-Nothingism, Whigism, or Barnburning. A purist might demand that the campaign of 1856 be included, but that campaign was developmental; it had none of the elements of greatness that the campaign of 1860 exhibited. The Republican party was too young and untried in 1856; Abraham Lincoln was still unconverted to Republicanism in that year, and called himself a Whig.

A century has passed since that campaign, but the end of the century, surprisingly, finds the Democratic party uncomfortably close to the same split condition it found itself in in 1860. The biggest issue then, as now, is race, whether it be complicated by the economic factors of slavery, as in 1860, or the social factors of ingrained prejudice, as a hundred years later. The end of that century, sadly, finds the Republican party neither so brash nor so brave as the Republican party of 1860, although a good deal wiser.

The symbols of the two parties, the braying jackass and the jumbo elephant, were invented by one man, cartoonist Thomas Nast, who also dipped his pen in acid and drew an elongated, mangy tiger that was to haunt New York's Tammany Hall.

Nast was a worshiper at the feet of Ulysses Simpson Grant and extolled Grant's virtues to the skies in his cartoons in *Harper's Weekly* during the '70s, even after the Whisky Ring and other incontrovertible bits of larceny were unearthed. One of Nast's great cartoons, with the jumbo and jackass as motif, rose out of the Democratic New York *Herald*'s cry of "Caesarism" against Grant in 1873. Nast sat down and drew a cartoon that depicted an ass, which was Democracy's newspaper editor Bennett, cloaked in the skin of a lion (Caesarism), stampeding a group of animals, including the elephant, labeled as the Republican party.

Contents

1

In the beginning it was a nation led by revolutionaries, and we should never forget that. These men, who first dissented, then rebelled to save themselves from prison or hanging, were of many different types. The ascendant type was the aristocrat, typified by George Washington and Thomas Jefferson. These were the men of action and lands and leisure. But there were other types: the nervous-fingered writer Thomas Paine, the shrewd but placid burgher Benjamin Franklin, the wild-eyed silversmith Paul Revere. And the types, themselves, became confused. Alexander Hamilton, a brilliant bastard from the Antilles, became the epitome of the aristocracy; Jefferson, the true aristocrat, became the symbol of states' rights and the common man.

The times were violent and these were violent men. Political dissent was more restrained than now, for to call a man or his party "traitor" invited sudden death at the end of a rapier or looking down a gun barrel.

At first the revolutionaries concentrated on survival. Then, as their little nation was welded together, they found room for argument on national rather than regional questions. The first election, in 1789, was non-partisan. But by 1793, Thomas Jefferson had resigned as Secretary of State to devote his efforts to the cause of the new Republican party. In 1796, Jefferson ran against John Adams, who represented the Federalists the central-government advocates. Adams received 71 electoral votes. Jefferson, second in the field with 68 votes, was elected Vice-President. Then, in 1800, Jefferson was elected President and the Republicans (fathers of the Democrats of today) began a quarter century of rule. The two parties deteriorated and by 1828 had really disappeared. In that year John Quincy Adams ran for the National Republican party, a strong federal-government party, and

Andrew Jackson ran as a Democratic Republican—an advocate of economic and political equality. After Jackson's victory the name of the party was shortened to Democrat.

The opposition formed the Whig party—named for Britain's Whigs —to oppose what they termed Jackson's highhandedness and in the next twenty years elected two military heroes to office: William Henry Harrison in 1840 and Zachary Taylor in 1848.

But in the 1850s all other issues paled beneath the black cloud of slavery. Slavery's rot tinged every corner of American life, from the stern kitchens of New England to the haciendas of Texas. For wrapped up in the word "slavery" were questions of money, of trade, of industry, of agriculture and markets, of sex and morals, of racism, of habit, and, above all, of religion and the dignity of humankind. Each side could and did quote the Bible to prove that God was on its side. Slavery, the all-encompassing issue, saturated the United States of America from border to border, and past, into the virgin lands of the unexplored West. Men who were Whigs or Democrats, merchants, farmers, or professionals, laborers or ne'er-do-wells— these men were suddenly separated by a gap that transcended all others. Were they for slavey or against it?

1. The House Divides

The special quiet of a weekend evening came early to the federal offices in Washington on Friday, April 20, 1860. Congress would reconvene on Monday, but it was apparent that government affairs would stand still during the week to come. More important business was at hand.

The omnibuses that ran along Pennsylvania Avenue between the Capitol and the White House were strangely empty. Busiest places in town that Friday afternoon were the southbound railroad station and the steamer depot on the Potomac. At both spots streams of carriages rolled noisily in and out of the entrances, depositing loads of eager and anxious politicians, hangers-on and wire-pullers, all headed for the eighth national convention of the Democratic party at Charleston, South Carolina.

As the trains and steamers moved southward through the softening dusk, their passengers bore the hopes and worries of the entire political community. The supporters of Senator Stephen A. Douglas of Illinois were jaunty and assured. President James Buchanan's few friends were tense and angry with the "Little Giant" for obstructing the presidential efforts to compromise the slavery issue in Kansas. The leaders of the southern cotton states were fearful and uncertain of their northern brethren, but determined to stand their ground for slavery.

And everywhere the nation watched and waited. Even the members of the ebullient young Republican party, a party less than ten years old, were to watch fretfully for the latest telegraphed reports from steaming Charleston.

Douglas was the front-runner of the Democrats, just as Senator William H. Seward was the leading candidate for the Republicans, who would convene in Chicago in less than a month.

A few days before, the whole issue of the campaign, the essence of the arguments between Republicans and Democrats and the intra-party differences of the Democrats themselves, had been aired in angry senatorial debate over the admission of Kansas to the Union.

Seward had said that in the South the laborer was regarded not as a person, but as capital, while in the free states, the laborer had the rights of "personality."

Seward charged the Democrats with trying to force Congress to protect slavery.

The Republicans had only one avowed policy: "The saving of the territories of the United States, if possible by constitutional and lawful means, from being homes for slavery and polygamy."

Douglas said the Democrats "stand by the Constitution as our fathers made it," that the Republicans "repudiated the Constitution." He was referring to the pro-slavery Dred Scott decision of the United States Supreme Court in 1857, a decision that had been as bitterly criticized by Republicans in the North as were the Court's school integration decisions by the Democrats of the South a century later.

The square little Illinois senator with the giant head reaffirmed an unblinking Democratic position: the American government was made *by* white men *for* white men and *no* others. He would not allow any Negro to vote or hold office, where he had the constitutional right to prevent it. As for slavery, he said it was the states' business, not his. He disagreed with his party's "cotton senators." They demanded protection for slavery—not *laissez faire*.

Here was the Democrats' strongest leader, a man of indomitable will, great courage, and vast political sagacity. Douglas did not agree with the southern intransigence on protection of slavery everywhere. That was to be the issue at Charleston.

Rumors flashed back and forth across Washington now. Some said Douglas was assured of nomination on the first ballot, others that President Buchanan's supporters had pledged $2,000,000 to sink the Little Giant; still others claimed a secret deal had already been made by Douglas's many enemies.

The senator from Illinois had earned the bitter enmity of the Administration and the distrust of the South. He was father of the Kansas-Nebraska Act. That law set up two territorial governments. The inhabitants of the half million square miles between Missouri and Canada were to determine whether they would be "free" or "slave." But in 1855 some 5000 southerners from Missouri invaded the Kansas polls to vote for a pro-slavery legislature. There were already sixteen free states in the Union, fifteen slave states. The South demanded the balance in states to maintain the balance in Congress. The bootleg Kansas legislature drafted a constitution—the Lecompton Constitution—that would have made Kansas a slave state, had it been accepted by Congress. Douglas swung his influence, and the vote in the House of Representatives went against the Lecompton Constitution. By 1860, outraged southerners were determined that Douglas's "squatter sovereignty" would be abandoned for a clear party declaration protecting slavery everywhere.

The Democrats of the "cotton South" were as gritty as the black smoke of the trains that streamed through the silent Virginia night. Those trains carried a mixed bag of North and South down through the green pine forests of North Carolina, into the apple and peach country, where the blossoms and wild flowers brought the fresh smell of spring into the smoky, crowded cars.

Less than thirty-six hours from the capital the tired, bleary, but excited politicians reached South Carolina and the ninety-degree heat wave that had already scorched the South's life-giving cotton and corn. The searing heat was a fitting greeting for the Democratic convention of 1860.

Charleston—the brightest light in America's crown of home-grown aristocracy—had become overnight a blazing amphitheater. Hour upon hour crowds buzzed around the railroad depot at the lower end of Chappel Street. Other swarms of men and women swirled along the wharves on the Cooper River, awaiting the majestic steamers from the North that bore new hundreds of passengers past Fort Sumter, then in to land.

Hackmen bellowed out their destinations: "Charleston Hotel!" "American Hotel!" "Passengers for the Pavillion Hotel!" "This way for the Mills House."

As the horses drew the cabs through the broad streets, the starched and crinolined residents retreated shudderingly from their verandas and balconies, behind lush green foliage that protected their gardens from public view. The sedate beauty of Charleston was punctured, for a moment, by the hurrah of politics but not yet by the bitter schism so soon to lay the nation by the throat, to entomb the Democratic party for a quarter of a century.

Primed for the struggle, arriving politicians found housing where they could, in attic and assembly hall. Hotel rooms rented for the outrageous price of $10 per night—seven or eight times normal—and regular lodgers were evacuated along with the best furniture from the finer rooms of the handsome hostelries in the city.

The hall of the St. Andrew's Society, on Broad Street, was headquarters for Mayor Fernando Wood of New York, one of the early arrivals. Leader of Tammany Hall (he had taken over in the mayoralty election in New York six months before), Mayor Wood had arrived by steamer on the nineteenth, to begin maneuvers he hoped would end in the seating of his "hard" pro-southern delegation at the convention, rather than the "soft" pro-Douglas delegation.

Wood's New York City did a great deal of business with the South and of all northern cities was by far the most sympathetic to the southern cause. Nor was New York the only state in which the sentiments of the Democracy were divided. Even Douglas's Illinois sent dissidents who professed common cause with the Democrats of the cotton states. The issue of slavery—an economic, social, moral, and emotional issue—had been steaming within the party for years. Now it was rolling to a boil.

The physical temperature continued in the nineties; the political thermometer rose steadily. On April 20, three days before the convention began, Douglas's supporters ensconced at the Hibernian Hall claimed 117 votes for their candidate; 152 would be a majority, 202 a two-thirds majority, as had been required by previous Democratic conventions.

The Douglas men were now predicting his nomination on the fourth ballot. A delegate from Alabama offered to bet anyone $10,000 that Douglas would carry every southern state if he were nominated —but this same delegate said he would not vote for Douglas himself. And the rest of his delegation, along with that of Mississippi, Florida, Arkansas, and Louisiana, were talking that night about bolting the convention unless they found the party platform totally acceptable, or a candidate met their demands for protection of slavery.

On the eve of the convention, April 22, the slavery issue's reverberations could be sensed even back in Washington. President Buchanan scoffed, said Douglas would not win eighty votes. Senator Robert M. T. Hunter of Virginia was the favorite southern candidate of the moment, but the name of Kentucky's John Breckinridge was heard more and more often in the smoky corridors of the hotels that lined Meeting Street. The course of the convention was still unclear. The issue would be fought over the platform or the candidate, but which would come first?

When the delegates convened at the stone-columned, spacious South Carolina Institute the next day, the Douglas men and the cotton-state delegates were agreed on one thing: the battle would be fought over the platform. But before the platform fight, first must come the skirmishes over seating rival delegations from the various states. The struggle began with New York.

Mayor Wood's "hard" faction was openly pro-southern and anti-Douglas. The upstate "soft" delegation stood rocklike for Douglas. The convention had to hear the evidence and decide which delegation was entitled to be seated, as truly representative of the New York State Democratic voters, since both groups claimed the honor. Each charged the other with everything short of mayhem and murder—but mostly with fraudulent conduct.

The credentials argument lasted three days. It was resolved when Mayor Wood's delegation was turned out in favor of the Douglas supporters from New York. The platform fight, meanwhile, had grown even hotter, and William L. Yancey, the slight, stern, but rousing orator from Alabama, made it clear there would be a slavery plank, a southern candidate, or schism. Here again, Douglas agreed with the cotton states. Unaware of the depths of southern feeling, the Douglas men were even willing to let the Deep South secede from the convention, for Douglas believed he could hold the upper South.

On April 25 the South Carolina Institute's big hall was loaded with tension. The visitors' galleries, half empty on the first day of the convention, were so crowded with ladies that the delegates, in a grand and sweeping gesture, admitted several hundred of them to the floor, amid cheers and good-natured laughter. The nomination of Douglas seemed only a matter of hours.

But in Washington a lonely and fretful President Buchanan remained unconvinced. The nominee would be James Guthrie of Kentucky, he said, or Breckinridge. Buchanan, discredited as he was with the majority Douglas faction of his party, had an insight into the bitterness of the South, a bitterness against Douglas that he shared.

After nearly four years of dodging the slavery issue and satisfying no one, the President had so little standing with the convention that while one delegate was reported to be carrying a letter in which

Buchanan declined the nomination, he was never called on to produce it; the name was never mentioned except in epithet.

Yet Buchanan's men worked hard—against Douglas.

Douglas, for his part, made his position clear in a wire to his men at Hibernian Hall. The Douglas supporters could accept the platform drafted four years before at Cincinnati, which endorsed "squatter sovereignty"; they were not to compromise on any plank, demanded by the South, if it would require Congress to protect slavery throughout the land. They could accept the Supreme Court's Dred Scott decision of 1857, which declared that a slave was personal property. But they could go not one step further.

Mississippi, Texas, Louisiana, Florida, Alabama, Georgia, and South Carolina were now primed to leave the convention.

On April 27 the Democrats debated the two opposing platforms. Both sides agreed on acquisition of Cuba, aid to the transcontinental railroad, protection of American citizens, native and foreign-born, at home and abroad. Both sides condemned state legislation that tried to subvert the federal fugitive slave law, under which all citizens had to return runaway slaves to their masters. But there the Democratic factions parted company. The slave states, joined by Oregon and California, said neither Congress nor any territorial legislature had the right to interfere with slavery. The Douglas men said only the Supreme Court had the right to decide these issues.

Laughter had disappeared in the South Carolina Institute. At the end of the ten-hour session of April 28, General Caleb Cushing of Massachusetts, the practiced and gentlemanly president of the convention, bedeviled by the shouting and catcalling of a hundred delegates, threatened to leave the chair. That night two members of the Ohio delegation threw plates at one another across the dining room of the Mills House, justifying Major Nickerson's fears for his furniture, and one drew a gun on the other. At the same hotel Colonel Craig, a delegate from Missouri, and a newspaperman named Longmore of the St. Louis *Republican* came to blows, but agreed to settle their differences in a duel on their return home.

Two days later the convention passed the northern platform, by a vote of 165 to 138, amid shouts of "swindle" from the southerners. William Yancey announced that his delegation was walking out. Alabama was followed by Mississippi, Louisiana, Florida, Arkansas, South Carolina, and Georgia. They called a convention of their own at 7 P.M. in Saint Andrew's Hall. There Alabama's Yancey spoke of principle and states' rights before a large audience. Ladies threw him bouquets on the stage as he defended the position of the cotton South.

Now that the most radical southerners were out of the way, the regular party convention could go back to work. But Douglas was not to have the nomination so easily. The delegates voted to retain the famous two-thirds rule, initiated by Andrew Jackson in 1832 when he called the first Democratic party convention together. The rule provided that two-thirds of all the votes in the convention must be given to a candidate, to nominate. A candidate must either be an all-out favorite, or his supporters must make deals with several other hopefuls. Under the conditions of 1860 no one could be nominated at this point. The cotton delegates had walked out but were still officially members of the convention. A candidate for the Democratic nomination had to secure 202 votes; yet there were only 250 votes in the convention. Douglas needed 80 per cent of the votes remaining. He led from the beginning, trailed by Hunter, Guthrie, and others. But on the fifty-seventh ballot Douglas still had only 151½ votes. It was obvious that no one could be nominated. The delegates adjourned, to try to patch up their differences with the South, then to meet again on June 18 at Baltimore.

Down the street the seceding cotton-state delegates had been joined by individual members of other delegations in the regular convention. Men from northern and western states joined in. New York's Mayor Wood, denied access to the main convention floor, looked in on the seceders' proceedings. But with matters so unsettled, the southerners adjourned too, agreed to meet in Richmond the second Monday in June, and invited delegates from all states that approved of an anti-squatter-sovereignty platform.

The Democrats went home dissatisfied, confused, and angry, and the aristocratic citizens of Charleston moved out onto their verandas and balconies again. The proprietor could now return his best furniture to the rooms of the Mills House. The happiest man in the city was probably the correspondent of Horace Greeley's arch-Republican New York *Tribune*, who had predicted, in the swelter of the opening moves, that "a pretty hot time may be confidently counted upon."

Less than a week later the new Constitutional Union party held its first, and last, convention. They met at the old First Presbyterian

Church in Baltimore, in a flag-draped hall dominated by a full-length portrait of George Washington, where Martin Van Buren had been nominated by the Democrats in 1835. The party deliberately did not adopt a platform, pledged itself only to support the Union, the Constitution, and the nation's laws. Delegates were mainly former Whigs, and members of the American party. They had come from every state and territory except Oregon and South Carolina, hoping to capitalize on the rupture in the Democratic party and the growing fear of the Republicans by the South.

It was a dull convention, marked more by evil weather than political brilliance. Sam Houston, incumbent governor and twice president of the Republic of Texas, was the front-runner for the Constitutional Union nomination as the convention opened. But on the second ballot on May 10 the laurels went to John Bell, an honored statesman from Tennessee who had been a Whig in his more virile days. The party's vice-presidential hopeful was Edward Everett of Massachusetts, who had already distinguished himself as congressman, ambassador, and president of Harvard College.

That second week in May also marked the twenty-seventh anniversary of William Lloyd Garrison's Anti-Slavery Society, prayerfully deliberating at the Cooper Union in New York.

Some Republicans claimed that the Republican party had been born in the abolitionist Anti-Slavery Society. These stalwarts compared the Republican platform of 1856 to the anti-slavery declaration signed on December 4, 1833, by representatives of ten northern states.

That week was also the twenty-fourth anniversary of the American Temperance Union, whose members celebrated the closing of five thousand drinking houses in New York City in the preceding twelve months.

"Whether the Republican or the Democratic party is in power makes no difference to us; the Rum party is always in power," the secretary, Dr. Marsh, told an enthusiastic but temperate crowd at the Puritan church in Union Square.

Both the Abolitionists and the temperance workers hitched their wagons to the star of the brash young Republican party. It was fitting enough, for the new party was a loose and spontaneous coalition of various interests. It was a party so heterogeneous, indeed, that credit for its establishment has been claimed by at least four different states, Wisconsin, Michigan, New Hampshire, and New York, and the origin of the name credited variously to the fifty-three men who met at Ripon, Wisconsin, in March 1854, to Horace Greeley, and to Joseph Medill, editor of the Chicago *Tribune*.

But whatever its origin of name or place, the party's purpose was unmistakable. It was a group of men brought together initially in the 1850s in indignation against the Kansas-Nebraska Act and the principle of "squatter sovereignty." The men who became Republicans were anti-slavery Democrats who had first become Free-Soilers, anti-slavery or Conscience Whigs, members of that strange secret society of a party, the Know-Nothings, Barnburner Democrats (named after a story about a Dutchman who went to the extreme of burning down his barn to get rid of rats), Abolitionists, teetotalers, and Germans. The party had no single major leader at the start, and the beliefs held in common, in the beginning, went little further than the non-extension of slavery.

By 1855 the party emerged as a force in American politics and that year in New York merged with the Whigs. Judge J. W. Culver of Brooklyn performed a mock marriage ceremony, uniting the widow Mrs. Whig and Mr. Republican. In the fall the Republicans elected their candidates for governor and lieutenant governor.

By 1856 the party was strong enough to put up a candidate for national office. It chose Colonel John C. Frémont. Frémont ran only fairly; Abraham Lincoln was so cautious about the party that, while he served as a presidential elector and spoke for Frémont, he avoided reference to himself or his fellows as "Republicans." It was a crusading party, and many of its founders and early leaders were extremists, of Puritan New England stock. Woodrow Wilson wrote that the party got its "radical and aggressive spirit from the Abolitionists whom it received without liking." Perhaps that is why the party did not appeal to Lincoln in the beginning. Abe Lincoln was a hardheaded politician, who had little use for the emotional outbursts of the Anti-Slavery Society and the other Abolitionists.

But by 1858, when he ran for the United States Senate against Stephen Douglas, Lincoln had joined his fortunes to those of the Republican party in Illinois. And by 1860 he was its acknowledged leader in the West. This was not as important as it might seem, since party strength was concentrated in the East. In the elections of 1858 the Republicans had carried local elections in every northern state but Indiana and Illinois. In the spring of 1860 even Douglas was a much more important man in his home state than was the gangling Abe Lincoln.

But as far as politics was concerned, Lincoln had one tremendous advantage: the convention was to be held in his political bailiwick.

Chicago, a lusty, rawboned, and windy city, was the perfect site for the Republican convention that year. By May 10, almost a week before the meetings, some 3000 politicians and their allies were in the city; by convention day the number swelled to an estimated 75,000 laughing, scheming, boisterous, and energetic temporary citizens who jammed the three dozen hotels to overflowing, paraded day and night, and amazed the citizens with their capacities for talk and whisky.

On the pleasant spring evening before the convention, a Democrat made so bold as to attempt a political speech for Douglas in front of the Tremont House. The good-natured crowd heckled and interrupted him ceaselessly, marveling at his courage and bad judgment at the same time. But finally, overcome by temper or stronger spirits, the sidewalk orator became quarrelsome, was finally arrested and hauled off by the police to contemplate his errors in quieter surroundings.

As the convention opened the name Seward led all others. William H. Seward, tempestuous, admirable, and long-hating; Seward, twice United States senator from New York, one-time governor, was at fifty-nine by far the most prominent leader of his party. In 1838, as a Whig, Seward had been elected governor of New York by a tremendous majority. In the early '50s he became one of the first to espouse the cause of the Free-Soil movement that proved to be of such importance in the formation of the Republican party. Seward had labored hard and long for the party. Now, at fifty-nine, his emissaries were arriving in Chicago to claim his reward, the presidential nomination.

Scores of delegations were pledged to Seward's cause. Among them were the delegates from "Bleeding Kansas," so much in the political eye for its citizens' fight against legalizing slavery in the territorial constitution. On April 12, at Lawrence, the state Republicans had instructed "five gentlemen" and "John P. Hattersheidt, German," to back Seward as the first choice of the people of Kansas.

Of course, there were other candidates, among them Judge

Edward Bates of Missouri, Senator Salmon P. Chase, who was later to be Secretary of the Treasury and still later Chief Justice of the Supreme Court, Pennsylvania's Senator Simon Cameron, and as a compromise candidate, Illinois' Abraham Lincoln. But Seward's name led all the rest among the 466 delegates. As the delegates were called to order, at noon on May 16, in the wooden "Wigwam" built for the convention, Seward's representatives needed only sixty more votes to assure his nomination. Thurlow Weed, the senator's chief strategist, was supremely confident. Even Seward's worst political enemy, *Tribune* editor Horace Greeley, admitted that the New Yorker's chances were too good for his liking.

Those last few hours before the convention opened, Thurlow Weed had been busy. On the morning of the arrival in Chicago of the Kansas delegates, Weed invited them into his parlor at the Richmond House. Pledged or not, he wanted to make sure of his men.

"We are facing a crisis," the New Yorker told the Kansans. "What this country will demand is a man of the highest order of executive ability . . . well known to the country and of large experience in national affairs . . . We think we have in Mr. Seward just the qualities the country will need . . . We expect to nominate him on the first ballot . . ."

But hardly had the delegates from the prairie country gotten back to their quarters at the Briggs House, when in walked the delegate from Oregon (by proxy), Horace Greeley, dressed in his famous light drab suit, blue eyes twinkling from a sturdy pink and white face, "like a well-to-do dairy farmer fresh from his clover field."

Greeley tossed his soft felt hat carelessly on the table and began to speak.

"I suppose they are telling you," he drawled, "that Seward is the be-all and the end-all of our existence as a party, our great statesman, our profound philosopher, our pillar of cloud by day, our pillar of fire by night. But I want to tell you boys that in spite of all this you couldn't elect Seward if you could nominate him. You must remember as things stand today we are a sectional party. We have no strength outside the North. Practically, we must have the entire North with us if we hope to win. Now, there are states of the North that cannot secure electoral votes enough to elect. So to name Seward is to invite defeat. He cannot carry New Jersey, Pennsylvania, Indiana, or Iowa, and I will bring you representative men from each of these states who will confirm what I say."

Greeley then proceeded to do just that. He brought Governor Andrew Curtin of Pennsylvania, Governor Henry S. Lane of Indiana, and Governor Samuel J. Kirkwood of Iowa.

"I am a Republican candidate for governor," said Curtin. "I could not win with Mr. Seward as our candidate." His two fellow governors expressed the same sentiments: Seward couldn't carry the key states.

But if Seward was not the man, who was? Greeley wanted Bates, had put out a circular two days before the convention opened, calling for Bates's nomination. The circular was a disaster for Bates; it lost him more support than it gained to have would-be kingmaker Greeley behind him.

Greeley, and the other easterners, didn't have too high an opinion of the fifty-one-year-old Lincoln. Not that they disliked him; they knew him as an adroit politician who had actually gotten more votes than Stephen A. Douglas in the Illinois senatorial election of 1858, even if Douglas was chosen to go to Washington by the deciding votes of Democratic holdovers in the legislature. They knew, too, that Lincoln had comported himself admirably in the series of debates on the slavery issue preceding the 1858 election. Even though the Lincoln-Douglas debates were highly technical, they had been widely reported, since they dealt with the important issue of the day and concerned that most widely known politician, Senator Douglas.

And Lincoln's Cooper Union speech of February 27, 1860, had been widely publicized. It was reprinted, in English and German, by Greeley's *Tribune* for sale as a Republican campaign document along with Seward's words about the "irrepressible conflict" between slavery and freedom.

Yet the eastern Republicans discounted Lincoln for his lack of experience. He had served a term in Congress, but he had not distinguished himself.

That made no difference to the Republicans of the West and the border states. Lincoln went into the convention with the firm support of the Chicago *Tribune*. His campaign manager, the mammoth Judge David Davis, was as seasoned and wily as any candidate could desire. Lincoln was a westerner. The West wanted him.

As the convention went into its preliminaries Davis began to chop quietly at the roots of Seward support. On May 17, Davis was laboring behind the scenes as the delegates settled the question of seating southern Republicans, a question that arose because of the intense feeling against slavery. The southerners were seated. The party adopted a seventeen-plank platform that declared for the Union, for states' rights, against the Lecompton Constitution that would have turned Kansas over to slavery. But they voted for admission of Kansas as a state, knowing that anti-slave citizens were in the majority. The Democrats were lambasted for the corruption and extravagance in Buchanan's administration. The platform also showed early pro-business leanings in a pledge to support high tariffs. It favored government land grants for homesteads in the West, support for the railroad to the Pacific, and equal rights for the foreign born, an important plank in the Republican platform since many party members came from the ranks of the jingoist Know-Nothing party that had tried to suppress those rights. The Republicans came out solidly against legalizing slavery in any territories of the United States, and against the Dred Scott decision.

The platform resolved so quickly and so enthusiastically, the convention then turned to selection of a candidate. Had the tally sheets for the balloting been ready, it is quite probable that Seward would have been the candidate, nominated on the second day of the convention. But the sheets were not ready, and a request to adjourn was accepted, starting a busy and sleepless night for the Lincoln men. Judge Davis sent Cassius M. Clay of Kentucky and a group of thirty mountain men to visit the Kansans, a key delegation because of the territory's martyrdom. Clay was a model of the Kentucky colonel, dressed in a faultless suit and sparkling linen. He was handsome, cultured, and fascinating, and his keen eyes swept the room as he spoke:

"Gentlemen," he said, "we are from the South and we want you to know that the South is preparing for war. If the man that you nominate at this convention should be elected on the platform you have already adopted, the South will attempt the destruction of this Union . . . You must give us a leader at this time who will inspire our confidence and our courage . . . We have such a man—a man who we will follow to the end. We want your help. We want you to name Abraham Lincoln . . ."

Clay made the same speech to delegates from key states. He was followed by the more reasoned arguments of Governor Lane, of Indiana, a state the Republicans had to carry, along with Illinois, Pennsylvania, and New Jersey.

The Lincoln men made deals all night long. Some of these deals, such as the offer of a cabinet post to Pennsylvania's Cameron, were later to haunt the Republican candidate. For the moment that was unimportant. The deals were successful, and on the third ballot on May 18, Lincoln was nominated. A few hours later on a second ballot, Senator Hannibal Hamlin of Maine was chosen as his running mate.

Then bands of Republican volunteers—the Wide-Awakes—paraded far into the night, their way lighted by the eerie flames of 2000 blazing tar barrels set along the streets. The Germans, who had secured their platform plank of equality, staged their own parade in honor of the candidate, and bonfires and rump political sessions flamed on a half-dozen street corners, in front of the Tremont House, the Metropolitan Hotel, and the Wigwam convention site.

The next day, May 19, convention president George Ashmun and the chairmen of the state delegations made the trip to Springfield to inform Lincoln officially of his nomination. He had been told, of course, on the day before, and had been serenaded at home by the Young America band. When the crowd demanded a speech, he noted quietly that he did not suppose all this fuss was in honor of Lincoln the private citizen but of the Lincoln the representative of a great political party.

He was right. Across the country, from west to east, the Republicans were shocked at the nomination of Lincoln.

In Albany, on hearing the news, the Republicans first refused to believe Seward was not their candidate. But by nine o'clock that night State and Broadway were jammed with men intently discussing the curious chain of events, by eleven the party organization had managed a fireworks display, and later the newspapers reported State Street was a "perfect sea of fire" from burning tar barrels that lit up the milling, parading mob.

In Chicago, the Michigan delegation, which had been solid for Seward, nevertheless planned to take the campaign trail home. Governor Austin Blair told his men to forget their disappointment and go to work; so early on the nineteenth, they set off in a special Michigan Central train, decorated with bunting, large portraits of Lincoln, and campaign slogans and mottoes. The governor telegraphed ahead to assure good turnouts, and the train stopped at all the big towns from Niles to Detroit. The crowds emerged, all right, to hear and cheer the governor, but during the entire day not one crowd offered a cheer for the presidential candidate.

"Lincoln?" asked the Republican man on the street. "Abe Lincoln of Illinois? Who's he?"

But in Washington, Senator Stephen A. Douglas received the news very thoughtfully indeed. Abe Lincoln—he told intimates—was the strongest candidate the Republicans could have nominated.

2

The issue was half resolved now. The South knew what it had to face. If the Republicans, by and large, were really convinced that the South could be backed down, they would have to learn the hard way. Lincoln was not so foolish as some of his partisans, but to the South he was the Black Republican personified, and there was no temper in the cotton states for sober consideration of the man's merits.

Outside the Republican party Lincoln's virtues were almost unknown. His spotty political record gave little promise. But in Washington it was a different story. . . .

2. Explosion

Senator Douglas worried. The Democratic problem seemed more serious than ever. The Democrats could not count on the enemies Senator Seward had made in his long political career to help them win the presidency again. Douglas now lost some of his assurance. Against Lincoln it was not certain he could carry the election without the South.

In an effort to placate the cotton states Douglas sought a meeting with Alabama's William Yancey. Yancey came to the Douglas house one night at ten o'clock, just a few days before the bolting southerners were pledged to meet in Richmond.

Douglas and Yancey talked for a long time, behind closed doors. Later, Douglas supporters told Yancey he could have the vice-presidential nomination. At a party Yancey was offered Douglas backing for the presidential nomination in 1864, if he could bring the Deep South to Douglas this year. The Douglas men reminded Yancey that Douglas was not well and that two presidential terms were out of the question.

But Yancey turned them down cold. He could not sacrifice the principle of states' rights for personal ambition.

Other attempts to smooth over the party's basic differences in principle came to no more. When the Richmond convention met on schedule—June 11—the southern delegates merely deferred action, until after the regular party meeting in Baltimore on June 18. Some southern Democrats went on to Baltimore. The rest waited in Richmond.

Baltimore's Monument Square was the center of both informal debate and loud recrimination. On one side of the square stood the house of Reverdy Johnson, former Attorney General of the United States and a powerful Douglas supporter. His mansion was open, day and night, offering cots and committee rooms to those who could squeeze in. The Johnson house was flanked on one side by Barnum's Hotel, where both northern and southern delegates held forth. On the other side of the Johnson place the Gilmor House was unofficial southern headquarters.

Across the square was Guy's Monument House, in which Douglas supporters occupied one end and secession-minded southerners the other. Each night Douglas forces at one side of the square and southerners at the other outdid one another in heaping invective on the shoulders of the opposition.

Yancey, as leader of the dissident southerners, controlled the fate of the convention as much as anyone. This issue had not changed: Slavery must be guaranteed protection in the party platform or the South would walk out.

Delegates and sight-seers swarmed around the Gilmor House, hoping to catch sight of the fire-eating leader of the secessionists. What they saw was a small, light-complexioned and convivial man, a well-mannered gentleman who might be found in the bar lifting a glass or two as he talked with great earnestness of the right of the states to choose their own way of life.

Like John C. Calhoun, Yancey believed that powerful influences in the North threatened the Union and the agrarian economy of the South. Undoubtedly Yancey believed secession might be necessary, but he also believed that a united and firm resistance by the South was the best means of preserving its constitutional rights within the union.

When the Baltimore convention opened at the Front Street Theater on June 18, the seating of delegates was the first order of business. The Charleston convention had instructed state parties to fill vacancies caused by the walkout of the Yancey group.

The next day various delegations appeared before the committee on credentials. W. C. Whiteley, one of the seceding delegates from Delaware, and a Mr. Townsend, a Douglas delegate from the same state, began arguing over Delaware's seats. Townsend made several especially uncomplimentary remarks before they separated. At five o'clock the next morning Whiteley walked into Maltby House, where Townsend was staying, and sat down in the passageway to the washroom. About fifteen minutes later Townsend came downstairs, laid his cane on the counter, and walked toward the washroom. As Townsend passed, Whiteley rose and struck him a violent blow on the side of the head. Townsend shook his head, seized the other by shirt and necktie and hustled Whiteley across the room, then fell on top of him.

The frightened landlord yelled for the police and in a few minutes officers separated the two. But as they rose Whiteley reached into a breast pocket. Townsend watched him carefully, then saw Whiteley's ten-shooter on the floor and picked it up.

"I will take care of this for the moment," he said. Then he straightened and walked out.

The Whiteley-Townsend fight was typical of the atmosphere. The real crisis neared on the twenty-first; two members of the Pennsylvania delegation exchanged harsh words over distribution of admission tickets to the convention hall. Delegate Montgomery questioned delegate Robert Randall's motives in handing out passes to the convention gallery. In the argument that followed, Robert Randall, Jr., half rose from his seat to challenge Montgomery. Later, at the corner of Gay and Fayette streets, Montgomery was deep in political discussion with friends when young Randall walked up, recognized his father's detractor, and struck him squarely on the face. Nose streaming blood, Montgomery hit young Randall on the ear, knocked him down, and was about to kick him when a Texas delegate offered the younger man a gun. The crowd stopped it before it became murder.

That same day the whole convention perspired more than even the summer heat would indicate when a section of the theater's wooden platform collapsed. Primed for a fight, delegates began to overturn furniture. Others, not primed, ran for the exits. But Chairman Cushing finally restored order and called for a cheer. In momentary good humor the convention recessed so the carpenters could repair the platform.

The wooden platform was reparable, but the political one was not. The following day, when the Douglas forces won control and began seating new delegations to replace those who had walked out at Charleston, the cotton states seceded.

The South did not walk out alone. When the seceders met at noon on June 23 across town, they were joined by delegates from such non-slave states as California, Oregon, Vermont, Massachusetts, New York, and Minnesota. Caleb Cushing of Massachusetts had deserted the chair to join the South. Cushing was promptly chosen president of the southern convention. It was not a grab-bag or bobtailed aggregation either. There were 230 delegates in attendance, representing all but eight states. The rebels nominated John Breckinridge for the presidency. Yancey was offered the vice-presidential post by acclamation but declined, and General Joseph Lane of Oregon was honored by acclamation.

These nominations were later confirmed by the Richmond convention on June 26, a day on which Douglas was hanged in effigy at Wilton, North Carolina, as "traitor to the South, the Union, and the Democratic party."

At the now gloomy regular convention in Baltimore's Front Street Theater, one delegate carried a letter of withdrawal from Senator Douglas, but refused to submit it. So on the second ballot Douglas was nominated over Breckinridge and Guthrie. Benjamin Fitzpatrick of Alabama was nominated for second place, but declined. Later Herschel V. Johnson of Georgia was selected by the national committee to replace him.

Now *two* groups claimed to be Democratic parties. President Buchanan declared that neither convention carried the official party torch, and authorized Democrats to vote for either Douglas or Breckinridge. But almost immediately Buchanan began throwing the administration's slender strength against the Douglas faction, and spoke for Brechinridge at a Washington demonstration on July 9.

Both Democratic campaigns were vigorous, if confused. In Bangor, Maine, one Charles Howard's arm was blown off while he was helping fire a cannon salute for Douglas. Torches and burning tar barrels again seared the air of Albany, New York, and store fronts echoed the thunder of a hundred-and-eight-gun salute for Breckinridge. Two nights before Albany's State Street had been ablaze with tar in honor of Senator Douglas.

General Lane appeared at a Philadelphia meeting, to be greeted by loud cheers from the Breckinridge supporters, but hisses and catcalls from the Douglas men there to heckle.

And in New York, General Lane met the newly organized National Democratic Volunteers who would support the Breckinridge ticket. The Douglas forces gathered at Tammany Hall, then trooped over to the Fifth Avenue Hotel to serenade their leader.

The Democratic party bigwigs were disturbed. On July 6, Mayor Wood of New York had suggested that Douglas be run in the North and West and Breckinridge in the South to beat Lincoln. After they won the election, thus, the Democrats could meet to decide who would occupy the White House.

This proposal brought a contemptuous editorial snort from Horace Greeley in the *Tribune,* but the idea of almost any kind of fusion had great appeal to a disunited Democratic party.

When Georgia's Governor Herschel Johnson spoke in behalf of Douglas in Macon, the crowd cheered Breckinridge so that Johnson was forced to desert his prepared speech, was eventually driven from the platform.

There was one overriding issue in the South: slavery. Breckinridge stood for unqualified approval and protection of slavery; Douglas was in effect an apologist; and Bell's Constitutional Union party was a straw blown listlessly in the wind, neither abolitionist nor pro-slavery, but searching out the moderate voter that held Union above all else.

Even at this late date the compromisers were still trying. Jefferson Davis reported that both Breckinridge and Bell were willing to withdraw from the presidential race if Douglas would do the same. But the Little Giant said it was impossible because his support in the North would then be thrown to the Republicans.

The Breckinridge and Lane committee of New York continued to talk fusion, in the hope that the state would be carried against Lincoln. They called on William Yancey to help win for the anti-Republicans, and Yancey then embarked on a remarkable tour. He delivered some twenty major speeches in seven weeks of rough-and-ready travel through the northern, central border, and southwest states.

From Chicago the Republican campaign had begun slowly enough, but once the party recovered from its initial shock over Seward's defeat, spirits began to rise. Seward saved the day. Concealing this bitter disappointment a few days after the convention he embarked on a speaking tour of the West.

Lincoln did not leave Springfield, and made no speeches. But earlier speeches, statements, and correspondence were resurrected; so there was no shortage of Lincoln material for the newspapers and his vocal supporters.

In the North and West slavery was important, but it was not an overwhelming issue. In the South it was life or death of a social system. The average northerner did not see this clearly. Nor were many northern voters convinced that southern talk of secession was anything more than the old plaint that had been heard within the Union almost continually for nearly eighty years.

In the House of Representatives, Democratic Representative Barksdale of Mississippi had warned the North: "Disband your Republican party; disband it; you threaten the peace of the Union."

But the North had simply smiled at this misplaced zeal.

"The people of the state of Mississippi may walk out," smiled Republican Representative Thomas Corwin of Ohio, "but the state never will . . . Why, sir, I have heard of this thing ever since I have heard anything in public affairs. In 1833, South Carolina was determined to go out of the Union, because of what she deemed an excessive duty on foreign goods. Pennsylvania was going out because we taxed her whisky in 1794; and Massachusetts thought the Union was endangered when Louisiana was purchased. I have been through three dissolutions of the Union myself [great laughter from the House] and the Union is stronger today than when its dissolution was first threatened—stronger than it was in the beginning."

Abraham Lincoln's position on slavery and the platform of the party were clear enough: slavery would not be extended to the new territories if the Republicans won.

The South and the Abolitionists knew that this meant strangulation of a way of life. But north of the Mason-Dixon line industrialists were more interested in the high protective tariff the Republicans promised, laborers and farmers in the free grant of farming land that the homestead plank promised.

Not that slavery was shorted in the North. "The Democracy of today," Lincoln had written a year earlier, "hold the liberty of one man to be absolutely nothing when in conflict with another man's right of property. Republicans, on the other hand, are for both the man and the dollar, but in case of conflict, the man before the dollar."

And on April 22, even as the Democrats had descended on Charleston, the Reverend Dr. George B. Cheever preached at New York's Church of the Puritans to a full house. His subject: "Northern Strikers and Southern Slavery, God's Bill for Unpaid Wages."

On the eve of the Republican convention the New York *Tribune* published a fiery murder story from Buchanan, Texas, omitting names in respect for "the feelings of a fond mother and sisters to whom ignorance is bliss."

The report described in gory detail how a young man had been attacked as a "Damned Yankee abolition book peddler," had been flogged and robbed of his wagon and its load of books. When a slave came running by with a forged free pass in his pocket, the mob lashed the Negro to a tree and beat out a confession that the book peddler had given him the pass. The slave pointed to the young man, "well knowing who his captors wanted him to accuse."

The mob now numbered a hundred and fifty slave owners, their overseers and sons. "Six of the most furious" dragged the wagon under a tree, covered it with dry branches, tied the peddler, immersed him in tar, poured the remainder on the wagon, passed a rope around his neck and over a tree limb. They lifted him until his toes barely touched the wagon, and then forced the Negro to set fire to the pyre.

Stories like this fired hatred in both the North and South. The Abolitionists told embellished tales of conditions that were evil enough to begin with. The southern planters countered with their own tales of cruelty, wage slavery, and child labor in the factories of the North.

Harriet Beecher Stowe had come out in 1852 with *Uncle Tom's Cabin; or Life Among the Lowly,* first having published the book as a serial story in the *National Era,* an anti-slavery paper in Washington. The story of the slave and his friends was a great convincer for the abolitionist cause in the North.

Neither *Uncle Tom's Cabin* nor *Dred: A Tale of the Dismal Swamp* caused more than a few ho-hums in the South. Generally slave owners looked on Mrs. Stowe's writings as ridiculous penny dreadfuls dreamed up for the ignorant northern trade.

But the slave South *was* impressed, outraged, and frightened by another book, published in 1857: *The Impending Crisis of the South.* Its author, Hinton Rowan Helper, a native North Carolinian, tore no bleeding heart over the morals of slavery but warned, coldly and statistically, that slavery was destroying the economy of the South.

Now, all four presidential candidates were pledged to defense of the Union—but what different Unions they defended. Lincoln's was Union with slavery protected, but not extended to one more inch of territory. Breckinridge's was Union with complete freedom and protection of slavery. Douglas's was Union with the issues of slavery left to the courts and to the will of the majority in the new territories. The colorless Bell was for Union at any price and under any conditions.

Bell's platform was the simplest to defend; also the most annoying to both Abolitionists and slavery men. But what Bell lacked in color and the platform lacked in substance was made up by the enthusiasm with which the Constitutional Union party conducted its campaign, particularly in the border states.

The Bell campaign was all basket picnics and mass meetings. Parades featured beautiful, well-groomed horses, their tails and manes flashing in the air, followed by uniformed companies of men marching to popular tunes. "Bell ringers" clanged all kinds of bells —tea, dinner, cow, and locomotive—to applaud the rousing words of their favorite orators.

In Tennessee and Kentucky, Bell supporters hauled a 2000-pound bell in a huge furniture van, awaking the countryside for miles around with its clanging.

Yancey formed the League of United Southerners to urge the protection of states' rights. The South covered its own eyes, unable to see the indignity of slavery from behind its dimming veils of high moral purpose and righteous indignation.

As the campaign warmed up, Douglas and Bell charged Breckinridge with disloyalty to the Union. They described the Southerner's League as a secret society dedicated to disruption. Their followers circulated copies of a document that purported to be the constitution of the league with the motto: "A southern Republic is our only safety."

But this, like many documents in many campaigns, was a forgery. The southern Democrats wanted to preserve the Union, but on their terms. It was refusal of either side to compromise that broke the party, more cleanly than any subversive efforts could have.

If the Democrats were divided in 1860, the Republican campaign was not all champagne and cheering, either. In the campaign the differences between Horace Greeley and Senator Seward were aired in Henry J. Raymond's New York *Times*.

Raymond charged that Greeley had been nursing a grudge against Seward for six years, because the senator had refused to support Greeley's aspirations to the governor's chair. Greeley denied that "considerations of personal ambition" had anything to do with his maneuvers against Seward, but the charge had the ring of truth.

Even so, the Republicans were so confident of victory that their leaders felt impelled to warn them. It was hard to restrain GOP confidence in the face of the wild exhortation of the Abolitionists and the untrammeled enthusiasm of the Wide-Awakes, the political-cheering association that led the parades and provided suitable background noise (and protection) for Republican meetings.

The Wide-Awake order was born on February 25 in Hartford, Connecticut, long before the presidential campaign. That Kentucky spellbinder, Cassius Clay, had come to speak for the Republicans in the Connecticut capital. Young Republicans in the city massed for a torchlight parade in his honor but, fearful of spilling torch oil on their clothes, decked themselves in black oilcloth caps and capes. After the parade one Republican was attacked by a Democrat, and in the indignation meeting that followed the Wide-Awakes were created, to act as a special escort for all parades.

A week later the marching and protective association numbered fifty members under Captain James S. Chalker, a man who had slugged the pugnacious Democrat with a torch on the night of the twenty-fifth. The movement spread. By convention time Wide-Awake organizations covered the North and West, and on October 3 the Wide-Awakes organized a great rally in New York.

Union Square was jammed by the bustling, swaying crowd, lighted bright as day by 10,000 torches and the flickering candles in the shop fronts of merchants who were Republican enough to brave the dangers of fire. The police moved tortuously through the mass to nab pickpockets and maintain a narrow trail along Broadway, while the ralliers oohed and aahed at the slashing bursts of red, green, diamond, and crystal fireworks.

As the parade turned down Fifth Avenue, matrons and young ladies peered shyly from behind rich draperies of the mansion windows. Occasionally one flashed into sight as she threw a bouquet or waved a kerchief at the heroic young men on parade. Floats foreshadowed the glories of Republican victory; one showed a White House, labeled "Abraham Lincoln's New Home." Bands, interspersed every two or three hundred yards, stirred the marchers to manly precision with "Hail Columbia," "Yankee Doodle." Republican spirits soared, and even Horace Greeley and rival Henry Raymond put away their long knives for a time. But, as the Republicans prospered, Democratic fortunes had fallen low. The Douglas campaign was drooping like a daffodil in summer, the Breckinridge

Democrats were not yet organized in the North, and the Bell party was making a great deal of noise, but little else.

Finally, three anti-Republican groups got together to try to carry vital New York State. On October 8 enough enthusiasm was diverted from the coming visit of the Prince of Wales to allow a great fusion rally at Cooper Union in behalf of Douglas, Breckinridge, and Bell —now known loosely as the "Democratic triumvirate." If this ill-assorted crew could secure enough popular votes, and enough electoral votes to split the college, the election would then be thrown into the House of Representatives, where all three parties felt they could carry the day.

Spurred by the Republican parade, on October 23 the fusionists held their own. "Minutemen" came from New Jersey and Albany, Philadelphia and Boston to join the local youth in the line of march from New York's City Hall up Broadway to Union Square. There they respectfully doffed their hats before the equestrian statue of George Washington, then moved across to Fifth Avenue, up to Twenty-sixth Street, and turned toward the Bowery and back downtown.

A team of high-stepping horses drew a float on which was seated a beautiful Goddess of Liberty. Knights of the Union—thirty-four of them—rode in full armor. A boy dressed as Young America rode under a canopy topped by a full-rigged miniature ship topped by flags of all nations. Behind, a wagon warned: "No Rail Splitter Can Split This Union."

The Young Men's Independent Club of the Seventh Ward—five hundred strong—marched in checkered shirts, "An Allied Army Against Black Republicanism."

And toward the end of the procession a rattletrap cart labored along bearing a seedy caricature of Horace Greeley. By his side sat a large Negro girl whom he caressed from time to time. The crowds laughed and jeered in derision of the "Nigger-loving" Republicans.

Election day, November 6, was marked by the usual challenges, long lines at the polling booths, and hurried canvassing for unvoted regulars in party districts throughout the land. But in New York election day was marked by unusual sobriety. Wards noted for riot, blasphemy, and bloodshed were as quiet as a courthouse on a Sunday afternoon. As the polls opened an earnest Irish Republican lugged a drunken friend out of his cellar at what must have seemed dawn

to the inebriate, to insure his voting "airly." Around midnight, opposite the Astor House, a Wide-Awake procession engaged in a knife-
and-pistol battle with a gang of what might have been Democrats.
But in the hours between, throughout the land, the business of getting
out the vote was sober and serious.

The Democrats opened election night boisterously at Tammany
Hall, with announcement of the usual Democratic majority in the
Thirteenth Ward. But as the returns piled in the air turned leaden,
and by nine o'clock silence had stolen over Tammany's headquarters.
In their headquarters opposite the old New York Hotel on Broad-
way, the Republicans greeted the first returns uncertainly. If the two
Democrats and Bell carried the city by less than 25,000, then
Lincoln was certain of victory in the state, but the fusionists already
claimed a 45,000 majority.

Yet as the reports began pouring in to the election center established at police headquarters, it became apparent that the Republicans were winning. When the returns were in Lincoln had defeated
what Horace Greeley called the "hybrid, tesselated, three-legged anti-
Republican ticket" by more than 50,000 votes, even though that
strange animal had polled more than 300,000 votes.

Lincoln had spent part of the early evening at the Cheny House
in Springfield, telling stories and chatting, calm as an icebound
lake, while the returns began to come in. Then he went to the telegraph office to wait.

Lincoln had carried the North solidly. The fusion campaign had
failed—it won three electoral votes in the state of New Jersey. Nowhere else did it make even a ripple on the surface.

Senator Douglas was in the South, ending a last-minute speaking
tour, when the news reached him. The defeat staggered him, but
he continued his tour, now urging the people of the South to accept
the verdict. But in Charleston the news of Lincoln's election was
received with shouted demands for a Southern Confederacy.
Federal Judge Magrath, District Attorney Connor, and the collector
of customs immediately resigned their jobs.

Sadly enough, the electoral vote was cut cleanly on a sectional
basis. Lincoln with 1,857,610 popular votes and 180 electoral votes
carried every state in the North but New Jersey and there he got
4 votes; Breckinridge with 850,082 votes carried every state in the
cotton South with 72 electoral votes; Douglas with 1,291,574 popular
votes carried only Missouri. Bell with 646,124 popular votes and 39

electoral votes carried the eight upper South and border states. Lincoln was elected. The fusion efforts had accomplished nothing, except perhaps to remind the Democrats that if they could have selected a single candidate they would have won the election handily. But it was obvious to all concerned, except the Republicans, that real fusion was impossible in a nation so divided.

Even before the election South Carolina was talking secession if Lincoln were the new President, and on November 5 as he called the presidential electors into convention Governor Gist also called for a state convention to consider secession.

On the evening following Lincoln's election Alabama's Yancey spoke at a citizens' meeting in Estelle Hall in Montgomery.

Yancey was sure there would be no war. He was sure there was no will in the North to resist, nor any constitutional or physical "power to direct a gun against a sovereign state."

The slave states contemplated a new nation based on the economics of agriculture. The North basked in the fond hope that the southerners' tongues were longer than their swords, but the southern states began to make plans for secession.

This news drifted north. The shock was violent, perhaps the more so because northern Republicans and their newspapers had scoffed so loudly at secession talk. On November 16 the most influential Republican newspaper of all, Greeley's *Tribune*, told the South to go ahead and secede if it wanted. It was quickly joined by the New York *Times*, the *Courier*, and the *Inquirer*; the Abolitionists and the Radical Republicans preferred no union to one with slavery.

But the Abolitionists were not so popular now, as the people began to realize the South meant what it had been saying for twenty years. On December 3 an abolition meeting in Boston, called to commemorate the first anniversary of the execution of John Brown, was routed by a mob that denounced both abolition and the Anti-Slavery Society.

On December 16 another abolition meeting denounced the actions of the mob. Wendell Phillips, one of the prime movers in the Anti-Slavery Society, was escorted home by a hundred policemen.

A few days later 22,000 citizens of Boston petitioned Congress for concessions to the South to avert secession. Republican office holders and candidates in local New England elections were swept aside by an electorate that suddenly realized that either war or disunion was upon them, possibly both.

On December 20, South Carolina seceded. On January 9, 1861, Mississippi went out. Then events moved faster: Florida and Alabama seceded on January 11, Georgia on January 19, Louisiana the next day, and Texas on February 1. When Lincoln started to Washington for his inauguration, the whole South had risen. Warned of a plot against his life, he rode the last part of the way in a sealed train to take up the reins of a government whose states he could not even count.

The Democratic party, and the South, were heeding too well the words William Yancey spoke after Lincoln's election:

"As for myself, rather than live on subject to a government which breaks the compact at will and places me in a position of inequality and inferiority to the northern free Negro, though that life be illustrated with gilded chains, by luxury and ease, I would in the cause of my state gather around me some brave spirits who, however few in number, would find a grave which the world would recognize, my countrymen, as a modern Thermopylae."

Mr. Yancey might have been looking into a crystal ball.

3

Slavery had not burst out, politically just in the year 1860. Four years before, the Republicans had organized to the point where they could offer a presidential candidate and they selected John C. Frémont, military man and explorer of the West. Frémont was a logical enough selection as a hero, and as a believer in the need for abolition of slavery. The Republicans hoped, despite the sectional nature of their party and their paucity of organization, to unite all the anti-slavery elements in the nation. They did not succeed.

Millard Fillmore, the former President by vice-presidential succession, was nominated by the American or Know-Nothing party, a strange cabalistic and supernationalist group. Fillmore also secured the support of the Whigs, but the budding Republicans were cut from the withering Whig branches.

James Buchanan, who had the extreme good sense or political luck to be out of the country during the Kansas-Nebraska argument, was nominated as a compromise candidate by the Democrats. He was able to straddle the slavery issue, and stall for a few more years, after his election to the presidency. Buchanan received fewer popular votes than Frémont and Fillmore, but he had the votes where they counted, and won the electoral college.

His election was hardly a service to the nation. Buchanan's position was very difficult, of course. But the new President neither understood the Abolitionists nor recognized the growing strength of their cause. He had precipitated the Kansas crisis by appointing a governor with assurance that he would adhere to the will of the people on the question of freedom or slavery for Kansas. But almost immediately President Buchanan began agitating to bring Kansas into the Union under the pro-slavery Lecompton Constitution.

On the face of it, Buchanan had all the makings of a great

*President. He had vast legislative experience in Congress. He had
been a Secretary of State in President Polk's cabinet, and minister
to St. Petersburg and to Great Britain.*

*But Buchanan would not face up to slavery as an issue that must
be resolved. And in this he failed as President—failed so completely
that by the end of his term the people of North and South had
forgotten his long years of public service and his great abilities as
negotiator and compromiser. After election day, 1860, James
Buchanan simply hung on at the White House, doing what he could
to appease a South that would stand for no appeasement.*

3. Stop the Slaughter

The Buchanan administration was drawing to its close in a cold and cheerless Washington. The President labored without hope against the appalling march of southern withdrawal, for neither North nor South would listen to a President only living out the ghostly days until March 4.

Senator Stephen A. Douglas returned from political defeat with but one aim: to save the Union. As the thirty-sixth Congress reconvened in December, Douglas turned to the old magic of compromise that had poulticed the wounds of secession in 1820 and 1850.

But now the South was in no mood for compromise. Rebellious hands grasped Union military installations below the Mason-Dixon line. By February only three were left in Union hands, two in Florida and Fort Sumter in Charleston Harbor.

If the South had its back arched, so did the President-elect. On December 13, Abraham Lincoln warned the Unionists to hold firm as a chain of steel against compromise of any sort on the extension of slavery.

Two months later, to the day, Vice-President John C. Breckinridge led the gentlemen of the United States Senate into the chambers of the House of Representatives just after noon, took his seat on the right of Speaker Pennington, and began the count of votes of the electoral college.

The Capitol was excited, the House galleries were overflowing. Ladies found their way into the cloakrooms to await the occasion; some occupied the seats of members who had surrendered them with handsome gestures.

There was no irregularity, except Arkansas Representative Thomas Hindeman's bitter remark that the Army Chief of Staff General Scott could now be informed that there was no further use for his "janizaries about the Capitol."

Neither was there any end to the tension that had gripped Washington since election day, nor to the rumors of assassination plots against Lincoln.

The Republicans, fearful of anarchy, appointed Senator Grimes and Representative Elihu Washburne as a committee of public safety. These two persuaded General Scott and New York's Chief of Police Kennedy to send secret operatives to Washington, Baltimore, Richmond, and Alexandria, where the sleuths, dressed in slouch hats and seedy coats, chewed tobacco, smoked cheap cigars, drank bad whisky and damned the Yankees while they pried into the anthills of rumor.

As inauguration day drew near, Senator Seward and Washburne were delegated to assure Lincoln's safe travel to Washington. By midmonth they had heard enough about an assassination plot said to be brewing in Baltimore to convince themselves that Lincoln must not appear there.

Lincoln had left Springfield in mid-February, planning a leisurely trip to the capital. Baltimore held no fears for *him*. On the twenty-second Senator Seward sent his son Frederick to Philadelphia to warn the victorious party of the Baltimore threat. The next day Lincoln was scheduled to attend a reception of the Pennsylvania legislature in Harrisburg. Young Seward, Detective Pinkerton, and Lincoln's friend Norman Judd persuaded the new Chief of State to take a special train to meet the night Washington train at Philadelphia. They ordered their operatives to cut the telegraph wires from Harrisburg, and the plan went into effect.

That night, unaware of the Harrisburg trip, since the wires were down, Washburne and the elder Seward met the regular train from Philadelphia. No Lincoln. They were worried but agreed to meet the night train from the North when it arrived at the old Washington and Baltimore depot just before dawn.

The plot-conscious Washburne arrived early and hid behind one of the pillars, where he could watch the passengers without being seen. The train arrived. Car after car was emptied, but still no Lincoln. Finally, as the station quieted, he saw three men climb slowly off the last sleeping car: one of them, his man, dressed in a soft low-crowned hat, swathed in a muffler and short overcoat. Washburne emerged from behind his pillar and hailed them. After

Lincoln had identified him to his suspicious companions, the congressman drove them to the Willard Hotel on Fourteenth Street and Pennsylvania Avenue.

There this unheroic party encountered a breathless and apologetic Senator Seward, who had overslept. They all waited in a small anteroom while the night porter attended to straightening up a room for the new President of the United States.

Three days after Lincoln's arrival Douglas went to see the President-elect. He and Seward, party lines forgotten, tried to persuade Lincoln to call a constitutional convention on an amendment that would prohibit interference with slavery. That effort to delay the issue made but little impression on Lincoln, although he did mention it in his inaugural address.

After walking arm in arm to the Senate chambers with the retiring Buchanan for inauguration, the new President bent his long legs awkwardly and strode up the steps to the rostrum on the east front of the Capitol. Lincoln paused. He could find no place to hang his high silk hat. Douglas strode forward, reached for it, and held it during the speech.

And when he learned that Washington's predominantly southern society planned to snub the Lincolns by not appearing at the inaugural ball, Douglas spread the word that he was going to be there, and that he would take it badly if the snub succeeded. On inauguration night Senator Douglas escorted Mrs. Lincoln into the ballroom on his arm. Mrs. Douglas, a gracious southern lady, went out of her way to be kind to the gauche new first lady from the backwaters of the West.

Unhappily the Douglas position was not that of his party or of the South. The Democratic party no longer existed, as such. It was fragmented by the events of 1860 as the nation was to be in the four years to come. And even as Lincoln and Douglas worked to maintain the Union, that Union was dissolving around them. On February 9, 1861, the Congress of the Confederate States of America had elected former United States Senator Jefferson Davis as President of a new nation.

As conflict neared, even the loyalty of northern Democrats was opened to question. But when the Confederate government in Richmond foolishly gave the order to fire on Fort Sumter on that April day, Democrat Douglas declared, "Every man must be for the

United States or against it. There can be no neutrals in this war; only patriots or traitors."

The telegraph wires clacked with the news of the Fort Sumter attack and Douglas sped to the White House for an interview with Lincoln. The President read Douglas his proposed proclamation; a call for 75,000 troops to be mobilized immediately. Douglas said that it should be 200,000.

In such agreement the two—the tall, saturnine Lincoln and the short, stocky senator—moved to a wall map of the United States and stood in whispered conference. Later Douglas said that he was fully prepared to sustain the executive in the exercise of all his constitutional functions to preserve the Union. He told friends there could be only two parties: the party of patriots and the party of traitors.

Douglas proved a good friend to Lincoln. There was trouble in Illinois, where the southern half of the state had always been for slavery. The President asked Douglas to go to Illinois and quiet the state for the Union. Lincoln's prime political opponent entrained for the Northwest to help their joint cause. First, Douglas spoke in Springfield, then in Chicago, where 10,000 people filled the Wigwam. Douglas warned that there could be no neutralism, that there was now no place for political division within the nation.

A few days later, exhausted by the efforts and anxieties of the last months, Douglas fell ill. He lingered for several weeks, but on June 3, from his sickbed in Chicago's Tremont House, the senator sent a last message to his sons. "Tell them to obey the law and support the Constitution of the United States," the Little Giant whispered. Then he died.

Now, a grieving Lincoln had no concern for party lines. The Republican party, as such, was submerged, replaced by the Union party, which encouraged the adherence of all who believed in preservation of the federal union of states.

Stephen Douglas had been a man of great and generous heart, despite his small stature and almost gnomelike appearance. But his brother Democrats were not all of Douglas's caliber. Old enmities and allegiances are not readily forgotten, even in the heat of common danger, and in his determination to restore the Union, Lincoln took steps that clearly went beyond his constitutional powers, violating both the letter and spirit of the law of the land. Had Douglas been alive to counsel with him, perhaps these steps would have been tempered, but Douglas was not there. Armed with even more zeal and less good sense and determined to hold the border states in the Union, Lincoln's subordinates went further, as in General McClellan's arrest of the entire Maryland legislature, when he suspected that legislature of disloyalty to the Union.

One thoughtless radical who was to give Lincoln a great deal of trouble was Major General John C. Frémont, the Republican presidential candidate in 1856.

In 1861, Frémont had been placed in command of the western department of the army in Missouri. Missouri then was badly split between the radical "Charcoal" faction led by B. Gratz Brown and the pro-Lincoln "Claybank" faction led by Lincoln's friend Representative Francis P. Blair.

Almost immediately, Frémont's hatred of slavery led him to side with the Charcoal group. In August 1861, Frémont freed the slaves of southern sympathizers; to the great glee of the Abolitionists, the "I told you so's" of the Confederate states, to the white-hot anger of the Democrats and slave-holding border states, and to the intense embarrassment of Lincoln. The President privately tried to persuade Frémont to modify the order. Frémont refused. Lincoln finally rescinded his general's command, and thus set up another issue for the Radicals to fume about.

By 1862, Lincoln's prestige had fallen very low. The war had not gone well, and Lincoln's attempts to create unity among the leaders of the North backfired. These failures laid him open to charges of bumbling, which his enemies used again and again. The President now could do very little to suit the Radical members of his own party. On Wednesday, February 5, possibly prompted by a socially ambitious wife, the President gave a party at the White House. Some five hundred invitations were sent out to government leaders. The next morning the party was pronounced a success. But Lincoln was again castigated by some of those selfsame guests, armed with the ammunition of a fresh look at his unpolished western countenance, which only confirmed their worst fears for the war.

These were not political judgments, but the snarling emotions laid bare when a war is failing. Politics as such had been given a seat far back in the theater; no one talked internal politics; the influential Leslie's Weekly carried no political reports at all between January and April 1862. Even Lincoln's most vicious detractors were to be found within the ranks of the Union political movement.

In the spring of 1862—a congressional election year—Lincoln raised the important political issue of emancipation in a more sensible manner than Frémont's. On March 6 the President recommended gradual, subsidized emancipation of slaves in the border states.

This move was formally endorsed by the House of Representatives and was generally praised in the press. But it raised the old issue of abolition. The quiescent Democrats were aroused, prompted by this and by the abuses of the freedoms of speech and press that the Administration had countenanced since Lincoln had suspended the writ of habeas corpus. In Pennsylvania, Ohio, Illinois, and New York that fall the Democrats elected nearly every state officer. It was not so much a triumph of the Democratic party as a verdict against the Administration, from a country sick of incompetent management of the Army, and what it saw as vacillation.

In New York, to the annoyance and worry of the Administration, the Democrat Horatio Seymour was elected governor. On learning this news, Lincoln remarked that he felt like the boy in Kentucky who stubbed his toe while running to see his sweetheart. "The boy said he was too big to cry, and far too badly hurt to laugh," a remark that was later to be revived by a presidential candidate from Illinois.

Some Democrats favored wholehearted prosecution of the war, but many others wanted the war ended, even if it meant the permanent separation of the South from the Union.

Most prominent of the anti-war Democrats was Clement L. Vallandigham, a representative from Ohio. In April 1863, Vallandigham was mending political fences in Columbus when General Ambrose Burnside of the Military Department of the Ohio outlawed any criticism of the Administration or the war effort.

Vallandigham had already spoken out many times against the war. This, he told friends, was a crisis in civil liberties. Someone had to stand up to these violations of the Constitution. He would be that man.

Vallandigham stepped up his blunt criticisms. On May 1 in a speech at Mount Vernon the congressman called the war "wicked, cruel, and unnecessary." He said the war was being waged "for the freedom of the blacks and the enslavement of the whites," and that war could have been ended months before, were the Administration not trying to establish "a despotism in this country more cruel and more oppressive than ever existed before."

These strong words were heard by two members of the 115th

Regiment of Ohio Volunteers, Captain H. R. Hill and Captain John A. Means, who had attended the meeting in civilian clothes.

At two-thirty on the morning of May 5, Vallandigham was roused from bed by insistent pounding on the front door of his house. Captain Charles G. Hutton of Burnside's staff had arrived to arrest him, reinforced by a detachment of soldiers.

Vallandigham offered no resistance, but refused to come down or let the soldiers in. They could not force the front door, so they chopped their way in the back, then broke down two more doors in the house before they encountered the congressman, fully dressed, looking down the barrels of their muskets.

That morning Vallandigham was taken under heavy guard to the Cincinnati military prison.

Public reaction to his arrest was violent. Crowds massed throughout Ohio to condemn the military and the war. Bloody riots erupted in Dayton. Burnside declared martial law throughout the county, and public opinion was further enraged.

A few days later, incensed by criticism in the Democratic Chicago Times, Burnside ordered the paper closed, but this so infuriated the whole North that Lincoln revoked the order.

Representative Vallandigham's attorneys sought his release on a writ of habeas corpus, but that constitutional right had been suspended by Lincoln himself. A few days later Vallandigham was convicted and sentenced to prison for the remainder of the war.

The furore rose and spread across the North. Lincoln saw that Vallandigham was becoming a martyr and ordered Burnside to deliver Vallandigham to the Confederate lines, since the congressman seemed eager to espouse the rebel cause.

But Vallandigham was not to be dismissed by such treatment. He demanded status as a prisoner of war from the Confederates, later made his way to Canada, and by May was settled in a suite of rooms at Hiron's House, near the foot of the ferry landing at Windsor, across from Detroit.

The anti-war sentiment of the Democrats hurt the Administration. But it hurt more, in the beginning of 1864, when the Radical Republicans began moving openly against Lincoln. They believed him too conservative on emancipation and reconstruction. They wanted all the slaves freed right then, and they wanted the South to pay bitterly for the war. These Radicals were mostly Republicans, but their leading presidential aspirant was Salmon P. Chase,

Lincoln's Secretary of the Treasury, who had been a Democrat before the war. Other potential presidential candidates of the opposition to Lincoln were General Benjamin F. Butler and Frémont, who had resigned from the Army to seek the presidency. In October 1863 the well-organized German minority had called a convention in Cleveland and had adopted a policy that demanded abolition and a scorched South. In February 1864, B. Gratz Brown and several members of the Missouri legislature began laying plans for a third-party convention in May.

Lincoln won an immediate victory, however, when his friend and supporter Senator Edwin D. Morgan of New York called the Union party's National Executive Committee into meeting on Washington's Birthday, at his home. The leaders chose June 7 for the date of the party's one and only national convention. The site was to be Baltimore. It was a victory for Lincoln because his Radical enemies wanted to delay the convention as long as possible, hoping that public opinion would turn against Lincoln. Joseph Medill, editor of the Chicago *Tribune*, was so alarmed at the growing opposition to Lincoln in the West that he asked the President to return Frémont to command. Nor was Lincoln under any illusions about his popularity at this point. The President sent Thurlow Weed of New York to offer the Union nomination to the Democratic governor of New York, Horatio Seymour, who had defeated the Unionists in the 1862 elections, but Seymour evinced absolutely no interest in such an offer.

As spring spread slowly across the warring land, the national and military picture began to brighten a little. General U. S. Grant's Army of the Potomac had finally won a victory at the battle of Spotsylvania Courthouse. E. C. Ingersoll, a Republican, had been elected on May 10 to Congress from the Fifth District of Illinois, ending a nasty trend toward Democrats that had begun in the President's home state two years before. And the economic problems of the Confederacy were becoming more insoluble every day. In Richmond flour was selling for $350 a barrel, calico at $15 per yard, shoes at $300 a pair; and it took 18 Confederate dollars to make one U.S. dollar, 28 Confederate dollars to a gold dollar.

Yet opposition to the Lincoln administration was blooming. At the anniversary meeting of the Abolitionists' Anti-Slavery Society in New York, Wendell Phillips publicly stated his doubts and fears of President Lincoln as too soft for the job at hand. William Lloyd Garrison supported Lincoln, but Phillips was for Frémont.

The Democratic party state convention in San Francisco declared the war was being waged to abolish slavery, and demanded peace on just and honorable terms (without abolition). The convention elected nine delegates to the national Democratic convention in Chicago and adjourned with three cheers for "the Constitution as it is and the Union as it was, and for the downfall of Abraham Lincoln."

On May 22 the Reverend Dr. Henry Cheever, a prominent Abolitionist minister, preached in New York. His topic was "The Claims of the Colored Race Before God to a Republican Form of Government and the Guilt and Peril of Denying Them Those Rights." A week later Dr. Cheever gave the same sermon before the full House of Representatives in Washington, then left the next day for Cleveland, as a delegate to the convention of Radicals who were trying to organize a party that could unseat the Administration.

The Radical Cleveland convention opened on Monday, May 30, seating 350 delegates. A dozen states were represented, but the strongest delegations came from Missouri, Illinois, Iowa, Arkansas, Ohio, and Pennsylvania. Only 158 delegates actually signed the register, but there were no rules for seating this strange mixture of personalities.

As the session opened, the war Democrats from New York wanted U. S. Grant as their candidate, with Frémont for Vice-President. (Lucius Robinson, the controller of New York, sent a letter to the convention, announcing that Grant would beat Lincoln in New York by 100,000 votes.) But John C. Frémont won this nomination by acclamation, General John Cochrane won the vice-presidential nomination with only a few negative votes.

The solution to the war, this rump group said, was to present a tough line to the South and a strong nationalist front to the world. The Cleveland convention passed resolutions calling for a radical reconstruction policy to be administered by Congress, a one-term policy for the presidency, direct election of the President, and confiscation of the lands of the rebels and their distribution among soldiers and settlers of the North.

A number of Democrats were present. They hoped to join the Grant men in offering Grant as a compromise candidate who could unite both the war effort and war Democrats against Lincoln. But when Frémont was nominated these war Democrats lost interest.

The convention broke up after naming itself the Radical Democratic party. In New York, Horace Greeley's *Tribune* was so incensed by this desertion of the Republican fold that it carried no word of the last day of the convention. The Philadelphia *Evening Bulletin* described the delegates as "broken-down politicians," *Harper's Weekly* insisted that the convention was held only for revenge against Lincoln, and Henry Raymond's New York *Times* called the meetings a "form of mental hallucination."

Nevertheless the Union party coalition was seriously concerned—so much so that when their convention met on June 7, at Baltimore, Lincoln had primed his friend Senator Morgan to open the meeting with a call for a constitutional amendment outlawing slavery.

Lincoln remained in Washington, and despite assurances that he would be the nominee he was worried lest the Radicals manage somehow to unseat him. A few days before the convention he expressed his pessimism to Senator Alexander McClure of Pennsylvania. When McClure tried to reassure him Lincoln shook his head grimly.

"Well, McClure," he said, "what you say seems to be unanswerable, but I don't forget that I was nominated for President in a convention that was two thirds for the other fellow."

Lincoln knew that the Radical Senator Samuel C. Pomeroy had been trying to arrange for a special "people's convention" in Baltimore to meet when the regular Union convention assembled. In fact, the malcontents had managed to rent the Baltimore convention hall—and the assembling convention suddenly found itself with no place to go. There was talk of moving to Philadelphia, but finally the convention rented the Front Street Theater—the scene of the bitter last-ditch fighting of the disintegrating Democratic party in 1860.

Two days before the Union convention the National Grand Council of the Union League of America went into session—a radical hotbed if there ever was one. Here, Lincoln's opponents paraded accusations of malfeasance, tyranny, corruption, favoritism, frivolity, and vulgarity in office. Finally Senator James H. Lane of Kansas, who had been asked by Lincoln to protect the President's interests, unleashed a withering diatribe against the Radicals. One by one he refuted the charges, and man by man he flayed the opposition, until at last the meeting voted for renomination of Lincoln and Hamlin.

One crisis was past and the next did not really exist, except in Lincoln's mind. While his enemies had been fulminating noisily, the people of the country quietly but steadily declared their support of Lincoln. Union conventions in Massachusetts, Kentucky, Delaware, Maine, and a half dozen other states either pledged their delegates or recommended Lincoln. On the floor of the Front Street Theater it was hot all right, but it was only the heat of a Baltimore June.

Physically, it was so hot, in fact, that the committee removed the scenery and curtains from the stage and threw open the back of the theater. Since the theater was located on one of the busiest and noisiest corners in Baltimore, this made for some confusion.

Yet even in the confusion there were only three problems: 1) settlement of the status of contested delegations, 2) adoption of a platform, and 3) nomination of a vice-presidential candidate.

The platform was solved by declaring to win the war and to abolish slavery. The convention did not know it, but Lincoln had already finessed the vice-presidential nomination.

Earlier in the year the President decided he wanted Andrew Johnson, the former Tennessee Democrat and slave-holder. Lincoln told half a dozen of his friends of this—cautioning each to keep it to himself. He asked Pennsylvania political boss Simon Cameron to work for Johnson's nomination and, unknown to Cameron, asked Senator McClure to do the same. At the convention each persuaded the other to back Johnson, each probably marveling at his statesmanship in selling the proposition with so little trouble. Just in case of a hitch, Lincoln had primed Secretary of State Seward and Henry Raymond as well.

There was no hitch, despite the opposition to Johnson's slave-state background by such Radical leaders as Pennsylvania's Representative Thaddeus Stevens. Very early in the convention Cameron rose and demanded the renomination of Lincoln and Hamlin, very pleased with himself because he had thus diverted suspicion from his efforts for Johnson. The convention nominated Lincoln quickly enough; only Missouri's John Hume had the courage to cast twenty-two votes for Grant on the first ballot. He changed his tune as quickly as he could in face of the howls, angry stares, and "lynch" murmurs that spread through the room. Hamlin didn't have a Chinaman's chance for the vice-presidency. Cameron and others had done their work, and Andrew Johnson was nominated in short order. Then the convention adjourned. Summing it up, John Hay, Lincoln's secretary, wrote thoughtfully in his diary: "There was little drinking, little quarreling, an earnest intention to simply register the expressed will of the people and go home."

Home they went; most but not all went happily. Radicals, like Thaddeus Stevens and Henry Blow of Missouri, went home scowling, determined to do something to defeat the ticket they hated.

Now the two active political organizations in the country were badly divided. The Republican party was splitting into moderate and radical wings, and the Radicals were not yet through in this campaign. The Democratic party had divided into three groups. First were the war Democrats, who tended to join with the Union party. Second were the moderate Democrats who favored the war but avoided the Union party because they did not approve of Lincoln's disregard for civil liberties and his policies on emancipation. Third were the Copperheads, the peace Democrats, some of whom actively opposed the war effort and worked for peace, even if it meant recognizing the Confederacy.

Following his nomination, Lincoln's political fortunes took a turn downward. Early in the summer of 1864, Greeley's influential paper said flatly that Lincoln could not carry Missouri if Frémont did not withdraw as candidate of the rump group. By the middle of August, Senator Charles Sumner, Governor John A. Andrew of Massachusetts, Thurlow Weed, and twenty other prominent Republicans held a despair meeting in New York. They proposed a new Republican convention, to be held after the Democratic meeting in Chicago, to select a GOP candidate who might be electable.

These Republican leaders were convinced that Lincoln had no chance. Thurlow Weed took the awful news to Lincoln. Later Henry Raymond wrote Lincoln that Illinois, Pennsylvania, Indiana, and New York were in danger. Perhaps, he said, Lincoln should abandon the whole idea of abolition. Then perhaps the South would end the war.

Even as the Democratic convention met in Chicago the frightened Republicans were arranging for Senator Zachariah Chandler of Michigan to visit Lincoln and demand dismissal of several members of the cabinet—in an attempt to force Lincoln to withdraw.

Chandler was one of the Radicals, a real two-fisted, Copperhead-hating Republican. On the night of May 26, while sitting with his wife and children in the dining room of the National Hotel in Washington, he had been assaulted by a pair of them, men named Voorhees and Hannegan, of Indiana.

Chandler was talking to Dr. E. M. Clarke of Detroit—discussing the firing of a Copperhead politician in Detroit in a rather loud voice.

Suddenly Voorhees stood up in anger and faced Chandler.

"This conversation, sir, is evidently intended for me," he said. Whereupon the senator rose to his full height, in apparent surprise. "Who are you? What is your name? . . . I don't know you," he declared.

Mr. Voorhees said he was inclined to doubt this, and in a moment blows were struck. Dr. Clarke tried to separate the two men, but before he could Hannegan seized a water pitcher from the table, stepped toward the senator, and struck him full on the head with it. Then Hannegan abandoned the pitcher, picked up a straight-backed chair, and hit the senator on the head with this bar-room weapon, dropping the senator to his knees.

Small wonder that Senator Chandler did not like Copperheads.

But while he and other Republican leaders were worrying about the impending defeat of Lincoln if Frémont stayed in the field, the Democrats were yielding to the Copperheads and building the plank in their platform that would fall through and carry the whole Democratic position to ridiculous defeat.

Clement Vallandigham was the hero of the Democratic convention as it met on the bright cool morning of August 29 at the special convention hall built on the shore of Lake Michigan. Twenty-five thousand visitors came to the Windy City for the festivities, and 15,000 of them were on hand for the opening session, even though the Midwest was just recovering from one of the worst storms in its history, with winds so fierce they had blown a Chicago-bound Indianapolis and Cincinnati train completely off the tracks.

Commenting on the festivities, Horace Greeley snarled: "A more appropriate title would be the Jefferson Davis convention." Indeed, as the session opened, Gilmore's Boston brass band played "The Star-Spangled Banner," but when it struck up the traditional "Dixie Land" the applause and storm of cheers filled the hall.

General George B. McClellan was the man of the hour. As a Union general, he represented loyalty to the Union. As a general deposed by Lincoln, he was a logical candidate for the Democrats. New York political boss Dean Richmond put the Democratic sentiment bluntly: "By God, McClellan shall be nominated and this damned war must be stopped."

McClellan was obviously already tapped by the party bosses as the candidate, although a handful of other names were put up, including that of a former president, Franklin Pierce. Another strong runner, Horatio Seymour of New York, declared himself unavailable.

One small voice was raised in rebellion against McClellan after the general was nominated. J. M. Harris of Maryland got up and demanded the floor. As the room quieted he announced that his state opposed the nomination.

"Maryland," he said, "which has suffered so much at the hands of that man, will not submit to his nomination in silence."

Thereupon Mr. Harris read the order of arrest McClellan had issued against seventeen members of the Maryland legislature. But as he read the hall rose up against him, hissing and shouting him down, so he could scarcely be heard above the racket.

"Vote for Jeff Davis," they yelled.

Harris struggled vainly on, but in the confusion no one could hear his statement of charges.

On the platform President Seymour tried vainly, for minutes, to gavel the convention to order.

". . . an assassin of states' rights, and if he is nominated, he will be beaten as he was at Antietam. I would not vote for him——"

The convention bellowed, and Harris was forced to stop.

"Mr. President," shouted delegate Corrigan of Pennsylvania. "Mr. President."

When he got the floor Corrigan turned on Harris. If the delegate from Maryland would not vote for the candidate selected by the convention he had no right to be there at all.

Harris retreated in complete defeat. General Morgan of Ohio soothed the delegates in his eulogy of McClellan's fair name. Finally Harris rose again. In a very small voice he explained that what he was saying before was that he could not go before the people of Maryland and ask them to vote for McClellan. He did not mean, he hastily added, that he would not support McClellan. He would abide by the will of the convention.

That settled it. McClellan was nominated on the first ballot, and George H. Pendleton, three times congressman from Ohio, was selected as his running mate.

But Vallandigham was the key man of the convention and the

key to the campaign that followed. On August 27 he spoke so strongly in favor of ending the war that rebel sympathizers began cheering, "Hurrah for Jeff Davis."

As the convention got to work Vallandigham was made chairman of the committee on resolutions and was responsible for the plank in the Democratic platform that declared the war to be hopeless and the Union position untenable.

The Republicans jumped on that plank. They called it a "Copperhead convention," and declared that the Democrats had once and for all proved themselves to be the party of treason. (This was not the last time the Republicans were to so charge.)

McClellan accepted the nomination but rejected the peace plank in the platform, whereupon the New York *News,* a Democratic paper, rejected McClellan, much to the delight of the South.

The Union campaign began to unfold. The Unionists charged that all the speeches, deliberations, and activities at the Democratic convention were treasonable. The New York *Times* went further: Every man who attended the convention, it said, was a "blackhearted traitor."

Despite his rejection of the peace platform, McClellan was smeared. It was rumored that he had volunteered his services to the confederacy, that he had given ammunition to Lee during the battle of Antietam.

Pendleton was called "The Great Dodger." Unionists said that whenever a bill beneficial to the Union was being voted on in the house Pendleton invariably dodged into the cloakroom to avoid having to vote for it.

The Democrats were hurt, too, by the extraordinary viciousness of their own kind—the War Democrats—who were convinced that the party had gone over to the South, and now allied themselves with the Republicans in the Union front. A contemporary historian, Daniel S. Dickinson, writing in August 1864, prophesied that the Democratic party "has the taint of disloyalty, which whether true or false will cling to it, like the poisoned shirt of Nessus, for a century." He was wrong—the taint lasted only twenty years.

The vindictive and bitter Union campaign was probably prompted, as much as anything else, by the very real fear and belief that Lincoln could not win the election.

Six days before the Democrats assembled Lincoln wrote the following note:

This morning, as for some days past, it seemed improbable that this administration will be re-elected. Then it will be my duty to co-operate with the President-elect so as to save the Union between the election and the inauguration, as my successor will have secured his selection on such grounds that he cannot possibly save it afterwards.

August 23, 1864   A. Lincoln.

This note was endorsed on the back by all members of the Cabinet, who had no idea what they were signing, sealed, and committed to the safekeeping of Gideon Welles, Secretary of the Navy, with instructions that it should not be opened until after the election.

But if the Union campaign was bitter, so was the Democratic campaign against Lincoln. No act of the Administration was too insignificant to spit upon, and the dragging, bloody, dreadful war was hauled out on every street corner, flaunted in every hall, as the Democrats harangued, pleaded, and argued against the Administration.

The Democratic convention broke up; the dissatisfied Union political leaders began to plan a new convention to be held in Buffalo, to dump both Lincoln and Frémont, and pick a compromise candidate who might stand a chance of winning.

Then, on the day that Senator Chandler was to have his showdown with Lincoln, General William T. Sherman announced the capture of Atlanta.

The rebellious Republican leaders were nonplussed. It was hard to stop wheels already grinding. On September 8, Greeley, Raymond, Henry Ward Beecher, and Thurlow Weed still talked of a new convention, in a depressed sort of way. But their major issue had evaporated, now the claim that the war was a failure would seem just so much claptrap to the voters.

Depressed as they were, the Republicans were afraid to try changing horses. Greeley announced reluctantly that he would support Lincoln, and the others began to fall in line, one by one.

So, Chandler was deputized to get Frémont out of the picture and opened negotiations at New York's Astor House with three Frémont leaders. After several days of fencing it was agreed that Frémont would withdraw, if his old enemy from Missouri days, Montgomery Blair, was fired as Postmaster General.

On September 22, Frémont carried out his part of the bargain but couldn't refrain from one last lash at Lincoln.

"I consider," he said, "that his administration has been politically, militarily, and financially a failure and that its necessary continuance is a cause of regret to the country."

Lincoln did not reply. On September 23 the President asked Montgomery Blair to resign. The Missouri man did. Frémont, at least, had the satisfaction of dragging one of his principal enemies out of high office.

The campaign proceeded with acrimony. Lincoln took no active part except to make a few speeches to soldier groups, but throughout the nation mass meetings were held day and night. Henry Ward Beecher and other preachers filled churches and public halls to deliver political sermons in behalf of Lincoln's Union cause.

Money was poured out by both sides, even on elaborate and highly colored posters pasted lavishly on the sides of buildings and fences throughout the Union.

But the issue was the war—and the Union forces kept rolling up victory after victory now, each step toward Richmond making the Democratic claims look more foolish and more disloyal.

Finally the balloting put an end to the political warfare. Lincoln won by 400,000 popular votes. It was apparent that the political Cassandras had been right: had Frémont stayed in the race, Lincoln would have gone down to defeat. But as it was, the Administration was preserved, as was Union control of the Congress.

The war against the Democrats was won, for two years. The war against the Confederacy was nearly won. It was obviously only a matter of months before the South would collapse. But an equally important struggle, the war within the Republican party for control of the Union's reconstruction—this was just beginning.

4

Everyone but the most stubborn Confederates knew the war could not go on. No one knew quite when the Confederacy would be finally defeated, but no nation could get started if it subsisted on a single crop, and that crop's markets were suddenly shut off, the fertile lands captured and burned, and the men who grew the crop were fighting and dying in battle.

All the Confederacy was on starvation rations in 1864. The newspapers were printed on wallpaper, and only printed thus to announce the tightening flow of government restrictions.

It was a bitter war, fierce in the bloodletting. The North suffered some 360,000 casualites and the South, which could less afford it, some quarter of a million. Yet the dispirited, nearly beaten South was not ready to give up in 1864. The election of Lincoln, and the frightening rise of the Radicals in Congress, spurred the South in the last desperate months of the war.

In the North the sweet taste of victory at Atlanta and Mobile Bay had suddenly begun to turn sour. More than the South, by far, sober businessmen in the North saw the destruction that war had wreaked. Among the hotheads of Congress bent on revenge and among those motivated even more basely by personal gain, there were men who wanted justice and reasonable treatment for their erring brothers of the South.

Lincoln's strange gentleness gave these men hope as the year 1864 flickered to its end, and the President moved ungracefully but steadily toward his appointed goal.

4. The Bloody Shirt of the Rebellion

On the cold and drizzly morning of March 4, 1865, the melancholy Lincoln stepped into his carriage before the White House and was driven rapidly through the rainy streets of Washington to the Senate chambers. A few minutes later he and the new Vice-President, Andrew Johnson, moved outside to the east front of the Capitol.

Lincoln stepped forward on the platform, to be greeted by a roar of applause from the crowd, a roar that was repeated again and again as he stood quietly holding a single sheet on which was written his second inaugural address. Then, the crowd hushed as the President began to speak:

". . . With malice toward none; with charity for all; with firmness in the right, as God gives us to see the right, let us strive on to finish the work we are in; to bind up the nation's wounds; to care for him who shall have borne the battle, and for his widow and his orphan—to do all which may achieve and cherish a just and lasting peace among ourselves and with all nations."

That was the Administration's policy as the Civil War drew to its end. But there was to be no such reconciliation. On the night of April 15, six days after the surrender at Appomattox, Lincoln was dead. Within a few hours Andrew Johnson, the dark-haired, deep-eyed tailor from Tennessee became the seventeenth President of the United States.

The Radicals in Congress viewed this change with mixed emotions. "Johnson, we have faith in you," said Ben Wade, the blunt and recalcitrant senator from Ohio. "By the gods, there will be no trouble now in running the government."

But Thaddeus Stevens of Pennsylvania, leader in the House, and Charles Sumner, the cold, idealistic senator from Massachusetts—

these Radical chiefs were not so sure. Stevens and Sumner were determined to punish the South for its rebellion, were absolute in their demand that the Negro should have full, practical, immediate equality.

As spring warmed into summer President Johnson began to rebuild the nation as Lincoln had planned, the southern states began demolishing the wreckage of war, and in the North every state political convention, Republican and Democratic, approved the Administration's moderate program except Pennsylvania and Massachusetts.

But by spring 1866 the Radicals in Congress were strong and united against the Administration's program. On June 16, Congress passed the slavery-ending Fourteenth Amendment on to the states for ratification. The Fourteenth Amendment not only gave the Negroes equality, but it forced the South to count Negroes as voters or lose representation in Congress; forbade Confederate soldiers to hold office; and outlawed the Confederate debt. By midsummer, as bitterness increased between a forgiving Administration and a vengeance-bent Congress, it was apparent that the congressional elections would decide the fate and control of reconstruction of the South. On August 14 the National Union convention, representing conservative Unionists of both South and North, endorsed Johnson's policies; on September 25, in Pittsburgh, the South-hating Radicals condemned him with equal vigor.

President Johnson took to the stump. He was invited to Chicago for dedication of the new Douglas monument and took this opportunity to make a political tour, accompanied by several members of his cabinet and by General Grant and Admiral Farragut. The latter had won the sweeping victory of Mobile Bay that did so much to elect Lincoln and Johnson two years before.

Johnson spoke in Philadelphia, New York, Albany, Buffalo, Cleveland, St. Louis, Indianapolis, Louisville, Cincinnati, and Pittsburgh. It was a trip to rival the political tour of the South's William L. Yancey in 1860, and it was equally fruitless, for the slack-lipped President fell to arguing with the crowds, about responsibility for the war and proper treatment of the South, and his manner was such that he was accused of drunkenness on the platform, time and again. As the reception grew more unfriendly, the President responded in kind. At the end of the trip, Johnson had defeated his

own moderate program by immoderate action. The Radical victory
was now certain.

In the split between the moderate Republicans who supported
Johnson and the Radicals who fought him, the Democrats hoped to
pick up new support. But by election time even the Democrats were
so distrustful of Johnson, and he of them, that the weld came apart.
Lincoln's Union coalition was beyond redemption.

The congressional elections were a debacle for both Johnson and
the Democrats. The Radicals captured two-thirds control of both
House and Senate; they did more: the Fortieth Congress was to
contain only twelve Democratic senators and fifty Democratic
representatives.

The Democrats were to have little to do with legislation, except to
serve as an opposition (often castigated as disloyal) and, allied with
moderate Republicans, to stop the Radicals from going to the worst
extremes.

By fall all the states of the South but Tennessee had rejected
the Fourteenth Amendment, to the indignation of the Radicals.
When the Thirty-ninth Congress went back into lame-duck session
the radicals were dedicated to two propositions: their own reconstruction bill, and impeachment of President Johnson, to punish him
for resisting their efforts to enforce the will of Congress on the nation.

Both houses fully expected the President to veto the reconstruction
bill. They were not disappointed.

At one-forty on the afternoon of the next to last day of the session
the House clerk began reading the President's veto message. He
finished at two thirty-five. An hour later the bill was passed by a
vote of 135–48, the largest majority given any measure in that session,
against a backdrop of applause and cheers from the galleries. The
Senate concurred.

The next morning Senator Ben Wade called the Senate into
session, signed a bill that would enable the YMCA of Washington to
form a joint stock company, and adjourned the Senate of the Thirty-
ninth Congress. At twelve-fifteen he called the Senate of the Fortieth
Congress to order. Stern reconstruction was now the law of the land,
and a stern and sometimes venomous Congress began to put that law
into effect.

It was a busy spring. Jefferson Davis sat imprisoned in Fortress
Monroe in Virginia, while the lawmakers debated endlessly over his
fate. Horace Greeley took an editorial swipe at southern "women

who boasted they never made a bed nor swept a room until after Lee surrendered" and "soured sullen, discontented restless ex-rebels" but noted that there were more people at work in the South than ever before, advised them to patch their old fences and put in crops, and noted cheerfully that "the South will pull through." Later that year he signed Jeff Davis's bail bond, and in doing so committed political hara-kiri.

President Johnson held his tenth and last state dinner of the season on March 19. He invited new members of the House and Senate. They attended the dinner but the next day were back on Capitol Hill looking for evidence to impeach him.

Impeachment finally came to a head a year later—on May 17, 1868. President Johnson did not appear before the Senate, although he was called. Instead, he told them to take their impeachment to the devil, and sat stern and brooding in the White House while a test vote on one charge in the Senate failed 35–19—one vote less than the two thirds needed.

And so it stood, though not without recrimination and false heroics on the part of the Radicals, who vowed to try every other charge when they returned from the Republican convention in Chicago.

The GOP convention, which began almost immediately, was marked, as was the Democratic convention later, with the emergence of a new political group. The veterans became a real political force, for the first time. Republican soldiers held their own convention on May 19 at Turner's Hall on North Clark Street, after a long procession led by a war eagle, "Old Abe," which belonged to the Wisconsin delegation. Serenaded by the Light Guard band, and singing old battle songs, a thousand men marched into the hall and sat down to applaud Radical speeches, cast their weight behind General U. S. Grant, and demand "reconstruction on a basis of equal and exact justice to all men."

General Grant, the scraggly-bearded general who had many times scoffed at the thought of his own candidacy, had finally been persuaded that he was a man of destiny and that he should make the race in the interests of the whole nation.

As the Republican convention opened on May 20 at Chicago's Opera House, there was no question about the name of the presidential nominee. The vice-presidential spot, however, was still open. That nomination was being sought by two Radical leaders: Schuyler Colfax, Speaker of the House, and Senator Ben Wade.

Wade's strength seemed to be growing in the indignation over the failure to impeach Johnson. A vote for Wade would be a vote for a new effort to impeach the hated President.

But that was the extent of the convention's disagreement. After the preliminaries General John A. Logan of Illinois nominated Ulysses Simpson Grant for the presidency.

When the roar of applause had died down a delegate from South Carolina moved that Grant be nominated by acclamation, but he was shouted down by a convention that demanded the right to show its enthusiasm for its candidate. The voting began.

"Alabama casts 18 votes for U. S. Grant."

Arkansas cast 10 votes for Grant.

California's chairman shouted, "We come here, 6000 miles, to call our vote for U. S. Grant."

Governor Brown of Georgia arose. "The Republicans of Georgia, many of whom were the original secessionists, recognizing the wisdom of the maxim 'Enemies in war, in peace friends,' and heartily desiring to speed the restoration of the Union, harmony, peace, and good government, instruct me through their representatives here to cast 18 votes for General Grant."

From Kansas came the word: "The John Brown state gives 6 votes for Grant . . ."

Massachusetts primly announced its 24 votes for Grant. Then came Mississippi: ". . . the home of Jeff Davis repudiates the traitor and offers her 14 votes for Grant."

Missouri's leader announced that his delegation was under instruction of the state convention to vote for Grant on a Radical platform, and, having that platform, "We have confidence Grant will carry out its principles." Twenty-two more votes for Grant.

Nebraska, "the last state admitted to the Union and the first to adopt impartial suffrage," gave 6 votes for Grant.

New Jersey gave her 14 votes for the general as a "victorious soldier but conspicuous for his calmness of judgment, sincerity of patriotism, and personal honesty."

New York laconically announced her 66 votes for Grant.

It was time for South Carolina, the original secessionist, and her orator was not to be outdone.

"The birthplace and home of Calhoun and the doctrine of states' rights, the first to withdraw herself from the Union, directs her representatives, sent here by a majority of 43,470, returning as we do to the counsels of those who desired only to preserve the Union; arm in arm and heart to heart with Massachusetts, gives her twelve votes for Grant."

Tennessee, claiming honor as the first southern state to reconstruct and be readmitted to the Union, and praising her "liberal Republican government," cast her votes for Grant, "with the solemn pledge never again to present the name for President or Vice-President of such a traitor as Andrew Johnson."

Texas, "the empire state of the South, containing 275,000 square miles and capable of sustaining 20,000,000 of people," cast her eight votes for Grant.

So it went. Vermont, Virginia, "rising from the grave that General Grant dug her in the Appomattox," the strangely carved state of West Virginia, Wisconsin—650 votes in the whole convention—all went for Grant.

Then the convention was unleashed. Amid the wild cheers, the band struck up "Hail to the Chief." Someone launched a dove bearing red, white, and blue ribbons, which flew around the hall several times before roosting on the rear of the stage. The bunting on the stage opened, to reveal a grandiose drawing by the cartoonist Thomas Nast of a heroic uniformed Grant before the White House portico, while a benign, white-robed Columbia challenged the Democrats to "match him if you can." The band whooped into "Rally Round the Flag," then a new campaign song: "Hurrah for Grant!"

Four ballots later Indiana's Radical Schuyler Colfax won the vice-presidential nomination. The impeachment of Johnson died with Ben Wade's candidacy.

Five weeks later on the day that a convention of Democratic sailors and soldiers pledged themselves to fight Radicalism, the tenth convention of the Democratic party convened on July 4 in the spanking new Tammany Hall near New York's Union Square. It was a hot day, so hot that the triumphal arches of evergreen, flags, and bunting across Fourteenth Street wilted over the portraits of Jefferson and Jackson; "too hot for the warm work on hand here," Salmon P. Chase's daughter Kate informed her father, the Chief Justice of the United States Supreme Court.

There was no pre-picked Democratic candidate. The dignified, ambitious, chin-whiskered Chase was a front-runner, to be sure. So was gimlet-eyed George Pendleton of Ohio, whose escort of three hundred and fifty men paraded through the sticky streets on July 2, wearing linen dusters and badges shaped of five-dollar bills to plump for "Gentleman George" and payment of war bonds in greenbacks —paper money backed by the federal government.

Greenbacks were backed merely by the promise of the federal government to pay in metal money. Unlike gold certificates, there was not a dollar in gold in the treasury for each of these greenbacks. This kind of paper money had been issued during the Civil War, as an emergency measure. In reality, the greenbacks were promises by the U. S. Government to pay for goods and services in "good" money, at some future time. When the greenbacks were first issued it was understood that they would all be called in at the end of the war and destroyed. But when the war ended the federal emergency did not end. The Union government, faced with reconstruction and a destroyed and impoverished South, did not have the funds to retire the greenback currency. War bonds were coming due. Large armed forces still had to be kept up to keep the South in control, and, while the South was to assume part of the Union war debt, all these matters took time.

Now, too, money was scarce, and the poor in the United States wanted to see war bonds and other debts paid off in the greenbacks. In 1865 the greenback value had fallen to about half its face value— when one wanted to exchange a greenback note for a note on which the government promised to pay in gold.

Naturally, farmers and debtors—who were mostly Democrats, it seemed—wanted to pay their debts in this cheap currency. Naturally, too, the businessmen and creditors of both parties wanted the government to retire the bills and force payment of both government and private debts in metal money or government paper money that could immediately be exchanged at the treasury for metal. For "hard money" men in those days thought of paper money only as a convenience—it was easier to carry than metal money. They did not appreciate the concept, held by the paper-money advocates, that money was the declaration of the government to honor the debt —because they did not believe government could manage affairs, or should manage affairs, so that the price and value of unbacked currency would remain stable.

This issue opened in the campaign of 1868, but it was to continue for many, many years, growing in intensity. Even today there are bankers, businessmen, and especially men in the mining business who became choleric on the subject of hard money.

Now, at Tammany's grand establishment on Fourteenth Street, Gentleman George Pendleton thought he had a good chance of rallying the western farmers and the poor men of the party to him by plumping for cheap money—the "Ohio idea." He was exactly right. And since he came from the West, where money was hard to come by at any time, this position could not hurt him at home, no matter how the sharks of Wall Street might take it.

Horatio Seymour, a New Yorker of open face and impeccable manner, was the choice of the New York delegation. He was a hard-money man, as any good Democrat had to be in the biggest capital center in the country.

But Seymour was a Chase supporter himself, so the New Yorkers decided to cast their votes for Sanford E. Church, then await a trend. A bluff military man, General Winfield Scott Hancock, was the first choice of the soldiers' and sailors' convention, and a strong candidate as the Democratic convention developed.

The South was present at a national Democratic convention for the first time since 1860, but it was walking a very cautious path, much more concerned with the platform of the party than with nomination of a candidate. For the record, the South supported President Johnson in the early balloting. Actually, the southern delegates were nervous and ill at ease, ready to blow with the wind and concerned lest they say too much.

The balding, halo-haired Seymour was chosen president of the convention, which then voted to take up the platform before nomination of candidates. This was largely hailed as favorable to Pendleton's cause, since some of the states that could not be counted on for him did espouse the greenback plank, and if that were voted the chances of a hard-money candidate like Chase looked slim.

One announced issue before the convention was preservation of the power of the President. Another was protection of the judiciary. Both were touted by the conservatives as slaps at the high-riding Radical Congress.

But the real issues were the venality of southern reconstruction, the equality of the Negro, and the financial question of hard or soft money.

The Democratic platform weaseled on the race question; it established a Democratic precedent, declaring the right to vote was the problem of the individual states. The Democrats did come out strongly for greenbacks, which would help all the poor, including the South, and denounced harsh reconstruction laws passed by the Radical-controlled Congress.

The Democratic platform pleased very few of the party's northern supporters outside the convention. It was attacked as "a mass of catch phrases" and "nearly as good as the Republicans could have desired," and this was just about the whole truth. The platform's sniping at the reconstruction laws laid the party open immediately to attack as disloyal.

The war was over, to be sure. But no one in the North was quite certain the South would not try to rise again. So the word "Copperhead," even in 1868, retained almost its wartime concept of treason and contemptibility.

There was plenty of bitterness on both sides of the Mason-Dixon line. But on the northern side the voters wanted to be sure the Civil War stayed won. They were not sure—could not be sure—from the Democratic platform that a Democratic government would not favor the South or destroy the battlefield victories in congressional default. Their fear, their uneasiness, and the recurrence of Copperhead and questionable names in the Democratic convention gave the Democrats a very difficult selling job, and the Democrats were not close enough to the voters at that moment to see what they were doing.

The convention had been called to order on Independence Day but adjourned over the weekend. On Monday the flimsy platform was adopted unanimously and enthusiastically, an unpleasant job well done, since Democratic seers said it offended no one but the Radicals. On Tuesday the business of selecting a candidate began.

The name of Salmon Chase was held back, for the party now had a greenback platform. Very few of the politicians believed in it, and no one expected the platform to control selection of a candidate, but since Chase was a hard-money man, his chance lay in striking at exactly the proper moment.

The first six ballots were cast on Tuesday. They were totally inconclusive. The canny delegations were nominating favorite sons for the record and sniffing the wind for a trend. The serious candidates mentioned were Pendleton, Hancock, and Johnson. On Wednesday the name of Thomas A. Hendricks of Indiana was proposed by a delegate from his home state. Hendricks was an imposing candidate, handsome and craggy of feature. After the seventh ballot New

York retired, dropped her next-to-most favorite son, Church, and switched to Hendricks. The object was to eliminate Pendleton. On the ninth ballot it was still Gentleman George, Hendricks, and Hancock. Then California was called—and gave a half vote for Salmon P. Chase. Perhaps this was it? The murmur ran through the convention.

By the eighteenth ballot Pennsylvania had manipulated a swing to Hancock, who now held 144½ votes to Hendricks's 87 and Pendleton's 56½. Still no word from the Chase support.

Illinois had been voting as a unit for Pendleton, but on the seventeenth ballot Illinois split. Almost half went for Hendricks.

On the eighteenth ballot the Illinois delegation first announced solidly for Hendricks, but one delegate objected. He wanted to vote for Pendleton. Chairman Seymour ruled that each delegation would decide how it was going to vote. Then the argument and a few fist fights spread throughout the hall. The convention was suddenly getting out of hand!

A Massachusetts delegate moved for adjournment. Seymour called for a vote. The affirmatives whispered; the nays thundered. But in the manner of chairmen before and since, Seymour whacked down his gavel, declared for the affirmative, and left the chair.

The day's work was over, and a dirty day's work it was by the anti-Hancock men, declared the Hancock supporters, who could smell a landslide for their man on the next vote. Grumbling but undismayed, the Hancock boys rallied in front of Tammany to fire a premature cannon in honor of Hancock's nomination. Several incautious newspapers announced the selection as a fact.

In the small hours of the night that overwhelming Hancock sentiment went up in smoke and demon rum. On Thursday, before the nineteenth ballot, Ohio's Vallandigham secured the floor and stunned the convention with George Pendleton's letter of withdrawal from the race. That opened 56½ votes, so Hendricks gained steadily.

By the twenty-first ballot Hendricks had 132 votes, and it began to look to some as though the landslide was now his. Others noted that the Chase men, so quiet all this time, had picked up four votes in California. Was this, then, the swing to Chase?

The twenty-second ballot started, a seesaw between Hendricks and Hancock. It looked like the kind of deadlock that might open the field for another candidate.

Then the roll call stopped at Ohio.

An old war horse, General McCook, gave the delegates their second shock. He nominated Horatio Seymour of New York. Seymour gaveled for attention, and declined, although the delegates would have none of it. Seymour said no again—but he then left the platform.

Vallandigham said the Seymour nomination must stand. New York's delegates agreed. Then Seymour returned to the platform, determined to decline once more. The New York *World* later reported that he was planning to suggest Chase's name to the convention at that point.

But before Seymour could get the floor he was stopped by a scheming Democratic ward heeler, Joseph Warren of Buffalo. Warren hustled him off the rostrum, out the rear door, into a carriage, and into seclusion at the Manhattan Club. It was reported that on the stairs, meeting his proper friend Peter Harvey of Boston, cheeks wet with tears, Seymour exclaimed, "Pity me, Harvey, pity me."

But off Seymour went. Some suspected that New York's Samuel Tilden had engineered "the nasty moves by which Seymour was thus rushed from the convention and held incommunicado." True or not, Seymour was nominated, without another ballot.

That was the climax of the convention. Francis P. Blair of Missouri and of the walrus mustache, who had served with considerable distinction as major general under Sherman, was chosen vice-presidential candidate on the first ballot. The ticket and the platform had been selected. There was only one problem. The Democrats had nominated a presidential candidate who did not want to run. Would he accept?

Horatio Seymour did accept, although he later said it was the worst mistake of his life. Chief Justice Chase must have agreed, for had Seymour spoken his name on the floor, there was a very good chance that Chase would have been nominated by a tired and easily stampeded convention. Even after the convention a moment arose to persuade Seymour to decline and substitute Chase. But it came to nothing and Chase disappeared from the election scene, after scotching talk about a third party.

The convention had declared support of President Johnson, although he had been elected as Lincoln's running mate on the Union ticket of 1864.

Candidate Blair, an announced enemy of radical reconstruction, had said President Johnson should refuse to enforce the reconstruction laws as unconstitutional. So Blair became the focus of the Republican attack. Election of the Democrats, said the Republicans, would mean revolution and repudiation—revolution against the law and repudiation of the currency. Not satisfied with this, the Republicans found other charges. The *Nation* reported the handsome General Blair's bill for two days at a Hartford hotel as $10 for board, $65 for lemons and whisky. Whenever Blair failed to meet a speaking engagement the Republican press indicated he had been drunk.

The Democrats began their campaign in spirits that were high enough. They saw a trend in the local elections of 1867, when they had carried all of New England, all of the Middle Atlantic states except Delaware and Maryland. They carried West Virginia, Kentucky, Tennessee, Ohio, Michigan, Minnesota, Wisconsin, Iowa, and California. In 1866 the Republicans had carried all these states except Maryland and Kentucky, but in 1867, Democratic majorities increased in every case, or Republican majorities were cut.

In Massachusetts the vote for the Democratic candidate for governor had increased from 36,000 to 70,000 in 1867. Boston, of all things, elected a Democratic mayor.

Negro rights and the rebellion had been key issues in 1867 in Ohio, where the Republicans carried the state by 42,000 votes in 1866. That next year the Republicans campaigned on slogans like "Honest Black Men Are Preferable to White Traitors"; "Democrats Murdered Our President"; "If Any Man Pull Down the American Flag, Give Him a Post Office—A. Johnson."

And the Republicans sponsored a constitutional amendment guaranteeing Negroes the right to vote.

When Ohio voters went to the polls in October, Republican candidate Rutherford B. Hayes won the governor's chair over his Democratic opponent by less than 3000 votes. The Democrats won control of both houses of the legislature, and the Negro suffrage amendment was defeated.

Those local elections paved the way for the 1868 campaign. The Democrats saw a rosy future. The Radical Republicans were frightened into rushing reconstruction, to bring Negro votes of southern states into the fold. By election day, 1868, nine southern states had ratified the Fourteenth Amendment, most of them through the efforts of carpetbaggers and scalawags.

At the end of the Civil War leather was scarce and expensive in the North and almost non-existent in the impoverished, defeated South. The carpetbaggers got their name through that combination of facts. When the northern Radicals took control of Congress, strengthened the hand of military government, and determined to put local governments into control in the South that would do Radical bidding, and vote Republican, a number of ambitious men saw their chance for fame and fortune. Most of these were of fortune so slim that they could load all their earthly belongings into a single handbag—and, times and costs being what they were, those bags were made of carpet material. Hence the name of the men whose fame soon sped across the world, a name that would for a century characterize those loose of morals, perfidious, salacious, covetous, thieving, dishonorable, rapacious, and Republican in the South.

Scalawags were an even lower species of humanity, in the eyes of the now poor but still magnolia-trimmed South that could not forget the ante-bellum days of plantations and the good life.

A scalawag was generally poor white, in origin. He had the same rapacious spirit as the carpetbagger, but because he was not a Damn Yankee he was even more hated by the men and women he betrayed into the hands of the Radicals.

The Democrats could see the advantage of a Negro vote to the Republicans, when the veterans of the Confederate Army—and this was just about every able-bodied man—were still without full citizenship in the United States. In 1868 this Negro vote question meant control of the South and was a very large reason for intense Democratic opposition to the Fourteenth Amendment as it stood. But it was not the only reason: the Democrats still proclaimed themselves guardians of states' rights. They saw the amendment as a flagrant invasion of state sovereignty.

The money issue was far less important. No one really believed Seymour would stand on the greenback plank. Charles Francis Adams, the Democratic candidate for governor of Massachusetts, denounced it outright. The Republicans charged the greenback policy would force payment of bonds in currency that was worth only seventy cents on the dollar; the Democrats countered that Republican extravagance was the reason for 1) high taxes, 2) the failure of the greenbacks to reach par with gold, and 3) the recession the country was still suffering. If Seymour were elected the Democrats promised an end to the expensive Radical reconstruction policy that kept thousands of troops on occupation duty in the South.

But these were lesser issues. "Revolution"—the Democratic opposition to the Negro vote and the Fourteenth Amendment—was the big issue. The other party played it for all it was worth.

The Republicans built a hefty war chest. Much of the big money of the campaign came from war fortunes like those of Jay Cooke, the war-bond salesman, Commodore Vanderbilt, the Astors, and others who had a strong interest in railroads. The Republicans would continue to get land in county lots; the Democrats were pledged against the land grants.

The Democrats weren't nearly so well off as their opponents. The most notable contributions of the Democratic campaign came from eight men, who gave $10,000 each. H. T. Helmbold, a New York patent-medicine manufacturer, felt strongly enough about the Democratic chances to stake a million-dollar bet against all comers, but his announced contribution to the campaign was only $40,000.

Then, as now, the Democrats made a strong bid for labor support. Seymour was pictured as the workingman's friend, a man who favored labor organization and the right to agitate for the eight-hour day.

Both parties passed the hat among federal job-holders, in these days before civil service. The Democrats noted that every dollar given in September would be worth ten given in October and the Republicans suggested "a voluntary offering in aid of the work."

One Democrat, R. W. Latham, thought of bribing the whole Washington press corps for Seymour. He said the newspapermen could be controlled for $3500 a month. The Republicans had been dickering for press support but made payment contingent on a Grant victory.

"This don't suit," Mr. Latham reported. It had to be cash on the barrelhead. Apparently the Democratic National Committee didn't think the press corps was worth the investment.

Seymour conducted a sedate campaign. He was as reluctant as a candidate as he had been for the nomination, and he was so impressed with the high dignity of the office that he felt it unseemly to stump for himself.

The Democrats disagreed among themselves on the money issue, Blair's bold calls for defiance of the Fourteenth Amendment made them nervous, and the party spent most of the campaign defending itself against charges of treason and revolutionary intent.

The Republicans pulled out all the stops. Grant was a bona fide war hero. He was no speaker, and knew it, and preferred to stay home in Galena, Illinois, and let the politicians do the work.

So the Radicals had a field day. They were smart enough to preserve Grant's reputation as a conservative, even while they charged conservative Democrats with treason. The Radicals organized "Tanner Clubs," honoring their candidate's peacetime occupation, "Boys in Blue" to keep the war alive. The Republicans made sure war veterans were readily available for mass meetings but kept the generals relatively quiet. Sherman and Sheridan accompanied Grant on a trip to Denver, but nobody made speeches except the politicians.

The Republicans hung President Johnson around the neck of Seymour, since Johnson had been a candidate for the Democratic nomination.

Southern generals, like their northern cousins, had little to say, but southern politicians conducted a vigorous campaign for the Democrats. Southern orations on reconstruction probably did as much to help Grant in the North as the Radicals did. *Harper's Weekly* noted that the issue of the campaign was simple enough: Grant and Peace or Blair and Revolution.

Finally, northern Democrats were so distressed that they persuaded General Lee and thirty other leaders from ten southern states to sign a letter noting that slavery and secession were dead issues, the South was now loyal to the Union and wanted only peace, self-government, and relief from misrule. It was a statesmanlike document, but it had little effect, for the Democrats, in trying to woo Negro votes, did not stop at barbecues and cajolery. The Ku Klux Klan, formed in 1866, was beginning to extend its sphere, and while party leaders denounced violence there was trouble from time to time.

At Camilla, Georgia, on September 19 a band of armed Negroes ran afoul of a sheriff's posse. Eight or nine Negroes were killed and several whites wounded before the pitched battle ended. The Democrats declared this was a case of mob suppression; the Republicans charged deliberate slaughter of the Negroes.

Generally, the North and West believed the Republicans. In September and October state elections were held in Vermont,

California, Maine, Nebraska, Pennsylvania, Indiana, Ohio, and West Virginia. The Republicans carried every state but California.

Now the Democrats were shocked into action. Seymour took to the field. Until October he had made only two speeches. At Albany he had carefully refrained from discussing campaign issues. At the Saratoga agricultural fair he had eulogized the farmer. But after refusing to speak in Pennsylvania, and noting the disastrous results, he embarked on a tour that took him as far west as Chicago and lasted until November 2, the day before election.

Hearing of Seymour's decision, President Johnson spoke out for the first time, wired Seymour his hopes for a Democratic victory.

The Democratic National Committee was very glum, and some party leaders nodded solemnly when the Democratic New York *World* called for the withdrawal of Blair as a smudge on the ticket. Seymour offered to resign, but the committee refused to let him, or to let Blair quit.

The Republicans laughed out loud, and three weeks before the election settled back to count their votes. Grant and Colfax were elected, by electoral votes of 214 to Seymour and Blair's 80. Yet, while Seymour carried only eight states, the popular vote was much less one-sided.

Grant's conservative position, his war record, his expression, "Let us have peace," won him the election. The whole country wanted real peace and no more trouble in the South. Even Chief Justice Salmon Chase was content with the result.

"Well, the election is over," Chase said. "I believe the result is the best for the country, though I could not bring myself to make a choice. Anything is certainly better than Blair and revolution."

Seymour attributed his defeat to the greenback plank in the Democratic platform. The facts show that while Grant won by 300,000 popular votes, there was, for the first time, a Negro vote of 700,000. The Democratic party was still the majority party in the country, but the former slaves looked to their liberator Grant and to the Republicans, the party that promised them equality. The Republicans seem to have won the election because they saw the trend of reaction against them in 1867, moved in Congress to increase the number of sure Republican votes, waved the "bloody shirt of the rebellion" night and day, and chose a candidate who could have been elected on a laundry ticket.

5

Eighteen sixty-eight. Three years after the end of the war the nation was still suffering the effects. This was not surprising, but the vindictiveness that blossomed among the politicians was shocking. The pre-war Abolitionists became the postwar Radicals. After the election of Grant, President Johnson was scorned even more thoroughly than Buchanan; after Johnson's impeachment attempt was begun in 1864 no one paid the slightest bit of attention to him. Even the Democrats, who had entertained some thoughts of running him, shied away as though the President were a carrier of the pox.

Lincoln had laid plans for quiet reconstruction of the South, and President Johnson tried to carry them out, but civil government was not restored in the way either had wanted. General amnesty was not given to the men of the South. Negroes did not receive limited suffrage but unlimited suffrage, which they were ill equipped to handle. The carpetbaggers and scalawags were the more equal, the aristocracy of the South was the less equal now.

5. Carpetbag and Ku Klux Klan

The election of Ulysses Simpson Grant to the presidency opened a kind of Pandora's box in America. Demons of avarice, treachery, skulduggery, bamboozlement and outright theft seemed to be lying in wait for the hero of Appomattox.

President Grant, unfortunately, tried to run the White House as General Grant would have. His military aides, transposed to civil affairs, fell easy prey to corruption by the school of sharks who wanted something from the government.

President Grant's life was further complicated because he saw himself as an administrator. It was his job, he felt, to carry out the policies established by Congress, for he believed Congress reflected the direct will of the people. But poor Grant was saddled with a Congress in which venality was the rule.

From the beginning in 1869, Grant's White House staff led the chase for gold. Hardly was General John Rawlins installed as Secretary of War when he conspired with Cuban rebels to wrest their land from the hands of Spain. A less intelligent sellout could hardly be imagined. The deal was made for $28,000 in bonds valuable only when the island was annexed to the United States.

The miserable, tubercular Rawlins died within the year, but Grant replaced him with General William W. Belknap, whose luxurious entertainments and princely habits shocked even cynical Washington. The price of a Belknap appointment to a lucrative post: a share of the loot. One such was an annual $12,000 fee paid to Mrs. Belknap by a trader in Fort Sill, Oklahoma Indian Territory, for what must have been a license to steal from the Indians.

Yet official waywardness was a very small drop in a very large bucket. The biggest crooks of the day roamed the floors of the stock exchanges, wined at Delmonico's, gossiped at the President's table, and slept in four-poster beds in their mansions, secure in the knowledge that they had bought the scurvy souls of every salable legislator in office.

The railroad magnates, knighted by an administration that gave them vast land grants, made the lobbyist an important factor in government. These new barons preferred to work indirectly, so they employed lawyers, newspapermen, and former office holders to educate and convince the lawmakers. Collis Huntington of the Central Pacific, Jay Cooke of the Northern Pacific, and Oakes Ames of the Union Pacific all spent millions of dollars explaining things. One lobbyist of the period was given a $60,000 contract as an explainer, and, like his fellows, he roamed the capital, buttonholing, cajoling, and distributing facts, liquor, cigars, and money.

In 1869, after the Union Pacific rail line was finished, Mr. Ames kindly arranged for legislators to see the masterpiece. They journeyed across the continent in private trains at a cost of $10,000 per train. News of this gigantic persuasion spread even to Paris, where Ambassador Elihu Washburne was seriously disturbed, for in his congressional days this tough old man from Illinois had been known as the watchdog of the treasury. Washburne wrote James G. Blaine, Speaker of the House, praising his friend's good sense in not taking the junket and expressing worry over the political implications of the free-loading. "Keep clear of all entangling alliances," Washburne warned.

But Blaine was too busy to listen—too busy managing the handout of public lands to railroaders and supervising the cutting of the juicy fiscal pies in the hands of Congress.

The Administration had the best part of the spoils. After eight years of Republican government—even in coalition with war Democrats and other Union men—there weren't many Democrats to nudge from the public trough, yet every job, from Cabinet to country post office, now came under the masters of patronage in the various states —party bosses whose greatest motives were political and personal gain.

When the "Mephistopheles of Wall Street," Jay Gould, planned to corner the gold market he found Grant's brother-in-law Abel Corbin and made him a minor partner in the Erie Railroad fraud. Corbin's job was to keep the naïve President blindfolded as Gould bought more and more gold; to keep Grant from ordering the

Treasury to prop up the market as the price jumped. The plot worked, until Black Friday, September 24, 1869, when Grant saw gold rise to 162½. Even as the President ordered the Treasury to open its doors, Gould had the word and was able to take his profit before hundreds of legitimate businesses collapsed as the price fell thirty points with the public announcement.

No pocket was too small to pick, no treasury immune from rape as the freebooters of business and politics filled their carpetbags and wall safes.

Colonel Orville E. Babcock, once Grant's military aide, now chief of his "kitchen cabinet" and principal adviser, became an informal partner in a combine that milked the District of Columbia treasury and ran up a public debt of $17 million in three years.

When Brevet General John A. McDonald learned of the Black Friday scandal he was so impressed that he asked Grant to introduce him to Jay Gould and his worthy partner Jim Fisk. Grant caviled at this, but on Babcock's advice appointed McDonald Supervisor of Internal Revenue at St. Louis. The job only paid $3000 a year, but General McDonald made it up in fringe benefits. When Babcock found it necessary to travel to St. Louis, from time to time, he came home with diamond baubles and cigar boxes full of thousand-dollar bills, for McDonald had set up a doughty business with whisky distillers in which they paid taxes to him instead of the government. As Washington contact Babcock kept St. Louis informed of complaints and suspicions that found their way to the White House.

This system worked admirably. Best of all, from the viewpoint of Republican politicians, was that the party now found a gold mine in St. Louis.

The collector's office was a gay and fun-loving place. Lawmakers could always count on a campaign contribution from St. Louis. In later years, when the Whisky Ring had been unmasked to the public, McDonald reported that at the height of the campaign of 1872 Indiana political boss Oliver Morton had visited him to refill the whole state's campaign chests.

Elsewhere, also, reconstruction offered all kinds of opportunities for ambitious and hard-working men. The Radical Republicans of Congress were committed to rebuild a South that would never again rebel, where all men would be equal, and as many as possible would be Republican. Determined to insure the freedom of the Negroes, visionaries like Senator Charles Sumner of Massachusetts unwittingly set the South up for pillage. The Radicals encouraged election of Negro legislators. Northern carpetbaggers and southern scalawags promptly employed the Negro vote in every conceivable way to get the boodle.

"To the victors belong the spoils," said the Administration, even as the spoils rotted the foundations of government. As corruption spread, so did the determination of southern whites to regain control of their governments. The Ku Klux Klansmen rode through the night in white sheets, masquerading as the ghosts of Confederate soldiers to frighten superstitious Negroes. Plunder and fraud begot violence and murder as the whites banded together to take back their governments, even though hundreds of thousands of white southerners had already been disfranchised by the Fourteenth Amendment.

The North was slow to realize the extent of the plunder. With the 1870 congressional and state elections a season away, Horace Greeley, with a straight face, complimented his party in the New York *Tribune*:

"We do not think it is assuming too much when we say that probably no party has ever been governed so much by its principles and so little by selfishness as the party that has ruled the country during the past decade."

But by election time, 1870, some citizens were growing restless under this constant drain of the nation's wealth into a handful of strongboxes.

In the South the congressional program of reconstruction had been completed by the midyear. It was just a question of fixing the state laws so the carpetbaggers could take over.

These worthies already had control of Louisiana, which became a sea of putridity that washed across the southern shores. In 1868, Henry Clay Warmoth was elected the first governor of Louisiana, under the reconstructed constitution. Governor Warmoth was a native of Illinois who had served with General Grant until Grant dismissed him from the service for theft. At the end of the war Warmoth had drifted to Texas, and there had been indicted for stealing cotton, but only indicted.

When he appeared in Louisiana, Warmoth moved quickly to the top of the Republican party, for he was young, intelligent, imaginative, and completely dishonest. Warmoth promised the Negro voters to invent a machine to pump black blood out of their veins and replace it with white blood. That campaign promise was an immediate success. He was elected, along with a Negro house painter who became lieutenant governor, and a predominately Negro legislature.

In two years Warmoth ran the Louisiana state debt from $6 million to $50 million, saved $100,000 a year on a personal salary of $8000. In four years the governor had quarreled with other worthy white Republicans in the state. He denounced the carpetbag government as crooked and in 1872 voted the Democratic ticket.

South Carolina's reconstruction House of Representatives was composed of 124 members: 23 white, 101 Negro. The speaker, clerk, doorkeepers, pages, and chaplain were all Negroes, ill educated for the most part—but glorying in their power as they laid down the laws of the land, as the twenty-three whites sat grim and silent, waiting.

By 1870 the disaffected and disgusted white Democrats and conservative Republicans rebelled in an unsuccessful attempt to take legislative control from the corrupt radicals.

Elsewhere, particularly in the border states where race was not such an important issue, the reaction against reconstruction was quicker. In Arkansas the Republicans divided into regular or "minstrel" and liberal or "brindle" groups; in 1870 the Democrats gained by the split, and the liberals elected nine members to the legislature.

In the Deeper South, in states like Alabama, the Democrats were gaining control. The night riding of the Ku Klux Klan and the revulsion against Radical excesses began to create the solid Democratic white South.

But the worst shock to the Administration in Washington was Missouri's ingratitude. B. Gratz Brown deserted the regular Republicans, to be elected governor on a Liberal Republican ticket, over the specific and public objections of President Grant, who called these dissenters "traitors" to the party.

This Missouri movement became the Liberal Republican party, as wartime passions cooled and conservatives began to see the effects of Radical policy.

The Radical Congress had passed a high protective-tariff act in 1870, to the hearty applause of a president who was now effectively under their thumb. Free trade, civil service reform, and reconstruction were issues in the 1870 congressional campaigns. After elections the Republican majority in the House was reduced to 37 seats in the Forty-second Congress, and the party lost four senatorial seats.

The Democrats gained 16 seats in the House from Virginia, Tennessee, West Virginia, and Missouri. The Democrats also elected senators from Missouri, Tennessee, West Virginia, and North Carolina. The South was rising again, in national affairs, but that did not tell the full story of the Republican loss. Among the Republicans elected to the House, 43 were tariff reformers, 35 of them from the Middle West.

The Democrats won that year in Georgia, too, but General Alfred Howe Terry illegally expelled twenty-four white Democrats and Conservative Republicans from the legislature to keep the Radicals in power. As the Radicals said: "Law or no law, we want to keep this state government in power."

In 1871 the pattern for the solid South was set. The excesses of the Radicals had driven the native white into a unified Democratic opposition. In the North, and West, the Republicans quarreled among themselves over spoils and fell out over the inefficient and dishonest civil service system, scandalous southern policy, and the high tariff, advocated by the East and hated by the West.

The country was now ripe for change, it seemed. Certainly the anti-Radicals thought a change was needed. The corruption and excesses of vengeance against the South had begun to sicken many who had felt their own share of hatred for the rebellious southerners during the war and just after it. But now the war had been over for seven years. This was 1872, not 1865. Many were tired of the constant strife.

Many more were tired of the corruption and the evil-doing and the slackness of Washington and its long fingers of government.

President Grant had made enemies, as any President will through appointments in his own party, and the lack of them; through public and private actions and public and private friendships and enmities. Besides, he had been in office for four years. Consequently the glamour had rubbed off for some of his supporters. They thought it was time for a change.

Cassius M. Clay, the Kentucky colonel who had done so much to win the 1860 Republican nomination for Lincoln, was one of these. He was an original sponsor of a movement in 1871 to nominate Horace Greeley instead of Grant on the Republican ticket in 1872. Greeley was a not too reluctant candidate. In the spring of 1871 he toured the South, where he was generally well received. The

Administration, sensing danger, made some attempt to appeal to the moderates and reformers, but the old ways and the boodle won out. Senator Carl Schurz of Missouri, one of the newly elected reformers, spread his doctrine all over the South and West, and the New York *Herald* began calling him "the great political missionary, laboring for the defeat of General Grant next year."

Schurz and Governor B. Gratz Brown were the leading figures at the Liberal state convention at Jefferson City, Missouri, on January 24. They set forth the issues of the 1872 campaign: universal amnesty for the rebels of the Civil War, lower tariffs, civil service reform, and an end to federal interference in states' rights.

The Missourians invited all Republicans who wanted reform to a national convention at Cincinnati on May 1. Now that the Tweed Ring's power was destroyed and Jim Fisk dead, Horace Greeley could see corruption in the Administration. But the Liberals' tariff policy stuck in his protectionist craw, and it was not until March that he convinced himself the corruption of the Administration was a greater evil.

Greeley's new conviction was helped along by events at a pair of minority party conventions in the early months of the year.

The Labor Reform movement at Columbus, Ohio, on February 21 gave Greeley eleven votes for nomination, although Judge David Davis of Illinois and Governor Joel Parker of New Jersey were the candidates finally selected.

The next day 194 delegates from 9 states met at the Prohibition convention in Columbus to denounce the evils of rum and to nominate a candidate for the presidency. As a red-hot teetotaler, of long standing, Greeley was again mentioned prominently and favorably, although James Black of Pennsylvania became the candidate and John Russell of Michigan his running mate.

By spring 1872 the revolt of the anti-administration Republicans was serious, and Greeley, once that most ardent of regular-party men, had begun to question the unquestionable.

The taste for public office was not a new sensation. In 1848 the *Tribune* editor had served a three months' term in Congress—appointed to fill a vacancy—and there he had introduced the first homestead bill, which gave small tracts of government land to actual settlers.

In 1861, Greeley had run for the Senate but had been defeated. In 1867 he had been considered for the Senate nomination, but came out so strongly in favor of universal amnesty for the southern rebels that it was unthinkable to nominate him and give these obnoxious views a place of honor in Congress. In 1869, Greeley had been Republican candidate for state comptroller, in a Democratic year, and in 1870 he ran for the House of Representatives but fell ill during the campaign.

Now, at 61, Greeley was one of the most controversial characters in the Republican party. He affected a long white duster and strange, distinctive clothing. He detested woman's suffrage, thought theaters the spawning place of the devil, and opposed divorce. A great and fearless editor, he had no business sense and was prone to investments in desiccated egg companies, well-salted mining stocks, and patent looms. By 1872, when he felt the presidential itch, Greeley owned only six of one hundred shares of the stock in the *Tribune* he had started in 1841.

More and more disgusted with the excesses of the regular Republican party, he began calling attention to some of the strange political shenanigans going on.

As the rebellious conventioners began assembling in Cincinnati in the last few days of April, the loyal Republican New York *Times* was openly derisive of the "soreheads" who had flocked together. It would be less than kind, but probably accurate, to suspect that some of the *Times'* derision was occasioned by the rivalry between editor Raymond and Greeley.

Delegates had assembled from nearly every state. But whom did they represent?

A colored preacher in Cincinnati called on several colored delegates from Louisiana and expressed surprise at their desertion of the Republican party that had freed them from slavery.

"You see, they wanted some colored men to make a show," the delegates told the preacher, "and offered free tickets and expenses paid; so we came along for the fun of the thing."

Altogether, Henry Raymond's men thought it a gang "from which the nation may devoutly pray to be saved." As for Greeley, why, "His very portrait would call forth yells of laughter when presented as that of a proposed occupant of the presidential chair."

Greeley was no front-runner in the contest. The now venerable Salmon P. Chase was mentioned, of course. His name was brought up by both parties in those confused postwar days. The leading figure at Cincinnati was Judge David Davis of Illinois, whose supporters had already gotten him the Labor nomination.

Charles Francis Adams, governor of Massachusetts, was the choice of the reformers, for he was sympathetic to the Liberal cause and had no major difference with the Democrats.

Sixteen hundred delegates rattled around in an exposition hall that could seat six thousand. But if they did not draw the big crowds of the regular party conventions, the Liberals suffered no shortage of scheming and maneuvering in the best tradition of both major parties.

The Illinois supporters of Judge Davis had provided transportation and paid the bills for all the Republicans they could persuade. Until just before the convention opened the professional politicians hoped to turn the rebel reformers over to the Davis machine.

The New York and Pennsylvania delegations, directed by Senator Fenton and Colonel A. K. McClure, planned to work with the Davis group to put up Davis and Greeley.

But on the night of April 29 four leading independent editors, all ardent reformers, upset the political apple barrel and declared in a joint newspaper release that they would not support Davis under any conditions. When Senator Fenton heard the bad news he gave up and went back to Washington.

The reformers were jubilant. Missouri's Senator Schurz, permanent president of the convention and leader of the reform movement in Missouri, warned the delegates that "beat Grant" was not enough. The political bosses agreed with him. The bosses fought off efforts to nominate Adams or anyone else. They were determined to carry the convention for Greeley, and the pale, red-haired Gratz Brown of Missouri. The cantankerous old *Tribune* editor was in a terrible fix, for he was a "ferocious" advocate of the high protective tariff, and the tariff was the cause of the principal fight over the platform.

Finally in an all-night session the tariff problem was resolved by an uneasy compromise. The reformers submitted, since they believed they were going to put their candidate into the driver's seat.

Then came the deal: B. Gratz Brown agreed to take second place and throw his support to Greeley. It was all over but the shouting. On the fifth ballot Adams was fifty-one votes ahead, and within thirty-three of the nomination. On the sixth ballot, when Greeley began to show gains, his managers decided the moment had come, so they called for their "spontaneous demonstration." It was the greatest convention display since Judge Davis and company had invented this claque system to overwhelm the Seward forces in Chicago's Wigwam in 1860.

"As the voting wore on," wrote an ardent young reformer later, "Adams strengthened, and by the time the fifth ballot was reached, Greeley was plainly on the decline. Then came the spontaneous rally which had been carefully planned the night before. The hall was filled with a mechanical pre-ordained, stentorious bellowing. Hoary-haired, hard-eyed politicians, who had not in twenty years felt a noble impulse, mounted their chairs and with faces suffused with a seraphic fervor, blistered their throats hurraying for the great and good Horace Greeley. The noise bred a panic. A furore, artificial at first, became real and ended in a stampede."

Convention President Schurz, seeing his reform movement flying into the hands of the hard-eyed ones, brought up his parliamentary rules to stop the tide. But he was shouted down, and the convention nominated Horace Greeley.

It seemed to have been done in a moment. First the room was shocked into silence. But then hundreds of delegates began stamping their feet and swearing. Old Judge Hoadley of Ohio, a trenchant reformer, "shook with rage." Scores of delegates left in disgust, even before the vice-presidential nomination. But Brown was nominated with speed, if without enthusiasm.

Washington was as surprised as the delegates. When the news hit the floor of the House of Representatives it sent up a loud and general laughter of disbelief.

Senator Trumbull, one of the principal leaders of the reform movement and a prime contender for the nomination, was visibly shaken. As he retreated behind his newspaper—the pages quivered.

In New York as Greeley stepped from the *Tribune* office into Printing House Square he was surrounded by a crowd of grinning, cheering newsboys who followed him to the horse-drawn tram that would carry him uptown to the Union League Club. But at the club, a Republican stronghold if there ever was one, Greeley was greeted by stony silence. He stopped to pick up a bundle of letters from his postal box. He walked into the club reading room. There several members engaged in animated conversation suddenly stopped. The silence was intolerable. It was not long until Greeley left the club for more congenial surroundings.

In Wall Street, in the stock exchanges, the gold room, the merchants' news rooms, and the cotton and produce exchanges the nomination was regarded as a "huge joke" or a tragedy.

At the Democratic Manhattan Club one member announced loudly that of course he would vote for Mr. Greeley—he would vote for the devil himself rather than U. S. Grant.

And at the fashionable Fifth Avenue Hotel a gathering of prominent citizens agreed among themselves that the Democrats would not support this farce or their lifelong enemy. It was preposterous.

But whatever the initial reaction, Greeley was now a full-fledged candidate for President, and if his platform included a rickety plank on the tariff issue, the whole platform raised some embarrassing questions for the regular Republicans.

The platform called for equality of all men before the law. That meant universal amnesty and restoration of the civil rights of white southerners. It also proposed return to self-government after the South accepted the war amendments to the Constitution. These were measures designed to wipe out the bitterness of the Civil War—measures whose inclusion on a party platform showed how tenuous and destructive the boondoggling reconstruction program had become.

The Liberal platform also demanded civil service reform, restriction of the presidency to one term, tax reform, a return to payment in metal money, opposition to land grants, and "just dealings" with foreign nations—a slap at Grant's fairy-tale attempt to make Santo Domingo an American possession.

The Greeley nomination brought great glee to the hearts of the regular Republican organization. The platform reflected truly the issues of the day. Theft and rottenness in government were not regarded as bitterly then as now. There was, indeed, great admiration for thieves and rascals like Jim Fisk, Commodore Vanderbilt, and Boss Tweed, all the more for those who stole and defrauded without getting caught.

The three surviving members of Lincoln's cabinet, Salmon Chase, Gideon Welles, and Blair, supported the new group.

The Democrats were faced with a serious problem that year. They had the support of nearly half the voters, but they lost election after election, by so few votes as to make them gnash their teeth in rage. Under the majority system their 45 per cent meant very little. In the Forty-first Congress the Republicans had a majority in the House; in the election of 1868, Grant's 300,000 majority over Seymour was as effective as if it had been 3,000,000. What the Democrats needed was control of states, and thus guaranteed electoral votes. But the party was in trouble, for it had still not regained control of the South—its source of prewar strength—and the Tweed scandal of New York had broken its strength in that key state.

The Liberal platform had one great appeal to the Democrats: it got them off the hook of the Civil War. Maybe this new movement was not ideal, but it would be good enough to bury the albatross of treason. This new movement was not a Democratic movement. Greeley was a well-known Republican. The old bloody shirt of rebellion could not be waved against him. Even the irreconcilable old Clement Vallandigham, leader of the peace Democrats, had finally accepted the war amendments to the Constitution—the measures that guaranteed civil rights to the Negro. The Democrats wanted to get back into the election race, and a good share of the party urged support of the Greeley-Brown ticket. For others, reformers as well as Democrats, this ticket was harder to swallow. On May 2 some two hundred delegates from eleven states met together at Cincinnati—in the heat of the Liberal Republican convention—and banded together as the Reunion and Reform convention. It was understood that Reunion and Reform would endorse the Liberals, but when Greeley was nominated the shock was too much for the reformers. They adjourned.

The regular Republicans met at Philadelphia on June 5, to preserve the status quo and solve the question of the vice-presidency. Schuyler Colfax was the Vice-President, but he had made his quota of enemies, including a number of Washington newspapermen. Grant was nominated by unanimous vote, and Henry Wilson of Massachusetts was chosen on the first ballot as Vice-President—defeating Colfax by forty-three votes.

In May the Democrats of Tennessee had instructed their delegates to the national convention to support the Greeley-Brown ticket. So had the Democrats of New York.

The other states began to fall into line, but not without incident.

On June 27 in the debate of the Virginia Democratic Convention all the delegates favored Greeley, but one. The ancient and honored Extra Billy Smith, twice governor of Virginia, answered the recalcitrant:

"Give me Jew or Gentile, dog or devil, I care not which, so we can beat Grant."

In response to which the unhappy one, Colonel J. H. Lacy, coined a phrase and established a campaign issue: "I kin eat crow," he said, "but I don't hanker arter it."

In all, when the Democrats assembled at Baltimore on July 9, eighteen states were primed to feast on the black scavenger. The Liberal platform was adopted 670 to 62, and after the two-thirds and unit rules were adopted Greeley was nominated with 686 votes, Brown for Vice-President with 713.

But the Democratic party was not to be united against Grant, no matter what its bosses might say. On September 3, at Louisville, Kentucky, the party's bolters nominated Charles O'Conor, and Charles Francis Adams, defeated candidate for the Liberal nomination, for Vice-President.

O'Conor promptly declined the nomination. The convention then nominated James Lyon of Virginia, but he declined. Adams refused to take anything but the vice-presidential nomination, and not even that unless O'Conor were presidential candidate, so the rump Democratic party retired in confusion, after renominating the unwilling O'Conor.

Party discipline had been thrown to the winds by both major parties, and now the field was wide open.

The Liberal Republican Revenue Reformers party, free-trade advocates, met in New York. They nominated William S. Groesbeck of Ohio for President and Frederick Law Olmsted of New York for Vice-President. Their greatest claim to fame was a call for direct election of the President and Vice-President, and elimination of the convention system of nomination.

Victoria Claflin Woodhull became the first woman to seek the presidency. Her candidacy was supported by Theodore Tilton, a newspaperman, superintendent of Henry Ward Beecher's Plymouth Church Sunday school, and Mrs. Woodhull's publicly avowed lover. She was a spiritualist and strong suffragette, but her platform included free love as well.

Another candidate was George Francis Train, one of the backers of the Union Pacific and a sponsor of the Crédit Mobilier of America, a venture formed ostensibly to finance building of the railroad. Train espoused communalism, which he had encountered in France, and woman's suffrage. He was nominated by the Train League, a group he had thoughtfully founded.

Train's candidacy was notable because he was in the know on part of the Crédit Mobilier scandal, which the New York *Sun* exposed in the first week of September as one of the juiciest and most awe-inspiring swindles of all time in which major political figures were embroiled, fleecing the public of millions of dollars.

It was quite an array by now—candidates to fit just about anyone's prejudices. The parties were splintering, and changing character, to a degree. But more than that, the splintering reflected dissatisfaction with the corruption of the Grant administration, dissatisfaction with the continued harassment of the southern whites, and a desire to settle down.

There was never any real question in the election, except between Grant and Greeley. And no one really expected Greeley to win, partly because he was such a strange political figure, partly because the combination of reform-Democrat-crackpot support did not seem a realistic base for the presidency, and partially because the Democrats really knew Greeley wasn't their candidate, and Greeley really knew his compromise on the tariff issue changed his public profile considerably, and unfavorably.

The campaign of 1872 started as a war of ideas, but when it was over Senator Carl Schurz, the reformer, complained that it had become a "campaign of personalities." Greeley noted ruefully that it was hard to tell whether he was running for "President or the penitentiary."

Grant took no part in the campaign, which was probably the smartest thing he could have done. As usual, he neither attended the party convention to preside at his own nomination, nor did he make a speaking tour. His speechmaking was not that impressive, anyhow. Most of the political season he spent at his summer home in Long Branch, secure in the belief that he would win the election.

Gratz Brown wasn't much of a help to Greeley. In July he came East to attend a Yale University commencement, got drunk at the alumni dinner, and made a fool of himself at the hotel that night.

The Springfield Republican demanded that Brown withdraw from the ticket—a request the vice-presidential candidate did not honor.

Senator Charles Sumner, who had been ousted as chairman of the Foreign Relations Committee after a fight with the Administration in 1871, on the proposed annexation of Santo Domingo, came out for Greeley at the end of July. But Sumner's support was purely moral. He left in September for Europe and did not return until after election day.

The Republicans threw every charge in their book at Greeley. They accused him of giving bribes in Washington, of participating in the Tweed Ring. They pictured him as a slave trader, as a secessionist, a friend of the Ku Klux Klan.

The Liberals and the Democrats assailed the corruption of the Administration, and while Grant's personal honesty was generally recognized, his opponents belittled his associates and friends, his proclivity for putting his own and his wife's relatives on the public payroll.

The Liberal platform weaseled on the tariff question, to the disgust of those who had joined the growing move for free trade. There was little to choose between the naïvete of Grant and that of Greeley, and none of the other candidates was seriously in the race.

The businessmen, merchants, and manufacturers poured money into the Republican coffers in bundles. The country seemed prosperous; they remembered Lincoln's warning not to change horses in midstream. The corrupt officials of the Grant administration now gave some of their loot to the common cause—staying in power. The loot of the Whisky Ring was invaluable in shoring up weak positions around the country.

At the end, just before election, Greeley's wife fell ill and he lost interest in a campaign that was going badly, anyhow. Greeley remained at his wife's bedside until she died on October 30. Then came election day. It was generally quiet, with no more than the usual amount of fraud. The suffragettes provided comic relief. In New York, Victoria Woodhull tried unsuccessfully to vote for herself. Upstate, Susan B. Anthony and a dozen others wheedled Rochester officials into letting them vote under the Fourteenth and Fifteenth amendments; and in Oregon, officials let four women vote, just to keep the peace, but threw their ballots out after they left the polls. Almost all these women voted for Grant, though Greeley had given women's rights good play in the *Tribune;* the Negro vote went for

Grant, though Greeley, not Grant, was the old Abolitionist; the business vote went to Grant, though Greeley was the stanch Republican rock of protectionism.

It was a strange election, General Sherman said, in describing it to his brother, a Republican senator:

"Grant," he wrote, "who never was a Republican, is your candidate, and Greeley, who never was a Democrat, but quite the reverse, is the Democratic candidate."

The outcome was predictable long before election day. Grant had too much money behind him, the Republicans had too much at stake; the reformers and Democrats were too badly split; the Liberal platform was too confused; and Horace Greeley too strange a man, proving that great newspapermen are not necessarily even fair politicians.

Grant won decisively, 3,597,132 to Greeley's 2,834,125; O'Conor's 29,489 and Prohibitionist Black's 5608. Greeley carried only a half dozen states. The death of his wife, the load of the campaign, and the vicious charges of old friends were too much for him. He died soon afterward, leaving the field to the incumbent Grant and an era of corruption that was now beginning to send up its stench.

6

Quite aside from the political boodling of the Grant administration, the country was undergoing considerable social change during this period. Mrs. O'Leary's cow had kicked over the lantern in Chicago, and the resulting conflagration eliminated a good deal of the city's old-time construction.

Elsewhere in the nation, the effects of the industrial revolution were making themselves felt. There was a general stirring of labor which was still deluded into believing the protective tariff protected the working man. Besides the Vanderbilts and Fisks who were lining their pockets, men were moving West, discovering new lands and new resources. The Northwest was opening as a whole new section of the nation, and the transcontinental railways were knitting the country together as an economic unit. The West was still a colony, and would be for a long time to come. But the whole country was growing, and feeling the need for new ways of doing things. The Civil War still rankled, but the bloody shirt was growing frayed.

6. The Fraud of 1876

"How Crédit Mobilier Bought Its Way Into Congress," exploded the headline in Charles Dana's New York *Sun*. It was the first week in September, 1872, and Dana's paper linked a dozen of the most prominent names in Congress with the gigantic Crédit Mobilier—a firm organized to finance construction of the Union Pacific Railway.

It was election year. The charges were extravagant, although they were generally true. The fact was that the Crédit Mobilier had stolen more money from the United States Government than most citizens could possibly imagine.

Here's how it was done:

When the clamor for a railroad across the continent had reached its height during the Civil War, the men who were promoting the Union Pacific Railroad secured grants of twelve million acres of land. Further, they persuaded the federal government to lend them $27,000,000 and take a second mortgage for the money. The first mortgage was held by earlier investors whose money had been poured into the pockets of the promoters.

Then the promoters took over a little investment company called the Crédit Mobilier. The promoters, as Crédit Mobilier, made a deal with themselves as the Union Pacific: Crédit Mobilier would actually build the railroad. The Union Pacific would pay Crédit Mobilier a price about three times the cost of doing the work.

The federal government now held a second mortgage on a worthless piece of corporate property known as the Union Pacific Railroad. If it had gone broke at any time in those days, it is hard to see how the government would have been able to recover a cent of its investment, or any of the value of the land grant.

In order to keep this gigantic bit of personal thievery quiet it was necessary that no one in Congress ask how the Union Pacific was faring or ask for a look at the railroad's books. And this could best be accomplished by ringing the individual members of Congress into the act.

No one paid too much attention to the *Sun* charges, because it was election year. But those charges were repeated and garnished by anti-administration politicians throughout the land. The *Sun* was a Democratic newspaper, and the whole campaign of 1872 was so vicious that this exposure fell quietly among the rest, causing hardly more than passing notice—at first.

But once the election was safely won, the very men who had been charged with wrongdoing called bravely for an investigation: Speaker James G. Blaine of the House of Representatives and Representative James Garfield were among the loudest to demand proof or exoneration of the fair name of Congress.

When the Forty-second Congress reconvened in December 1872, Representative Luke Poland of Vermont was assigned a special committee and the job of getting the facts. Blaine himself had been falsely charged with accepting ten shares of Crédit Mobilier stock from Representative Oakes Ames, the millionaire plow manufacturer who was hip-deep in the scheme. The Speaker knew the charge against *him* was untrue; apparently he believed there was no more truth to any part of the scandal.

But in the investigation the testimony of the lawmakers began to indicate strange, naïve misunderstandings by other guardians of the public weal.

Several congressmen had purchased shares in the Mobilier from Ames. Some admitted it. But they became strangely forgetful when asked if they knew that they bought the shares at less than half their market value or that it was unusual for any seller to finance the sale, as Ames had in many cases.

The investigation disclosed shabby performance of duty. Ames had lied flatly on September 18, when he told the newspapers: "I never gave a share of stock, directly or indirectly, to any member of the Congress." Actually, he had only dispensed about $65,000 worth of stock since 1863. The accused congressmen were losing their integrity over amounts that in most cases involved only a few hundred dollars each. It was nothing compared to the estimated $40 to $50 million dollars the real backers of the Crédit Mobilier stole in the building of the Union Pacific.

Dana's *Sun* had accused sixteen congressmen of wrongdoing, but the two investigating committees, sympathetic to their colleagues, to be sure, found strong evidence against only three of them.

At first the lawmakers cried for their heads, but Speaker Blaine worked to lessen the punishment. Finally the three escaped with a censure for unbecoming conduct.

Saddest of all were the fates of Vice-President Henry Wilson, who had returned his ill-gotten stocks, and Schuyler Colfax, who until this time had been regarded as a presidential possibility. Colfax denied that he had accepted anything from Ames, but the investigators had his bank statement, which showed a $12,000 deposit on the day Ames said he had given Colfax $12,000.

That was the end of Colfax and Wilson as political figures.

The Crédit Mobilier scandal was still stirring in March 1873 when the Republican Forty-second Republican Congress unwisely voted itself a retroactive raise in pay. Then on September 18 came the unexpected collapse of the great banking firm of Jay Cooke, the biggest contributor to the Republican campaign of 1872. The panic of 1873 was on. Daily hundreds of businessmen fell by the wayside. The nation, seemingly so prosperous a few months before, sank into the tortures of depression, and in the shadows of the panic the "Salary Grab" of Congress was even more unpalatable to the voting public. While many members of the Forty-third Congress refused to accept the raise they had voted the damage was done.

In 1872, on Grant's coattails, the Republicans had elected 194 men to the House; the Democrats 92; the Liberals 14. But in the reaction of reform and hard times, in 1874 the Democrats captured control of the House: 169 Democrats, 109 Republicans, 14 Liberals. For the first time since 1860 the Republicans' control of Congress was shattered. And in the anti-Republican reaction even Massachusetts —which had given the Republicans majorities ever since the birth of the party—elected a Democratic governor.

That same election in 1874 saw the official birth of the Greenback movement, which was to flash across the sky of American politics during the next few years, then to fade away—completely, by 1882— as prosperity returned. The Greenback party picked up a platform plank the Democrats discarded after their defeat by Governor Hayes in the Ohio elections of 1874. Earlier the western wing of the Democratic party had favored an increase in the use of federal greenback currency, those bills that were not backed specifically by metal money, in the Treasury but were guaranteed by the government.

When it became apparent that the greenback plank would not be urged in the Democratic convention of 1876, the soft money men from both major parties got together to form their own crusade.

The Republicans laughed at the fanatics. The Democrats were feeling their muscle now. After winning control of the House the Democrats felt certain they would win the presidency in the elections of 1876. President Grant, of course, was a threat to their hopes, but he was serving out his second term, and the continued eruption of scandal in his administration was weakening the position of even this hero.

Grant would have liked a third term, but he wanted to be coaxed. The Pennsylvania Republican state convention in 1875 passed a resolution opposing the third term for any President. Noting this, Grant wrote the president of the convention that he did not want a third term, any more than he had wanted a first term, but that circumstances might arise when it could be unfortunate to make a change at the end of eight years. Grant did not foresee any such circumstances, of course, and he "would not accept" nomination unless it was made "an imperative duty."

This was an invitation to the party to draft the general. But the party demurred. Just after the Forty-third Congress reconvened in December 1874, Democratic representatives from Illinois laid it on the line:

". . . in the opinion of this House, the precedent established by Washington and other Presidents of the United States in retiring from the President's office after their second term, has become by universal concurrence, a part of our republican system of government, and that any departure from this time-honored custom would be unwise, unpatriotic, and fraught with peril to our free institutions."

Every Democrat in the House that day voted for the resolution— but even worse, so did 70 of the 88 Republicans. The result was 234 to 18. The third term was dead. Or at least stunned.

Colfax and Wilson having been ruined by Crédit Mobilier, the strongest Republican candidate was James G. Blaine. He had been Speaker for six years and was now minority leader in the House under the Democratic Congress. But while Blaine was cleared in the Crédit Mobilier investigation he was now charged with corruption in connection with the Little Rock and Fort Smith Railroad Company.

The charges were no help when he sought support of the strong reform movement that had rejoined the Republican party. The reformers liked Benjamin H. Bristow, an honest Kentucky lawyer, and the Secretary of the Treasury who had been responsible for stirring the country against the Whisky Ring that had stolen $4,000,000 between 1872 and 1874 alone. Bristow was the favorite candidate of those Republicans who were down on the Administration—but the Adminstration still had powerful adherents. Grant had turned against Bristow when the Secretary brought Whisky Ring charges against Colonel Babcock. Grant's loyalty to his friends was a notable attribute, not one to be abused with impunity. As a carrier, if not a cause, of embarrassment to the President, it was not long before Bristow resigned his cabinet post. The Whisky Ring exposure finished Collector McDonald, who was convicted of theft. It finished Babcock, who had to resign his White House job. Two big fish, again, got away.

Far less controversial than Blaine or Bristow was the Governor of Ohio, Rutherford B. Hayes, a citizen of spotless reputation. Further, Hayes had one of those handsome war records—he had been made a temporary major general for bravery in action at Fishers Hill and Cedar Creek during the Civil War. And he could win elections. Hayes had won the governorship of Ohio three times, including 1874 when Republicans were dropping like flies all over the North and West.

As spring drew on the charges against Blaine were still under investigation and the party was split in two. The convention promised to be hot, even hotter than Cincinnati in June.

But first the lesser parties would have their innings. On May 17 the Prohibitionists met in prayerful session at Cleveland. They suggested Green Clay Smith of Kentucky and G. T. Stewart of Ohio as a combination that could save the country from sin and sour mash. This had some relevance to real politics since that same day the widow of John Leavenworth, the pay-off man for the Whisky Ring, testified in St. Louis that the ring had been organized for political gain. Her husband, she said, had sometimes kept as much as $7000 in the house over weekends, when he had failed to contact various minor government officials on Saturday. It was his job to assure the proper ratio: the distillers preferred to pay taxes on only one third of the whisky they produced.

As Mr. Smith received the dry accolade, what was left of the revolutionary Liberal movement of 1872 was meeting at the Fifth Avenue Hotel in New York. New York's practical Thurlow Weed and Missouri dreamer Carl Schurz were both there. The venerated Peter Cooper stuck his white whiskers in the door for a few moments, but his heart was in Indianapolis, where the Greenback, or Independent National, party was setting up shop at the Opera House, despite the overpowering humidity and breathless heat. On the eighteenth of May, Cooper was nominated by the Green-backers. He declined at first, said he was too old, but was nominated anyhow, since the party could agree on no one else. The 239 delegates from 19 states also nominated Senator Newton Booth of California as Vice-President. Booth declined and meant it; Cooper's running mate became General Samual F. Cary of Ohio, who had espoused just about every new political cause that came along.

Meanwhile the reformers in New York decided they liked Bristow or Samuel Tilden, the former Democratic governor of New York who had done so much to rid the city of the Tweed Ring, but they were in no position to do anything about it. The New York *Times*, loyal as usual to the Republican party, called Tilden a "political trickster" and saved its praise for the forthcoming Republican convention in Cincinnati.

That convention was most anxious to cultivate the Liberals, who had contributed spectacularly to the Democratic successes in the elections of 1874. Now, Carl Schurz, lampooned for years as a visionary fool by the Republican party press, was suddenly seen as a respected statesman. Schurz was pleased, but wary. Even President Grant made gruff peace with the Liberals. In December 1874, after the House had been lost to the Democrats, Grant offered an important customs job to A. W. Bradford, a leading Liberal from Maryland. The Democrats were strong now and grew stronger during 1875 as competition was exposed at a frightening rate. On October 12, 1875, Rutherford Hayes wrote in his diary, "Defeat in the next presidential election is almost a certainty." In the spring of 1876 scandal followed scandal, much to the delight of a Democratic House of Representatives.

The Republicans, if they had a chance of winning in 1876, had to be "clean as a hound's tooth" and they knew it. So the Liberal reformers were wooed accordingly, and their demands, spurned so sneeringly in 1872, were now accepted.

On June 10 the Cincinnati hotels began filling up, as the delegates arrived for the sixth Republican National Convention. Blaine was strong in Illinois, Colorado, and Wisconsin but weak in New York and Connecticut, and his enemy Roscoe Conkling had the pledges of 70 delegates who stepped off the Pennsylvania Railroad's crack train from New York. Pennsylvania's 58 delegates were instructed to vote for a favorite son—General John F. Hartranft. Senator Morton had 30 votes from his own Indiana and about 100 more from southern delegates. Bristow was reported to have about 100 votes. Only if the votes for all the others could be put together could Blaine be beaten. That's how strong the former Speaker was, as the Republican National Committee met in room 108 of the Burnet House on May 12, to settle, first of all, the question of convention-hall tickets for the delegates.

It was unmercifully hot in Washington that week. Mr. Blaine had just gratefully accepted an offer by the Western Union Telegraph Company to install a private wire in his library. It would save him much trouble, particularly in the blistering heat.

On Sunday morning there was some talk in the Blaine household of taking a carriage to church, but Blaine preferred to walk the five blocks to the First Congregational Church at Tenth and G streets. But at the Tenth Street entrance to the church the former Speaker suddenly slumped, sat down on the steps, and mopped his head with his handkerchief.

". . . sunstroke," he murmured. ". . . take me home . . . Dr. Pope. . . ." And he fell unconscious.

Mrs. Blaine and his friends hailed a passing omnibus and took Blaine home where the doctor came and began applying plasters to the representative's breast. At two o'clock in the afternoon the word was circulating around the outside of the house that it was all up with the former Speaker.

"I'm afraid he is dying," said Surgeon General Barnes.

And in a moment that ill-chosen word was on its way to Cincinnati.

At four o'clock on Sunday afternoon Blaine regained consciousness. By Tuesday he was well on the way to recovery. What had he suffered? No one was saying.

Blaine was still the strongest candidate at the convention, but his strength was now challenged in the hectic jockeying. To counteract Hayes's strength in his home state, someone reported that Blaine could count on five to seven thousand "anti-Catholic Democratic

votes" in Ohio. The Morton men of Indiana accused Conkling's
heroes of trying to buy the colored vote, and hired spies to watch the
Conkling forces day and night, but without catching anyone in a
desperate act.

Conkling's men offered to pay the California and Nevada delegations' convention expenses if the westerners would throw their
support to the New Yorker. Conkling got no satisfaction there.

The betting still ran heavily for Blaine, in a field of eight, with
Grant trailing badly. On June 13, the day before the convention
opened, the New York *Times* polled the delegates, found the
following support:

Blaine	279
Bristow	127
Hayes	51
Conkling	86

That night, in front of the various hotels that served as headquarters for the opposing forces, the warm evening of Cincinnati
was broken by shouting and singing. Blaine's men rallied in front of
the Burnet House, to hear a telegram read from their leader assuring
them of his complete recovery. Bristow's forces rallied at Pike's
Opera House. Conkling's supporters, not to be outdone, appeared
before the Gibson House. Hayes, in home territory, apparently felt
no need for such a show of strength.

The convention itself began the next day, June 14, in Exposition
Hall, where Horace Greeley's flittering comet had risen in 1872. But
this time the hall's six thousand seats were filled, and the mass of
perspiring, buzzing humanity, plus the intolerable acoustics of the
building, made hearing a fine art. But if the delegates could not hear
the discussions at least they could read them in full; newspapermen
from all over the country were there. The Western Union office had
supplied twenty telegraph wires for the reporters.

As the convention went into session Blaine's recovery from his
illness seemed to be progressing. His candidacy did not. In Washington, Senator Morton felt sure that he would follow close on Blaine
in the first ballot, and gain strength thereafter. And at the convention
the bettors now favored Conkling.

The Democrats in Congress were so confident that it would be
Blaine that they ordered special printings of reports of hearings
linking Blaine with the Crédit Mobilier scandal.

First, however, the Republican platform had to be settled.

Most notable of the seventeen sections were two which again charged the Democrats with treason—this eleven years after the end of the Civil War.

Section 15 lamented "all sectional feeling and tendencies" and warned that success of the Democrats, who counted on a "united South" would "reopen sectional strife and imperil national honor and human rights."

Section 16 charged the Democratic party was the same "in character and spirit as when it sympathized with treason." It charged the Democrats used control of the House of Representatives in the interest of "the nation's recent foes"; applauded "unrepentant rebellion"; repudiated government financial obligations; thwarted justice; and finally, it said, the Democrats were incompetent.

The nominations began with two new fillips. One rule ended the practice of "stampeding" that had worked so well to nominate Lincoln; under no conditions would the roll call be eliminated on any ballot, nor could a state's vote be changed on that ballot after it was once announced. And in a fight within the Pennsylvania delegation the famous "unit rule" which bound delegations to a single candidate, was broken for the first time. (After one more fight on the rule, four years later, the unit rule was to be abandoned by the GOP.)

Blaine led the race for six ballots, but he was not fooled. Even as the sixth ballot was being cast, he predicted the nomination of Hayes, and before the seventh ballot was concluded he had telegraphed Hayes on the instrument so handsomely provided in his library, to promise support in the state of Maine.

A nonentity named William A. Wheeler, a party wheel horse and representative from New York, was chosen to run with Hayes, the party press declared it "an invincible combination," and the race was on.

Hayes was inoffensive, "a third-rate nonentity, whose only recommendation is that he is obnoxious to no one," wrote Henry Adams. He was also a handsome man; for the times, an ideal candidate.

At fifty-four Hayes looked ten years younger, his massive head, blue eyes, and old-fashioned, middle-class puritanism made him spokesman for the "clean bureaucracy" that had to be promised, no easy job on the dunghill of the Grant administration. Hayes began, in his acceptance letter, by stressing three points: civil service reform, guaranteed "hard" currency, and pacification of the South.

He scored immediate victory. Carl Schurz came out for him—and this meant a large helping hand from the reformers, even if many of Schurz's fellow independents were now committed to the Democrats. The Democratic Cincinnati *Enquirer* might refer to Hayes as "his accidency," but if the Republican party had not chosen an irreproachable candidate there would have been no question of the outcome of the election. The Democrats would have won.

Two weeks after the Republican meeting the Democrats opened their national convention at the Merchants Exchange in St. Louis. It was not a stirring convention. Lean, graying Samuel J. Tilden held such a lead over his nearest opponents that his nomination was a sure thing from the beginning. He went into the convention with more than 400 of the 744 delegates, and even with the two-thirds rule and unit rule operating the outcome was never in doubt. When his name was presented there was no cheer, or even applause. While Tilden was well known, since he had been governor of New York, he was not the lovable type—far from it. Tilden was a corporation lawyer who had poor health and good manners, liked books, fine wines, and intellectual companions. In forty years of politics he had become a great practitioner of the arts of persuasion and control; indeed, it was Tilden who was credited with maneuvering the Democratic nomination out of the hands of Chase, Hendricks, and Hancock and into those of an unwilling and tearful Horatio Seymour in 1868, by the simple expedient of kidnapping Seymour and holding him incommunicado.

Tilden was also rich. Before he became known as the Great Reformer, he had sometimes been called the "Great Forecloser." His personal fortune was estimated at $10 million, and he lived in a fashionable brownstone house facing New York City's Gramercy Park.

Tilden's running mate was Thomas A. Hendricks of Indiana, still an active, handsome man.

The Democratic platform consisted of nine planks this year, most referring to reform. The ringing words spoke of "abuses, wrongs, and crimes" in sixteen years of Republican rule, "corrupt centralism," "carpetbag tyrannies," "waste and fraud," and "hard times."

The party referred to the "profligate waste of public lands, and their diversion from actual settlers by the party in power, which has squandered two hundred million acres upon railroads alone."

One real issue, skillfully avoided by both parties, was the money question. Both major parties tried to straddle it, because both were worried about the Greenback party's easy-money plank, but neither party wanted to advocate an easy monetary policy at that time.

Hayes went one up on that, for he saw the problem and moved quickly to declare himself for hard money. Tilden, who also believed in metal money, avoided the issue.

Tilden managed his own campaign. He ran it intelligently enough; but, again, by running it himself he did not gain the enthusiastic support of would-be political generals who would be cabinet officers or White House advisers.

The Democratic campaign operated on two levels. First was the cry for a "Solid South," a new technique that frightened the Republicans because all Tilden needed for election *was* the South, plus New York, New Jersey, and Connecticut.

The other campaign was for reform. Tilden promised to sweep away corruption and oppression by replacing "grasping centralization" that had caused all the nation's ills with "limited constitutional government."

"Hold the Fort for Tilden" was the favorite Democratic campaign song:

> See the ring, the combinations,
> Whisky, railroad, land.
> Wicked schemes for peculations,
> Rife on every hand.
>
> See our taxes, swelling, rising,
> Money almost gone.
> Produce falling, no one buying.
> Farmers' faces long.
>
> See the officeholders' ticket
> Running in Grant's track;
> If elected, "no removals,"
> No reform, in fact.

> Ho! ye voters, pure and honest,
> Rally with us, then;
> Vote for Tilden, vote for Hendricks,
> Vote for honest men.

As the Democrats rode the tide of opposition to the "ins," the Republicans became frightened.

"Our strong ground," Hayes wrote Blaine, "is the dread of a solid South, rebel rule . . . I hope you will make these topics prominent in your speeches. It leads people away from 'hard times,' which is our deadliest foe."

Good as his word, Blaine began waving the "bloody shirt of the rebellion" all over again. He knew as well as the next man that the Republicans had to rekindle sectional fear and hatred if they were to stand a chance of victory. The Democrats responded with louder cries of "scandal," and the infighting began.

The Republicans charged that Tilden was a tax dodger. During the fifteen years just passed he had filed returns in only four years, and in 1862, when he received one railroad fee of $20,000, he filed a return on an income of $7118. Government agents, working for the Republicans and their jobs, tried to get evidence enough to indict him, but could not, and Tilden ignored the accusations. In the North the Republicans called him "Copperhead" (he had no war record) and "Barnburner" to raise the prejudices of slavery days.

Tilden's managers were not worried. Their campaign was building with an almost religious fervor.

The times were hard and the political gleanings lean in 1876. Tilden's wealth was the envy of the Republicans, who (little knowing their man) thought he was spending his own money to win the election.

Collector McDonald, who had been so helpful in the past, sat in prison, and there was no money from the Whisky Ring. In August, Indiana political boss Oliver Morton told Hayes the state was slipping badly, he would need $100,000 for money and speakers in the ninety-four counties. He didn't get it. The state went Democratic in the local elections in October.

Luckily, the Republicans were not completely without resources. A new financial prop was invented; the Post Office Ring, headed by Senator Stephen Dorsey, a carpetbagger from Arkansas, and Thomas Brady, the Second Assistant Postmaster General. The Post

Office Ring dipped into federal postal funds to supply the needful money for strategic states—with special emphasis on the South.

Through bribery, corruption, and violence, the Republicans had established unscrupulous party machines in the three remaining carpetbags of the South—South Carolina, Florida, and Louisiana.

Money was scarce, but they thought of a better plan, anyhow. On October 17, following the outbreak of rioting by white southerners in South Carolina, Republican Governor Chamberlain called on President Grant for help. Grant proclaimed a state of insurrection in South Carolina, and two weeks before election day sent thirty-three companies of troops into the state. They were there to help count the returns.

Thirty-eight states participated in the election of 1876, including Colorado, admitted to the Union in August. As the polls closed on November 7, the Democrats were sure of victory, for they had carried New York, Indiana, New Jersey, and Connecticut—and there was every indication that southern voters had heeded the call. The total electoral vote was 369. If the assumption of the Democrats were true, Tilden would have 203 votes, Hayes 166.

The battle seemed to be won. At Democratic headquarters in New York, Tilden was already receiving the congratulations of party leaders, late on election night, and the Republicans were almost in a conceding mood. Almost, but not quite.

The hour was growing late, and the tension of the long night was wearing on everybody. Three states were still doubtful—South Carolina, Louisiana, and Florida. If the final word would only come, the victory was assured.

Bumbling William A. Barnum of Connecticut was so thoughtless as to ask the New York *Times* for the latest telegraphic report. The *Post*, the *Sun*, the *Herald*—all these he could have asked without incident—but he had to turn to the Republican *Times*.

The editor on the desk when that early morning inquiry came in, tired as he was, sat up and took notice. If Democratic headquarters wasn't sure of its position in the three disputed states, then there was still a chance for Hayes.

This editor went immediately to Republican headquarters and confided his intuition to a tough little campaign manager, the first man he saw as he entered the door. Together they rushed upstairs to roust a fat and sleepy Zach Chandler from his couch of defeat. As he rubbed his eyes, the head of the Republican National Committee saw the opportunity and had hardly sat up in his nightshirt before telegrams were humming along the wires to the carpetbag bosses. Could they hold their states, keep the outcome at least in dispute? And to Florida, suddenly the key to the election, further information: Chandler was on his way, Florida could have a man in the cabinet. Florida could have anything, if only Florida could win for Hayes!

The Democrats had been no more scrupulous than the Republican reconstructors in their election methods. In all three states white Democrats had organized "rifle clubs" under what had come to be known as the Mississippi plan of intimidation and skulduggery.

Under this plan the white citizens of Mississippi had taken government back from the Negroes and the carpetbaggers in 1875. The whites organized rifle clubs, displayed these weapons before election and at the polls, printed the word "Republican" on Democratic ballots, and stuffed the boxes magnificently. So did the Republicans, where they could. The Ku Klux Klan had voted itself out of existence as a general organization, but in various localities the white-sheeted knights of the evening rode wildly through the countryside. The Klan might have died, but its spirit had not.

The blueprint worked as well now in 1876 as it had in 1875. The result was Democratic majority in all southern states, including the three in dispute. Zach Chandler's job was to convert Democratic majority into Republican victory, and there was only one way to do it—get Democratic votes thrown out. It took time to get election results in these days, and time for counting and transmission also meant time for ballot-stuffing and cheating.

In Louisiana, Tilden had a majority of 6549 votes. In Florida, Tilden had a majority of 92 votes, of a total of 48,774. In South Carolina, too, Tilden had a majority.

Chandler and money were sent to the South. All through November he sent coded telegrams to headquarters for money and assistance. President Grant ordered the federal troops to be watchful, to see that the election boards were unmolested. Grant invited a number of Republicans to help assure honesty by observing the count in Louisiana. Immediately, a companion group of Democratic politicians set out for New Orleans to watch the Republican watchers.

The pressure was on. Chandler and his associates bought and sold, harangued and wheedled, entertained and corrupted. The Republicans promised fat federal jobs to the key men they needed.

They were not alone. Tilden's nephew, Colonel Pelton, and Smith Weed, one of the Tilden campaign managers, were bargaining, trading, and carrying on a furious correspondence of their own, in secret code. But they were not as strong-minded as the Republicans, nor was their candidate tough enough.

Weed tried to buy three of the seven members of the South Carolina returns board for $80,000. The money was to be held in escrow until the votes had been cast for Tilden. It seemed fair enough, so Weed asked Colonel Pelton to get the money and arranged to meet him in Baltimore. When Pelton arrived he had no money, but a sad story:

"The old man is against it," Pelton reported.

Two weeks later Pelton raised money to buy a Republican elector in Oregon, but the elector wanted $10,000. Pelton haggled too hard and too long, and the cash finally arrived to complete the deal after the electoral college had already met.

Another Tilden adviser, Manton Marble, wired from Florida: "Have just received proposition to hand over a Tilden decision of board and a certificate of governor for $200,000." And a Republican carpetbagger in Louisiana offered that state's vote to the Democrats for another $200,000.

But nothing came of these efforts. Votes of Democratic districts, and even whole counties, were thrown out. The Democratic majority of 6549 votes in Louisiana became a Republican majority of 4807. The slim Democratic majority of 92 in Florida became a Republican majority: 922. The Democratic majority in South Carolina became a Republican victory by 974 votes.

And when the electoral college met it voted 185 for Hayes, 184 for Tilden.

Now the vote of the electoral college had to be accepted by the Congress, and a compromise electoral commission was established to certify the count.

The count began on February 1. Each party was prepared to hold out for victory—the Republicans to protect their theft, and the Democrats to overturn it.

The commissioners were chosen by "partisan" vote, with feelings running so high there was talk of a southern march on Washington. Just talk? President Grant did increase the military forces around the city. The commission would settle disputes.

When the count reached Florida it stopped. The Florida matter was referred to the commission. On February 10 the commission submitted its findings to Congress. All the Republicans had voted one way, to accept the Republican election, all the Democrats, for Democratic victory—and there was one more Republican vote than Democrat. The two houses, the Republican Senate and the Democratic House, disagreed on acceptance of the decision. It was stalemate, but under the original compromise the decision of the commission stood, since the two houses could not agree on rejection.

The count proceeded. Maine, Mississippi, Missouri, Louisiana . . . There it stopped again.

Louisiana had two governors, one Republican and one Democrat, two sets of statistics and two sets of electors. Which were to be accepted?

On February 16 again eight Republicans voted to accept the Hayes electors; seven Democrats voted no.

On the nineteenth the two houses again disagreed. On the twentieth the count was resumed, but the dispute continued, more vitriolic than ever. How was it to be resolved? If no real compromise could be reached the very function of government was threatened. If the dispute continued along straight party lines the least that could be expected was an extended filibuster by the Democrats, destroying the process of government.

The Republicans, the "ins," had a strong position made stronger by the procrastination, worry, and indecision of Tilden. By now, according to his intimates, Tilden was a brooding, tired invalid, more dedicated to self-justification than to struggle for power. His associates, the northern Democrats, were bowing their backs and digging in for a fight, but the candidate was little help.

The days of Congress were drawing to a close. So were those of the Grant administration. What if the dispute was not settled by March 4, the date the newly elected President, whoever he was, should take office?

The southern Democrats resolved the issue. On February 26, at Wormley's Hotel, leaders of the two parties met to try to work out a compromise. "If we are saved," James Garfield had written, "it will be by the southern rebels." And by the rebels it was. They would agree to accept the election of Hayes if the Republicans would agree to remove the federal troops from Louisiana, Florida, and South Carolina. It was more important to them to get the troops out than to win this one election.

The "gentlemen's agreement" was made. The count could continue.

Hayes entrained for Washington, now confident, or as confident as he could be without actually knowing, that his election would be certified.

That certification came, just after four o'clock on the morning of March 2, two days before the scheduled inauguration of the new President. Senator Thomas W. Ferry, President of the Senate, picked up the special eagle-quill pen that had been prepared for the job and signed the certification. As he rose to announce the result to a joint session of Congress a Democrat shouted:

"Come, Democrats—let us not remain to witness the consummation of this infamy."

In a few moments most of the Democrats in Congress had withdrawn and Ferry turned pale as he grimly announced Hayes election. At 4:10 A.M. it was done.

The New York *Sun* appeared that morning dressed in the same black border it had used to announce the death of Abraham Lincoln. Later the Democrats of Congress passed a resolution that shouted fraud. Tilden supporters refused to dignify Mr. Hayes with the title of President, and the Democratic party press referred to the new President of the United States as "His Fraudulency."

Tilden did not come off scot-free. His own party charged him with indecision and even cowardice. By anybody's count Tilden had won the popular election. Even the Republicans gave him that:

Tilden	4,285,992
Hayes	4,033,768
Peter Cooper	81,737
Green, Clay Smith	9522

But Hayes was the new President. True to his word, on April 10 he removed the soldiers from the South. The election-returns boards of the three disputed states got their pay-off; the Louisianians moved quickly into the U. S. Treasury Department, as all the carpetbaggers and scalawags moved out of the South.

The New York *Tribune* uncovered the secret correspondence of the Tilden group and ran a sensational "exposé" of the Democratic attempt to "steal" the election. Interestingly enough, while the coded telegrams of the Democrats were produced in abundance, all those of the Republicans had somehow disappeared. And the fact was that none of the corrupt boards voted for the Democrats—all went Republican.

Long after it could help, S. B. McLin, chairman of the Florida returns board, admitted that Tilden had carried Florida and that money and federal jobs had been used to corrupt the board.

But the Democrats won a signal victory in one respect. After twelve years, during which the South had been despoiled and ravaged, the states were turned back to the white southerners. Between 1860 and 1872 the ten southern states' debts had been increased from $76 million to $291 million, while that of the twenty-seven other states was $88 million less. In Mississippi alone, when the Democrats regained control of the legislature in 1875, in one year they reduced the cost of government from $1,130,192 to $547,816. Now, finally, after the elections of 1876 and the bitter presidential dispute, the South was free, white-controlled, and solidly Democratic.

The Negro, having enjoyed a brief period of political power, when his vote was controlled by unscrupulous whites, would be submerged on account of that brief period for nearly a century.

7

With the removal of troops from the South the temper of the nation changed subtly. The war was really over now, and at last politics was to grow away from the issues between North and South. This period of the 1870s was marked by struggle between labor and capital that threatened to become class warfare of the European type. Time and time, strike and riot turned into deadlock and bloodshed.

This was truly the age of industry. At the moment the industrialists were on top, discovering to their woe that the laboring man was not a tabby cat but, when aroused, a lion, showing his organized strength. The great fortunes continued to grow, and the workingman's lot seemed little better than before, yet little by little the seeds of reform were being sown in American society. New inventions were speeding the manufacturing processes of the nation, brought steel manufacture, a rash of bridge building, and practical electricity for lighting city streets. The telephone had been invented, and the distances between cities grew steadily shorter, as speed took the nation's fancy.

President Grant had been out of office for four years now and had made his tour of Europe and the warm countries of the South. Grant's die-hard supporters had not changed much in the past four years, and they still controlled a remarkably large segment of the Republican party, but the nation had gone far beyond them in almost every way.

The intense feelings about the South were no longer an issue, although the South had moved firmly to the Democratic column. The great waves of European immigration were on. Most voters, now, had no personal feeling about the Civil War of twenty years before. Newer problems claimed their interest and brought forth men and *issues that had more connection with the times, issues like the tariff, cheap money for the undeveloped West, and cheap Oriental labor that threatened the domestic laborer's wage standards.*

And there were other changes. Nearly every state had a firmly established system of public education. By now, fully half the people of the United States lived in cities, read newspapers, and knew something of matters other than those that affected their own bread and butter.

7. The Solid South

As New Yorkers began stirring on the morning of May 27, 1880, it was apparent that it was going to be another scorcher. The newspapers had so predicted in the midst of the heat wave that seared the eastern seaboard; the heat had already persuaded Coney Island resorts to open two weeks early. The newspapers were right. In midafternoon the mercury hit 94 degrees in comparatively breezy Central Park and hovered around 96 downtown. In Great Neck, Long Island, the temperature climbed to 100, and in the blazing sun in Newark some brave soul clocked the heat at 109 degrees. It was the hottest May 27 in the region's history.

In Washington, Congress was engaged in dispute over a Democratic proposal to buy the private papers of Confederate generals Bragg and Polk. The families of these two southern heroes needed the money. But the Republicans could not refrain from reminding the Democratic majorities in both houses that only a few years before, when a Republican Congress had bought certain Confederate state papers, the Democrats accused them of nest-feathering and corruption.

Senator James G. Blaine was not engaged in that postbellum debate. He was just leaving New York for the capital city, escaping the frightful heat of New York after a short stay at a plush Fifth Avenue hotel. Blaine was confident of nomination by the Republican National Convention that would meet on June 2 in Chicago. "The plumed knight from Maine" was playing it carefully and was not available to newspapermen on the twenty-seventh.

Blaine had no intention of traveling to the Chicago convention. As a leading candidate for the nomination it would be most unseemly. Thurlow Weed, the old Republican tartar of the '60s, had planned to make the trip in easy stages, for if nothing else he wanted to warn the Radicals of his beloved party against trying to force the nomination of Ulysses S. Grant for a third term. But at his advanced age Weed was afraid to make the trip during the intense heat. Reluctantly he called the journey off and, instead, presented his views in a letter in Whitelaw Reid's *Tribune*. From a limp couch in the library of his home the feeble old politico told newspapermen that Grant just couldn't win; to nominate him would be to hand the election to Samuel Tilden on a silver platter. (Tilden hadn't been nominated yet, but Weed was sure the Democratic candidate of 1876 could have the spot for the asking.)

The heat didn't stop General Horace Porter and a hundred fifty other Republicans-for-Grant who entrained on the Pennsylvania for Chicago. Porter, who had been the President's secretary, told the press, "We are bound to nominate Grant this time," as he stepped onto a private car. But from the North, New Hampshire delegates set forth in a special five-car train of New Englanders, first decorating their car with a poster announcing their support of Blaine.

In his parlor at Chicago's Grand Pacific Hotel, former Governor Dennison of Ohio, one of the principal campaign managers for John Sherman, Secretary of the Treasury, had just about given up hope. It was apparent, even a week before the convention, that Sherman's chances were very slim. Dennison was equally certain that Grant would not get the nomination. Sentiment in Chicago was very strong against the nomination of the ex-President. Grant's position was not strengthened any, either, by the strong-man tactics used by Senator (and General) John Logan in seizing control of the Illinois state convention, a few days before. Illinois' forty-two votes were now made safe enough for Grant, but the bulldozing had cost the Grant movement dear, as his managers were to discover.

Those stalwart supporters of the ex-President were led by Logan, red-mustached and bespectacled Republican National Committee chairman Don Cameron, senator from Pennsylvania, son of Simon Cameron, and Senator Roscoe Conkling, the fiery-tempered New Yorker whose dislike for Blaine knew no bounds. All three men had gained control of their state conventions and thrown their votes of these vital states to Grant.

More than a week before the convention, the Grant men had engaged rooms at the Palmer House, where the national committee would also hold forth. From there they maneuvered as best they could to bring about Grant's victory. The political generals had already sent the two-time President on a two-year trip around the world after he had failed of nomination in 1876, and in that voyage he had met the crowned heads and best brains of Europe. His advisers had shipped him South, even more recently, to Mexico and Cuba when it became apparent that his presence in the United States was not preserving the mystique necessary to break General Washington's two-term precedent.

Through their power in the national committee, the Grant men had managed to get Chicago named as the convention site, on the principle that it would be best to fight the battle on the former President's home ground. Now they claimed 400 votes for Grant on the first ballot with only 378 needed to nominate, but to their horror they found sentiment in Illinois so overwhelmingly anti-Grant that they wished the convention were being held anywhere else.

A New York *Tribune* survey showed that Grant had 315 votes, Blaine 272, Sherman 110, Senator George F. Edmunds 36, Elihu B. Washburne 13, and Senator William Windom of Minnesota 10.

President Hayes had declared, even in his election campaign, that he would not run for a second term. Grant was the front-runner. Even so, the Grant men at the Palmer House were anxious to make a deal with Secretary Sherman. They offered him second place on the ticket, if those 110 delegates could be transferred. But Sherman would have no part of the deal. He was pledged for first place or nothing. The Sherman men in Chicago were planning to co-operate with the supporters of Blaine and Washburne, to keep the Grant faction from capturing the convention at its opening, as Senator Logan had captured the Illinois state convention at Springfield.

There were some ominous signs. General Chester A. Arthur had arrived in Chicago, along with other stanch Grant supporters—stalwart third-termers, they were called, or just Stalwarts.

The committee on arrangements asked that the convention hall in the exposition building be turned over to the committee—eight days before the convention. In 1876, the local committee had kept control until twenty-four hours before the meeting began. This unusual request brought grave suspicion that the Grant men had something up their sleeves, for the national arrangements committee was controlled by the pro-Grant forces.

The Grant men were anxious to enforce the unit rule at the convention and thus pledge whole delegations to vote by majority rule. Many delegations were pledged to oppose him—and in some cases individual delegates had been replaced by state conventions when they objected to the pledge.

Jeremiah Haralson, a Negro who had represented the carpetbag Alabama government in Congress, arrived in town and immediately paid a call at Sherman headquarters. There he was collared by the Grant men, who promptly offered him free room at the Palmer House. Haralson declined the offer. Like many other southern delegates, Haralson had a problem. He was pledged to Grant, but he didn't believe Grant could win the election.

Willard Warner of Tecumseh, another Alabama delegate, had no such offer of free room from the Grant men. Warner had refused to pledge himself to Grant, and the Alabama convention had asked his district to replace him as a delegate. But only eight of nineteen district delegates participated. Warner was replaced, but he shouted fraud and came on to Chicago, planning to stand on his district credentials. He and former Governor Smith, both replaced by their state convention with Grant men, would demand seating as the representatives of their districts. So it was certain that when the convention met, the issue of credentials and unit rule would be joined on the first roll call.

Grant, himself, was getting ready to leave his home in Galena, and travel to Dubuque, Iowa, to avoid the steady stream of telegrams and letters that deluged the telegraph and postal facilities. But his brash son Fred had already created amusement among the hard-bitten politicians by his obvious enthusiasm for a paternal third term.

"Father has got a sure thing," Fred told Governor Dennison.

Dennison wasn't convinced. Nor were others, such as Wharton Barker, a Pennsylvania delegate, who announced in Philadelphia just before he left for the convention that there were 10,000 Republicans in the city who would not vote for Grant, and 15,000 of the same mind in the rest of the state. If Grant were nominated he thought the state would be doubtful for the GOP. (Barker had an idea that a representative named Garfield would be the best man.)

Grant's motives weren't clear to most of the party. Even before the convention got under way opposition to his third term was largely based on principle, rather than personality or issue.

"This country does not belong to General Grant or to any other one man among its forty millions of free citizens," said the New York *Tribune*, in as strong a statement as it thought proper. Other newspapers were asking what would happen in 1884 if Grant were elected in 1880. The Grant supporters avoided that issue but let it be known that Grant had "offered himself" because he thought he alone could revive the Republican party in the South, where in 1878 four Republicans and a hundred and two Democrats had been elected to the House of Representatives.

That talk outraged the Chicago *Tribune*, which brought the matter into the open in a forty-count indictment of Grant's two administrations. It was a personal attack on the former President, using such terms as: "contempt for law," "deception," "false statements," "violation of law," "indecency," and "contempt for public opinion." The *Tribune* attack came as a shock, for Grant had been treated gently by his party in the past, and those who were outraged by the conduct of his two administrations generally thought better about accusing the hero of Appomattox.

Unafraid, the Democratic New York *Herald* said that only Grant's nomination at Chicago would decide the third-term issue once and for all and recommended this course to the Republicans. Only this "and his overwhelming defeat in the election" would settle the question.

If the unit rule could be maintained half the *Herald* hopes would be fulfilled, for the Grant men controlled enough political machinery to do the job.

Then, as the convention went into session on June 2, Representative (and former General) James A. Garfield was selected to head the rules committee—the group that would determine the fate of Grant.

As Garfield's name came up in discussion on the floor, early in the convention, it gave rise to tremendous cheering, without any apparent cause. "A put-up job," reported the *Herald* correspondent the next day. "Keep your eye on Garfield."

Roscoe Conkling, in no way confused, sent Garfield a quick note, scrawled on a scrap of newspaper: "I congratulate you on being the dark horse."

Garfield's position was most delicate. As second to Senator Sherman in the Ohio delegation, Garfield was bound to support his senior's candidacy, and was, in fact, chosen to nominate Sherman. For that, he was to have a seat in the U. S. Senate.

But as the days wore on, Garfield moved his seat from the side to the center aisle and his mellifluous voice was heard on the floor perhaps more than was strictly necessary to the conduct of his business.

Sherman's chances were nil. But Garfield, though otherwise prompted by his Pennsylvania friend Barker, had to remain true to the cause until released. Garfield concentrated his efforts on whipping the unit rule in committee.

The days dragged a bit as the obvious candidates traded for position and the lesser lights fabricated a platform for the party.

On June 4, Mr. Warner and Governor Smith, the anti-Grant delegates from Alabama, were seated by the credentials committee and the Grant men saw they would have a fight on their hands. The convention hall was jammed, waiting for the battle to begin, but it was not jammed with all the right people.

Tickets were selling for $15 each at the entrances to the hall, but five hundred that had been ordered reserved for Union veterans suddenly could not be found. The Grant men, sure of the support of the Union veterans' group, were up in arms. Senator Logan decided something must be done.

When party chairman Elihu Root walked into the lobby of the Palmer House on his way to the national committee's rooms that day, a crowd began hooting at him. Up the stairs he went, into the committee parlor, and locked the door, while behind him a milling, howling mob of fifteen hundred collected on the stairs and jammed into the hall of the mezzanine.

Turning from the locked door, Root encountered Kirk Hawes, a dissatisfied delegate, who put the question of the mob: Where were the tickets?

"They are all given out," said Root.

"I don't believe a word of it."

"It is a matter of small consequence to me whether you believe it or not," replied the chairman.

"You are a liar and you know it!"

"You lie yourself when you say so!"

"You have used misrepresentations about these tickets," shouted the delegate, "and you have lied to me and you know it. I want nothing more to do with such a man."

A disquieting discussion. But outside the room the shouting grew louder. It was apparent that the crowd was not going to wait much longer for the door to be opened, and Root was not about to open it. Somehow they got Potter Palmer, proprietor of the hotel, into the room and somehow Mr. Palmer got word to two of his porters, who sneaked a ladder around back and up against the Monroe Street side of the building.

Root, with as much dignity as he could put together, climbed down the ladder into the street—and just in time, for the mob broke down the door and ransacked the room. They found twenty-five tickets that had been reserved for Senator Hoar, the chairman of the convention. He did not ever see them.

The delay in getting to the nominations was doing nothing for the tempers of Grant's supporters. Conkling had managed, by a vote of 716-3, a resolution that every member of the convention was bound to support the nominee, whoever he might be. That was to assure control, once they nominated Grant.

But Logan, at least, was not so sure of the outcome that he was willing to put any money on it. The night before the nominations began Logan encountered Lieutenant Governor Woodford of New York on the stairs at the Palmer House. "I'll bet you we've got 'em," he said, "and I'll bet you $1000 that Grant is nominated."

Woodford declined the bet, good-naturedly enough, but Assemblyman William J. Youngs, an alternate delegate from the Empire State, offered to take the Illinois senator's wager. Logan stalled. Youngs got the money from his room, found the senator in Parlor Q, and said he had come to cover the bet.

Logan denied that he had made a bet that Grant would be nominated.

"I certainly understood you to mean that," said Youngs.

"You know a goddamned sight better," said the senator, "and if you repeat that I'll slap your chops."

"I don't want to get into any personal difficulty," said Youngs. "Use milder language, please."

"Damn you, sir, this is my room," shouted the senator.

"Who the hell are you, anyway?" chimed in young Fred Grant, a member of the Logan following.

By now a Chicago delegate named Burke arrived, and was so unwise as to state that he had heard Senator Logan offer the bet, whereupon the senator offered to mash him in the face. But, finally, the argument broke up without violence or settlement.

Late the next day, June 5, the business of nomination finally began. Garfield's committee had recommended against adoption of the unit rule, and it was defeated on the floor. In nominating Grant, Conkling made his supreme effort, using every bit of energy in the Grant claque which was so carefully marshaled on the floor. Blaine's man had done the same with much less success, and then Garfield made his appeal for Sherman, in the interest of party harmony. Garfield's speech for compromise was a speech for Garfield as well. This was not his intent. Garfield, on the record of his letters, was wholly without presidential ambition. He was satisfied with his Senate seat, did not even want to manage the Sherman campaign, much less be proposed as a compromise candidate.

When the voting began both the Grant and Blaine forces held firm. In twenty-eight ballots Grant's strength fluctuated only between 302 and 309 votes; Blaine's between 275 and 285. It would take 378 votes to nominate. A tired convention adjourned for the night.

On June 6 there seemed to be a swing to Sherman. On the thirtieth ballot his vote rose to 120 but had absolutely no effect on the Blaine or Grant support. So no compromise was to be expected with Sherman as candidate.

Then on the thirty-fourth ballot sixteen Wisconsin votes were swung to Garfield; he rose to protest, but was overruled by Chairman Hoar, who later confessed that he was afraid Garfield "would say something that would make his nomination impossible." Garfield did tell a reporter that he had not sought the nomination and protested the use of his name.

But the Garfield choice was popular, and on the thirty-fifth ballot he picked up a bloc of Blaine's votes. Then Sherman released the Ohio delegation, and the stampede to Garfield was on: a stampede that was not shared by the stalwart Grant men. Garfield was nominated by 399 votes on the thirty-sixth ballot, but at the very last Grant held 306. Grant's supporters were disgruntled and sullen at the outcome. It was clear that while the convention had nominated a candidate, the party was split. Blaine, defeated for the second time, was tranquil enough. "I should much prefer to see the party defeated with Garfield or some other candidate, to winning with Grant," Blaine said. President Hayes was delighted with the nomination.

Conkling, of course, had engineered the resolution of total support for the candidate, whoever he might be, and above all others Conkling was honor bound to back Garfield. He asked that the nomination be made unanimous, but in barely good grace, and with so little enthusiasm that the bitterness showed through.

To ease the pain the convention chose General Chester A. Arthur as Vice-President: a straight concession to the Grant wing of the party. This seemed to heal the breach as well as it could be healed on such short notice. Back in Galena, Illinois, Grant mumbled his satisfaction at the nomination of Garfield.

Hardly had the smoke of the Republican battle blown from the air of the Windy City when the Greenback party came to town. The month before, a newspaper correspondent in Cheyenne asked General Benjamin Butler if he knew he was under consideration for the party's nomination. At that point Butler looked most thoughtful.

The Greenback party had been a real threat to the two major parties by 1878, less than two years before. The chief recruits of the Greenbackers came from the frontiers of the West, where men believed in the "nationalization" of money, strong federal government, and, particularly, regulation of interstate commerce and transportation. The Greenbackers proposed to take government out of the hands of the bankers and put it in the hands of the governors. It was a frightening policy, and the newspapers and pulpits of the East thundered against these un-American beliefs, this advocacy of the rights of laborer and farmer. It was a radicalism, said the press, that had to be stamped out.

In 1878 the prospects for stamping out Greenbackism had not seemed too bright. That year the party polled more than a million votes and elected fourteen representatives to Congress. It was enough to make both jumbo and jackass shudder with fright and tremble with rage. But by 1880 the teeth of the Greenback party had fallen out. In the Hayes administration Secretary of the Treasury John Sherman had conducted a thorough financial housecleaning. Hayes himself had eliminated the odor of corruption from the federal government. At the end of his first year of administration the Grant shenanigans were an almost forgotten nightmare.

It had taken almost six years, but by 1879 the panic of '73 was only a dim memory too. Times were good, wheat prices were high on the European market, and the national economy was expanding again. The Democrats, in control of both houses of Congress, asked no aid from the Greenback men who suddenly found their hopes of establishing a strong third party whisked away along with corruption and the end of depression.

By 1880, when they met in Chicago, the Greenbackers were a poor and undernourished party. One of them complained:

"There is no money to pay the ordinary and necessary expenses of a campaign. There is no press to advocate organization, to lead public opinion . . ."

And, with the return of optimism, there was little interest in reform of a currency that seemed to be meeting the national needs. The Greenback convention was on, but it was a convention of echoes. Gaunt, sad-eyed General James B. Weaver of Iowa, an Abolitionist, once a Radical Republican, and then leader of the Greenback party in the House, was chosen as the presidential nominee. The newspapers of the country paid scant attention to the party's convention or their campaign.

At that, the Greenbackers were better off for publicity than the Prohibitionists. The anti-rum men met at Cleveland on June 17, and true to the fashion of the year nominated a general, Neal Dow of Maine, with A. Thompson of Ohio as Vice-President.

The party was represented by 142 delegates from 12 states. It made so little impression that the major newspapers carried no reports of its proceedings.

Thurlow Weed had been sure that Samuel J. Tilden, defrauded of election in 1876, would be the Democratic candidate in 1880. But Tilden, the withdrawn, gentlemanly Sage of New York's Gramercy Square, was no help to his friends in the months before the convention. He did not say he wanted the nomination, nor did he say he would decline if nominated. Altogether, it was hardly the performance of a man determined to run for public office—and it was so accepted by the majority of Democrats. Tilden, who had actually *won* four years before, went into the convention at Cincinnati with scarcely a third of the delegates plumping for his nomination.

It was, said the New York *Herald*, "The Gathering of the Unterrified at Cincinnati" on June 22. But it was also the gathering of average men—no giants appeared on the convention floor to demand the nomination by presence or prescience. If there was one outstanding development it was the complete rout of Tammany Hall in the meeting. "Porkopolis," as Tammany was known, had no standing with the delegates this year, and after much wrangling before the credentials committee the New York delegation was excused from voting altogether.

At the start Tilden sent a letter "renouncing" the nomination, but again, in such a way that he could be nominated if the party wanted him. The party wanted no disinterested or pallid candidate. Tilden was taken at his word, and his name was dropped from consideration.

Senator Thomas F. Bayard of Delaware had a considerable following in the South, Thomas Hendricks of Indiana was again under consideration, as was Horatio Seymour, the Democratic nominee in 1868. But Hendricks no longer had the support of past years, and Seymour made it quite clear, this time, that he would not accept the nomination, so they left him alone.

The Democrats decided to do the Republicans, Greenbackers, and Prohibitionists one better. They nominated a general too, not only a general with a handsome Union war record, but one who was still on active duty. General W. S. Hancock was commander of the Division of the Atlantic, with headquarters at Governor's Island, New York, and it was there that he received news of his nomination.

The Democratic convention was a quiet affair. On the second day, after the platform had been accepted, the candidates were presented, and on the first ballot Hancock led Senator Thomas F. Bayard of Delaware, the candidate of the South, but the combined vote for the two was not a majority. The next morning Hancock gained handsomely on the second ballot and won.

The strange part of it all was that no one cared very much. Hancock's own supporters indicated they were willing to abandon him in a moment if someone came up with a better ideal. No one did.

The contest for vice-president was hardly more spirited: William H. English, governor of the key state of Indiana, was nominated by acclamation over Richard M. Bishop of Ohio.

The two important platform issues became the protective tariff and the election frauds of 1876. The Republicans favored a high tariff for protection and revenue; the Democrats had equivocally endorsed "a tariff for revenue only," and the Republicans shouted that the Democrats were wild free-traders, without concern for the interests of American industry.

The Democrats did all they could to make the frauds of 1876 the principal issue, but their record of fraud and intimidation of southern Negroes in the congressional elections of 1878 did a great deal to take the wind out of that storm.

The Hayes administration record helped the Republicans too. In a table in their history of American politics Thomas V. Cooper and Hector Fenton noted that the Hayes administration showed fewer losses from corruption than any administration in the past, including those of Washington and Jefferson. Washington, with a revenue of $56,448,721, lost $210,552 to private pockets before the treasury ever saw the money. Hayes, with a revenue of $1,728,979,-907, lost none. The total losses in Hayes's time, from revenue and disbursements, seem unbelievable when compared to seven billion under Lincoln (which included the war), four and a half billion under Johnson, and two and a half billion under Grant's two terms. The general feeling was that Hayes's administration was clean.

The campaign itself was really remarkable for the savage assaults on both sides, but principally those directed against the character of Garfield.

Garfield's name had been raised in the Crédit Mobilier scandal; it had appeared in Oakes Ames's little black memorandum book, the one in which he kept the names of the men he bribed with stock, and the amounts he gave them.

Ames had contradicted himself in testimony about Garfield's part in the affair. First, he said he had sold Crédit Mobilier stock to Garfield. Then he said he hadn't. Garfield denied any such dealings, unequivocally and flatly. The amount was not large—$329 in Ames's book. Garfield said it was borrowed to pay the rent on his house and it had been repaid. Unfortunately, anxiety of the investigating committee to exonerate all the congressmen whose names were mentioned in the Crédit Mobilier scandal resulted in considerable obfuscation of the truth. Nothing much came of the investigation. As a result the men who had been tarred unfairly were forever after to wear the same stigmata as the guilty.

The whole affair now was nearly twenty years old, but the Democrats dusted it off to smear Garfield. The number "329" began appearing on sidewalks, doors, walls, and in the newspapers. It was a conversation piece, a sneer. And the sneering did not stop there. Garfield was charged with having taken other bribes and having "arranged" advantageous contracts for businessmen. In the language of the twentieth century he was charged with "influence peddling." If the charges were false they still gained currency by constant repetition.

Backed by the solid South, the Democrats again needed only a few key northern states to carry the election. As the summer wore along, their chances looked very good indeed because the Republican organization had not yet recovered from the split over Grant and the third term. If New York went Democratic, Hancock would win the election.

In August, at the demand of the national committee, Garfield reluctantly left his farm at Mentor, Ohio, to travel to New York in an attempt to heal the breach with Conkling. An impressive group gathered at the Fifth Avenue Hotel for the peace meeting: Senator Blaine, Senator Logan of Illinois, Secretary Sherman. . . . All these, but not Conkling.

In September the Democrats and Greenbackers won the Maine elections on a fusion ticket. If the Republicans were to win the election they had to carry Indiana, Ohio, and New York, and Indiana and Ohio were holding state elections on October 13. The result of those elections would forecast the results in November.

So the Republican breach was finally healed in a meeting between Hayes and Conkling, and Conkling and Grant took the stump for the Republican ticket, although neither had anything to say for Garfield personally.

The Democrats counterattacked with a fraudulent document, "the Morey letter," supposedly written by Garfield to an employer, defending the mass importation of cheap Chinese labor. Both parties had come out for strict regulation of Chinese immigration. So if the Morey letter were valid, it should swing a great many votes to Hancock.

The Republicans lost no time in raising the cry of forgery. They tried to trace it to the Democratic National Committee, but without success. It was impossible to *prove* that the letter was a fake, and it cost Garfield a great number of votes, especially in California.

The Republicans were not without weapons in this campaign, nor were they afraid to throw mud at the Democratic general. Just after Hancock's nomination the Republican press pointed out that in the 1867 military campaign against the Indians of the plains Hancock had spent "nine million dollars to kill two Indians." Specifically, the story went, Hancock had launched an expedition from Fort Larned against the Cheyennes in Kansas, had searched high and low, and with a force of fifteen hundred men had captured and killed two Indians in a camp at Sand Creek—an old man and a demented girl who was raped before she was murdered. The fact that this was a monstrous oversimplification of the Indian pacification campaign was immaterial to the Republicans. It made good reading.

The Republicans won in Ohio and Indiana, and Garfield rested easier at his farm, busy with details of plowing and seeding the gardens around the house and harvesting the beets. The Democrats were having a hard time making the corruption issue stick, since the Hayes administration was so upright, and the Democrats never did get the economic issue before the voting public. Times were too good.

On election eve Garfield was at the farm when returns began to come in at about 6 P.M. At midnight he gave supper to two dozen friends and at 3 A.M. he went to bed, confident of election and of carrying all the northern states, except New Jersey, and the Far West.

Thirty-eight states were represented in the election of 1880. Garfield won 214 electoral votes to Hancock's 155, but his popular margin was not quite 10,000 votes: 4,454,416 for Garfield, 4,444,952 for Hancock. Weaver, the Greenback candidate, polled only 308,578— a third of the Greenback vote in 1878—and Neal Dow, the Prohibitionist, found 10,305 voters who hated liquor above all else.

It was a personal triumph for Garfield and a serious defeat for the Democrats, who not only lost the presidency again but lost control of the House. The Democrats, recalling the actual victory of Tilden over Hayes in 1876 and the Democratic trend since in Congress, had begun the campaign fully confident of victory, and perhaps that was the trouble.

After his inauguration Garfield had scant time to make his mark on the American scene as Chief Executive. On July 2, 1881, in Washington, he was shot down by a fanatic, disappointed Stalwart office seeker, Charles J. Guiteau. For eleven weeks Garfield clung to life with stubborn will, but on the night of September 19 he died. Chester Arthur, an old Grant man, became the President of the United States, as the Stalwart cronies of the Grant administration chortled. They believed Arthur would bring back the "good old days" of the '70s.

Arthur, who had been collector of customs for the port of New York, had been removed from that post by President Hayes in his drive to stamp out corruption in the government. Arthur's nomination at Chicago had been the single crust thrown to the Grant supporters, and now the anti-Grant men winced as the Grant men rubbed their hands in anticipation of the spoils. The Republicans, like the

Democrats, had espoused a strong civil service plank in their platform, but with the Republicans it had been all show. When the matter was brought up on the floor of the convention, a Texas carpetbag delegate shouted:

"What are we up here for? I mean that members of the Republican party are entitled to office, and if we are victorious we will have office."

That was the position of the thirty-eight state party machines, despite any highfalutin talk about "civil service reform." Conkling stood for the greedy patronage system, and, as Conkling's man, President Arthur was expected to reopen the public trough that Hayes had guarded so carefully, to the disgust of the party machinery.

The spoilsmen could not have been more wrong.

Arthur became a solid, conservative President.

*Perhaps the most remarkable aspect of Chester A. Arthur's admin-
istration was the devotion this old spoilsman showed to the concepts
of ability and fitness as requisites for federal jobs.*

*Grant's boodlers could not understand it, but Arthur proposed
establishment of a civil service based on merit, and the Democratic
Congress of 1883 obliged nobly. Arthur also backtracked on the Republican tariff position. The national economy began to suffer from
depression in 1882, depression caused largely by the extremely high
taxes on imports that the Republicans had imposed. To the horror
of the high-tariff men in the GOP, Arthur backed tax reduction and
was supported by a coalition of Democrats and "revisionist" Republicans.*

*America was changing rapidly now. The Land of the Free was
also becoming a land of cities, a great manufacturing and commercial
nation. Tariff revision opened foreign doors to American goods, and
the business centers seemed likely to prosper as never before.*

*In 1881, south of the border, the French engineer, Ferdinand de
Lesseps, began digging a trench across the Isthmus of Panama. He
envisaged a great canal that would connect the Pacific and Atlantic
oceans as he had earlier connected the Red Sea and the Mediterranean and made passage to India possible without the weary trip
around Cape Horn.*

*In 1882, Germany, Austria, and Italy formed the Triple Alli-
ance, but the United States paid little attention, for Americans
were too busy with their own affairs to meddle in matters that did
not concern them. European power politics were incomprehensible,
anyhow.*

Thousands of Europeans eyed the shores of America with awe and hope, and many of them took the jump into the new world in search of fortune and happiness.

    But by 1884 the power of the nation to thrive on change was paralyzed, temporarily. On May 5, 6, and 7, Wall Street—and then the rest of the nation—was seized by financial panic. Prosperous banking houses collapsed; personal fortunes were wiped out in a moment's turn of the market; and with them, into political oblivion, traveled Chester A. Arthur's hopes for a presidential term of his own. His ruin was as final as the ruin of the financial firm of Grant and Ward, whose failure wiped out the personal fortune of former President Ulysses S. Grant.

8. The Reformer from Buffalo

At fifty-four, James G. Blaine had enjoyed the highest honors the people of the United States could bestow, save the presidency itself. He had been elected to the House of Representatives from Maine and chosen by his fellows as Speaker of the House. He had been senator, Secretary of State in the Garfield cabinet, and an intimate of that President. By many, Blaine was regarded as Garfield's heir apparent. He was attractive, benign, and as slick a politician as had ever paced the halls of Congress or mulled a problem of state in a Cabinet meeting.

A sharp wit and biting tongue brought Blaine many admirers and many enemies. Not the least of the latter was Senator Roscoe Conkling of New York, so bitter a foe that Blaine's selection for the Cabinet had been a prime factor in Conkling's resignation as United States Senator. It was not the only factor—Conkling resigned in a fight over patronage—but the enmity between Conkling and Blaine had been blazing for ten years, often flaming in rage on the Senate floor.

Blaine had stout friends, too. These men had supported his bids for the presidency in 1876 and 1880, and they were determined that the honor should not escape him a third time.

Blaine, in the spring of 1884, was not so sure of himself. He saw, as clearly as anyone, the three-way split in the Republican party. His support had been bolstered by the addition of some of the Stalwarts who had supported Grant through thick and thin. Even so, President Arthur claimed most of the Stalwarts, as an old machine politician from New York. But after Garfield's death Arthur's negative attitude toward spoils shocked the section of the party that had been smacking its lips in anticipation of a renewed three years of Grantian feasting.

The third Republican faction in 1884 was made up of leftovers from the old Greeley Liberal campaign, men now calling themselves "Independents." They were reformers who had opposed Grant's nomination in 1872, who had supported Bristow in 1876, and had cheered for Garfield in 1880. The Independents were irrevocably anti-Blaine, although not noticeably opposed to President Arthur.

Blaine had been described—had described himself, in fact—as the Henry Clay of the Republican party, in view of his high standing as a legislator, his wealth of experience and forensic skills; but most of all because he, like the golden-voiced Whig, had been passed over time and again for the presidential honor he coveted.

The "Plumed Knight from Maine" (as Blaine was christened in 1876) had a bad case of Potomac fever. When he resigned from the Cabinet on Garfield's death, in September 1881, he did not go home, as unhorsed politicoes usually did in those days. Instead, he began construction of a large house in Washington, a project he supervised personally when not busy writing his memoirs, *Twenty Years of Congress*.

Blaine's opponents charged that behind this façade of husbandry and literary effort lurked the most shrewd and scheming politician of the era, making every effort to snatch the Republican presidential nomination at the Chicago convention.

At any rate, Blaine was out but not forgotten, unlike his nemesis, Roscoe Conkling, who was so far removed from the scene of politics by 1884 that he did not even attend the Republican convention.

In the winter of 1883, Blaine's supporters had met in New York. Those men included Whitelaw Reid of the New York *Tribune*, William Walter Phelps, and Charles Emory Smith of the Philadelphia *Press*. The purpose of the meeting was not to settle the "if" of the Blaine movement, but the "when."

The Blaine movement was launched once again that year. But Blaine himself was cautious. Only a month before the convention he told his campaign managers not to spend money in behalf of his nomination. "I never want it," he said, "unless it be the unbought, unbiased will of the nominating power." He ordered them specifically *not* to purchase votes.

On the eve of the convention Blaine returned to his constituency in Augusta, Maine, and from his home there anxiously awaited the decision of the nominating power assembling in Chicago's exposition building.

The Republicans were in high spirits. Even the Democratic New York *Herald* referred to "Mr. Arthur's conservative and respectable administration." The public odor of the Grant administration was wiped out at long last.

But if Blaine had cautioned his supporters against pouring money into the campaign for the nomination, they had counseled among themselves and decided they knew better. Blaine money flowed freely in Chicago. It was obvious that he was the most prominent candidate, could be defeated only if President Arthur's men and all the others worked together.

Powell Clayton, former senator from Arkansas, had been designated by the Republican National Committee as the temporary chairman who would start things off before the convention elected a permanent chairman. The temporary chairman's job was an important one at all conventions, for he set the keynote of the convention in his opening speech, and by maneuvering in the organizing stages of the convention he might have great influence on the final results. Clayton, the 1884 Keynoter, was a Blaine man.

On June 2, Chicago was struck by a sudden freak hail storm. "Stones as big as pullets' eggs" pelleted the city, an apt meteorological forerunner for the rocks the anti-Blaine men would throw a few hours later.

As the convention went into session Blaine claimed 340 of 818 delegates. It was a strong showing. Clayton was nominated from the floor for the chairmanship. All was proceeding according to plan. But before the eyes of the 8000 men and women who crowded into the auditorium, two of the party's striplings, Henry Cabot Lodge and Theodore Roosevelt, proposed John R. Lynch, for the chairman's job. Lynch was a mustachioed Negro from Mississippi, a congressman in the carpetbag days and a figure who demanded the emotional support of a great number of delegates, if only by his race.

It was a bombshell! Had the Arthur men and other anti-Blaine forces managed to unite?

It looked that way. Lynch was elected to the temporary chairmanship by 431 votes to 387 for Clayton.

The next day John B. Henderson of Missouri was chosen permanent president of the convention, and the Blaine men, warned, were beginning to rally their support.

On June 5 the conventon adopted its rules; one set a precedent that would take control of the national committee out of the hands of government officials. "No person," it read, "shall be a member of the committee who is not eligible as a member of the electoral college." Here was an important move, one that would put control of the party, and to a large extent control of the patronage system, back in the hands of the national convention.

The same amendment established the nomination of delegates by the method under which congressional representatives were chosen. State Republican conventions were to have the power to choose delegates-at-large. This made each congressional district all-powerful in choosing its own delegates. It killed the unit rule as a control of state voting.

The nominations were made, with all the oratorical gusto at the command of the nominators. On the first ballot Blaine carried 334½ votes, President Arthur 278, and the remaining six candidates 205½. It was odd: every state convention of the party that year had endorsed Arthur's administration, but 196 of his 278 votes came from the southern states, whose delegates were really chosen by Republican officials, since in the South the Republican party consisted of a few Negro malcontents and transplanted Yankees. The voters of the South were overwhelmingly white and Democratic.

On the fourth ballot Blaine was nominated, 541 votes to Arthur's 207, with a holdout bloc of 41 for Senator George F. Edmunds of Vermont and 24 votes scattered between Senator John Logan of Illinois, the old Grant Stalwart; Joseph R. Hawley of Connecticut; and Robert T. Lincoln of Illinois, old Abe's son.

The Grant men were mollified by nomination of Senator Logan as Vice-President. The problem of the anti-Blaine Republicans was not really solved at all. These were the reformers, men who remembered too well the Crédit Mobilier scandal and the charges made against Blaine as a railroad agent and profiteer. The reformers took no overt action. They made no threats at the convention. But the revolt was there, simmering.

Blaine's friends and neighbors in Maine were excited and happy. A special train came from Bangor to Augusta crowded with Republicans who wanted to be among the first to congratulate the candidate. From Chicago the whole California delegation traveled all the way to Maine to do the same, they said.

Across the land Republicans and the party press crowed their pleasure in the nomination.

But the dissident reformers were not yet heard.

On June 12, E. L. Godkin, a sober leader of the reform Republicans, wrote, in *The Nation:*

. . . the Chicago ticket does not present simply a triumph of somebody else's man, but represents to the dissatisfied a distinct outrage on their moral sense. It represents to them the success of rascality and corruption in the party councils, and an attempt to place the presidency for four years at the disposal of jobbers, speculators, intriguers.

A large segment of the Republican party was willing to bolt —and a number of Republican newspapers were willing to support a rebellion. Yet, except to snarl their anger at the Republican nomination, they had nowhere to go, as yet. The existing candidates had little appeal for them.

The first national convention of 1884 had been held by the Anti-Monopoly party, which met at Chicago, May 14, representing only half the states and the District of Columbia. This party was dedicated to the alliance of labor and capital, government regulation of big business, and government economy.

General Benjamin F. Butler of Massachusetts, former Democrat, Radical Republican, sometime Greenbacker, was nominated as the Anti-Monopoly candidate for President. The vice-presidential spot was left open—to be filled by the national committee. Why? Well, when the Greenback, or National party, met two weeks later at Indianapolis, it also nominated General Butler, and General A. M. West of Mississippi for Vice-President. The Anti-Monopolists then accepted West, and the two had a kind of fusion, for what it was worth. The dual nomination was no accident. Butler's aides worked their heads off to bring it about for the former governor of Massachusetts.

This lunatic fringe was certainly no place for the dissident Republicans, particularly when Ben Butler announced that not only did he carry the banner of both the Anti-Monopolists and the Greenbackers, but was going to Chicago now to sit in on the Democratic convention—as a Democrat.

The puzzled anti-Blaine Republicans, Missouri's Carl Schurz and the others, would not support an omnibus candidate—could not support a man they believed immoral and unfit for public office.

Independent committees were organized in New York and Boston. There and elsewhere the reformers played cautiously with the Democrats. Nominate acceptable men, said the reformers, and the Democrats could look forward to a considerable amount of Republican support.

There was nothing very formal or binding about the reform offer, but it had considerable influence with the Democrats. There was such a man. Grover Cleveland, the double-chinned, stout, but still handsome young governor of New York, had been elected by the enormous majority of 190,000 in 1882. Cleveland was known as the "reformer from Buffalo," a description bound to be impressive to the reform-conscious Republicans. They were equally impressed by the bitter opposition of boss-ridden Tammany Hall to Cleveland's candidacy.

Two weeks after the Republicans adjourned, Cleveland supporters set up shop at Chicago's Palmer House, prepared to do the advance work. One Cleveland lieutenant, William C. Hudson, had a list of all the New York delegates. As each New Yorker arrived, Hudson began to compile all the information possible about the man, his habits and his morals. Daniel Manning, an old Tilden lieutenant, now a Cleveland backer and Democratic state chairman of New York, told Hudson they had to win the doubtful and undeclared delegates, or their man's chances were nil. ". . . we must subject them to pressure . . . but first we must learn the sort of pressure that should be applied," said the old pro.

It was not an easy job. Tammany Hall was already at work in Chicago, too. Thomas F. Grady, a state senator whose re-election Cleveland had opposed, was spreading largesse among the members of the press, trying to fix the newspapers against Cleveland. Grady was joined gleefully by Blaine's lieutenants, who considered Cleveland the most dangerous of the potential Democratic candidates. A prime target of both groups was the Irish, to whom Cleveland was painted as a pious, blindered Presbyterian, a hater of Rome and all its works.

Tammany came to Chicago in force, six hundred strong, although only a handful of the ragged tigers wore delegates' badges. Tammany men came for only one purpose, to defeat Cleveland and regain control of the Democratic party in New York State for their society.

The Tammany men worked hard. Even on the morning of the New York delegation's caucus the Cleveland men were not sure of victory. Cleveland leaders finally won control by two votes—the two votes represented by two delegates who had been virtually kidnaped and put under pressure. One of them walked into the caucus with the promise of a state job, if he would vote for Cleveland.

The fourteenth Democratic convention opened on July 8 with a bang. Almost immediately the Cleveland opposition in New York made its first move. When the routine motion to adopt the rules of the previous convention came up, Tammany's Grady asked an amendment that would outlaw the unit rule. By anybody's calculations, the New York delegation of 72 was split thus: 50 for Cleveland, 22 against him. If the unit rule prevailed New York's 72 votes would go to Cleveland.

The amendment was defeated, 463 to 332, but Tammany continued the fight against Cleveland's nomination. Declared boss John Kelly, "I will not lift a hand for him."

At midnight on the third day, the first balloting began. Cleveland's nomination had been seconded by Governor Edward S. Bragg of Wisconsin, who declared the young men of the party loved Cleveland "for the enemies he has made." That remark looked right down Tammany's throat.

The other candidates were Thomas F. Bayard, Allen G. Thurman of Ohio, John G. Carlisle of Kentucky, Samuel J. Randall of Pennsylvania, Joseph McDonald of Illinois, and George Hoadly of Ohio.

On the first ballot Cleveland had 392 votes—more than twice as many as Bayard's 170, but still 155 short of the two thirds needed under the standard Democratic rule.

The convention recessed for the night. Then Tammany really went to work.

Boss Kelly met with General Benjamin Butler, the Anti-Monopolist, Greenback Democrat, and planned a "spontaneous" stampede for Thomas A. Hendricks of Indiana, who had gotten one vote on the first ballot. The stampede was to be triggered by Hendricks's appearance the next morning on the convention floor.

They "fixed" the convention sergeant at arms. He let them pack the galleries with men pledged to raise a hullabaloo for Hendricks as soon as this perennial candidate's name should be mentioned.

But the permanent chairman got the word. He sent a messenger to every member of the convention, except the Tammany men, and told each what would happen the next day.

Morning came, and so did Hendricks. The stampede began. The galleries rang with shouts, cheers, and applause for the great gentleman from Indiana. And the gallery noise was joined by the brave little knot of Tammany men on the floor. All other delegates, nearly eight hundred of them, sat in stony silence and watched the Tammany men, as the spontaneous stampede faded limply into silence.

On the second ballot Cleveland gained but at the end was still 72 votes short of nomination. Under the revised rule of the convention the states could change their votes once the roll call was completed. When the changes were registered Cleveland had 683 votes. Tammany was disgraced. Cleveland did not need the hand boss Kelly had refused to tender, and throughout the hall rose the cry, "We love him for the enemies he's made."

Hendricks, the sacrificial cow in Tammany's last-ditch stand, was nominated for Vice-President. It was a Democratic ticket the dissident reform Republicans could espouse with enthusiasm.

"The Democratic party," declared Carl Schurz, "has never presented a candidate whom any friend of good government, Democrat or Republican, could see step into the presidential chair with a greater feeling of security."

A few days later, on July 22, some five hundred accredited Independent Republican delegates from sixteen different states rejected a motion to form a third party, but did make their views known, flatly and clearly.

Blaine, they said, was "a candidate who is an unfit leader, shown by his own words and his acknowledged acts, which are of official record, to be unworthy of respect and confidence; who has traded upon his official trust for his pecuniary gain; a representative of men, methods, and conduct which the public conscience condemns and which illustrates the very evils which honest men would reform."

These renegade Republicans came to be known throughout the land as Mugwumps. The term was subject to a crude, joking definition: A Mugwump was a man with his mug on one side of the fence and his "wump" on the other. The real origin of the term is cloudier. It was not new: it had been used to characterize the Greeley Independents in 1872. Some said it came from an Indian name meaning big chief. The regular Republicans, running both frightened and bitter, said the term meant Ishmaelites, Dependents, Soreheads, Pharisees, Goody-Goodies, or Assistant Democrats.

The last had more than a grain of truth in it. For after the two clean Republican administrations of Hayes and Arthur the country, except for the solid South, had developed a habit of voting Republican. The Democrats needed assistance, all they could get, if they were to win the election.

There was not much to choose between in the platforms of the parties. The two parties, as always, had opposed views on the question of the tariff. This year the Republicans tried to push the issue, the Democrats to play it down. The Republican campaign textbook of 1884 devoted almost half its 170 pages to tariffs, Blaine more than half his letter of acceptance of the nomination to the same subject. If the Democrats won, it was assumed, the country would overthrow protection and go wild for free trade.

Seldom in American history have there been times when party labels had meant less than in the years 1881–84. In Congress there were no great partisan issues; the Republicans were split into "Stalwart" and "Half-Breed" camps, and the issues like Mormon polygamy in Utah, Chinese immigration, and civil service reform led to splits more along sectional lines than party lines.

In 1882 the Democrats had won 196 seats in the House of Representatives of the Forty-eighth Congress, the Republicans, 118. The Senate was Republican by four seats. The Democrats also won local elections in a number of important states. The smashing victory of Grover Cleveland in New York, was, in itself, a warning that the trend in American politics was away from "boss rule." In 1883 the Republican National Committee considered a pair of proposals that would have revolutionized the convention system—one of which would eliminate the influence of the southern Republicans, mostly Negroes, whose numerical influence in the party councils far outweighed their ability to pull votes.

But in the end the committee settled for a milder reform, to preserve the rights of minorities within the state conventions and guard against hamstringing of the national convention by preventing state meetings too early in the year.

Several new political forces did emerge in the campaign of 1884.

For the first time labor was important enough and organized enough to be an important political factor. Both parties asserted their devotion to the working man, the Republicans by favoring a national bureau of labor and enforcement of the eight-hour day, the Democrats by a pious declaration that labor should be "fostered and cherished" and by espousing the rights of workers to organize.

The Federation of Organized Trades and Labor Unions of the United States and Canada, grandfather of the AFL-CIO, had been formed in 1881. The new depression hurt the workingman. Economic conditions grew worse in 1883, and wages were cut 10 to 20 per cent in most industries; 10 per cent of the industrial working force was idle. In 1884 wages were cut again, and 20 to 35 per cent of the men were idle in basic industry.

The Knights of Labor and the International Typographical Union appeared before the Republican convention this year to press their case for the kind of legislation they wanted. The printers appeared, to complain about Reid's New York *Tribune*, which had solved its labor problems, temporarily at least, by hiring non-union printers. The union's local No. 6 wanted the convention to repudiate Reid. The convention did not, and the printers came out against Blaine, their candidate.

The Prohibitionists were to play a more important part in this election than before. On June 19 the American Prohibition national convention had held a mass meeting in Chicago and nominated Samuel C. Pomeroy of Kansas for President. But this was not the regular Prohibition party and Pomeroy's name did not appear on the ballot of any state. Pomeroy represented a rump group that had split off over peripheral issues—not involving rum. On July 23 at Pittsburgh the National Prohibition party—the real dry movement —met to choose its candidate. The name of Dr. R. H. McDonald of California was brought up, but quickly hushed when, of all things, it was whispered that he had manufactured and sold alcohol in "a medicine called bitters." John St. John of Kansas was nominated again. Prohibition was a growing issue, particularly in the Middle West. It had been the main issue in the election of 1883 in Ohio— and the Democrats, who said liquor was not a fit subject for legislation, defeated the Republicans, who wanted to put the question to the people.

In the party platforms the Republicans ignored the issue while the Democrats took a sidelong slap at "laws which vex the citizens and interfere with personal liberty."

But the real importance of the Prohibitionists in 1884 was that they provided a haven for many Republicans who could not stomach their party's ticket, would not join the Mugwumps and support Cleveland, or espouse the cause of the Greenbackers and that old chameleon Ben Butler.

Twenty years had passed since the silencing of the fratricidal cannon at Appomatox. The new generation of voters had much less interest in the causes and effects of the Civil War than in the cause and control of economic depression. Even this gave way to the issue of personal morality, which enveloped the political consciousness of the nation in a swirling emotional fog.

The Mugwumps started it. They didn't even wait until Blaine could get up from his hammock under the fruit trees of his Maine garden before they were attacking his personal honesty.

Many important publications announced, from the beginning, that they would not support Blaine. Among them were the New York *Times* and the Springfield *Republican*. Carl Schurz, George W. Curtis, and Henry Ward Beecher led the Mugwumps. There were anti-Blaine men, Theodore Roosevelt, Henry Cabot Lodge, and Hamilton Fish, who refused to bolt the party.

The Mugwumps again linked Blaine with the infamous Crédit Mobilier. They charged that he had accepted stock in the Little Rock and Fort Smith Railroad in exchange for favors. Senator Thurman had introduced a bill which would compel the Union Pacific Railroad to pay 25 per cent of its earnings to the government, until it canceled its huge indebtedness. Blaine, said the Mugwumps, had proposed an amendment to the bill that would have prevented Congress from passing any further laws to regulate the Union Pacific for twenty years. When the amendment was defeated Blaine voted against the bill.

They said Blaine had never failed to make any possible use of his positions of trust for personal gain.

These were strong charges. At first the Republicans did not know how to respond. They began the campaign just as in the past, waving the Union flag and recalling the bloody rebellion. They talked of treason, the threat of the "solid South," and the vote thefts of the Democrats. But nobody was listening.

The Republicans, hopefully, tried the tariff. Voters were inclined to yawn. But the voters gulped at news disclosed by the Buffalo *Evening Telegraph* on July 21. The newspapers charged that Cleveland had lived, out of wedlock, with a Buffalo widow named Maria Halpern, some eight years previously, and that their union had been embarrassed by the birth of a child. If that were not enough, said the *Evening Telegraph*, Cleveland was a drunkard and a libertine who had no business running for the highest office in the land.

The story flashed across the nation's telegraph lines right into the public consciousness. Cleveland admitted that he had lived with Mrs. Halpern and that while he was not sure of the child's paternity he had contributed to its support.

Now it was the Republican's turn to raise the roof. The GOP lost no time. Party strategists distributed the Buffalo story. Republican ministers began thundering in their pulpits against this "moral leper."

In New York the Republicans organized a demonstration that tramped up Fifth Avenue, singing:

"Ma, Ma, where's my pa?"—a marching cry, repeated up and down the avenue by thousands of voices, sneering, laughing, and counting cadence to the words.

The Democrats countered, in a parade of their own:

> "Ma, Ma, where's my pa?
> "'Gone to the White House,' ha, ha, ha."

Henry Ward Beecher, who later stood accused of adultery with one of the members of his Plymouth Church congregation, expressed shock at the adultery charges but repledged his Mugwumpism in a letter of support to Cleveland. Cleveland, in a letter that was saccharine even by the flowery standards of the *Times*, replied that Beecher reminded him of his mother. At the next Republican rally, this was the party refrain:

"Mrs. Beecher, Mrs. Beecher, you remind me of my mother" . . . as 16,000 Republican "businessmen" marched down the city streets. And the Democrats, at their own rally, had an even stronger contingent of lawyers, merchants, and workers, shouting:

> "Blaine! Blaine! James G. Blaine!
> The con-ti-nen-tal liar
> From the state of Maine."

Cleveland behaved better than either his enemies or his friends. He made no attempt to deny or justify the charges, refused to take any hand in putting out similar charges against Blaine, and warned his men against blackguarding the opposition.

"Whatever you do," said Cleveland, "tell the truth."

The Mugwump Committee of One Hundred was carrying on a propaganda campaign against Blaine in pamphlets that showed the Republican candidate as dishonest, tricky, greedy, unscrupulous, and disloyal to his friends.

But the Mugwump campaign was forgotten for a moment, on August 8, when an Indianapolis newspaper charged that Blaine had raped his wife before marriage and had married her at the point of a shotgun. The proof, the newspaper said, lay in the cemetery at Augusta, where the headstone over the grave of Blaine's son Stanwood showed he had been born less than nine months after the couple's wedding.

Blaine promptly filed a libel suit against the paper. On the night of August 17 someone stole into the cemetery at Augusta and chiseled the date of birth from Stanwood Blaine's tombstone, burying, as they say, the evidence.

The fighting continued with fresh stimuli. General Ben Butler finally decided that he *was* the nominee of the Anti-Monopoly and Greenback parties and began running for office. Butler had taken care, before the Democratic convention, to refrain from committing himself as candidate of the two minor parties. At the Democratic convention Butler's alliance with Tammany Hall's attempt to defeat Cleveland was undertaken to get the nomination for himself.

Butler did claim the adherence of much of the labor vote that year, since his two parties stood for everything the workingman of the day asked for. And as the campaign wore on, the Democrats were as worried about the votes Butler might draw from them as the Republicans were about the Mugwump vote that would go for Cleveland.

Cartoonists had a field day with this campaign. Blaine was shown as the tattooed man by Democratic cartoonists, as a knight in armor by his adherents. Thomas Nast, the great political cartoonist of *Harper's Weekly*, began early and worked late to paint Blaine as a dishonest, ward-heeling politician.

In September, anxious about the way things were going, Blaine was persuaded to take to the stump, to appeal for votes in the West, where Ohio and West Virginia were still clinging to the outdated practice of holding state elections in October. On his route Blaine stopped off in New York State, where he was met by one admiring group after another.

While he was on tour the Democrats unveiled a set of damning letters that again indicated Blaine had used his official position in Congress to feather his own nest. This particular scandal had begun during Blaine's Congress days when a discomfited clerk named Mulligan had released a series of letters relating to financial transactions. Now came a new packet of "Mulligan letters," correspondence between Blaine and his railroad friends that showed the Republican candidate in even worse light. One was a letter to Blaine's business partner Warren Fisher, written on April 18, 1876—a week before Blaine had gone before the House to read and explain the original letters in the investigation of charges against him. It told how he had arranged to have his partner copy and sign a letter of Blaine's composition, to be used as favorable testimony in the investigation.

"Burn this letter," Blaine had written at the close. But Fisher was not so wise. The letter fell into the hands of the bitter Mr. Mulligan, then into the grasping fists of the Democratic politicians. Soon the cry was heard:

> "Burn this letter! Burn this letter!
> Burn, burn, oh burn this letter!"

So another marching song for the Democrats had been written in the ink of Blaine's own pen.

Now the campaign was coming to a close. The Republicans seemed destined to hold most of their northern states, although Massachusetts was a little doubtful in view of the great triumph of Mugwumpishness, so strong in Boston that the rebels twitted the regular Republicans in all the best clubs.

Cleveland, they said, would carry the solid South, Blaine the rest of the North, and the West would split. The four key states were Indiana, New Jersey, New York, and Connecticut.

The Catholics in New York and New England had been persuaded that Cleveland was not only anti-labor but anti-Catholic as well. Then Blaine came back to New York, on his way home from the western trip, flushed with success, but underneath it sallow and tired from the slogging, jolting campaign. It was October 29, just a handful of days before the election. Blaine was met by a delegation of clergymen who wanted to assure him of their support against Cleveland and his friends.

"We are Republicans," said one frocked worthy, the Reverend Burchard, "and don't propose to leave our party and identify ourselves with the party whose antecedents have been Rum, Romanism, and Rebellion. We are loyal to our flag. We are loyal to you."

Blaine, nearly sick from his grueling tour, paid no attention to the words. That night, he attended a dinner at Delmonico's; there was money to be raised for those last all-important days.

At Delmonico's two hundred men assembled. Jay Gould, Cyrus Field, John Jacob Astor, Levi Morton, Cornelius Bliss, Henry Clews —the list read like a bluebook of millionaires. The candidate appealed hopefully for a king's ransom. They gave him an ovation, and a beggar's pledge.

"LUCULLUS ENJOYS HIMSELF WHILE THE COUNTRY SORROWS," said Joseph Pulitzer's New York *World* the next day.

And beneath was a cartoon that showed Blaine surrounded by fat, diamond-studded capitalists, while a poor starving worker and his emaciated wife and child pleaded for crumbs.

That was bad enough. Worse was to come.

"Rum, Romanism, and Rebellion," shouted the Democrats. That was how Blaine regarded the Catholics, the party brayed, in fliers posted everywhere, to inform the Irish of the mortally insulting words of the bigoted Republican. The handbills were not too concerned, either, if readers got the impression that Blaine himself had said these words.

The Catholics got the idea.

Five days later the country went to the polls. The unpleasant patter of raindrops assailed the ears of the rural Republicans of upstate New York. The Democrats were out in force, and even Tammany Hall had finally come out for the party's candidate, after all its caterwauling.

The early returns showed that Cleveland had carried all the southern states. That was to be expected. The Republicans had carried all states outside the South except Connecticut, New Jersey, Indiana, and New York. That was to be expected, too.

New Jersey, Connecticut, and Indiana fell to the Democrats. Bad news, but not necessarily fatal.

Both parties claimed the key state—New York. First, the New York

Sun gave the victory to Cleveland. The Associated Press gave it to Blaine. Three days later all New York papers but the *Tribune* conceded to Cleveland, but the Republican party had not.

The returns were slow in coming in . . . too slow for the New York crowds, who suspected Jay Gould of using his control of Western Union to his own ends. "We'll hang Jay Gould to a sour apple tree," they shouted as they descended on the Western Union building. But Gould was not there to be hanged; he was safe on his yacht in the middle of the Hudson River.

Finally, the tenth day after the election, the Republicans were forced to concede a Democratic victory for the presidency. Grover Cleveland had won New York by 1149 votes. He had 219 electoral votes to Blaine's 182. For the first time in twenty-four years a Democrat would again occupy the White House.

Cleveland polled 4,874,986 votes; Blaine 4,851,981; Ben Butler 175,370, and John St. John 150,369. It was a banner day for the donkey, but one that its rider took calmly enough. All during the waiting and the disputes over the count Cleveland had remained at his desk in Albany, carrying out his duties as governor of New York. Finally, he was told: he had won. The Republicans had conceded.

"I am glad of it," said the big man quietly. "Very glad. There will be no trouble. If they had not, I should have felt it my duty to take my seat anyhow."

9

In the 1880s the captains of American industry came into their own.
Cornelius Vanderbilt left a fortune of more than a hundred million
dollars when he died in 1877. Jay Gould, a pauper before the war,
ran his luck, influence, and brass up to eight million dollars in
the fabulous '80s. John D. Rockefeller now counted his wealth in
hundreds of millions and his corporations by the score. Andrew
Carnegie was becoming the steel king of the world.

Labor grew with capital, and the clashes began. It was an era
in which the big businessman had things all his own way for the
most part, but the seeds of rebellion were sprouting. The railroad
men—barons of privilege—were also acquiring bad reputations along
with their good fortune. Congress began to step in, gingerly at first,
to regulate the industrialists.

Europe overshadowed the world, but the United States had no
interest in world affairs, except as they directly affected this nation.
There was more interest in Latin America, and some citizens were
talking about annexation of territories. Cuba, perhaps. But most
Americans were much more concerned with expansion of business
at home. . . .

9. The Tariff Wall

Cleveland's administration was respectable enough. The only serious scandal was the case of the Pan Electric Company and the Bell Telephone Company patents, which involved Attorney General Garland.

Garland owned a large block of Pan Electric Company stock. The Department of Justice began an anti-trust suit that attacked the validity of the Bell patents. Had the suit been successful, Pan Electric's value would have skyrocketed.

When the Republicans uncovered these facts the halls of Congress resounded with screams of "foul," but the Democrats refused to get excited, and by studiously ignoring the issue they found that it *did* go away.

It was an era of great change in America. The old politicians who had fought the Civil War at the polls ever since 1865 were now dying off—Grant in July 1885, Vice-President Thomas Hendricks in November. Horatio Seymour, the Democratic candidate of 1868, died the next year. Samuel Tilden, the great Republican preacher Henry Ward Beecher, and the old Stalwart Roscoe Conkling were carried to their graves in the next two years. With their passing the temper of politics was changing too, even the Republican newspapers now referred to the Civil War with restraint. The New York *Tribune* went so far as to express the belief that service in the Confederate Army did not necessarily disqualify a man for federal office. And visitors to Washington were pleased to see Union General Phil Sheridan and the Confederacy's Joe Johnston sitting quietly on a couch at a party in friendly discussion. At this late date one could hardly have expected the two soldiers to draw on one another, but in the air of ostentatious forgiveness, such events were self-consciously noted.

President Cleveland had to contend with a Democratic House of Representatives, a Republican Senate, and 100,000 loyal members of the Democratic party who felt they were now eminently eligible for federal jobs after twenty-four years of Republican administration. The Republicans suddenly showed wholehearted interest in civil service reform, especially as it would freeze their men in their jobs. The Democrats, who had advocated civil service reform so ardently under Republican administration, were scrambling for juicy government posts, and their idea of reform now was to turn out the rascally Republicans, put honest Democrats in their places, then freeze the jobs.

Cleveland's time was monopolized by hungry office seekers. His limited patience was sorely tried, for Cleveland really did believe in civil service reform, and to the outrage of his party the new President tried to practice what he had preached. The party bosses often accused him of appointing "the wrong kind of Democrat" to office, for Cleveland preferred capable, honest, and industrious men to the backroom boys who got out the vote.

The New York *World* warned: "Cleveland must remember the obligations which an administration elected by a great historical party owes to that party."

The President answered, in a letter to a friend: ". . . the damned everlasting clatter for offices continues . . . and makes me feel like resigning, and hell is to pay generally."

The Missouri reformer Carl Schurz warned that if Cleveland tried to please both the Democrats and the Independents he would be "sitting between two chairs." The President once asked one of the party's spoilsmen, "Do you want me to appoint another horse thief?" But in the four years of his first administration he replaced two thirds of the 120,000 officeholders in the federal government.

The old-fashioned spoils-loving New York *Sun* bragged that Cleveland had been forced to yield on the "bunkum" of reform, and the Republicans agreed wholeheartedly, if bitterly.

Of 2379 first-class postmasters, 2000 had been changed; of 52,609 fourth-class postmasters, 40,000 had changed; of 33 foreign service ministers, 32 were changed; of 21 secretaries of legations, 16 changes; of 111 collectors of customs, 100 changes; of 85 collectors of internal revenue, 84 changes. All territorial governors appointed under the Republicans were removed.

Cleveland's own tendency to reform the government was not

calculated to hold party loyalty, nor was his veto of a measure that would have guaranteed practically every Union war veteran a pension of $12 per month.

The friction showed in the congressional elections of 1886. The Democrats retained control of the House of Representatives, but lost 15 seats. The party press attributed this loss to Cleveland's civil service "nonsense," but, in fact, the party could not agree on either issues or policies. In 1888, in an industrial economy where the rich were growing richer and the poor poorer, issues once again were to determine the course of the election.

Laboring men were discontent. They did not feel they were getting their fair share of the nation's prosperity.

In industry the watchwords were growth and monopoly. "Corporations," Cleveland told Congress, "are fast becoming the people's masters." But if corporations were moving toward monopoly so were the labor unions. Sometimes the clashes between the two were severe. On the Texas and Pacific Railway, when a mechanic, a prominent member of the Knights of Labor, was discharged the union struck and paralyzed six thousand miles of railroads. The men pulled pins from the trains, sabotaged locomotives, wrecked the rails, and intimidated and assaulted the "scabs" who tried to work. In East St. Louis a squad of deputies fired on a crowd, killing several people. The crowd quickly became a mob and burned railroad buildings. After seven weeks the strike was broken, but not the movement.

Now labor began to agitate for an eight-hour day. The convention of the Federation of Organized Trades and Labor Unions in 1884 set May 1, 1886, as the date for the eight-hour day to begin. When that day arrived, in Chicago 10,000 lumbermen marched through the streets; 40,000 workingmen struck. At the McCormick reaper works strikers who were attacking strikebreakers were fired on by police. Four strikers were killed. The next night a mass meeting in Haymarket Square was broken up by bombing. Sixty men were killed or injured, and, although political anarchists had thrown the bomb, organized labor suffered the consequences.

Disgraced for the moment, the labor movement continued to seethe. The federal government legalized the right to organize and established the Interstate Commerce Commission to regulate national industries. State governments created labor departments with the machinery to end strikes and began regulating employment conditions, particularly those of women and children.

Strikes continued: long, bitter, violent strikes that often resulted in more cracked heads than benefits. At the beginning of the second week of January 1888 workers were on strike in the coal mines of the Reading Railroad. At Philadelphia the coal shortage made it likely the city government offices would have to close. In Chicago the typographical union was moving in on the non-union Chicago *Times*. In New York a butcher shop owned by John Stimmell was boycotted because Stimmell also owned the German Assembly Rooms and didn't hire union labor there.

The Cigar Makers International Union in New York City was planning to strike because employers had cut wages, and the local steam fitters held a meeting at their hall on Grand Street to demand higher wages.

But the vital issue of the coming campaign was the tariff. For years the two major parties had been moving in opposite directions. The Republicans now tended to favor a heavy tax on foreign goods, not so much to gain revenue for the federal government as to make the prices of foreign goods so high that Americans would "buy American." The Democrats had vacillated from the extreme of free trade to the moderation of a semi-protection tariff policy.

In 1884 both parties had been pledged to reduce the tariff because by that year the continual government cash surplus was hurting the national economy. During the Arthur administration the annual surplus had stayed around $100,000,000 a year. But by 1888 it appeared that the surplus would be nearly $140,000,000 despite the government's retirement of nearly $200,000,000 in bonds.

The financial community was worried, quite seriously. The government had nearly $600,000,000 in unexpended funds in the treasury. That was more than a half-billion dollars withdrawn from circulation, and the only way to get it back into circulation was either to spend it "recklessly" or to cut taxes. The welfare state was beyond the comprehension of most politicians in 1888.

President Cleveland decided to cut taxes. Specifically, he decided to cut the tariff, which he called a "vicious, illegal, and inequitable system of taxation." The Republican Senate immediately charged him with advocating free trade. Within his own party the President was in for a bitter fight, for the Democratic congressman from industrial districts had a political stake in the preservation of the high tariff.

A Gloucester fisherman symbolized the nature of the problem when he said that in general he was for free trade, with one exception. Obviously, there ought to be a high duty on herring.

In April 1888 the chairman of the House Ways and Means Committee introduced a bill that would reduce internal revenue taxation by $24,000,000 and the tariff by $53,000,000. The majority of his committee, Democrats, were for it, the Republican minority against. The lower tariff would increase the surplus by stimulating imports, the Republicans said.

The debate in Congress began on April 17 and continued until July 21, long after both party conventions had come and gone, to the delight of the Republicans. The tariff gave them the strongest capitalists in America on a silver platter. Clothing manufacturers and the iron and steel industry lined up with the Republicans against Cleveland's "free trade." The capitalists had been reluctant to disgorge funds at the emergency Republican meeting at Delmonico's on the eve of the 1884 elections. Now, with the tariff issue, the Republicans would not have to plead for funds in this campaign.

But before the Republicans could get together to begin raking in contributions farmers and two conventions of an awakened labor movement were to meet. In Cincinnati on May 15 the Union Labor party met at one hall and the United Labor party at another. The Union Labor group was composed of 220 delegates representing twenty states. By acclamation, this party nominated A. J. Streeter of Illinois for President and Samuel Evans of Texas as its vice-presidential candidate.

This group was noteworthy for its espousal of several revolutionary doctrines: equal pay for equal work of both sexes, women's right to vote, a graduated income tax, and direct popular election of United States senators instead of selection by state legislatures.

The other agrarian-labor group held what it termed a conference, rather than a convention, but it did nominate Robert H. Cowdrey of Illinois for the presidency and W. H. T. Wakefield of Kansas for Vice-President.

On May 30 the national Prohibition party held its convention in Indianapolis and nominated Clinton B. Fisk of New Jersey for President, John A. Brooks of Missouri for Vice-President. This time the Prohibitionists advocated a constitutional amendment to outlaw liquor.

In the face of continual official rebuff and even physical danger, the drys kept on preaching their heady gospel. On February 19 the Reverend O. W. Still of the Baptist church had been slightly inconvenienced when the front porch of his house was blown off by dynamite in upstate Connecticut. The Reverend Still and a Mr. Allen had been conducting a personal campaign of righteousness, seizing and destroying liquor at various drinking houses in the city. The night before the Reverend Still's house was bombed Mr. Allen found enough arsenic in his well to lay out a small city. But were they daunted? That Sunday the minister told his flock he was going to resign his pastorate. He felt the call, he said, and must now take to the lecture field, to devote his whole energies to stamping out the curse.

On June 5 the Democrats, always regarded as the rummier of the two major parties, met at St. Louis to select their slate and proclaim their policies. The presidential issue was hardly in doubt. President Cleveland was the first Democrat to have been elected President since the Civil War. Nobody in the party machinery was crazy enough to desert a winner, no matter how much the bosses might dislike some of Cleveland's radical ideas or lament his foolhardiness in tackling the tariff head on.

The latter, in particular, worried the back-room boys, who were already sure Cleveland couldn't be re-elected. For two years the pros had pleaded not to make the tariff an issue. But Cleveland was deaf.

"What is the use of being elected or re-elected, unless you stand for something?" said the President.

The politicians shook their heads sorrowfully. What could you do with a fool who talked like that?

In New York the Tammany men talked about a deal with the Republicans. If the Republican machine would help re-elect David Hill as governor of New York, in exchange, the Democratic organization of the Empire State would throw Cleveland to the elephants.

Ugly rumors about Cleveland's personal life started up again. If Mrs. Cleveland left the White House, even for a day's shopping in New York, the report was out that she had left the President and would not come back. A busybody wrote to her asking if it was true, as the local newspaper had reported, that the President's family relations were less than congenial. The First Lady wrote a flat denial, but no one paid any attention.

After a conference of Baptist ministers in Washington, many went home to spread the word about Cleveland's immorality through pastoral call and Sunday school, and in letters to their confreres. It was vicious stuff.

Even at convention time there was hint that an awful scandal about the President would be launched with the nomination.

Could the party jettison Cleveland, without saying, in effect, that his administration had been a failure?

Tammany thought so. A pamphlet circulated at the convention, eighteen pages of unexcelled vituperation against "The Beast of Buffalo."

But Cleveland plodded along. A week before the convention he had drawn up his own version of the party's platform, with particular emphasis on the tariff plank. When it was done he gave the document to Senator Gorman and told him to see it through.

Cleveland's nomination, by acclamation, was no surprise to the President, nor was he under any misapprehensions about his popularity with the party bosses. When delegates invoked the names of Horace Seymour and Samuel Tilden—both dead—they raised emotional outbursts far greater than that for the President. But Cleveland knew the party dared not repudiate him, that he had the respect of the rank and file of the party, and that he had the most skillful managers at the convention.

When Senator Gorman received the tariff plank the wily senator had not run to the platform committee to proclaim this as the President's will. Instead, Gorman casually showed the document to Robert Randall, the Pennsylvania political boss, with the strong inference that it represented Gorman's views only. Randall nodded. It was all right with him, he said, but "the Cleveland crowd will kick."

Gorman expressed the hope that he could manage to convince the Cleveland men that this was the best that could be done, and Randall pledged his support to push this version through.

It was done.

There was scarcely more opposition to the candidacy of old Allen G. Thurman of Ohio, a presidential candidate in 1884. Since Vice-

President Hendricks had died someone had to run for Vice-President.

Judge Thurman had bad attacks of rheumatism, was even more spavined than one might expect of a man well past threescore. In Columbus the good judge's physician stoutly denied any weakness: "He is naturally a man of splendid physique, especially from the hips up," said Dr. Van Selzer. An interesting defense, but it did not quiet the fears of the restless, and when Judge Thurman broke down completely during a campaign speech in New York, their saddest fears were realized.

The Republicans had no such easy choice as the Democrats. The only real veterans of the political wars were Blaine, now living in Europe, and old John Sherman, of Ohio.

The party leadership had changed considerably. In New York State the Republican boss was Thomas Platt; in Pennsylvania, Matthew Quay had fallen heir to the Camerons; in Michigan, Russell Alger was the man.

With the change in faces had come change in party procedure. The Republican organization, out of power, had no federal patronage to dispense and relatively few offices of any kind to sell. The big corporations had money to spend, and they had a stake in legislation and political privilege that no individual could match. It was a happy wedding of the haves and the have-nots, arranged largely through the offices of James G. Blaine, who three thousand miles away, was to maneuver the Republican convention in Chicago. Blaine had taken up the challenge on the tariff and fought a running battle with Cleveland. The Republican candidate of 1884 urged the party to work for the interests of American business.

In New York, from his court at the Fifth Avenue Hotel, the agreeable "Mousy" Platt was eager to please the princes of industry and commerce. Platt held conferences in the hotel bar on Sundays. From all over the state, party leaders came to attend the meetings and to say "Amen" whenever Platt announced a decision.

"State conventions would meet at Rochester, Syracuse, or Saratoga," said Chauncey Depew, president of the New York Central Railroad, "but the eight hundred members would wait before acting to hear what had been decided upon in the Amen Corner."

By June 19, 1888, when the Republicans met in Chicago, a good double handful of candidates had entered the field. Blaine had announced, repeatedly, that he would not be a candidate, but a few die-hards held out for him. On June 16 the New York *Tribune* reported John Sherman far ahead of all others. Sherman's campaign was being managed by a Cleveland capitalist named Mark Hanna.

Judge Walter Q. Gresham of Indiana was a strong candidate. He had been a general in the Union Army, always a plus, and had served in the Arthur cabinet.

But Gresham had butted heads with the big corporations. When the Wabash Railroad went into receivership Judge Gresham had the infernal nerve to administer the railroad in the interests of the defrauded investors and clients and not to line the pockets of the men like Jay Gould, who controlled the road.

Gresham would never do. "Nominate Gresham," said Chauncey Depew, "and he will Wabash all of us."

There were others: Depew himself, Alger, the political boss and match king from Michigan, and Benjamin Harrison, five and a half feet of rotund homeliness, the choice of the Indiana political machine that rejected Gresham as too controversial.

Harrison had several great attributes as a presidential candidate. He was the great-grandson of Benjamin Harrison, a signer of the Declaration of Independence and governor of Virginia, and grandson of President William Henry Harrison. This latest Harrison had never done or said anything of consequence and was almost completely noncontroversial in his own state. As the party campaign book said: "He had a good record and not too much of it." Harrison didn't like shaking hands and couldn't remember names, but those were minor difficulties.

Andrew Carnegie, the steel king, planned to try to nominate the Plumed Knight once again. Blaine polled a few courtesy votes in the first few ballots. After the fourth ballot the convention adjourned for the weekend. The rumor was out that on Monday the Blaine men would move, and that they had New York's Platt in tow. If that were true they might have as many as four hundred votes for Blaine, and if they could produce those on one ballot—when Sherman, for example, was polling about two hundred votes—the landslide could be put in motion. Pressure was put on Sherman to move over in favor of young William McKinley, one of his lieutenants; but Sherman was angry, and McKinley declined the honor.

Blaine crossed the eastern boys up. Over the weekend he sent two cables to the convention stating that he absolutely refused to accept the nomination.

On Saturday night the party bosses made a deal. Benjamin

Harrison was to get the Republican nomination. Platt was to name Levi Morton, a New York banker, for Vice-President and Platt was to get a cabinet seat and control of federal patronage in New York. On Monday, Harrison was nominated in short order. Morton was the vice-presidential candidate.

The issue was the tariff, and nothing else really mattered. "We are uncompromisingly in favor of the American system of protection," said the Republicans. "We protest against its destruction as proposed by the President and his party."

This year the Republicans were loaded for bear. John Wanamaker, the merchant and finance chairman of the Republican party, called a meeting of ten prominent citizens of Philadelphia, where he raised $100,000 just by asking for it.

Officeholders not yet under civil service were duly taxed for the campaign, but the returns were much less than these of the Republicans. Nor did the Democrats conduct the same kind of campaign.

Cleveland felt the dignity of the office kept him from making a personal speaking tour. His running mate with the splendid physique turned out to be worse than no speaker at all. The chairman of the Democratic National Committee, William A. Barnum, didn't really believe in his candidate—or the Democratic side of the issue. Barnum was a member of the American Iron and Steel Association and a high-tariff man himself. It was a ghastly combination.

Shortly after he had taken office President Cleveland had admitted bluntly that he didn't know a thing about the tariff. The President started to inform himself on the subject, but it took him almost two years to form the strong opinions he announced in 1887. The American public had to be informed in four short months. It was an impossible job, even if the Democratic party workers had wanted to do it. They didn't.

Harrison made ninety-four major speeches. He had no record to defend, and he had the tariff to whack at. Manufacturers didn't have to be sold, and it was surprisingly easy to convince many workers that if the low tariff became American policy it would bring even more unemployment and wage cuts. This was what the New York Central's Depew approvingly called the "cyclone of fear" campaign. Manufacturers panicked their workers with nightmares of unemployment. In the West certain manufacturers told their employees they would close the plants for the winter if Cleveland won.

In the last days of the campaign the Republicans were thrown into momentary panic themselves with a report that Cleveland would carry the Republican candidate's home state of Indiana. Wanamaker's task force went back to work and raised $400,000 to cinch the victory.

In New York, Democratic pressure was put on Cleveland to interfere in the election for governor. A few days before the election the rumor was out that Governor Hill and Tammany *had* sold Cleveland for those Republican votes. Then, the rumor was forgotten as the Sackville-West scandal broke.

Early in September a letter from Pomona, California, arrived on the desk of Sir Lionel Sackville-West, the British minister to Washington. One Charles F. Murchison respectfully asked the minister how, if he wanted to serve the cause of Britain, he ought to vote in the coming election. He was an American citizen now, wrote the strange correspondent but he had a soft spot in his heart for Old Blimey and wouldn't want to do anything to wrong the cause of Her Majesty's Government.

Quick as a lion, though hardly as bright, Sir Lionel took pen in hand and wrote back that the Democratic party certainly seemed friendly to England.

And what did Mr. Murchison do? He marched right down to Republican headquarters, because he wasn't Mr. Murchison the naturalized Briton at all but a Republican politician. Two weeks before the election the newspapers published the correspondence.

"If this letter is an audacious forgery," said the loyal Democratic New York *Sun*, "Lord Sackville should denounce it without an hour's delay. If it is genuine, Mr. Bayard should send him his passports before tomorrow night."

Secretary of State Bayard sent Sir Lionel his passports but not until after Cleveland had ordered it. The delay didn't help matters any.

The Republicans had their own scandal on election eve. The Democrats secured a set of final instructions issued by Colonel W. W. Dudley, Republican party treasurer, to Indiana Republican leaders.

There were an estimated 20,000 "floaters" in Indiana in 1888: voters who could be swayed by an application of cold cash to the palm.

". . . Your committee will certainly receive . . ." said Colonel

Dudley, ". . . the assistance necessary to hold our floaters and doubtful voters and gain enough of the other side to give Harrison and Morton a 10,000 plurality."

The colonel told his men to divide the floaters into blocks of five and put a trusted man "with necessary funds" in charge of each block. "Make him responsible," said the colonel, "that none get away and that all vote our ticket."

Vote prices had gone up in 1888 from the $5 ceiling of previous campaigns. The Republicans were to give out one twenty-dollar bill or three five-dollar gold pieces for each vote.

Matthew Quay, Chairman of the Republican National Committee, was upset when he saw the instructions printed in the newspapers. He shouted "lie" and began filing libel suits. But election day came. The Republicans carried Indiana by 2300 votes, and the libel suits were dropped.

David Hill won the New York governor's election by 19,000 votes; Cleveland lost New York by 13,000, and if Cleveland refused to believe that he had not been sold down the river his friends certainly could only shake their heads at his innocence.

Cleveland won a plurality of the popular vote: 5,540,329 votes to Harrison's 5,439,853. But Harrison had the votes where they counted. The Republican's electoral vote was 233 to Cleveland's 168. Prohibition's Fisk polled 249,506 votes, and Union Labor's Streeter 146,935.

The first Democratic President in a quarter century was defeated but not dismayed. He was pleased, he told a friend, to have created the tariff issue, and temporary defeat brought him no discouragement. He would fight again.

Republican Chairman Matthew Quay went to Indianapolis to congratulate Harrison. The little judge was both awed and pontifical. "Providence has given us the victory," he told the party chairman.

"Providence," said Quay, relating this naïve statement to an open-mouthed friend, "hadn't a damn thing to do with it."

The Johnstown flood of 1889 cost 2200 American lives and shocked a nation that had been relatively free from catastrophe since the end of the Civil War. President Harrison's administration moved back toward the days of boodle and political pay-off after his inauguration that year, and began whittling away at the federal government's surplus funds.

The Greenback party had died with better times, but good times did not bring help to farmers and the citizens of the West and South, who felt they were victimized by the industrialists of the East. They had all worked together, on a sectional basis, and had been successful in local and congressional elections, in both regions of the country.

Business was still growing. Labor was now organized into the American Federation of Labor, and although an infant it was growing fast.

Imperialism stirred in America, along with the growth of big business and establishment of huge personal fortunes. Americans were actively trying to overthrow the monarchy in the Sandwich, or Hawaiian, Islands and persuade Harrison to annex the territory.

The nation was beginning to sense that North America was closely linked to the world. Under Secretary of State James G. Blaine the nation was involved in serious arguments with Great Britain over fishing rights; with Italy over the mob murder of an Italian citizen in New Orleans; and with Chile over the killing of an American sailor in Valpariso.

But by and large, American interests still turned inward. . . .

10. The Rise of the Populists

On the last day of 1891 large numbers of Americans were down with the grippe, which periodically coursed America like the plague in the years before the discovery of wonder drugs and influenza vaccine. In Boston and Baltimore citizens anxiously scanned the pages of their newspapers, to see if the death rate was rising or falling. Lincoln, Nebraska, reported some five hundred cases of the dreaded influenza, and of the seven thousand souls resident in the little town of Seymour, Indiana, two thousand were stricken.

In the New York governor's mansion David B. Hill was suffering from another disease, one that seems endemic in Albany: presidential fever. Governor Hill's case was already severe, six months before the Democratic nominating convention.

The next day, January 1, 1892, was to be a banner day in the life of David Hill. On the first day of the new year he would forsake the governor's chair at Albany and move on to the United States Senate. It was a better place to advance his presidential hopes, much nearer the White House and much more visible to the eye of the national Democratic party.

The last night of the old year he was to sing his swan song in Albany. In the dawn of '92 the governor's chair would be filled by Roswell Flower, a strange man who seemed to have no ambition at all to be President of the United States. This festive night, at Albany's Kenmore Hotel, the main dining room was decked out for a party, a testimonial dinner for the retiring governor of the Empire State.

Secretary of State Frank Rice and State Engineer John Bogart, a pair of Governor Hill's closest associates, did not like the way the governor had set up the dinner. They had advised him to limit it to a few close friends. Hill had listened but presidential fever had overcome him, and he had demanded the presence of all the important Democratic officeholders in Albany who owed him debt. The great table of the Kenmore dining room was set for a hundred fifty places, flanked on either side of the hall by potted plants and tall vases of flowers. The mantel at the far end of the room was banked with more flowers, tastefully arranged to set off the half-size portrait of Governor Hill, resting with dignity beneath a draped American flag.

The shining linen of the table was spotted handsomely by well-spaced floral pieces. At the head of the table, directly before the governor's chair, stood the *pièce de résistance:* a masterful display of rare and lovely orchids.

As the guests filed into the dining room that night, there was noticeable grumbling from the impecunious office holders who had been forced to pony up $25 per head for the privilege of attending Governor Hill's last rites. Two dollars a man would have handled the expenses, one public servant remarked.

The souvenir menus were in keeping with the occasion, and the price. They were heavy cards embossed with flags and shields of the state of New York and the United States.

"Farewell, Governor," sighed a gallant line of type on one cover. "All Hail, United States Senator," shouted its companion joyfully, from the other side.

The conquering Governor-Senator beamed on the assemblage from his throne, flanked by Secretary Rice, and the Flower. Clanking of plates and silver gave way to the trickle of coffee and the haze of cigars. Governor Hill stood up, as the amenities were performed. Then the governor began to speak:

"These are the times that try men's souls. The hour of parting from the comrades of a long and arduous labor has come . . ."

The presidential campaign of 1892 was fairly under way.

A few days later, with Senator Hill safely in Washington and theoretically, at least, inculpable, the Tammany bosses of New York called a hurry-up state Democratic convention to meet in Albany on February 22, despite the fact that the national Democratic convention was not until June 21. This was promptly tabbed the "snap" convention. Its purpose was simple enough: to take the Democratic backing of his own state away from former President Cleveland and deliver it, with the Tammany tiger purring, to Senator David B. Hill. Indignant Democrats-for-Cleveland held a meeting at the Murray

Hill Hotel in New York City and began grinding out manifestoes and petitions against the dastardly plot. They were ignored by the Tammany men and brushed off by the conventioneers, so the dissidents called their own convention for May in Syracuse. What Cleveland termed the "cunning devices and shrewd manipulation" of Tammany ended as everybody knew it would, in the "snap" convention's support for Senator Hill. It was just as obvious, even then, that the Cleveland Democrats would support their man at the May convention.

By the end of April it was apparent that this was not to be a year of dark horses for either of the two major parties. President Harrison was not guaranteed the Republican nomination, for the political mores had not yet developed to the point where the President was automatically head of his party. Harrison would have to fight it out with Secretary of State James G. Blaine at the convention.

Who would win? In April the handwriting seemed less vague than usual to the Secretary of the Treasury, Charles Foster.

"Blaine is entirely out of the field and he will not, I think, ever be a presidential candidate again," Secretary Foster said. "Harrison will be nominated by acclamation. He has grown a great deal since he became President, and he is stronger now with the people than he was in 1888."

The Harrison men believed this prophecy of Republican victory, but a number of the shrewd heads in the party had serious doubts if 1892 was to be a Republican year.

Cleveland agreed with them, as wholeheartedly as only a Democratic candidate could. "The people are not dead, but sleeping," declared the ex-President. "They will awaken in good time, and scourge the money-changers from their sacred temple."

The Republican money-changers *were* in trouble. They did not know how bitterly their hard money and high tariffs were detested by a farmer, labor-debtor coalition. Cleveland hated the free-silver movement, which would put silver money on a par with gold, led by William Jennings Bryan, the able young Democratic congressman from Nebraska, and made no bones about it. But when Cleveland left office he left a healthy annual surplus behind him, and a treasury brimming with tax money.

Harrison's Republican administration had run through that surplus like a mouse through cheese. In four short years Harrison had destroyed an annual surplus of well over $100 million. The federal government was reduced to floating bonds to support deficit financing.

In part this was because the high tariff brought into effect by the McKinley tariff law of 1890 had knocked vast holes in the American economy. The Republicans had won control of both houses of Congress in the elections of 1888. It was a clear mandate for a high tariff, and a high tariff was what the Republicans put up. The general tariff level was raised some 12 per cent. Steep increases in textile and metal products, tariffs began immediately to erode the surplus in the treasury. Prices rose and people stopped buying in droves. But that was not all. The McKinley tariff eliminated the duty on raw sugar—the largest customs revenue producer of all. This cut revenue by $50 million.

The Harrison administration had promised veterans assistance so it was easy prey to the Grand Army of the Republic, now in its prime as the official association of the nation's saviors. The veterans put on pressure for pensions, and the Harrison administration yielded. Within four years the pension authorization increased from $81,000,000 to $139,000,000.

Congress cut off the federal government's prime sources of income, then went on a spending spree, and there was no stopping it, until the congressional elections of 1890. That year the Republican majority in the House evaporated, but while the Democrats gained, a new political force emerged—the Populists, who represented the discontented rural people of the nation. Since 1872 the farmers had been taking a beating, with the sudden rise and fall in the price of wheat, fluctuations not always free from the peculating fingers of the cigar-smoking boys in stovepipe hats, and heavy waistcoats. When the bottom fell out of the cotton market in the South, and when the boom of the western expansion slowed down to a steady but quieter roar, then the American middle class began to feel the pinch. One evil season seemed to follow another. In the late '80s and early '90s thousands of debt-ridden farmers lost their lands in foreclosures. Hard money was their curse, for it was hard to come by and harder to hold. They wanted currency control taken out of the hands of the national banks and put in the hands of a friendly federal government that would issue the greenbacks they remembered so fondly, cheap money with which they could pay the debt that was grinding them down.

In 1890 these debt-ridden men of the land began organizing. There were two principal organizations: the National Farmers' Alliance of the North and Northwest, and the National Farmers' Alliance and Industrial Union of the South. By 1890 a new political grouping, with all the religious fervor of a revival, was beginning to show signs of developing into a national political party.

In Kansas, Mrs. Mary Elizabeth Lease made a hundred and sixty speeches for the cause in the congressional campaign of 1890. "What you farmers need to do," this handsome thirty-seven-year-old Irish woman told her admiring audiences, "is raise less corn and more Hell."

The farm friends of "The Kansas Pythoness" seem to have believed her, for in the 1890 elections they helped the Democrats give the Republicans a thorough beating.

By 1891 the farm groups had joined Greenbackers, Single Taxers, and other reformers. The leaders of the movement called a national convention in the summer of 1892. It was apparent that a third party would be formed at that convention, and the strength of the groups it represented was enough to give spring nightmares to the old party professionals of both pachyderm and jackass.

On the day that Treasury Secretary Foster announced his confidence in the Harrison re-election, Foster also indicated his confidence in the McKinley tariff. Across the Atlantic all London was stirred up by a resolution passed by the Canadian House of Commons to offer preferential treatment to English goods—a direct reaction to the McKinley tariff. England, the old free trader herself, was sorely tempted to follow a course that might have led to the imposition of special duties on United States goods. It could have caused a major depression in the United States, had it been followed through. The report of the British reaction was carried prominently in James Gordon Bennett's New York *Herald* that day, and its implications did not go unnoticed in the sensitive financial houses of lower Manhattan.

As the political spawning season drew closer, tension grew in both Republican and Democratic parties. It was rumored that Senator John Sherman would withdraw from public life, to edit the letters of his brother, the great General William Tecumseh Sherman. It was a false rumor. The crusty old senator was preparing for the greatest fight in his long political career.

Slippery Senator Hill, quite puffed up by the support given him at the Albany "snap" convention, announced in May that the Democratic party "knows what it wants to do and has the ability to do it without delay." The Wisconsin and Michigan conventions of that omniscient and eager body promptly pledged their delegations to support Cleveland in the coming festival at Chicago. Governor Flower, in lonely Albany, told whoever was listening that all *he* wanted was to be left alone, and get out of politics when his gubernatorial term was up.

Less than three weeks before the Republicans were to meet at Minneapolis, there was a strange bustle of activity in Room 227 of New York's luxurious Plaza Hotel. Room 227 housed J. S. Clarkson, chairman of the Republican National Committee. Ugly rumor in the lobby had it that Clarkson was in New York to secure the GOP nomination for James G. Blaine.

Jesse M. Gove, an original Blaineiac, let it slip that he had it straight from the horse's mouth that Blaine could be talked into accepting the nomination, only if the Plumed Knight were certain Harrison could not win the nomination. How Blaine would determine that without putting it to the test on the convention floor was not announced. All this lively discussion began on May 22.

On May 23 the Secretary of State, James G. Blaine, happened to arrive in New York to visit his oculist. He looked every bit as ill as was reported, and it revived an old story about his health.

Republican Chairman Clarkson was supposed to have pressed Blaine to declare for the nomination months before, but Blaine demurred, pleading ill health.

"I should think that if you die as soon as you say, which is a most remote possibility," Clarkson replied, "the height of your ambition would be to die in the White House."

Perhaps it was only the long trip on the Pennsylvania Railroad's *Congressional Limited* that had made Blaine ill, or the fact that he had made the trip without lunch. Whatever it was, the Secretary got up the next day looking much more chipper, saw his oculist, and took Mrs. Blaine across the city to visit the grandchildren.

The buzzing continued around room 227, even though Blaine had said, time and again, that he did not want his name entered in the lists at Minneapolis. Polite but persistent disbelief was exhibited by the press. There were other question marks: the persistent reports of coolness between Blaine and Harrison; Mrs. Blaine's antagonism to the President, whom she regarded as holding office only because of her husband's power in the GOP; Harrison's refusal to promote Blaine's son-in-law over some twenty other army officers; the open machinations of the anti-Harrison wing of the Republican party, which saw in the President a sawed-off pip-squeak, do-gooder, do-nothing who couldn't beat his way out of a paper bag.

Harrison was not against nepotism. He gave offices to his father-in-law, his son's father-in-law, his daughter's brother-in-law, to his own brother, and to several of son Russell's college friends. And of course, like Presidents before and since, he gave important jobs to newspaper editors who had supported him. Whitelaw Reid of the New York *Tribune* was Minister to France. Thorndike Rice, editor of the *North American Review,* became Minister to Russia. Chairman Clarkson had been made first assistant postmaster, and had removed fifteen thousand Democratic fourth-class postmasters within a few months. By 1892, Clarkson was throwing Harrison to the wolves. It was a strange situation.

During those last few days of May, Senator Hill was in New York. So was his bitter opponent, Grover Cleveland, who had come up with Mrs. Cleveland and baby Ruth from their New Jersey cottage for a few days in the city.

Republican activity at the Plaza Hotel boiled. To add to the heat, Miss Anna Dickinson, a Republican spellbinder in the Harrison campaign of 1888, was suing the Republican National Committee. Miss Dickinson said she had been promised $1250 for her work if Harrison won. She had spoken six hours a day, traveled in the toughest part of Pennsylvania "where men were afraid to go," been rotten-egged, stoned, and had her hair parted by a bullet. Largely through her efforts, she acknowledged, Harrison carried Pennsylvania, but the Republican National Committee had never paid off.

Miss Dickinson lost the case on a point of law. Judge Truax recalled that the only valid election expenses were for printing and carriages to transport invalid voters to the polls. If Republican boss "Mousy" Platt choked on his morning coffee at the Fifth Avenue Hotel and Tammany's Croker had an extra one for the road on reading this bit of Alice-in-Wonderland legality, it was only in contemplation of the unsulliable virtue of New York politics, where not more than half the vote could be swayed by money.

But in the rest of the country something was stirring. The surging, squirming groups of farmers and labor men were preparing to meet in Omaha in July. Without organization the Populists had won two Senate seats in 1890. As a national party, what would they do in 1892?

The Republican convention had the Populists to worry about, plus the struggle between its President and his Secretary of State, as the delegates made their way to Minneapolis.

The convention was not to start until June 7, but the front men for the candidates arrived early, as usual. Less than a week before the convention party Chairman Clarkson was standing in the doorway of his room at the West Hotel when a reporter said Blaine had announced he would "write no more letters." He meant no messages disavowing his candidacy, as the secretary had done at the previous convention. Clarkson's interest in the reporter improved remarkably:

"When was the news sent?"

"This afternoon."

"I think it will nominate him," said Clarkson, and went back to his work with the arriving delegates.

The most malleable of these were the Negroes from the southern states, who had travel expenses, living expenses, wives and families back home, and very little money. Of the forty-eight Negro delegates at Minneapolis, it was rumored that forty-one were for sale. The Harrison men said Blaine's masterminds had a $40,000 fund to buy Negro votes. Blaine men complained that the Harrison men had pushed the price of colored support to $1500 a vote, with extra fringe benefits.

"They cost more than they did before the war," observed one disgruntled vote buyer.

One of the few Negro delegates who did not appear to be for sale was John M. Langston of Virginia. The Negro vote was anti-Harrison, he reported. The only Republican who could give the Negro justice was Blaine. Langston's statement was based on a letter President Harrison had sent to a group of ministers who deplored the lynchings, intimidations, and outrages against Negroes in the southern states. The President had deplored the situation, properly enough, but reminded the ministers that the Constitution prevented him from doing anything about it.

There had already been two outrageous lynchings in 1892. In Nashville, Eph Grizzard, a Negro charged with assaulting two white women, had been hanged from a bridge over the Cumberland River after a mob estimated at 10,000 overran the jail, disregarded the sheriff, and listened to the governor's pleas without response.

"Law is too slow. We won't wait," the mob shouted at Governor Buchanan, as he tried to stop the slaughter.

The other lynching was that of a Negro named Bob Lewis, and it happened at Port Jervis, New York, after Lewis was jailed for assaulting a young lady named Lena McMahon. Lewis was hanged with just as much violence, by just as angry and lawless a mob.

Vote trading, humbugging, and outrageous lying were the order of the day in Minneapolis, when James G. Blaine suddenly threw a wild skunk into the proceedings. On the morning of June 4, three days before the convention, the Secretary went to his office in the State Department at eleven o'clock. Blaine sat down and wrote out his resignation in his own hand and sent it to the White House by the hand of his private secretary, with instructions to wait for an answer.

Benjamin Harrison did not much care for people who told him what to do, and he felt he had been most forbearing in the case of Blaine, who had often tended to act as though he were shogun in charge of a half-idiot executive. The President read Mr. Blaine's letter, and when the secretary, Mr. Dent, asked if there would be an answer the Chief Executive shook his head.

The President would answer before the end of the day. Mr. Dent need not wait. Whereupon, consulting the time, President Harrison noted that he was keeping the common people waiting in the East Room downstairs where he held his tri-weekly reception for all who wanted to shake hands with the President of the United States. It was just after one o'clock. Mr. Harrison sent Mr. Dent about his business and went downstairs.

After the reception the President came back to his office, answered Blaine's cold resignation with a colder acceptance, and dispatched it by *his* private secretary.

Then, beaming, President Harrison told his son to get the grand-children ready for a drive and ordered his carriage sent around to the front gate. Last seen that day, the President and children were trotting off toward Georgetown in the carriage with driver and footman up.

The news of Blaine's resignation at this moment shocked the House of Representatives. Obviously his interest in the presidency was alive again. Speaker Crisp left the chair to check on the story.

He turned his gavel over to Representative Johnstone of South Carolina, but even Johnstone's broad and patient accent could not bring order to the milling, gossiping men on the floor.

What was Blaine up to? The House didn't know. Neither did the Minneapolis convention. But the timing of the resignation certainly indicated an interest in the presidential nomination. It was proof to Blaine's backers that they had his approval. It was proof enough for the non-Republican public that Blaine once again was after the highest office in the land.

Chairman Clarkson was delighted with the Blaine announcement. For the first time he now had a clear-cut candidate. But it was very late, and the Harrison men had not been idle. Thomas H. Carter of Montana, Harrison's campaign manager, had a satchel full of money under the bed and the President's authority to pass out patronage promises where they would do the most good.

As the convention opened, the ladies were very much in evidence. Wyoming had just been admitted as a state, the first to grant women the vote, and the end of the political convention as glorified stag party was at hand.

Mrs. Carson Lake of New York led the Blaine women from a spot at the front of the hall. She was a stunner, dressed to the nines and carrying a white umbrella topped by three beautiful, curling ostrich plumes.

As Blaine was named Mrs. Lake's voice rang loud and clear through the hall. "Blaine, Blaine, the man from Maine," she chanted.

The chorus was picked up. She said it again, leading now with her ostriches. And the men around the hall, seeing this handsome figure, were suitably impressed. The demonstration went on, and on, and on.

Finally Chauncey Depew, a Harrison man, tried to speak, but Mrs. Lake was still chanting and waving. He couldn't be heard.

Depew was saved by his wife, an aristocratic, pale lady in a gray silk gown adorned by a Harrison button. Mrs. Depew wasn't going to let that hussy get away with insulting *her* husband. She raised her voice for Harrison.

Mrs. John J. Ingalls unfurled a brave American flag for Harrison, the colors flickering against her wine-colored velvet gown. Mrs. William McKinley waved her flag with an enthusiasm she really felt only for her husband. Mrs. Lew Wallace fluttered a handkerchief, and the youthful, blossoming Mrs. Harry S. New, daughter-in-law of one of the principal Harrison leaders, blushed prettily and shouted with the rest.

Finally all the ladies were quieted and the business went on. Harrison was nominated on the first ballot. At the last moment some of the anti-Harrison forces tried to throw support to McKinley, the congressman from Ohio who had written the tariff law. McKinley shook off the draft, insisted that his vote in the convention be recorded for Harrison, although the rest of the Ohio delegation voted for McKinley.

Whitelaw Reid was chosen to run as Harrison's Vice-President, effectively alienating the labor vote as the Republicans were to do so often in the future. Reid was still fighting his running battle with the printers' union.

The Republicans stood solidly behind their high tariff, for both gold and silver coinage, for paper money, against intimidation of the Negroes in the South, and for temperance and morality (but not for prohibition).

The nominations were in and the platform built. That was the end of it. J. S. Clarkson looked around the big convention hall as the plumes and pompoms of the knight from Maine were removed. It was the end of an era. For five conventions James G. Blaine had stood as Mr. Republican himself. Four times he had lost the nomination, once he had won it to go down to defeat by members of his own party—The Mugwumps—plus, as Blaine said, "an ass in the shape of a preacher, and a rainstorm" (which had kept the upstate voters away from the polls).

As Blaine's men tore down the bunting and the plumes William McKinley was being raised to the shoulders of an admiring mob outside the West Hotel. It was a sticky, steaming day. Finally he escaped to his room and lay panting on the bed. In a moment Mark Hanna, the Cleveland industrialist, came in and began taking off his clothes, seeking relief from the intolerable heat. Hanna sat quietly, resting for a moment, then turned to McKinley. "My God, William," he said. "That was a damned close squeak."

For Mark Hanna knew he did not want McKinley to make Blaine's mistake when he got the GOP nomination in 1884. Hanna was sure of one thing: '92 for McKinley was like '84 for Blaine. It was the wrong year.

Two weeks later, at the summer solstice, 910 delegates to the Sixteenth Democratic National Convention met at Chicago, full of gall and scheming.

The miners of Missouri presented Chairman William Wilson with a pure zinc gavel, inscribed "We Need No Protection." McKinley's tariff was thrown to the resolutions committee for suitable reply. The resolutions committee was inclined to pussyfoot, but on the floor of the convention the Cleveland men demanded, and won, a flat condemnation of high tariff. The Democrats, like the Republicans, straddled the money issue.

One thing became clear to the Hill men and the other anti-Clevelanders lurking in the corridors. Almost nobody wanted Grover Cleveland's nomination for 1892—except the rank and file of the Democratic party. The ex-President was at his summer home in Buzzards Bay, Massachusetts, doing a little fishing and keeping tabs on the convention through a telegraph wire installed in the gun room.

A quick survey at Chicago had indicated a first-ballot strength for Cleveland of six hundred delegates. In other words, even with the two-thirds rule, Cleveland had just about enough votes for nomination on the first ballot if nothing upset the apple cart.

As the roll was called delegates nominated their favorite sons and the three senior candidates: Cleveland, Senator Hill, and Governor Boies of Iowa, the first man west of the Mississippi River ever to be offered as candidate to a Democratic convention. Hill's backers argued that Cleveland could not win, could not even carry New York, and that the New York delegation (the "snap" delegation seated by the convention) wanted Hill.

Long after midnight Tammany's golden-throated orator, Bourke Cockran, mounted the platform. He praised Hill and excoriated Cleveland. Cleveland had been nominated to please the Mugwumps, and the Democrats didn't need the Mugwumps. Let the convention remember Senator Hill's soldierly fight against the infamous Republican Force Bill, which would have put elections under federal control, stationed soldiers at the polls, in the devious name of protecting the rights of the Negroes of the South. Cleveland? Cockran sneered. The most popular man in America . . . except on election day.

Cockran went on for an hour and a half. Finally, he ran down. It was after four o'clock in the morning. The Cleveland household was sitting tensely in the gun room at Gray Gables now as the gray light of dawn began to push up over the Atlantic.

Without a word in Cleveland's defense, his lieutenants demanded a roll call. Tammany wanted adjournment; it was late, the delegates were exhausted, and there was much to do (including night visiting and vote buying).

The Tammany motion was overruled. The roll call began. As the sun came up across Buzzards Bay and stuck its fingers through the window of the Cleveland sunroom the vote was completed. Grover Cleveland was nominated by 617½ votes on the first ballot. He had won over the open opposition of the Democrats who controlled his own state, over the reluctance of the political bosses in his party's eastern wing. Adlai Stevenson of Illinois was nominated as Vice-President without fanfare.

Cleveland went fishing. He asked his sailing master to get the little sailboat out, and he and the captain skimmed Hog Island between Mashnee and Tobey and off to the rock-bass grounds. Cleveland wore a flannel shirt, blue scarf knotted carelessly around his neck, his trousers tucked in his boots, and a yellow slicker thrown across the seat, ready for a squall.

That afternoon the carriage was brought out. Mr. and Mrs. Cleveland with Ruth drove down to the village to get the mail. The villagers stood on the side of the road and waved handkerchiefs as the family went by.

Buzzards Bay was agog. There hadn't been so much excitement since that fellow brought the pool table to town just after the Civil War. Down at the post office the boys started an innocent little pool on the mail.

The very next day after the nomination the village carpenter was up at Cleveland's place putting a second ceiling and rock wool on the library. It took him all day, but he finished the job. Some of Cleveland's private conversation of the night before had leaked to the newspaper reporters who swarmed around Gray Gables, and the candidate was not going to have any more of that. The campaign strategy was being planned.

Tammany men, bedraggled as only wet tigers can be, limped back to New York after the convention. They had no part in this campaign, nor did they want any.

"Chicago," said Commissioner of Public Works Gilroy with all the venom in his tired frame, "is a hog town, and the people who live there are hogs." A shoeshine had cost twenty-five cents in the windy city and even buttermilk was twenty-five cents a glass.

But Tammany, unaccustomed to buttermilk, was drinking bitter tea as the campaign of Cleveland and Adlai Stevenson of Illinois began.

Cleveland wanted no part of Tammany, but his managers wanted to win the election. They asked the candidate to write boss Murphy. "I'll see the whole outfit to the Devil before I'll do it," Cleveland replied. But finally Cleveland was persuaded to bunch his big body uncomfortably into a dining chair at the Victoria Hotel and break bread with the Tammanyites.

Cleveland didn't much like the whole affair. At the end of the dinner he made that clear as he turned truculently to the New York power triumvirate, Murphy, Croker, and Sheehan.

"Well, gentlemen," said the candidate they despised, "what do you want?"

Promises that the organization would be properly recognized if he became President . . . ? Cleveland doubled up his fist, and crashed it down on the table until the silver rattled.

"I'll be damned if I will!"

What was he going to do, then?

Withdraw from the ticket! "I will tell the voters of the country that I cannot give any secret pledges, and that unless I do you will not support the Democratic ticket. I will tell the voters that I do not want to stand in the way of a Democratic victory. That is what I shall do. Then, gentlemen, you can pick out a candidate to suit you, and if he is a proper man and the candidate of the party I will vote for him."

Cleveland paused. Every eye in the room was on him.

"But I'll tell you one thing, Mr. Sheehan," he said very quietly. "In my opinion public indignation will snow you and your organization out of sight before the end of the week."

Tammany was tamed.

Between July 2 and July 5, at Omaha, Nebraska, the vague and irresolute yearnings of the dissatisfied farmers were forged into a new political party, the Populists, put together with a treasury of $50. James B. Weaver of Iowa was nominated for President; James G. Field of Virginia for Vice-President. They ran on a platform of "the common man," called in those days "the plain people." The

Populist movement was radical; it threatened to change the whole course of the American political movement. Weaver and his associates were not socialists, but they hated monopolies. They demanded a national paper currency, issued by the government and not by banks. They demanded free silver, and cheap money; a graduated income tax, government ownership of railroads, return of the land grants to the public domain. Their campaign appealed to a growing number of people. It was enough to frighten both parties, and it did.

The Prohibitionists met in Cincinnati on June 29 and nominated John Bidwell of California for President, J. B. Cranfill of Texas for Vice-President. They too wanted more money in circulation, and they had a new angle on the tariff: not for revenue, not for protection of American industry, but as a weapon against foreign governments.

The Socialist Labor convention was held at New York on August 28. Simon Wing of Massachusetts was nominated with vice-presidential candidate, Charles H. Matchett, of New York. This party wanted government ownership of the means of transportation, communication, and all public industry; income and inheritance taxes; women's rights; abolition of the presidency and the Senate; the recall of elected officers by popular vote; and the referendum, under which laws could be referred to the people.

The Socialist Laborites and the Prohibitionists did not pose much of a problem to either party, although the liquor issue always roused uneasy stirrings in the Puritan hearts of the Republicans.

The Populists—that was another story.

The Republicans saw how strong the Populist party was in the South. Here was an opportunity to get back into southern politics, and the Republicans wooed the new party as they had wooed the Negroes in '68. It wasn't just sweet talk; Republican money found its way into Populist hands.

The Democrats didn't let it go unchallenged. Florida, then other Democratic southern states, picked up segments of the Populist doctrine—the control of railroads, abolition of the national banks, free silver.

As the campaign wore on, the worried Democrats stepped up their efforts in the South. On election eve, in the black counties, the party provided barrels of whisky and plenty of food, and guardians who conducted the soirees, then marched the revelers to the polls the next morning and voted them right down the Democratic ticket.

In Augusta, Georgia, the home of Tom Watson, a Populist leader, the enthusiastic Democrats turned out a total vote double the number of legal, registered voters on the books.

In the silver-mining states, and in Kansas, the Democrats had no chance, in view of Cleveland's strong stand against free silver. The Democratic party fused with the Populists, and supported the Populist ticket.

On election day Cleveland polled 5,556,928; Harrison 5,176,106; Populist Weaver 1,041,021; Prohibitionist Bidwell 262,034.

Cleveland won 277 electoral votes, Harrison, 145. Weaver became the first third-party candidate to crack the electoral college since the Civil War, with 22 votes.

The Republican vote in Pennsylvania fell off 50,000, perhaps a vindication of Anna Dickinson's claims about her speaking tour in 1888. Most of the Republican defectors went to Weaver. So did the labor vote. The Socialist Labor party was already regarded as a lunatic fringe; its vote dropped from 147,000 in 1888 to 21,000.

The Democrats picked up 16,000 votes over 1888, almost all of them attributable to fusion with the Populists. The new party had made a strong showing, particularly in the West, where it carried Nevada, Colorado, and Idaho. Populist governors won in Kansas, North Dakota, and Colorado; the new party had seats in both the House and the Senate although the Democrats now controlled both houses. And the Populists could claim 50 state officials and 1500 county officials around the country.

Clearly they were a coming political force. If either party could harness these discontented farmers and workers, it would have a strong new wing. If the old parties could not take them over, the Populists might supplant them. What was to be done now?

11

The World Columbian Exposition was planned for 1893 in Chicago, and the men in charge of arrangements were determined to make this the greatest celebration in the history of the country. They were using structural steel in these days, and architects had developed a feeling for spaciousness and the handsome line, instead of the utilitarian and gewgawed buildings of the past. So the building that was in progress around Chicago's Jackson Park was something new, and exciting. Searchlights were brought in to reflect on the park's lagoons and to shine around the night sky in a manner to be affected by Hollywood drugstores and service stations a half century later.

But as the Exposition was building, so were tensions in the industrial affairs of the country. In 1892 steelworkers struck in Pennsylvania, and for the first time it was readily apparent that public sympathy was on the side of the strikers. Before, the well-to-do, at least, had looked on strikes as revolutionary outbreaks, to be put down with gun and club. But in the 1890s industry was growing fast, and if it was to grow healthily, the laboring man had to be made happy enough to do his job with competence and without rancor.

The Pennsylvania strike was called the Homestead strike. It was against the Homestead plant of the Carnegie Steel company, and it was fought over the employer's attempt to cut wages of pieceworkers who were using new machinery, on the then common theory that the machine made the work easier, so the men should not get so much money for it.

When an anarchist got into the office of one of Carnegie's assistants and tried to assassinate him, with both knife and revolver, the public good will was strained past the breaking point. The strike was finally lost by the workers, but the battle for organization of labor and decent wages was just warming up.

The next year, just a few weeks after the Administration changed hands, the Chicago exposition was set to open in a blaze of glory. The buildings were even finer than anyone had expected: truly a master stroke for native American architecture.

But then, in Wall Street, the stocks of the nation's industries took a tumble, when business discovered that President Harrison had not only wiped out that cursed government surplus—he had just about wiped out the government's reserves as well.

And on that somber note the fair opened.

The fun-loving spent time on the midway, where they could choose between Buffalo Bill's "Wild West Show" and the undulations of a belly dancer in a daring show called the "Streets of Cairo," in those days the epitome of the mysterious East.

For the more serious there were conferences on every possible subject, including the best way to get the country out of the economic ditch into which it had fallen. . . .

11. Silver and Gold
1896

The storm that hit Washington on the last day of February 1893 soaked the overalls of carpenters at work on the reviewing stand for the inaugural parade.

Editorial writers and optimists who hoped for sunny "Cleveland weather" were hollering down a rain barrel. The foulness continued on March 2, as the presidential party arrived at the Arlington Hotel to take over a suite reserved on the first floor. On the morning of March 4 the President-elect got up early and breakfasted with Mrs. Cleveland at eight-thirty. He looked out the window. Snow.

Cleveland's beswarded military aides clanked importantly in and out of the hotel, making parade arrangements and shivering in their overcoats. Shortly after ten o'clock Mr. Cleveland was notified that President Harrison's carriage was waiting outside. He got in, drove to the White House, and shook hands with the retiring President in an atmosphere of mutual respect. Each had defeated the other in the political arena.

The two warriors turned up their coat collars against the driving snow, as the presidential party made its way to the Capitol, then to the Senate chamber for the swearing in of the Vice-President. It seemed as though the room was jammed with women—all wearing or holding spring violets. The odor was overpowering. Mrs. Cleveland arrived, threw off her storm coat to reveal that she was wearing a fawn-colored street costume, the skirt trimmed with six rows of narrow brown chenille, a double cape of brown velvet lined with fawn-colored silk, a bonnet adorned with pearls and aigrette and ostrich plumes—and carrying another bunch of those damned violets.

The procession then straggled to the east front of the Capitol. Cleveland, fortified by a hooker of neat whisky, delivered his inaugural address in clear and ringing tones, while the freezing crowd stamped its collective feet, thrashed its collective arms, and breathed steamily in the wintry air.

When Cleveland was finished a mighty shout went up—perhaps some of it from sheer joy at the end of the torture. The ordeal was not over for the President and his party. He now traveled down to Fifteenth Street and Pennsylvania Avenue to review the inaugural parade.

> "Grover, Grover. Four years more of Grover!
> And now we'll live in Clover!"

So chanted Democrats who came from far and near to witness the great occasion, Democrats whose spirits were not to be dampened by rain nor frozen by the icy streets and sleety air of a semi-tropical capital suddenly turned frigid.

As it turned out the four years of clover became four years of bitter fighting within the Democratic party. The sleety air of inaugural day was positively balmy in contrast to the atmosphere that was to exist between Cleveland and the Democrats of Congress.

Cleveland was never one to run away from a fight, nor was he loath to speak his mind. He wanted the tariff reduced and he put the wheels in motion almost immediately, although his party wanted to fiddle and faddle with it. The Democrats began making common cause with the Populists, and Cleveland was totally and irrevocably opposed to what he termed their dangerous nonsense. The party was leaning to labor. Cleveland used troops to break up the Pullman strike of 1894. The chill settled, layer upon layer. And the Republicans rubbed their hands.

Any one of a dozen issues in the next four years would have made an election contest.

Cleveland said no to the annexation of Hawaii, which had been almost, but not quite, accomplished by the Harrison administration. After the death of King Kalakaua in 1891 the throne was occupied by his sister, Queen Liliuokalani. She was a despot; there was no denying that. The new queen tore up the constitution the Hawaiians had gained under her brother's rule. Her subjects rebelled, led by S. B. Dole, the pineapple king, and a handful of other rich Americans who wanted annexation. These worthies set up a Republic and sought annexation to the United States. Harrison favored taking over the islands and said so to the United States Senate. The matter was under consideration when Cleveland came into office.

Cleveland withdrew the treaty for "further study." The new study favored restoration of the Queen's monarchy. But the lives and actions of American citizens were involved. Cleveland could hardly take the part of a foreign power against Americans. The Senate settled the matter for him by ignoring his recommendations on restoration but refusing to use United States force to restore Liliuokalani. In effect, the Senate delayed the annexation of Hawaii until a more friendly administration came to power.

In the midst of this fracas the bottom suddenly dropped out of the economy. Republican politicians had suffered the effects of falling prices and sluggishness in 1892. The Democrats reaped the harvest of bad financial management in the Panic of 1893. It began in the summer after Cleveland took office.

The big Democrat with the walrus mustache had left Harrison a handsome treasury balance and annual tax surplus when he handed over the reins of government in 1889. General Harrison did not return the favor. Cleveland stepped back into the White House in 1893 to find $500,000,000 in paper money in circulation, backed by only $100,000,000 in gold. There was plenty of silver. Anyone who had a paper dollar could demand either gold or silver in exchange. Paper was all right as long as the people knew they could get the gold; it was easier to carry around. But when people worried even a little about the future, they wanted their money in metal. Metal has real value. In 1893 people were worried. Since gold was more valuable than silver all over the world, everyone in America demanded gold for their paper. And more and more people were exchanging paper money for gold, rather than using paper to buy commodities. Under the Sherman Silver Act of 1890 the government agreed to buy 4,500,000 ounces of silver a month and pay for it in paper money. The idea, originally, was to give the silver miners a market and to put more money in circulation; theoretically this stimulated business and industry too.

But three years of increased mining of silver in America depressed its world price. The more silver came out of the Rockies, the less rare it became, and the less rare it became, the less valuable in relation to the most valuable money in the world—gold.

Even silver miners were selling silver to the government, taking payment in paper money, and demanding gold for the paper. The government, instead of tearing up the paper money when it came in, reissued it in payment of debts, and the merry-go-round began to speed up.

Harrison had managed to stall off a public announcement of the government's dangerous position, but he had quietly prepared a bond issue to raise more gold. Cleveland had to face the problem immediately. Soon there would be no gold left in the treasury. If that happened the whole monetary system of the United States could collapse.

Cleveland called a special session of Congress, to repeal the law that made the government buy silver.

He called the special session, then left on a yachting trip. A desperate time for a President to be deserting his office, grumbled the critics. It *was* a desperate time, for the President. For several months Cleveland had been suffering from a sore on the roof of his mouth. By the first of July the sore had become an ulcer as large as a quarter, extending from his back teeth halfway across the roof of his mouth. The doctors thought it was cancerous. There was only one answer: operate.

In view of the shaky emotional climate of the country, Cleveland decided to undergo the operation in secrecy. He had traveled from time to time on Commodore Benedict's yacht, and while he might be accused of self-indulgence for taking another trip, press and public would hardly suspect the nature of his "pleasure."

The President took a train north and drove grandly down to New York City's Pier A. The next morning the yacht started along the East River. Cleveland started inhaling nitrous oxide, and when he was stretched on the operating table, unconscious, the doctors began the long and delicate operation. They cut away most of the President's upper left jaw. Five days later the yacht anchored in Buzzards Bay, and Cleveland walked up to the big house—Gray Gables. The doctors built an artificial jaw of vulcanized rubber, and after another minor operation the surgery was finished. Cleveland was very weak, and not at all sure that he did not have cancer or that it would not kill him. But he still had to prepare his message for the reluctant, angry Congress he was bringing back from its vacationing and fence mending.

In two thousand words Cleveland presented his case against silver. On August 5 he returned to Washington to lead the movement for repeal of the Sherman law. His own poll of the House of Representatives showed 114 men for silver, 173 against silver, and 69 whose position was questionable.

The President's special message was presented to Congress on August 8. Then the fun began. Congressman Wilson of West Virginia presented the Administration's repeal bill. But the opposition did not come from the Republicans. The Free Silver leader was Representative Richard P. Bland, Democrat of Missouri, who presented a bill calling for unlimited coinage of silver.

Still weak from surgery, Cleveland returned to Buzzards Bay for rest after a five-day stay in the capital. At first he was serene in his assurance that the mandatory silver purchases would be ended. But summer faded, fall waned, the Panic of 1893 flourished, and still Congress talked. Cleveland worried.

The President had been right the first time. Congress repealed the Sherman silver purchase law, but at what political cost to the Democrats! William Jennings Bryan, Democratic congressman from Nebraska, spoke for three hours for silver. The House was entranced by the personality and eloquence of "the boy orator of the Platte." It must have been. In his case the almost inviolable one-hour rule that governs speeches was extended by consent of the House.

In the end Congress split on the issue; the Free Silver Democrats were joined by Populists and Republicans from the mining states. The hard-money Democrats joined the Republicans.

The House repealed the purchase act by 239 to 109. After long and bitter debate the Senate concurred, 43 to 32, with 23 Republicans voting for the President's measure.

For the second time Cleveland had pressed a matter of principle to the point where it became the overriding issue of a presidential election. Cleveland made an issue of "sound money" in 1896 and 1888. But there was a difference. In 1888 the Democratic party followed its leader, albeit reluctantly. In 1896 the party split with most Democrats in favor of free silver with but a few still loyal to the old "sound money" policy.

The Panic of 1893 was no minor Wall Street flurry. In December the federal government added up the failures: 158 national banks, 172 state banks, 177 private banks, 47 savings banks, 13 trust companies, 6 mortgage companies. Gilt-edged stocks dropped fifty per cent on the New York market. In the South and West money—any kind of money—became so scarce that barter replaced cash transaction.

The nation had not recovered by 1896. Naturally, Cleveland was blamed for the depression, and after the Republicans won control of the House in 1894 it was generally conceded that the GOP could elect "a rag baby" over any candidate the Democrats might offer. The Democrats certainly were not planning to offer Cleveland. He had served two terms in the White House. This, alone, disqualified him with many voters. A movement for a third term had begun, but Cleveland had squelched it himself. It was just as well. The big Democrat from New York, a solid conservative, no longer represented the Democratic party. The party, in its virtual absorption of the Populists and its espousal of cheap money, had taken a turn that brought it as far from Cleveland as any party has ever wandered from its leader in four years. Cleveland was now philosophically more in sympathy with the Republicans, and in the distorted glass of 1896 it would be hard to see how he had ever been a Democrat.

Not a Democrat in the Senate was on really friendly terms with the President, not one would come to the White House without being called.

In this atmosphere Cleveland tried to get the tariff reduced, but the changes were so compromised as to be no changes at all, and the whole movement collapsed when he refused to sign the practically unrevised tariff law Congress did pass.

William Allen White, the Kansas Republican editor, characterized Cleveland almost lovingly as a militant obstructionist who prevented financial collapse, fended off anarchy, saved taxes, staved off the British attempt to move in on Venezuela, and protected the status quo.

Except for the tariff issue, said White approvingly, Cleveland acted like a Republican. Cleveland's administration represented "protection and conservation of property and privileges of capital during his second administration, while his party was taking the other road."

As convention time drew near, the Democrats had no solid candidate, but the Republicans were not so poor in material. The two rival hopefuls were Major William McKinley of Ohio, the congressman, and the three-hundred-pound, six-foot-three Thomas B. Reed of Maine, Speaker of the House of Representatives. Before the national convention the Republicans kept the silver issue in the background. Reed was a loyal party worker who had carried the Republican fortune wheel in Congress. But McKinley was the candidate of

Marcus Alonzo Hanna, the stout broad-shouldered wholesale grocer from Cleveland who became a big pig-iron man, then one of the leading industrialists of the country, and finally the first kingmaker of the Republican party. If the Republicans had been given lessons before in the uses of money in politics, it seemed like kindergarten stuff when compared to Hanna's methods. In '88, Hanna, as one of the chief fund solicitors of the Republican National Committee, had raised so much money the party was not able to spend it all before election! He returned the surplus on a prorata basis, to the surprise and delight of the donors. In '92 he had sweated to keep his protégé McKinley from being nominated in what he called a Democratic year.

Hanna felt things had changed by 1896. Major McKinley, "the busiest man in Canton," was at home, getting up at 7 A.M., eating sparingly, abstaining from liquor, and greeting itinerant politicans sent him by Hanna. In Cleveland, Hanna was writing letters furiously, mailing them by the hundredweight, and pulling every string to Wall Street, big money, and political influence that he could grasp. McKinley's efforts left him cool and relaxed on his veranda. Hanna's efforts put him flat on his back at the end of May, when he retired to his bed for several days suffering from complete exhaustion.

McKinley had his problems, but they weren't many. By the end of May the Cleveland *News-Herald* noted one of the more serious: the Republican jingle makers were having trouble with campaign songs and slogans. What rhymes with McKinley?

Unpoetic sloganeers got around it. "Bill McKinley and the McKinley Bill," they murmured. "The advance agent for prosperity." The silver issue was buried in the pre-nomination campaign, partly because McKinley had such an equivocal record on silver (he had voted for the Sherman Silver Purchase Act) and partly because the Republican leaders of the West had already served notice that they would bolt the party if it didn't come out for silver at the national convention.

It wasn't just the Democrats who were splitting on the money issue.

Indeed, even the Prohibitionists divided angrily into two camps, after their seventh national convention met in Pittsburgh on May 27. For once the Prohibition issue was not just war against the Demon Rum; it was silver, too.

The Prohis had been gaining strength: in 1869 the party polled 7000 votes. In 1892 it polled 280,000.

The Prohibitionists assembled this year in the wake of a tornado that swept through the Midwest, wrecked $20 million worth of property, and killed hundreds of people in and around St. Louis. Again, as usual, nature provided a fitting opening for the political season.

On the second day of their convention 1888's dry candidate St. John of Kansas declared for silver. He stood up and asked the convention to add silver, women's suffrage, public ownership of communications, the income tax—fifteen non-liquor planks in all—to the platform.

The rumble shook the rafters of Exposition Hall. Delegates stood on their chairs and shouted him down. A few minutes later 209 "broad gauge" Prohibitionists walked out of the "cold water" convention. The western silver men were bound together by an issue more important than politics or alcohol. They were determined to abandon all parties that did not support the mining industry and cheap money. The dissenters met the same night, May 28, to organize the National party, pledged to "work for humanity" by stamping out the liquor traffic and stamping out silver dollars at the same time. The Nationalists nominated the Reverend Charles E. Bentley of Nebraska for President, and James H. Southgate of North Carolina for the second place.

The "narrow gauge" Prohibitionists nominated Joshua Levering of Maryland and Hale Johnson of Illinois.

On Memorial Day, Major McKinley marched proudly in the parade through Canton's streets, in his Prince Albert coat and silk hat, with the GAR badge pinned to his lapel. The line of march passed his mother's house, and the eighty-seven-year-old lady sat on the porch, waving to the famous son whose trail was moving ever closer to the White House.

In New York, "Mousy" Platt, the manager of Levi P. Morton's ponderous campaign, was fending off Mark Hanna's McKinley steam roller as best he could. The nomination of McKinley would be "suicidal," Mousy said. McKinley had less to do with the Republican tariff than anyone realized, he was also an extremist on the tariff, and that was what had gotten the Republicans into so much trouble in 1892. Besides that, McKinley had voted for bi-metallism. Altogether, sniffed Mousy, McKinley was a narrow, untrustworthy, small-time politician who had no business aspiring to the highest office in the land.

As Mousy sniffed, Marcus Alonzo Hanna had 310 of the convention's 930 delegates pledged to McKinley, and there was still plenty of time before the convention met in St. Louis on June 16.

On June 2 the President and Mrs. Cleveland celebrated their tenth wedding anniversary and prepared to leave for Buzzards Bay. Cleveland was not interested in a third term, but he wasn't interested in attending the Democratic convention either.

Roswell Flower, the former governor of New York and one of the Democratic party's most disinterested observers, noted wryly that a lot of other Democrats were scarcely more interested.

"The prospects of a Democratic victory this year are not very encouraging, and I do not expect to see a scramble for the presidential nomination," said Mr. Flower.

Among the professional Democratic politicians of the East, this was regarded as the understatement of the year.

The Republicans agreed. When the GOP met on June 16 at St. Louis the convention ratified Mr. Hanna's man McKinley on the first ballot. Reed got only 84½ votes. Garret A. Hobart of New Jersey was nominated to run as Vice-President. The party was so confident of victory that it did not even straddle the silver question, but came out flatly for the gold standard and limitation of silver coinage. Senator Henry Teller of Colorado, leader of the silver men, made an impassioned plea to the deaf ears of Hanna and the rest. Teller left the podium and sat down sobbing. Hanna's long upper lip twitched, and his facial muscles jerked, but that was the only sign of emotion.

Utah's Frank Cannon spoke next for silver, and threatened to leave the Republican party.

"Go, go," shouted Hanna.

Cannon declared that the Republican party had left the course of truth and righteousness.

"Oh, my God . . ." blurted Hanna.

Cannon declared that this was the parting of the ways.

"Good-by," cried Hanna.

And then . . . as the silver men sadly picked up their hats . . . the convention picked up Hanna's chant. "Go, go, go," shouted the hard-money delegates, "go to Chicago. Take the Democratic train."

From a seat far in the back of the press gallery a handsome, square-jawed man with long wavy hair got up and walked down to the front of the hall to see better, stepping across the desks, for by now everyone was standing on top of them.

The handsome man watched the chanting, almost hypnotically. A gleam of triumph flashed across his regular face as Senator Teller walked sobbing from the convention hall.

This man, the happiest on the floor of the Republican convention, was the editor of the Omaha *World-Herald:* Democrat William Jennings Bryan.

For suspense, the convention was not very satisfactory. The outcome was so predictable that on June 8 the New York *Times* headline read: McKINLEY TO BE NOMINATED TODAY. The merchants, souvenir vendors, and those who hang about the fringes of political conventions were not satisfied either.

"See that feller?" queried one eagle-eyed gentleman loitering before the portico of the Southern Hotel and pointing across the way. "Well, he's from Ohio. He took a clean shirt and a ten-dollar bill, and he ain't changed neither since."

There may have been very little enthusiasm for the candidate at the convention, but most Republican party leaders were well pleased. After it was all over, on June 20, the New York Police Commissioner, Theodore Roosevelt, arrived in his mayor's office for a meeting, wearing an ivory-colored coat button the size of a silver dollar, a campaign button picturing McKinley and Hobart. It was the first one, said the commissioner proudly, that had reached New York.

And if Mousy Platt was so tired on his return from St. Louis that he would receive no visitors for two days, well, that was one of the consequences of backing the wrong horse.

New York didn't have a man on the Republican ticket this year, but it did claim one presidential candidate, Charles H. Matchett, a citizen of Brooklyn and foreman of a telephone-line gang. Mr. Matchett was the candidate of the Socialist Labor party, which met in New York on the Fourth of July to advocate a parliamentary system of government by and for the workingman. Mr. Matchett didn't really expect to trade his $18-a-week salary from the telephone company for the $50,000 a year paid the occupant of the White House. But in all seriousness the Socialist Labor party expected victory to come by 1925. Mr. Matchett was bidding for the job of elder statesman in a Socialist America.

Socialism's threat to the two-party system got little newspaper coverage in the first week of July, for the press was devoting its political columns to the great battle of Chicago. On July 7 the Democrats convened there. The metallic ringing in their ears seemed to drown out the names of any and all candidates. In truth there was no use talking about candidates until the metal issue was settled, for it was certain as God made little green apples that one faction or the other was going to split off from the party.

A survey showed that monetary policy was the issue in the local Democratic party in every state in the Union. The "gold men" were planning to contest ninety-four seats given by conventions to silver supporters from Illinois, Texas, and Nebraska. The silver men were equally determined to contest eight seats given gold men in South Dakota.

It was the West and South against the East all the way. The East had the national committee, the silver men had numerical strength; and numerical strength won the very first round. Virginia's John W. Daniel, a free-silver man, beat New York Senator David B. Hill, the hard-money candidate of the national committee, for the temporary chairmanship. From then on it was really no contest. The silver men had the majority and control. With the traditional unit rule in force, the representation of the territories which were pro-silver was increased from two to six members. Four silver delegates were seated in the contest with four gold delegates from Michigan, giving Michigan silver men a majority and, under the unit rule, all the twenty-eight Michigan votes. The gold delegation from Nebraska was unseated in favor of the silver delegation led by Congressman William Jennings Bryan.

The platform was free silver all the way. Bryan had written the money plank. Other planks—low tariff, pro-labor, and one ostentatiously opposed to a third term for any presidential candidate—could have fallen out and few would have missed them.

Cleveland received only a ripple of applause when his name was cast tentatively into the proceedings. A resolution commending his administration was defeated on the floor 564–357. A money plank hard enough to please the President was defeated, 626 to 303.

That vote showed the hard-money men that they could not prevent nomination of a silver candidate, even under the old two-thirds rule. They did not bolt, but neither did they offer a candidate.

The leader of the silver men was again Richard P. Bland. A good man, to be sure, but old, incensed with the single idea of silver, and equipped with a Catholic wife who would not be an asset in a political campaign. In these days religious feeling was running so high that the Republicans at St. Louis had enlisted a rabbi to open the convention.

While the other leaders of the silver bloc were expressing themselves forcefully on the convention floor, William Jennings Bryan had been closeted with the credentials committee, fighting for the admission of his Nebraska silver delegation. He was asked to take charge of the platform debate, since he was the only one of the prominent silver men who had not had a chance to address the convention in its early hours.

It was the voice that did it, that baritone, silvery, soft, penetrating voice that snatched the hearts of these groping, worried men who did not want to make another fight on the tariff, could not make a fight on the record of the Administration they had fought all the way.

When the convention met again the next day, Bryan felt as he always did before an important speech. He was limp in the pit of his stomach, half faint, and he wanted to rest. There was no time or place to lie down, so Bryan got a cup of coffee and a sandwich and waited for the call. Then as he moved to the platform the nervousness disappeared. . . . "I should be presumptuous indeed," said the young man from Nebraska, "to present myself against the distinguished gentleman to whom you have listened, if this were a mere measuring of abilities; but this is not a contest between persons . . .

"It is not a question of persons; it is a question of principle . . ." said the conscientious, studious young man.

"We do not come as aggressors. Our war is not a war of conquest; we are fighting in the defense of our homes, our families and posterity . . ." said the father of three, the husband, and editor.

"We go forth confident that we shall win. Why? Because upon the paramount issue of this campaign there is not a spot of ground upon which the enemy will dare to challenge battle . . ." said the brave young political leader, with all the confidence of a just cause.

". . . Having behind us the producing masses of this nation and the world, the laboring interests, and the toilers everywhere, we will answer their demand for a gold standard by saying to them: 'You shall not press down upon the brow of labor this crown of thorns; you shall not crucify mankind upon a cross of gold!'" ended the ambitious young knight, humbly, reverently, with just the proper amount of outraged righteousness in his voice to sway his receptive audience, the silver Democrats.

It was not a brilliant message. It was not even new. Bryan had delivered parts of it at various meetings a few weeks before; twice he had used the crown of thorns bit.

But this speech struck the silver-minded audience of the Democratic convention between the eyes. The crowd went wild, in a demonstration that was really spontaneous, really emotional, and as vigorous as any ever seen at a convention.

Bryan delivered his impassioned speech on July 9. He had not been blind to the possibility of his nomination, even before the convention. He had persuaded his wife to come to Chicago because he might be nominated. Now it was certain.

The next day Bryan turned his seat over to an alternate and stayed in his room in the Clifton House. He was nominated on the fifth ballot. He rushed down to the barber for a shave, then began greeting his well-wishers, who poured into the hotel. The convention was nominating Arthur Sewall of Maine to run as Vice-President.

Bryan was a remarkable young man. At the time of his nomination he was only thirty-six years old. He had already enjoyed a remarkable career in the House of Representatives. On the floor of the House he had battled against Cleveland's hard-money policy—and won, in a vote against an administration resolution to make a new bond issue specifically payable in gold. Since that time Bryan had been regarded as a comer, and, gazing into the mirror, he began to regard himself as a man of destiny. He ran for the U. S. Senate in 1894, but was defeated. Then he became editor of the Omaha World-Herald.

When the Bryans arrived back in Nebraska after the nomination they were greeted with tearful joy. Their house flew streamers from porch to eaves; small boys perched in rows along the roof, and the crowd overflowed the front yard.

In contrast to the yelling, screeching whoopee on the Nebraska prairie, the sombre quiet that emanated from Buzzards Bay was almost frightening. President Cleveland had installed a telegraph instrument at Gray Gables again, but he hardly went near it. On July 10, when the boy orator was nominated, the President went fishing early in the morning, returned late in the afternoon, and had nothing to say for public consumption on the platform or the candidate.

The silence was not fooling anyone. Neither Cleveland nor the hard-money wing of the party would support the candidate. Democratic newspapers openly advocated the election of McKinley.

What Bryan lost in Democratic support he gained in endorsement by the Populists. At their convention in St. Louis on July 22 the "People's Party" also nominated Thomas E. Watson of Georgia for Vice-President, because they did not like the Democrat's vice-presidential nominee, Sewall. This Populist convention also marked the political emergence of Eugene V. Debs, president of the American Railway Union. Debs had flatly refused the presidential nomination of the Populists. Almost immediately he was to organize the Socialist party of America. On September 2, at Indianapolis, a rump group of Democrats known as the National Democratic party nominated John M. Palmer of Illinois for President and General Simon B. Buckner of Kentucky for Vice-President on a hard-money platform, supported flatly but without illusion by a President Cleveland who preferred a Democratic defeat to victory for Bryan and the heresy of free silver.

"The Democratic party has survived defeats," said the National Democrats, "but could not survive a victory won in behalf of the doctrine and policy proclaimed in its name at Chicago."

Not long after, the New York *Herald* sponsored its own convention in the Monkey House in Central Park and reported its platform fully:

"The Simian party stands by its pristine prerogative and insists that if the currency must be monkeyed with its representatives are by birth and education best suited for such a task."

William Grinning Organmunk was the Simian candidate for President, said the *Herald*.

The *Herald* also hired its own expert "physiognomist" to discover Bryan's true character. The expert reported Bryan was a crowd winner, which everybody knew, and "but for the unselfish benevolent and altruistic trend of his ambitions as dangerous a leader as this country ever saw."

There was method in this, as well as fun. Bryan was handsome; Bryan was a man with a mission; Bryan had the makings of a demagogue. He frightened some people, he made others swoon in an ecstasy that was almost religious. The metal issue hardly sounds like a matter that could excite emotion, but Bryan's appeal was a sort of cross between that of Richard Nixon and Billy Graham.

It was a confused campaign. Long-term Democrats like Cleveland hoped for a Republican victory; such hard-bitten Republicans as Henry Teller openly argued the Democratic case; the Populists fought among themselves, even as they were sucked into the Democratic maw. The word "Popocrat" was added to the American vocabulary, to describe the fusion between Democrat and Populist. The Popocrats, men, women, and children, came in droves to hear the boy orator tell them of the evils of gold alone.

It was an arduous campaign. Bryan traveled 18,000 miles, made some 600 speeches to some 5,000,000 people. He spent every day but Sunday campaigning, at the end using cough drops, gargles, cough killers, and compresses to keep that golden throat in condition.

McKinley did not take to the hustings but remained in Canton in dignified quiet, receiving all comers, making speeches off the front porch, and keeping in touch with the ubiquitous Hanna. Wherever a businessman lurked, Hanna was likely to be, accepting a campaign donation, arranging to get the voters to the polls, or paying the money to get the farmers to leave their fields. He organized an old soldiers' touring special—a trainload of officers and soldiers left over from the Civil War, who made speeches to other old soldiers in behalf of McKinley and "the full dinner pail."

Before the conventions the country was counting on a Republican victory. After the conventions, when the pattern of party politics suddenly became a crazy quilt, there was a great deal of confusion. The Democrat-Populist-Silver Republican fusion was not to be sneezed at. Mark Hanna did no sneezing. He pulled every string, spent every dollar he could, left no banker or industrialist unturned.

> McKinley drinks soda water,
> Bryan drinks rum;
> McKinley is a gentleman,
> Bryan is a bum!

So went the song. The fact that it was not true—Bryan was also a teetotaler—meant nothing to the songsters, for this was a political campaign. But that was not the worst of it:

"The Harland and Hollingsworth Company of this city," wrote the *Morning News* of Wilmington, Delaware, on November 3, "have received a contract for a boat costing $300,000. One clause of the contract provides that in the event of Bryan's election the contract shall be canceled. If the boat is built here, $160,000 of its cost would be paid to Wilmington workmen for wages. The corporation wanting the boat feels that it would not be justified in having it constructed if Bryan should become President."

"Workmen were paid off on Saturday night before election," Bryan reported, "and notified that they might expect work Wednesday morning in case of Mr. McKinley's elections, but that they need not return if I was elected."

The head of the Steinway piano works told his men on Monday to vote as they pleased, ". . . but if Bryan is elected tomorrow the whistle will not blow Wednesday morning."

Finally it was all over. Hanna cried, "God's in his heaven, all's right with the world," and McKinley retired to his bedroom to pray. McKinley was elected, by more than a half million votes, 51 per cent of the popular vote to Bryan's 47 per cent. The Democrats could console themselves, perhaps, that they had made a fighting campaign in a year when they were not given a ghost of a chance; that the transfer of only 50,000 strategic votes would have given Bryan the majority in the electoral college; that they had won more counties than the Republicans. But none of these things counted.

The Cleveland Democrat, Palmer, got less than 150,000 votes, less than the Populist Bryan-Watson ticket polled when separated from the Democratic Bryan-Sewall ticket, and just a few more than the regular Prohibitionist, Joshua Levering.

Bryan might now lick his wounds.

He could count his prizes:

A stuffed alligator so long its tail was sticking out of the back of the express wagon when it was delivered;

one set of harness;

one pair suspenders;

one cane;

one band wagon;

one mule;

one silk bed quilt;
one watermelon in a gilded laundry basket;
one dog;
four volumes of Thomas Jefferson's works;
one ostrich egg;
one picture frame made from cigar boxes;
one frosted cake.

Et cetera . . . et cetera, in Mrs. Bryan's little black book.

Bryan was resigned to it, even on election night. "It is better to have run and lost," he said in the doggerel of the day, "than never to have run at all."

12

The lyrics of McKinley songs to the contrary, William Jennings Bryan was not a bum, but a hard-working man who wanted to be President.

Events of the next two years whirled him back into the political maelstrom. He went to war in 1898 with other patriotic Americans, when the Spaniards were so unfortunate as to get in the way of the imperialist juggernaut.

Eugene Debs had refused the Populist nomination. Now he formed the Social Democratic party, which was to become, in common terminology, the Socialist party. When war was declared in 1898, Debs fought against it, but war was popular and Debs, for the most part, was not.

Our war with Spain ended. Almost immediately the Filipino nationalists began a guerrilla war to secure independence from the United States. England was now engaged in the Boer War. The Turks and Greeks were still fighting, and even the Chinese were straining restlessly against the foreign bridle. From a matter of no importance, America's involvement in world affairs suddenly became an issue that would exert great influence in the election of 1900. Meanwhile, with new discoveries of gold, with better times, stimulated by war and industrial growth and with the public mind on other issues, the gold-silver issue lost some of its patina.

12. Imperialism and the Big Stick

Mark Hanna, the most astute politician of his age, was not one to worry about political niceties where something he wanted was involved. Having selected, groomed, and hand-fed the Republican candidate who became President of the United States, Hanna had no intention of releasing the reins. But the Ohio industrialist did not want to exercise his power as a member of the McKinley cabinet. Mark Hanna wanted to be a senator. He felt the Senate held higher honor.

There was no vacancy in the Senate seats allotted to Ohio, and even Hanna could hardly create a new seat for himself. So the senior senator from Ohio, the loyal and creaking John Sherman, was to become a sacrificial lamb.

McKinley demanded that Sherman resign his Senate seat to accept the post as Secretary of State. It was true that Sherman had a great name and had been a powerful political leader in the past. It was also true that he was seventy-four years old, and, if not actually senile, he was certainly bordering on senility.

With the pressure on, Sherman resigned and took the cabinet job. Governor Bushnell of Ohio immediately appointed Mark Hanna to the Senate seat. No one was the worse for the switch, except the people. The Ohio legislature confirmed the Senate appointment, reluctantly, after acrimonious debate over the manner in which the post had been secured for the man who had turned politics into a straight dollars-and-cents proposition.

Hanna joined a Republican Congress which proceeded to create one of the finest protective tariffs in the world—as far as manufacturers were concerned. By 1900, after the mid-term congressional elections strengthened his hand, McKinley put the country on the gold standard, to the relief of Europe and the disgust of the cheap-money men.

But the issues of the campaign of 1900 were to be raised over McKinley's foreign policy. Cleveland had warned McKinley to expect trouble with Spain, for Americans had been fishing in Spain's colonial waters in Latin America ever since Secretary of War John Rawlins's affair with the Cuban revolutionary bonds during the Grant administration. Trouble came in February 1898, when the battleship *Maine* was blown up in Havana Harbor. McKinley did not want war. Hanna did not want war either; he was afraid it would be bad for business. But things were dull and newspaper publisher William Randolph Hearst wanted excitement, and so did great numbers of men in Congress. Congress yielded quickly to public hysteria and passed a resolution demanding that Spain get out of Cuba. This resolution forced a declaration of war on the Spanish government.

The war lasted ten weeks.

"It has been a splendid little war," Secretary of State John Hay wrote Theodore Roosevelt at the end of it; "begun with the highest motives, carried on with magnificent intelligence and spirit, favored by that Fortune which loves the brave."

Splendidly or disgracefully, the United States had suddenly acquired an empire: Puerto Rico, Guam, and the Philippines. Some of the Filipinos were not anxious to be acquired, but a God-fearing America saw it as not less than duty to "take them, and educate the Filipinos and uplift and civilize and Christianize them," as President McKinley put it.

The Spanish-American War was a non-partisan war, too. Democratic generals, like Republican generals, went up hills and down again. Democratic admirals, like Republican admirals, were unafraid to "fire when ready." If there were Democrats who groused that Colonel William Jennings Bryan was not allowed to ride his shining black Kentucky stallion overseas and become a hero (simply because he was an aspirant for the presidency), there was an equal number of Republicans to deny that preposterous claim.

The war over, politician Bryan invaded the East just after the opening of the political season in 1900. The New Jersey legislature devoted earnest debate to a Democratic resolution that Bryan be given "freedom of the state."

What for? asked the Republicans. For "valiantly facing the dangers of fever and mosquitoes in Florida?" As if in agreement, the issue was referred to the legislative committee on public health.

Bryan was not seriously concerned about the freedom of New Jersey. He was on his way to New York to see about making up with Tammany Hall. In 1896, Tammany had shied away from the silver plank in the Democratic platform. Senator David B. Hill—indeed, most of the Democrats of the East—had fought the silver issue down to the wire. When a newspaperman had asked Hill if he was "still a Democrat," after the silver plank had been adopted in 1896, Senator Hill had epitomized the position of the East: A Democrat? Yes, he was a still Democrat, he said, very still.

Now, four years later, with an announced gold standard, silver was not an unresolved issue.

As Tammany got ready to entertain the visiting orator from Nebraska, big things were happening in far-off China. The Emperor Kwang Hsu had been deposed by the irascible old Dowager Empress Tz'u Hsi, and the Boxer Rebellion was growing serious.

On January 24, Tammany entertained Bryan at the Democratic Club in New York City. A year before, Bryan had refused to come to New York because he would not break bread with those who were against silver. But times change, and this was a presidential year.

By the time Democratic leader John W. Keller arranged the guest list thirteen were scheduled to sit down at the big round table in the center of the club's third-floor dining room.

Thirteen at dinner! What did Bryan think of that? the newspapermen asked.

"When I am hungry, I don't care how many sit at the table with me, and I am generally hungry at dinnertime," said Mr. Bryan. It may not have been the most brilliant statement of the year, but it indicated an admirable lack of superstition on the part of a man who had been nominated on Friday, wore opal shirt studs, and lost the election of 1896.

If Bryan wasn't superstitious, Keller was. They dug up Maurice F. Holohan, president of the New York board of public improvements, to break the jinx.

At the end of the dinner 193 members of the Democratic Club shook hands with Bryan, some of them twice, but they would not let him make a speech.

That was the love feast. As the Democrats ate, China burned.

When the Boxers forced all foreigners into the British legation in Peking, McKinley dispatched the battleship *Oregon* and sent a force of Marines into China. Was this more "imperialism"? The Democrats said it was. Carl Schurz, the old reform Republican, now passing a bit of time on New York's Lake George, declared, in a burst of enthusiasm, that imperialism was to be the issue of the campaign.

For a while the imperialism issue threatened to play a hand in selection of presidential candidates. Admiral Dewey, the hero of Manila Bay, had indicated his willingness to be drafted as a candidate. He did not much care which party nominated him. Admiral Schley, another hero of the "little" war with Spain, was approached by enthusiasts, but Schley, who knew his limitations, would not think of it. Bryan had comported himself well enough, even skillfully, by joining the Army, then resigning to oppose the "imperialism" of the Republicans. It was almost certain that he would be the Democratic candidate of 1900 and that he could expect, again, a good share of support from the Populists who had backed him in 1896.

The first political convention of the year was held just after Bryan's meeting with Tammany. A splinter of the Social Democratic party met in Rochester, New York, on January 27, pledged allegiance to international socialism, declared that *the* issue in American politics was between the working class and the capitalist class, and proposed to abolish private property in industry. Job Harriman of California was nominated for President. Max S. Hayes of Ohio was nominated for Vice-President.

A consolidated and much more important Social Democratic party of America convened in Indianapolis on March 6 to organize the workers of America. It also pledged allegiance to international socialism and sought support from organized labor. Eugene V. Debs of Indiana, who had been considered the year before for the Populist nomination, was the nominee. Job Harriman of California was the party nominee for Vice-President. The drop in Harriman's status really reflected the broadening of the party's base, between January and March. Debs brought a strong radical element with him, defectors of the extreme left from the Populists and the Democrats.

One branch of the Populists met at Sioux Falls, South Dakota, on May 9. Half a thousand delegates crowded into a circular tent, the sides of which bore pictures of Washington, Jefferson, Lincoln, and William Jennings Bryan. It was not hard to guess the name of the party's nominee.

There, the only question was Bryan's running mate. Bryan's friends in the convention wanted the Populists to accept the Democratic ticket. This caused John F. Kelly of South Dakota, who had been trying for hours to get the attention of Thomas Patterson, the chairman, finally to make his way to the platform in disgust and outrage.

"You," he said to the chairman, "are a miserable bunko steerer."

The crowd blinked.

"Lynch him," shouted an anonymous voice.

"Gag him," yelled another.

"Throw him out," screamed a third.

Delegates began removing their coats and eying one another. Chairman Patterson said he was only trying to be fair.

"You're a liar," said the irascible Mr. Kelly.

"There'll Be a Hot Time in the Old Town Tonight . . ." blared the convention band.

The band music quieted things down. By the time the concert ended, Kelly was under friendly restraint. Then Charles A. Towne was nominated Vice-President by acclamation and Bryan, President—but everybody had expected that.

This half of the Populist party continued to stand for free silver, income and inheritance taxes, government ownership of railroads and monopoly business, the initiative and the referendum, limitation of oriental immigration, direct election of senators, home rule for territories; and against imperialism, a standing army, and use of injunctions in labor disputes. It was quite a platform. Some of it would still have been avant-garde sixty years later, if the party had lived that long.

That same day, in Robinson's Opera House in Cincinnati, J. Clem Deaver banged a piece of gas pipe on the improvised podium and called to order the first meeting of the middle-of-the-road branch of the People's party—distinguishable from the other branch largely in its antipathy to that same William Jennings Bryan.

The crowd at the opera house came to order well enough (with the exception of Mrs. Killie's baby, sitting in its mother's arms on the stage and yelling to high heaven). A wry Minnesotan, Ignatius Donnelly, opened up by saying that Bryan would have been elected in 1896 "if the Lord had taken an inch off his lower jawbone and placed it between his temples." Wharton Barker of Pennsylvania was nominated. Ignatius Donnelly was unanimously nominated for Vice-President.

The Socialist Labor party met June 2 in New York and reaffirmed its platform of 1896. A total of eighty-three delegates from nineteen states nominated Joseph P. Maloney of Massachusetts for President and Valentine Remmel of Pennsylvania for Vice-President.

By now the Republicans were beginning to move into Philadelphia for their quadrennial session. Mousy Platt, the senator and Republican political boss of New York, had just broken the ninth rib on his right side and was confined painfully and unhappily to a plaster cast. But his broken rib pained him no more than did Theodore Roosevelt, the wordsy, quick-shooting, hard-riding erstwhile police commissioner of New York, later Assistant Secretary of the Navy, who had resigned to charge with his Rough Riders up San Juan hill and into the governor's mansion. When nominated for governor two years before, Roosevelt had indicated his willingness to take boss Platt's advice on appointments and other distribution of the boodle. Roosevelt had not reneged on the promise, exactly, but in his own ebullient way had flatly refused to do some of the things Platt demanded. It was embarrassing to a political boss unable to deliver on promises to the helpful and deserving. Mousy Platt decided that he had to have a new governor.

Roosevelt was too popular a figure to be simply shucked off. Platt decided the way out was to bury Roosevelt with the vice-presidential nomination. There was no problem of an incumbent: Vice-President Hobart had died in 1899. The fight would be with Roosevelt, who had no desire to leap into the political oblivion that awaited Vice-Presidents, and with Marcus Alonzo Hanna, who didn't like Roosevelt and who had some ideas of his own about the Republican ticket.

Hanna wanted Cornelius N. Bliss to be Vice-President in 1900. Bliss was an easterner, desirable since McKinley was from the West. Bliss had been Secretary of the Interior, and Bliss would make a good, tractable President for Hanna to manipulate in case of accidental succession to the presidency. But Mrs. Bliss did not want the job, and she was still so angry with Hanna for pushing her husband into the cabinet that Hanna had no heart to face her.

If there was any one man in the Republican party that Hanna did not want for the vice-presidency it was Theodore Roosevelt.

Neither Hanna nor McKinley trusted Roosevelt. The New York governor had been critical of the war, and was entirely too unpredictable to sit well with the conservatives of his party. And to Hanna the vice-presidency was one heartbeat removed from the presidency.

"If McKinley should die," said the little child to his mother, according to a story of the day, "will Hanna still be President?"

"I'm afraid so, my child," replied the mother.

Luckily, from Hanna's point of view, Roosevelt denied any interest in the vice-presidency. One of T.R.'s prime motives, as he stepped off the train at the Broad Street Station in his baggy old clothes on June 16, was to protect himself against railroading by Boss Platt into the mausoleum of the vice-presidency. Roosevelt warmed Hanna's heart when he told the Ohioan he had no intention of accepting the nomination.

The logical Hanna candidates were Jonathan Dolliver, congressman from Iowa, and John D. Long, former Secretary of the Navy. Both were safe, conservative Republicans.

There was no other real question. The nomination was to go to McKinley. The party would run on its record. All was right with Hanna's world as the convention machinery began to move.

That weekend the New York delegation kept busy. Senator Platt was confined to his hotel room with his painful injury, but he worked just the same, made a deal with Matthew Quay of Pennsylvania, who hated Hanna, to support the Roosevelt candidacy. On Sunday, Platt told the newspapers piously that he thought Roosevelt would be nominated for the vice-presidency. He hoped Roosevelt would reconsider.

Roosevelt knew why. His term as governor ended that year. Three months after the presidential convention the New York Republicans would meet to select their gubernatorial candidate. Furious, T.R. accused the delegates of arranging his political assassination. Some of them laughed and admitted it. Roosevelt planned to make his fight in the New York delegates' caucus, which would determine their vote on the nomination.

Roosevelt had been told there was a very strong western movement for his nomination as Vice-President, but he did not believe this, absorbed as he was in the power play of boss Mousy Platt.

On the morning of the nineteenth, as the convention assembled, Roosevelt got proof of the popular movement.

Hanna walked into the hall, about eleven-thirty. The band struck up "Hail to the Chief." If this was an error in protocol it was also an acknowledgment of a great political truth. Then "Teddy" strolled in, and the convention went wild. Hanna frowned, let it be known that this stampede was completely out of place. The demonstration continued. It gave T.R. something to think about. (Hanna, too.)

The convention proceeded. Temporary Chairman Edward O. Wolcott of Colorado gave the keynote address, which praised the status quo, promised more full dinner pails, and flailed the Cleveland administration, now dead four years, for bad handling of the nation's finances.

On the night of the nineteenth the New York Republicans were getting ready for their caucus when Roosevelt told the delegates if they backed his nomination for Vice-President he would expose Mousy Platt's vile plot to the whole convention. Platt's lieutenants listened uneasily, then went off to report to the boss. A few minutes later one of them returned with a summons for Roosevelt from the senator.

Roosevelt went up.

Platt stated his case in cold sentences. It had been decided that Roosevelt was to be nominated for Vice-President. They could not accept his refusal. He would have to yield.

Roosevelt refused.

Platt said that if Roosevelt did not accept the nomination he would be beaten for the nomination for governor.

A threat? Roosevelt bridled. Under no conditions would he accept the nomination. If there was to be war, there was to be war. He bowed and left the room.

Downstairs, Roosevelt told the assembling delegates what had just happened. He would announce immediately that he was a candidate for governor, would fight for the gubernatorial nomination, would make that statement to the full caucus, formally, then he would tell the whole story to the newspapers.

A Platt man asked Roosevelt to wait a few moments. Surely he must have misunderstood the senator.

Roosevelt laughed. He would wait.

A few minutes later Roosevelt was again summoned to Platt's room. Mousy was sorry. He was in pain from that broken rib, and maybe the drugs had made him a little lightheaded. He had expressed himself badly before.

Of course, in view of Roosevelt's strong feelings on the subject, the effort to nominate him for the vice-presidency would be abandoned. Of course he would have the support of all his old friends if he wanted to seek the governorship again.

The governor thanked the senator, bowed again, and went back downstairs. The caucus voted to present the name of Lieutenant Governor Timothy Woodruff, who wanted to be Vice-President, although Hanna didn't want him, either.

On June 20 the Roosevelt nomination seemed to be a dead issue. Roosevelt was talking about candidate Long but had not flatly declined to accept any nomination. Platt had quieted down. Hanna was doing everything possible to stop the talk about Roosevelt.

As usual, the credentials committee had the dirtiest job of the convention: settling disputes between rival delegations. The committee had started its deliberations early enough on the night of the nineteenth but was still in session at four-thirty on the morning of the twentieth. The deliberations became quite deliberate when W. H. Love, a delegate from McKinney, Texas, accused another Texan, Walter Burns, of making untrue statements.

Burns denied the charge.

Love called Burns a liar.

Burns struck Love in the face, and Love fell back, but bystanders kept him from falling down. Love then got a knife halfway out of his pocket, whereupon his friends held him back and forced it out of his hand.

"I'm through," said Burns, "unless he starts it again."

Mousy Platt was through too. He didn't care whether school kept or not, for there was no profit left for him in this convention. If Roosevelt would not be nominated, Roosevelt would run for governor again. Mousy took his aching rib back to New York.

But neither Mousy, Hanna, nor Roosevelt himself realized the strength and determination of the western delegates who were determined to return Roosevelt to national prominence. Roosevelt was ready to fight, but his friends won him over. Hanna was ready to fight too, but Charles G. Dawes of Illinois saw how the wind blew and called McKinley in Washington on that useful device new to national politics: the telephone. Dawes told the President that it would be very dangerous to pit the Administration against the will of the majority. Dawes didn't have to say it might threaten the renomination. McKinley agreed, and when Hanna was so informed he was persuaded reluctantly to give up the fight. For while Hanna was the kingmaker he still had to bow to the wishes of McKinley. As President, McKinley was in a position to win any open argument within the party. Hanna gave in, but he warned McKinley that Roosevelt was "a wild man."

McKinley was nominated by acclamation. So was Roosevelt, as his running mate.

Hanna became head of the Republican National Committee. He planned to run a sequel to the campaign of 1896 and after canvassing the country found that he needed far less money than before. He asked for, and got, only $2,500,000 from his business friends.

Platt accepted the Roosevelt nomination joyfully. This was a gift from the gods. But the senator could not resist a parting dig at the vice-presidential candidate: "There was doubt in the minds of some people," said the senator, "whether he could have carried New York State as a candidate for governor." In whose mind the doubt existed, Platt did not say.

McKinley, having accepted the will of the majority, put in his two cents' worth: "It was a very nice convention," said the President.

The Prohibitionists met in Chicago on June 27. The party had grown. It now represented 40 seats and boasted 735 delegates. They nominated John G. Woolley of Illinois for President on the first ballot and Henry B. Metcalf of Rhode Island for Vice-President. They condemned President McKinley as a wine drinker who had "done more to encourage the liquor business, to demoralize the temperance habits of young men, and to bring Christian practices and requirements into disrepute than any other President this republic has ever had."

As the GOP convention closed, the Democratic New York *Herald* tentatively started a boom for Cleveland for the Democratic nomination, but Cleveland shut it off with an immediate and brisk refusal. Bryan had worked for four years to get the nomination again, and there was small doubt that Bryan would have it.

The Democrats decided to hold their convention on the Fourth of July in Kansas City, and the silver Republicans decided to do the same. The silver Republicans, led by Senator Henry Teller of Colorado, nominated Bryan and then sat back to await the Democratic vice-presidential nomination, adjourning and leaving the mechanics of the endorsement to their party's national committee, which finally accepted the complete Democratic ticket.

The Democrats went into session at noon on Independence Day at the Kansas City Exposition Hall. First, the Declaration of Independence was read, "as a rebuke to the Republican party." A bust of Bryan was unveiled on the platform, and the delegates started yelling.

The platform, strong for silver and strong against imperialism, was adopted without a dissenting vote. This was completely misleading. The fight had been staged in the platform committee.

All the professional politicians were dead set against free silver this year, by a margin of 3 to 1. It looked suspiciously as though the convention would override Bryan on the issue.

Bryan would not hear of it. He released a letter to the newspapers, saying he was firm for a silver plank. It was apparent that he would refuse the nomination if the silver plank was not put in the platform.

In the platform committee the silver plank was saved—by one vote, cast by the delegate from Hawaii. The fight against it had been led by David B. Hill, one of the old gold Democrats.

There did not seem to be any question about Bryan's nomination now. Conforming to tradition, Bryan waited at home. In Lincoln, William J., Jr., rushed in and out of the house, bringing bulletins on the progress of the convention to his father, who sat in the yard as placidly as a candidate could sit when surrounded by a score of eager newspaper reporters.

Little Miss Grace, the female heir to the Bryan mantle, was impatient. From time to time she stopped her game of croquet and came running up to her father with the same question, "Papa, aren't you nominated yet?"

Bryan was nominated, praised by David B. Hill, to show the solid unity of the party, and seconded by a woman delegate from Utah, to show democracy. It was all unanimous, as expected.

The vice-presidency here, too, was the only issue. William Sulzer of New York wanted the job, fancied himself as a sort of poor man's Abe Lincoln, even though his only visible Lincolnian attribute was a certain cragginess of feature. Sulzer was a dreamer. From day to day he counted publicly the delegates pledged to him. Then Richard Croker, the grand sachem of Tammany, arrived.

"Bryan and Sulzer!" he snorted. "How long before everybody would be saying 'Brandy and Selzer'? Bill Sulzer for Vice-President? It's a joke."

Adlai Stevenson, Cleveland's Vice-President, was nominated for second place again.

Bryan began his campaign this year on the issues of imperialism and the trusts. The Republicans had declared against the trusts, but for "honest aggregations of capital." Senator Mark Hanna had written that segment of the platform himself. He was not afraid of identifying the party openly with the cause of big business. The United States was prosperous, wasn't it? Who wanted a change?

The undeniable prosperity took the steam out of the silver issue.

Never in history, said Elihu Root, McKinley's Secretary of War, was there a nation "so well fed, well clothed and well housed." The Republican reason: a wise government that did not interfere between capital and labor, but gave capital "that confidence in security for its investment which draws it from the hiding places of distrust."

Banker J. P. Morgan thought so well of *that* speech he asked for the manuscript, to keep alongside the manuscripts of Rousseau and Keats and the Shakespeare folios.

McKinley, feeling the importance of being "President of the whole people," refused to make a political tour, nor did he receive visiting political delegations.

Roosevelt was the great campaigner for the Republicans. Bryan again took to the stump for the Democrats, but with much less effect than in 1896. The campaign degenerated steadily, for the real issue, prosperity, made the Democratic talk about silver look old-fashioned. The attacks of the Democrats and the third, fourth, fifth, and sixth parties on "imperialism" did not strike a chord to an American electorate that seemed either to ignore or like a little bit of imperialism.

Day by day the newspapers recorded the number of speeches made by Bryan and by Roosevelt on their forensic marathon. What they said seemed less important than how many times a day they managed to say it. On one day, the Republicans bragged, Roosevelt made eighteen speeches. Bryan announced a plan for the next in which he would "see" his opponent and "go him two better," by talking to twenty separate audiences between 10 A.M. and midnight.

Bryan finally walked off with the record: thirty-two speeches one September day in upper New York.

Roosevelt, with his toothy grin, glistening spectacles, and falsetto voice, made a strange but lovable candidate. He and Bryan appeared on the same platform, in Chicago. Roosevelt soon got to calling Bryan "my opponent," to the outrage of the old GOP politicos, who wanted to know who was running for President, anyhow.

At Cripple Creek, Colorado, a stronghold of the silver men, Roosevelt declared for gold, and fought his way happily through the rioting mob. When Bryan charged that Republican imperialism would force the United States to support a huge and dangerous standing army, Roosevelt waved his arms at his crowds and called for the soldiers to stand. "There are your oppressors," Teddy shouted grandly, pointing at the half dozen figures who rose from the multitude.

The outcome was never really in doubt. But Mark Hanna was taking no chances, continually complained that not he but "General Apathy" was running the campaign.

When prosperity slowed a little in some parts of the country during the summer and early fall, Hanna urged his manufacturers to keep as many men on the payroll as possible until after election day. When a strike threatened the vote in the anthracite coal region of Pennsylvania, Hanna stepped out of character to put an end to it.

Toward the end of the campaign Hanna went on the stump himself, dismaying the Republican National Committee and President McKinley, who shared a shudder in contemplating the impression Hanna would make on the American people.

But Hanna had his reasons. Specifically, he wanted to go to Nebraska and to South Dakota. Nebraska was Bryan's own state, and Hanna wanted the pleasure of whipping him there. South Dakota was the home of Senator Richard F. Pettigrew, elected as a Republican, who had bolted on the silver issue and further had attacked Hanna personally on the Senate floor.

Hanna took along two assistant speakers, Senator William P. Frye and Victor Dolliver, brother of the late senator from Iowa. The pair had two prepared speeches each, which they delivered without fail or fervor. Hanna made seventy-two speeches from five minutes to an hour in length—and no two alike.

At seven o'clock in the morning the party's train would stop at a station in the country, where there didn't seem to be more than a half dozen houses. Yet three or four hundred people would turn out to hear Hanna speak.

In South Dakota the Populist legislature had prohibited political meetings within two hundred feet of the railroad track. This was to enable the Populists, who could not afford the luxury of special trains, to compete on even terms with the Republicans and Democrats.

As Hanna's train steamed into the station of the South Dakota town a carriage would draw up before the platform. Hanna would get off the train, drive to the meeting place, take over from a local politician who had held the crowd, speak for a few minutes, and when he heard the train whistle, stop talking and go back to the station.

Hanna had his hecklers, but he responded remarkably well to them. He had no prepared text with which to fumble. And he had a rough kind of humor that the crowds loved—not smart and slick, but sincere and slightly corny.

At Auburn, Nebraska, some 2500 people had come to hear him speak from a platform, and when a number of men and boys tried to climb onto the platform it suddenly gave away. Hanna and some fifty others fell six feet to the ground.

"Is Hanna hurt?" someone shouted.

Just then Hanna appeared from the debris, his eye twinkling and his hand raised to get the attention of the milling, worried mass.

"It's all right," he shouted. "No one is hurt. We were just giving you a demonstration of what is going to happen to the Democratic party. This must have been a Democratic platform."

Hanna left the East portrayed as a monster, lampooned invariably by the cartoonists as the man in the coat with the dollar signs.

In Nebraska, at one whistle stop, this immense placard greeted the campaign train.

POPULIST FARMERS
BEWARE!
CHAIN YOUR CHILDREN TO YOURSELVES
OR
PUT THEM UNDER THE BED
MARK HANNA IS IN TOWN

Despite this, despite the heckling he encountered, Hanna returned a minor hero, even more so when the Republicans won the most overwhelming victory since 1872. McKinley and Roosevelt had a plurality of 832,000 votes, a clear majority of 443,000. The Republicans controlled both the Senate and the House of the Fifty-seventh Congress by handsome majorities.

And dearest to Hanna's heart, Bryan was beaten in his own state, a job for which Hanna could take part of the credit. In South Dakota, Richard R. Pettigrew lost his seat in the Senate to a loyal Republican.

13

Carry Nation, the scourge of Kansas saloons, began her hatchet raids on the drinking palaces in 1900, and as she captured the public imagination, so the Prohibition cause grew.

Henry Ford had quit the Detroit Automobile Company and was working on his own tin Lizzie in private. The Wright brothers were alternating between their bicycle shop in Dayton and a sandy wind-swept beach at Kitty Hawk, North Carolina, where they lived in a shed, and tried to fly a giant glider that looked something like an awkward, spiderish kite.

The nation was serious now about its responsibilities in world affairs. The venture into imperialism had taught Americans that they had responsibilities to face . . . and not all of them .at home. . . .

13. The Radical Roosevelt—I
1904

The Pan-American Exposition at Buffalo was an important event in the spring and summer of 1901. It marked a new idea in American foreign policy, a belated recognition of the importance of neighborliness. Primarily the exhibiting nations came to show off their manufactures, agriculture, and fine arts, but the exciting program again included Buffalo Bill's "Wild West Show," as in 1893 at Chicago. Visitors came from all over the country. Diplomats from the entire Western hemisphere arrived to be seen and pay their respects. A special set of postage stamps was issued by the post office to commemorate the event, an unusual honor in days before the general craze for philatelic novelty.

The President of the United States, William McKinley, came on September 5 to deliver a memorable address on foreign affairs. In these fitting surroundings he declared America could never again be isolationist.

The next day, in the habit of American political figures, McKinley wanted to shake hands with the people. J. G. Milburn, president of the exposition, ordered the Temple of Music suitably arranged. A pair of secret service men, George Foster and S. A. Ireland, had been sent to protect the President. They were watchful for anarchists, since there had recently been several shooting and bombing attempts in Europe against chiefs of government.

But Europe seemed a long way away. President McKinley did not share the nervousness of his aides. The President planted himself under a floral bower at the end of an aisle lined with strips of purple bunting, flanked by Milburn and George Cortelyou, the presidential private secretary. Those who would shake hands with the first citizen had to come up the narrow aisle, under the eyes of the secret service men, soldiers, and police, and then pass out the other side of the building. The arrangements seemed safe enough.

The strains of Bach's "Sonata in F" surged from the great pipe organ at the end of the hall. Hundreds of awed Americans inched forward in the sinuous line to meet their President.

Suddenly Foster and Ireland noticed a suspicious character: a short dark-faced man with a heavy mustache, bloodless lips set in a straight line, black piercing eyes hooded by heavy knobby brows. This was one to watch, and they did, carefully, as he inched forward in the line.

Most of the crowd was as ordinary as Main Street—friendly smiling matrons, self-conscious men, slowly moving along in the shuffle. Not this one. He had a sullen look—no more like the slim youngster behind him than buzzard is like ostrich.

The crowd was growing too thick. Secretary Cortelyou stepped aside for a moment, to order the entrance closed until the crowd thinned out. Agent Ireland tensed, as his suspect approached the smiling, relaxed President, at ease in his Prince Albert coat and striped trousers. Ireland's eyes narrowed as the President took the dark man's hand and shook it warmly. The dark man was gone and the secret service man relaxed, even as the next young man reached his left hand across the sling that held his right arm, to catch the President's outstretched hand. President McKinley noticed the unusual effort, and turned slightly.

The turn brought his chest squarely before the snout of a revolver held in that treacherous, now uncovered, uninjured right hand. Two shots rang out. Ireland leaped forward as the President sank into the arms of Secretary Cortelyou. The secret service man was on the slim youth like a panther; so were a dozen others. Ireland wrenched the gun from the youth's hand. Agent Foster grasped the assassin by the throat, struck him full in the face with his clenched fist, knocked him through the legs of the police and soldiers. "You murderer!" the agent shouted, and started forward to hit the young man again.

Police and soldiers grasped the gunman. Others held Foster back. "I am an anarchist," proclaimed the pinioned youth righteously. "I did my duty."

The shocked police hustled the assassin upstairs as Cortelyou and the President's other aides hurried him to the emergency hospital on the grounds. A detachment of soldiers was assigned to guard the locked room, for the crowd was already talking of lynch law.

Outside, on the grounds, Dr. Edward Wallace Lee had just left the Buffalo Bill "Wild West Show" and was walking along, chatting with Colonel Cody himself, when the doctor was summoned to the hospital. Other doctors rushed to the President's side, Dr. Herman Mynter, the first to arrive, examined McKinley as he lay on the hospital table, pale and obviously in pain from his wounds, but lucid. There had been two shots. The serious damage was done by the second, which had penetrated the abdomen. There was no question, said Dr. Mynter. An operation was necessary—an immediate operation.

The President nodded. "I am in your hands."

Dr. Roswell Park was the surgeon. Dr. Lee assisted. "You remember me? We met at the Omaha Exposition," said Dr. Lee. The President focused, and nodded. Of course he remembered.

They moved the President into position, and on the gauze the ether began to drip.

"Thy kingdom come, thy will be done," McKinley murmured, and continued the prayer as he spun into unconsciousness.

The doctors moved swiftly, for they knew what was at stake. They opened the abdomen. The stomach had been punctured by a .32-caliber bullet that had coursed downward, through the abdominal cavity. The President had eaten a hearty lunch, and some of the contents of the full stomach had escaped into the peritoneum. Rapidly, the surgeons washed out the abdominal cavity, searched for a bullet they could not find. They sewed up the stomach with silk sutures, the abdominal wall with silkworm-gut sutures. That was all they could do.

The President was moved by motor ambulance to the Milburn home on Delaware Avenue. A tent for telegraph operators was installed on the lawn, and newspaper reporters sat down for a long vigil, informed and informing on the President's condition by hourly bulletins. Their newspapers made extras ready, to take the news to the homes of the nation.

The prisoner (who first gave his name as Frederick Nieman, then was identified as Leon Czolgosz) was transferred to the Buffalo jail under heavy armed guard. Before nightfall New York's financial world knew of the horrible affair. Luckily, the stock market in New York had closed by the time of the shooting. That night the principal men of Wall Street agreed to pool their cash resources to stave off the "recklessness of a timid public."

But these men, J. Pierpont Morgan and the others, were worried enough themselves. McKinley was a sensible and safe President, in an era of great business expansion. What about that unpredictable, charging bull named Roosevelt?

They, too, sat down to wait.

The first forty-eight hours were critical. Until they had passed, none of the doctors would venture any opinions at all.

In Burlington, Vermont, Vice-President Roosevelt had finished speaking at the annual outing of the Vermont Fish and Game League and had stopped off at the home of an old friend, N. W. Fisk, former lieutenant governor of the state. The telephone rang. It was an official of the New England Telephone Company, informing the Vice-President that McKinley had been shot, and asking him to join the Cabinet, immediately, in Buffalo. A course of action must be set. No one knew how serious it was. The nation could not go into panic.

"My God!" shouted Roosevelt, and dropped the phone.

At Cleveland's Union Club hefty, bald Senator Mark Hanna had finished a quiet lunch when someone told him that his old friend, the President of his own creation, was lying at death's door. At first Hanna thought it was a hoax. But when the report was confirmed again and again by newspaper dispatches, he was convinced. At four o'clock Senator Hanna stepped onto a streetcar to go to his office in the Perry Paine Building on Superior Street. There he made arrangements to have the Lake Shore Limited held for him, if necessary, so he could get to Buffalo immediately.

The next morning the whole nation knew.

The newspapers speculated on the succession, should McKinley die.

"VICE-PRESIDENT ROOSEVELT NEVER MINCED HIS VIEWS," said the New York *Herald*.

"It must have been the act of a madman," declared former President Cleveland at home in Princeton, New Jersey.

"A shock to the country," said an agitated William Jennings Bryan, in Lincoln, Nebraska, who declared war on anarchists everywhere.

The President's condition was a matter of intense national concern. Diagrams, of the kind that normally appeared only in patent-medicine advertisements, showed the course of the bullet through the presidential stomach, the probable further course as assumed from the angle of deflection and other information gleaned from doctors on the scene.

The hourly bulletins continued. On Saturday night, as the Cabinet began arriving, Dr. Charles McBurney had an announcement:

"His temperature is not too high. It is lower tonight than it was this morning. The pulse is better; the facial expression is entirely satisfactory; the mind is clear; there is no pain or tenderness, no nausea and no distension of abdomen."

The next day Vice-President Roosevelt and Senator Mark Hanna met the press in front of the Milburn home. So confident was he of the President's complete recovery, said Roosevelt, that he was leaving the next day to join his family in the Adirondacks. Senator Hanna was planning to return to Cleveland to attend the National Encampment of the Grand Army of the Republic.

The hourly bulletins seemed to indicate progress. At 9 A.M. the President's pulse was 132, temperature 102.8, respiration 24; twelve hours later pulse 130, temperature 101.6, respiration 30.

On Monday, Wall Street was buoyant. Stocks went up, the curled lips of the brokers came down, and recovery was in the air.

On Tuesday the doctors operated again; a minor surgical procedure, they informed the press.

On Wednesday they admitted the minor surgical procedure had been more serious than announced, but the President was doing fine.

On Thursday in Cleveland the GAR held a service of thanksgiving for the President's narrow escape from death. McKinley had been scheduled to attend a reception there for the GAR—this service was its substitute. The encampment's armory was jammed as Senator Hanna delivered an emotional, heartfelt speech of gratitude. But that night McKinley began to fail. His heart action was not just right. Then—something was drastically wrong. To the Hanna house in Cleveland came a shocking message from Secretary Cortelyou:

"The President is dying."

The Hanna party left at 5 A.M. for the Milburn house by special train.

Roosevelt was harder to reach. He was on a hike in the woods when tracked down by a messenger late Friday afternoon. Night had fallen by the time he got back to camp. Then he had to wait for a carriage, and drive fifty miles to the nearest railway station.

In Buffalo the President knew the end of the story, even as the messenger was informing Roosevelt. "It is useless, gentlemen," McKinley said to the surgeons. "I think we ought to have a prayer."

He sank rapidly. At 2:15 on Saturday morning, September 14, 1901, William McKinley died.

Unknowing, Roosevelt raced on to the North Creek Station, where a special train was waiting, to hurrry him to Buffalo. When the Vice-President arrived at North Creek, just at dawn, he learned that the President was dead. As soon as he could take the oath of office he would be President of the United States.

That same evening, at the home of Ansley Wilcox in Buffalo, Roosevelt took the oath, the third Vice-President to accede after the assassination of the elected President.

Roosevelt immediately announced that he would continue McKinley's policies.

It was easy enough to say that. The Cabinet was another matter. Secretary of State John Hay and Secretary of the Treasury Lyman That same evening, at the home of Ansley Wilcox in Buffalo, Roosevelt was not without guile, although many thought him a playful elephant rampaging through the delicate halls of diplomacy. Roosevelt told Hay he wanted him to remain in Washington because he was the next in line for the presidency, and Roosevelt didn't want "too many eggs in the same Pullman car." Gage was in Washington too. Oddly enough, Hay and Gage were the two men Roosevelt planned to replace immediately. He asked the others for their resignations, as was customary, but he planned to reappoint them.

On Sunday, President McKinley's casket was placed in the small library in the Milburn house, and Roosevelt came in with the six cabinet members to attend the first services. Senator Hanna was there, nearly out of his mind with grief and worry; grief for his dead friend, and worry over the nation that was being left in the hands of a man he considered unfit for high office.

The President and the Cabinet sat down near the casket. Hanna took a chair at the foot of the coffin and slumped over, with his head in his hands for a few moments, then with a visible effort straightened his back and smoothed out his face for the company.

After the services Herman H. Kohlsaat, editor of the Chicago *Times-Herald* and a confidant of both McKinley and Roosevelt, talked seriously to the new Chief Executive, at forty-two the youngest man ever to sit in the White House.

Roosevelt told Kohlsaat, confidentially, that he planned to replace Hay and Gage in the Cabinet. The editor was shocked: the stock exchange had closed on news of McKinley's death. To be sure, it was Saturday and the weekend had halted any possible panic, but the whole financial world was uneasy.

"What will happen when they open tomorrow?" Kohlsaat asked. Roosevelt had better remember that Wall Street thought of him as the "bucking bronco" of finance. If he fired Secretary Gage, whom would he appoint—some scatterbrain?

"It will probably cause a panic, and it will be known for all time as the 'Roosevelt Panic,' " the Chicago man warned.

Roosevelt made a wry face, then in the high falsetto that sometimes overcame him in emotion, said, "Old man, I am going to pay you the highest compliment I ever paid anyone in my life. I am going to keep both of them."

A few minutes later the new President burst into the parlor where the six cabinet officers were waiting to hear their fate, and announced grandly: "I have changed my mind. I am going to keep all of you."

The "Roosevelt Panic" was over.

For the next few days the executive business of government got slight attention. All honors had to be paid the dead President. First a special train would bear McKinley's body to Washington. Then the late President would be returned to his family home in Canton, Ohio, for burial.

On Monday, September 16, the funeral train left Buffalo for the thirteen-hour trip to Washington.

One coach was occupied by the presidential party, another by McKinley's friends, including Senator Hanna, and a third by the press. About two hours out of Buffalo a worn, bitter Mark Hanna unburdened himself to the sympathetic Kohlsaat.

"I told William McKinley it was a mistake to nominate that wild man at Philadelphia. I asked him if he realized what would happen if he should die. Now, look! That damned cowboy is President of the United States!"

It was a case of mutal misunderstanding.

Roosevelt complained that Hanna "treats me like a boy. He calls me Teddy." Roosevelt had nothing against Hanna, but it was hard to get along with a man who showed such obvious dislike.

Again, editor Kohlsaat tried to smooth things over. Did Roosevelt realize how powerful Hanna really was? Did he know that Hanna held the Republican organization in the palm of his hand? Did he know that if Roosevelt had an open breach with Hanna his administration would never get a measure Hanna didn't want through the Senate?

Roosevelt realized what he had to do.

Kohlsaat took the invitation for a private dinner to Hanna. After all, the senator had just lost his best friend. He was heartbroken. Roosevelt owed it to himself, and to Hanna, to try to make peace.

Hanna was outraged. "That damned cowboy wants me to take supper with him alone! Damn him!" But even Senator Hanna did not easily refuse the invitation of the President of the United States. He went to the President's drawing room—alone.

Roosevelt swallowed his pride. He told Hanna he wanted him for a friend.

"I will be your friend on two conditions," said the senator, taking the President's hand. "First, that you carry out McKinley's policies, as you promised."

"All right, I will," Roosevelt replied.

"Second, that you quit calling me 'old man.' If you don't, I'll call you Teddy."

"All right," Roosevelt grinned. "You call me Teddy, and I'll call you 'old man.'"

After dinner Hanna went back to his own car.

"He's a pretty good little cuss, after all," said the mighty senator.

The war was won, without a battle. From that day on, Roosevelt and Hanna respected one another, although Roosevelt was never to forget the political lesson. He began building a personal political organization loyal to him, and to root the tradition that the President is the leader of his political party in every sense.

That week, although he was busy with funerary affairs, President Roosevelt moved his family to the White House. The six children filled the mansion to overflowing; rooms in the basement had to be converted for staff use. But they made do, and by the end of the week the Roosevelt administration was in full swing. The President returned from the final ceremonies at Canton on Friday at nine-thirty in the morning. At ten he was meeting with Navy Secretary John D. Long, at ten-thirty with Secretary of State Hay, at eleven the new President held his first cabinet meeting. At twelve forty-five he discussed the Cuban situation with Secretary of War Root and Governor General Wood. At one-thirty he lunched with Hay. At four he met his first group of courtesy callers.

The murder of McKinley had made the men around the President nervous. They urged Roosevelt to take more precautions, and in his own way Roosevelt did. He almost always carried a large revolver with him.

"If any man is willing to give his life for mine," Roosevelt said, "there is no way that he can be prevented from making the attempt. But such a man must be quicker than I am in the use of his gun."

The first Roosevelt administration started slowly. Roosevelt had to have some time to get his feet on the ground. Within a few months he had begun fighting the great trusts that controlled the American business and industry. By 1904 some 236 such combinations had been established with a capitalization of more than $6,000,000,000. Roosevelt took the trusts seriously. Perhaps he was not very successful in breaking them up, but he was very successful in calling them to the attention of the public and making a political issue of Big Business. It was an idea he stole from the Democrats. In their platform of 1900 the Democrats had demanded that the affairs of the trusts in interstate commerce be made public. Roosevelt went them one better. He asked Congress to create a Department of Commerce, with a bureau of corporations that had the authority to investigate the history and practices of trusts. The trusts continued to grow, but Roosevelt's chief "trust buster," Herbert Knox Smith, began telling the American people what they were doing.

The next steps were to enforce the existing Sherman law, a clumsy statute, and to seek new legislation to control these vast combinations. Attorney General Philander C. Knox won an anti-trust suit against the Northern Securities railroad trust in 1904. The company was forced to dissolve, to the consternation of Wall Street, which saw an untimely end facing the hundreds of other monopoly groups that controlled business and industry.

Backed by public opinion, the Roosevelt administration gained in power.

The spring of 1902 brought a bitter strike in the anthracite fields of Pennsylvania. The mine operators, joined in the coal trust, would not negotiate in good faith with the United Mine Workers Union. The miners would not go back to work. Mark Hanna tried to talk sense into the heads of the operators, but with no success. Summer wore into fall. Still no settlement and the nation was beginning to suffer. Roosevelt decided to step in.

At a conference in Washington, President John Mitchell of the Mine Workers offered to submit the union's case to arbitration. The operators suggested that the President send troops into the coal fields to break the strike. The President had another idea. He would seize the mines in the public interest.

The operators were aghast but frightened enough of "that wild man" in the White House to yield to arbitration. Nobody was fooled by their acceptance of arbitration at the eleventh hour.

In 1901 the Hay-Pauncefote Treaty was ratified by the United States and Britain, after a good deal of nervous haggling on Britain's part. The treaty acknowledged the right of the United States to put a canal through the Panamanian isthmus and to operate it thereafter. In the politics of creating the canal the American government also carved a new Panamanian Republic out of Colombia, but that was not unusual for the times. While it provided the Democrats and wild-eyed radicals with something to shout about, Roosevelt's popularity continued to grow. By the time the election campaigns opened in 1904, Roosevelt was as good as nominated. He was the strongest political figure in the land.

Roosevelt managed to get along well enough with Mark Hanna, after the incident of the funeral train. There were some—not the least of them in and about Wall Street—who tried to get Hanna to run for the presidency himself. But Hanna was a shrewd politician. He knew Roosevelt was practically unbeatable. He also knew that Roosevelt had wrested control of the Republican party away from the Republican National Committee. It was done openly enough, by appointment and cultivation, and there was not a thing in the world that Hanna or anyone else could do about it. Roosevelt was condemned, of course, by members of his own party for not following the advice of the politicos in his appointments. His answer was that he agreed to consult the party, and did. He had not and would not agree to do everything they told him to do.

In 1903, Roosevelt began his campaign for the nomination of 1904, inviting politicians to the White House in order to consolidate his position. It wasn't that he distrusted Hanna. He didn't want to be under obligation to any man for his job. T.R. could not forget the power Hanna had exerted when he entered the White House.

Senator Joseph Foraker, Hanna's rival for control of the Ohio Republican machine, proposed that the party's state convention of 1903 endorse Roosevelt for the 1904 nomination. Foraker's shrewd maneuver put Hanna on the spot. Either Hanna could go along, which would throw Ohio local power into Foraker's hands, or Hanna could oppose the resolution, which would destroy him with Roosevelt. He tried to play it down the middle. Poor Hanna! Roosevelt was not that trusting a soul. T.R. saw his chance to pick up the commitment of another delegation. When Hanna wired him that the issue had been presented in such a way that the Ohioan would have to oppose it, Roosevelt was most unsympathetic. "Those who favor my administration and my nomination will favor endorsing both, and those who do not will oppose."

Hanna now had no real choice, unless he wanted to fight Roosevelt. He did not. The resolution was introduced, Hanna did not oppose it, and consequently Hanna lost a good deal of political influence and political power in his own state.

But it was to make very little difference. Mark Hanna was to be no help or hindrance to Roosevelt in the campaign of 1904.

On February 13, 1904, Mark Hanna died of typhoid fever and its complications. In those last days at the Arlington Hotel, Roosevelt was a frequent visitor to the tough old man, who had refused to give up lobster Newburg and other fancy foods even though his doctors had said they would kill him. There were few dry eyes among Hanna's acquaintances. For Hanna, the hard-bitten, cynical politician, was in the end a well-loved man, not the least-loved by the President.

Hanna's death left Roosevelt the undisputed leader of the party. A new chairman was needed. Roosevelt selected George Cortelyou, once McKinley's private secretary and now Secretary of Commerce and Labor in the Roosevelt cabinet. Senator Platt of New York opposed the Cortelyou nomination. So did the other party bosses. But Roosevelt, who had a few scores to settle with Mousy Platt, didn't give a hang, and if there was any doubt as to who was running the party Cortelyou's appointment settled it.

Hanna's death had another effect. The big-money contributors of the party, who had been trying to sink Roosevelt, suddenly began to try to influence him.

So it was when the Republican National Convention met in Chicago on June 21. Roosevelt controlled it, Roosevelt selected the temporary chairman, Elihu Root, his Secretary of War, and as permanent chairman Joseph G. Cannon, Speaker of the House of Representatives and a powerful Roosevelt ally.

It was all very unexciting. The platform was notable because it said so little about the problems of the day. The Big Issue—said the Republicans—was that everything was just fine. If this was not true it didn't seem to make much difference. Theodore Roosevelt had captured the hearts of the people. By slightly different means he had captured the mechanism of the Republican party. The delegates at Chicago, many of whom would have voted for anyone else, found that there was no one else to vote for.

Charles W. Fairbanks, the senior senator from Indiana, was nominated, unanimously, for Vice-President.

The platform paid lip service to the legality of the trusts and to the principle of high tariff. Roosevelt was really committed to neither policy. If he did not fight here, it was because he had battles that interested him more.

The Democrats met July 6 in St. Louis, but it was not the same party that had met in 1896 and 1900. They no longer swooned when the clear bell-like voice of William Jennings Bryan spoke of silver and gold. Two defeats had tarnished the metal issue. The conservatives were more persuasive than the silver men this year, and when the platform was stuck together there was no mention at all of the monetary issue. It had not been forgotten, but the sharp fighting in committee had been compromised in the interest of party unity.

Bryan was not a candidate this year. But he had torn the gold plank out of the platform after an impressive fight in committee, although he could not force a silver plank in. And Bryan, who still commanded the loyalty and love of the rank and file of the Democratic party, saved his nominating speech for the last.

First he eulogized himself. "You cannot deny that I have kept the faith."

This brought a great, enthusiastic, and really spontaneous demonstration.

Then he nominated Senator Cockrell of Missouri, a most unlikely candidate.

The name fell with a dull thud on the convention floor.

William Randolph Hearst, the free-swinging publisher who hated the trusts and championed the cause of organized labor, was also a candidate in 1904. Hearst was popular with the less conservative party members. But they were not in power; the convention was well stacked by the eastern political bosses and the conservatives who were running the party this year.

The conservative candidate was Judge Alton B. Parker, an eminently sane, eminently respectable, and abominably dull jurist from New York. Parker was nominated on the first ballot by 658 votes to 200 for Hearst, with a scattered 140 for the rest of the field. Even before the result was declared several delegations began changing their votes—for it took only 667 to nominate.

On July 7, Parker was sitting at his home in the little Hudson River village of Esopus, New York, chatting with newspapermen about the prospects of a new railroad station at Esopus, when the nomination was declared unanimous. He hadn't even bothered to have a special wire put in the house, but depended on the tenuous telephone connections of the village switchboard.

Having nominated its candidate and conducted a careful twenty-eight-minute spontaneous demonstration, the Democratic convention adjourned for the day.

The next morning the delegates reassembled to nominate a vice-presidential candidate. Waiting for them was a telegram from their new standard-bearer.

"I regard the gold standard as firmly and irrevocably established, and I shall act accordingly if the action of the convention today is ratified by the people," said Parker. "Inasmuch as the platform is silent on the subject, I deem it necessary to make this communication to the convention for its consideration, as I should feel it my duty to decline the nomination except with that understanding."

It was typical of their man: straightforward, scrupulous, and naïve.

The Parker telegram gave Bryan a re-entry, for it panicked the convention, which had not easily forgotten its two-time fight for silver. If the old pros had not managed a temporary adjournment Parker might well have been discarded, right then and there.

A reply was framed, but when the convention met again, Bryan tried to amend the reply, to save some of silver's strength. Finally, after having made several handsome but ineffective speeches, Bryan withdrew all opposition and sat down.

The battle within the party was won by the conservatives, but Bryan's retirement to his lonely tent convinced his followers that he had been outmaneuvered, that the Democratic party was in the hands of the economic royalists—"plutocrats," they called them. This was the end of Parker. Without personality, and now without the support of the one man in the party who had personality to spare, Parker was sunk.

The Democratic platform attacked the Republicans for entering into "entangling alliances." They favored both capital and labor. They sniped at Teddy Roosevelt's party giving, even though he paid for it out of his own pocket. But none of this was a substitute for a strong candidate.

The Democrats had it coming and going in espousal of an open door for world commerce in the Orient, without entanglement in Oriental and European affairs. They opposed colonialism. They favored freedom for the Philippines. They denounced the tariff and the trusts, demanded more of the reclamation T.R. was giving them, condemned the polygamy of Utah, favored direct election of United States senators, favored the Monroe Doctrine, and reduction of army and navy expenses.

The Republican administration, said the Democrats, was "spasmodic, erratic, sensational, spectacular, and arbitrary."

It was all those things, and apparently the people loved it. Or if they did not, they had little choice, for the Democrats had sidestepped the real economic issues of the day as neatly as had the Republicans.

The Social Democratic party of America again nominated Eugene Debs. The Socialists were just what they said they were; they pledged fidelity to the principles of international socialism. They also wanted more pay, less work, the income tax, women's suffrage, the initiative, the referendum, and the recall.

The Prohibitionists, at Indianapolis on June 29, nominated Silas Swallow of Pennsylvania and George Carroll of Texas on a platform that had a few new elements, too. The drys demanded justice "to all combinations of capital and labor," "wise application" of the initiative and referendum, direct election of senators, reform of the divorce laws, and "total overthrow of the present shameful system of the illegal sanction of the *social evil*, with its unspeakable traffic in girls by the municipal authorities of almost all our cities." Prostitution had become a political issue.

In July, meeting in New York as usual, the Socialist Labor party nominated Charles H. Corregan. All thirty-eight delegates assembled in Grand Central Palace in New York, on July 3 and conveniently divided the nation into moneyed and working class, demanding the "unconditional surrender of the capitalist class."

What was left of the Populists met in Springfield, Illinois, on July 4. The Democrats had raided their membership, stolen their issues, and corrupted their program. This year, 1904, Thomas E. Watson of Georgia was nominated for President, Thomas H. Tibbles of Nebraska for Vice-President.

The campaign of 1904 was the dullest since the Civil War. Teddy Roosevelt was colorful enough, but there was nothing to bring out the fighting qualities that made him glow, until the very end. Judge Parker was much too sedate to engage in the kind of political fisticuffs Teddy loved.

The platforms of the two major parties were such tiresome documents they did not even clash with enough vigor to make sparks.

Finally, there was one spark. Judge Parker noted that George Cortelyou, the Republican national chairman, had resigned as Secretary of Commerce and Labor to direct the campaign. As secretary, Cortelyou had access to a great deal of confidential information about the trusts. Parker charged that the Republicans were now using this information to blackmail contributions from the big-money men of the country.

Roosevelt waited until three days before the election to answer. Then he said Parker's statement was "unqualifiedly and atrociously false" and challenged him to prove it. Parker had neither the time nor the inclination to pick himself off the floor before the ballots were in and counted.

But the fact is that there was a certain truth to the charge. The big corporations had contributed $1,400,000 to the Republican campaign—all but a half million dollars of the total campaign fund. And while, in the beginning, to Roosevelt's knowledge, the national committee had not approached the men under investigation by the Administration for trust manipulation, those men had contributed, undoubtedly hoping to buy off the investigations.

That came out—but after the November election. The Democrats claimed they had been promised a $4,000,000 campaign fund from J. P. Morgan and the other Roosevelt-hating men of business, if they nominated a safe and sane man. They had nominated that man, but the money didn't materialize. Instead, they learned, J. P. Morgan had made his deal with Roosevelt.

On election day Roosevelt went to Oyster Bay, Long Island, to vote, then back to the White House that same night. First, the returns from Buffalo and Rochester, New York, showed great gains for Roosevelt over the McKinley pattern of 1900. Within the next few minutes he heard from Chicago, Connecticut, New York, and Massachusetts. It was obvious that a landslide was in the making. By the time the President sat down to dinner at seven-thirty, his election was assured.

The next day the Democrats began picking up the pieces. The Republicans had 58 seats in the Senate, 250 in the House; but the Democrats had 32 in the Senate and 136 in the House. Roosevelt had polled 7,620,331 votes to Parker's 5,079,041; and had won 336 electoral votes to Parker's 140.

Roosevelt's majority was the largest ever given to a presidential candidate. Roosevelt had carried every one of the thirteen western states, most of which had gone to free silver's Bryan in the past two elections.

If the Democrats could take any comfort it was from the strange fact that the Roosevelt who won was more like a Democrat than the Parker who lost. It was cold comfort.

But at least the Democrats still had a party, and they had polled nearly six and a half million votes. The real disaster of 1904 fell on the Populist party, which had its own candidate, unlike 1896 and 1900 when the party supported Bryan. The Populists polled only 113,258 votes, while even the Debs Socialists won 402,000.

Indicative of the fate of third-party candidates, perhaps, was the advertisement that was running in the New York newspapers that fall, an advertisement that featured J. B. Weaver, first Greenback candidate, the man who had polled enough votes to frighten both Republicans and Democrats in 1880. In 1904, twenty-four years after that impressive display, Weaver got his picture in the papers by endorsing a catarrh remedy called Pe-Ru-Na.

14

The Populists were dying now, although some would never forget and would rise to fight again under the farm and Progressive labels.

Teddy Roosevelt won all of America with his bluff, dashing, and yet patently honest ways. The era of worship of adventure and the great outdoors fitted right in T.R.'s pocket, and he fitted the era like a glove.

Thomas Edison and the Curies, muckraker Lincoln Steffens and novelist Henry James thrilled the nation in their several ways. The Wrights had progressed beyond gliders to fly an airplane at Kitty Hawk in the fall of 1903 and were now perfecting the device. They had wild visions of airfields dotting the nation, and airplanes as common as railroad trains. The Russians and Japanese had gone to war, and the Japanese victory bought a new respect for the yellow man, and with it, fear.

America's eyes turned anxiously around the western hemisphere, where the demise of Spain as a power was leaving chaos and from which sprang a succession of "banana republics."

Across the Atlantic the Russian people were ready to rebel, and in 1905 they did. The social revolution was stamped out by the Tsar's forces.

In the United States there was more consciousness of the rights of man than ever before, but concern for those rights and the responsibilities of the government to the governed was best illustrated at home. . . .

14. The Radical's Friend
1908

Theodore Roosevelt's "second term" often brought the people of
the United States to their feet cheering. It struck gloom into the
people of Wall Street. This was the era of Progress; it meant redress
of many corporate wrongs, and government interference with the
rights of business to monopolize, gouge, restrain trade, squeeze and
cheat. American business needed that restraint. It had gone too far,
and was now collecting its comeuppance. But Roosevelt was a reformer, not a revolutionary, even though he was pictured in
moneyed circles as a wild man.

Roosevelt had aroused the people to the need for law enforcement
against the rich as well as the poor. If he fought monopoly (and
the fight against monopoly was the running battle of both of
Theodore Roosevelt's administrations), he did so to preserve the
capitalist system. For Roosevelt regarded himself as a conservative,
protecting the constitutional system against the excesses of the very
rich.

In November 1906 the federal government brought suit against
the Standard Oil Company under the Sherman anti-trust laws. At
about the same time, the Department of Justice began an investigation of Edward H. Harriman's Union Pacific Railroad.

A Republican campaign committeeman called Harriman for a congressional campaign contribution. Harriman refused him a dime. He
told the caller that he had no interest in a Republican victory; quite
the contrary, since the Republicans were attacking the corporations,
he hoped the Democrats would win.

The Republican pleaded his case: The Democrats were much
more hostile to the big corporations than the Republicans. All
Roosevelt was doing was to refuse the corporations improper favors.

If the Democrats won, the capitalists would have more to fear.

Harriman brushed off the argument. He was not afraid. If he needed legislation, he said, it was a simple enough matter to buy enough senators and congressmen or state legislators to protect himself. If he had to he could buy the judges too.

But with people, rather than railroaders, Roosevelt was more popular than ever, by the end of the second administration. His fight to regulate the railroads and the oil companies, his backing of laws to protect the consumer against unclean foods and dangerous drugs, his visionary conservation practices—all had endeared Roosevelt to the voters.

But the President had lost the chance to run again. He had trapped himself with the phrase "second term." Roosevelt had served all but six months of McKinley's second term, to be sure, but it was not necessarily, under the political customs of the United States, Roosevelt's *first* term. When he took office Theodore Roosevelt had blithely ignored Bryan's request that he abnegate any kind of second term, a request delivered on one of those first feverish days after the death of the assassinated McKinley. But on November 8, 1904, when the election returns rolled in, giving Roosevelt an overwhelming majority, emotion overcame political sense and Theodore Roosevelt volunteered a statement to the press.

"The wise custom which limits the President to two terms," he said, "regards the substance and not the form, and under no circumstances will I be a candidate for or accept another nomination."

Roosevelt was to regret that statement, long before his first elected term was over. "I would cut my hand off right there," he once told a friend, pointing to his wrist, "if I could recall that written statement."

Since he could not recall it the next best thing Theodore Roosevelt could do was pick his own successor, subject, of course, to the approval of the voters. He wanted a man who would follow his own bent, a man who had no regard for money as such, who had great regard for power and would follow Roosevelt's "Square Deal" more heartily than Roosevelt had followed the McKinley program from 1901 to 1905.

The most likely personality seemed to be Elihu Root, who had become Secretary of State after the death of John Hay in 1905. Roosevelt and Root were in agreement on reform. Roosevelt had a high regard for Root. Once he said he would walk on his hands and knees to see Root made President. Yet this was impossible, for Root was a corporate man, and as such was distrusted by the West. He could never be nominated, said Roosevelt's advisers.

Governor Charles Evans Hughes was another possibility. Hughes was an astute politician. He had risen high in Republican circles in New York. But Hughes was too aloof for Roosevelt's taste, and too much his own man for Roosevelt to believe he would carry forward the Roosevelt policy.

There was William Howard Taft, who seemed to fit the Roosevelt pattern admirably. Taft had originally been a protégé of McKinley but came to national prominence as a Roosevelt man. Taft came from a wealthy Cincinnati family. His father, Alphonso, had been an ambassador and the Secretary of War in President Grant's cabinet of 1876. Taft had been appointed governor of the Philippines, at a time when the Philippines were much in the news, and had acquired a considerable reputation as an able administrator. He was big—six feet two inches—fat—almost three hundred and fifty pounds—amiable and able, and while Taft professed complete adherence to Roosevelt's policies, he appealed greatly to the hungry conservatives in the Republican party, men who had felt cheated since the death of McKinley, men who shivered when they contemplated the great strength of the roughriding Roosevelt.

Roosevelt had known Taft since the '90s, when Theodore Roosevelt was Civil Service Commissioner and Taft was Solicitor General of the United States.

Roosevelt liked Taft, he chose him as Secretary of War in 1904, and began to build him up as heir apparent to the presidency. Taft, on his part, had no desire to be President. He wanted to be Chief Justice of the United States Supreme Court. But Mrs. Taft wanted to be Mrs. President, and the quiet fat man was persuaded by his wife and his friend to become the Crown Prince of the Roosevelt second administration.

Taft assumed the mantle in all earnestness.

He stood unswervingly for the Roosevelt policy. If defeated because he was close to Roosevelt, Taft said, then he ought to be defeated. But first he had to get the Republican nomination. While this did not seem too great a problem since Roosevelt was strong enough to pick his successor, still certain plans had to be made.

Roosevelt sent William Loeb, his private secretary, and Frank

Hitchcock, the Assistant Postmaster General, out to sew up convention votes for Taft.

One of the first jobs was to secure the support of the Republicans of Ohio, Taft's home state. This was not as easy as it looked, because Senator Joseph B. Foraker, who had wrested a certain amount of power away from Mark Hanna in 1903, did not want Taft as his candidate.

At the end of July in 1907, the Ohio Republican State Central Committee endorsed Taft, over Foraker's outright objections. Foraker then tried to make a deal with Taft, to trade support for Taft's candidacy for Taft's support of Foraker for re-election to the Senate. But Taft refused him flatly.

One embryo politician was involved in this fracas. Warren G. Harding, the publisher of the Marion *Star,* had run successfully for the state senate some years before and was slowly becoming a figure in Ohio Republican politics. At first Harding sided with Foraker, but, seeing how the wind was blowing, he jumped into the Taft camp. Taft's strength in his own state was now assured.

There was, of course, talk of a third term, but Roosevelt put the thought resolutely behind him.

At first the Taft campaign for the nomination did not go so well, to the delight of the reluctant candidate. "The so-called boom for your humble servant," he wrote in his diary ". . . is now having all the gas let out of the bag."

But Roosevelt secured the help of Taft's half brother, Charles P. Taft, who put up a considerable amount of money for the pre-convention campaign and set up headquarters both in Washington and Cincinnati. Roosevelt appointed strong Taft supporters to strategic federal jobs, to give them plenty of time and opportunity to work for Taft's nomination.

In January 1908, dining with the Tafts one evening, Roosevelt relaxed after dinner in the library, threw himself back in an easy chair. Closed his eyes, and said:

"I am the seventh son of a seventh daughter. I have clairvoyant powers. I see a man standing before me weighing about three hundred and fifty pounds. There is something hanging over his head. I cannot make out what it is; it is hanging by a slender thread. At one time it looks like the presidency—then again it looks like the chief justiceship."

"Make it the presidency," cried Mrs. Taft.

"Make it the chief justiceship," exclaimed Mr. Taft.

Roosevelt was determined that it should be the presidency. By the end of April a clear majority of the 980 votes in the coming Republican National Convention was already pledged to Taft.

By mid-spring the Republican party was divided into two camps; the Taft men and the anti-Taft men, who gathered around Hughes as their only possible savior. The anti-Taft men did all they could to attract the special-interest votes within the party. To woo the Jews they indicated that Taft was anti-Semitic, they said he was anti-Negro; they claimed he had soiled the memory of U. S. Grant, they attacked him as anti-labor. But it was just so much wailing. Taft's strength continued to grow, as Roosevelt discouraged the third-term boom.

Taft was respected in Wall Street, although General Stewart Woodford, head of the Hughes movement, charged "Wall Street wants Taft, fearing that if they don't get Taft they may have Roosevelt for another term."

The placid giant from Cincinnati had no such appeal for the liberal Republicans. They didn't trust him—so he made a specific effort to charm them. Taft, a gentleman of the old school, a lawyer and club man, encouraged his portrayal as a bluff, hearty man of the people. Justice Brewer of the Supreme Court snorted, "Secretary Taft is the politest man alive," he said. "I heard that recently he rose in a streetcar and gave his seat to three women."

Roosevelt merely encouraged Taft to grin and bear it. "Smile," said the man-with-the-teeth. "I feel that your nature shines out so transparently when you do smile, you big, generous, high-minded fellow."

From spring on, Taft and Bryan, who was sure to get the Democratic bid, were fighting for the presidency, even before their respective conventions.

Fighting too were the bedraggled remnants of the once promising People's party. On April 2 the Populists met at St. Louis to choose their candidate for the presidency. On April 3 the Nebraska and Minnesota delegations began filibustering. Their object was to force the convention to adjourn until after the Democrats met. Then, if the Democrats did not nominate Bryan, these two delegations were sure the Populists would nominate him.

But this year the Populist convention was not buying the Bryan ticket.

T. H. Tibbles, imposing, snowy-haired leader of the Nebraskans, was speaking all around a minor issue before the convention, obviously bent on delaying the proceedings.

Chairman George A. Hanneker of Jersey City noted acidly that he could not understand what Mr. Tibbles was talking about.

"If some people can't understand things, I can't help it," said Mr. Tibbles in some heat.

"The chair cannot furnish you with the English to explain yourself," said Hanneker, fire in his eye.

"Nor can I furnish you with brains to run the convention," said the Nebraskan.

"The chair is fully aware that the gentleman cannot furnish brains," said Mr. Hanneker.

By this time both gentlemen were glaring and breathing hard. They finally shook hands. That same day Nebraska and Minnesota walked out of the convention when it became obvious that the Bryan cause was lost.

The Populists again espoused the cause of cheap money and government ownership of monopoly utilities; Thomas E. Watson of Georgia was nominated for the presidency. When he heard the news, in Jacksonville, Florida, Mr. Watson took that occasion to announce his antipathy to Negro suffrage. Watson did not believe that the Negro had any more political rights than the Indian or the Chinese. And he cheerfully announced that he was working to eliminate the Negro from American politics.

That same day Taft was in Chicago, making several important speeches. Two days later, on April 6, Taft invaded Bryan's own home state and added insult to injury by referring to Bryan as "the gentleman who still seems to have the power of leading the Democratic party against its will."

The next night Bryan, in Denver, said the charge "comes with poor grace from one whose nomination is being urged by all the President's officeholders."

Charge and countercharge continued for the remainder of the spring. The Socialists nominated Eugene Debs in May, to no one's surprise. In a way, the Socialists were becoming important politically now. They were lashed by Roosevelt, who claimed that only his

Square Deal could prevent the excesses of capitalism from collapsing in its own excesses and throwing the country into the hands of the Socialists. Roosevelt was waving the red flag! But to Wall Street the horrors of Socialism were only slightly removed from the horrors of the Roosevelt Republicanism.

Roosevelt was relaxed as the Republican National Convention met in Chicago on June 16. He had everything his own way. If he was not to have the presidency again, it was because he was determined to abide by his own word; he could have had the nomination for the asking.

The President's candidate was a shoo-in. On the day before the convention opened, Republican Herbert Parsons of New York telegraphed Governor Hughes in Albany, asking if Hughes wanted to withdraw before the state caucus since it was sure to be Taft on the first ballot. But Hughes refused, still hoping for that outside chance.

At Chicago's Union League Club, Speaker Joe Cannon was fuming at the "radicals" who were trying to force through an anti-injunction plank as the Republicans considered their platform. The same plank would exempt unions from the provisions of the Sherman anti-trust law.

Roosevelt cheerfully accepted responsibility for the final platform. He had dictated it. He was, as much as Andrew Jackson in his day, the real dictator of this convention, and the conservatives of the party could do nothing to stop him.

Nothing went wrong. The Ohio delegation showed up with a handsome portrait of Taft, as was expected, Roosevelt was cheered as expected, although the demonstration lasted forty-one minutes, frightening the Taft group. The candidates were nominated. The voting was to begin. Then a last-ditch attempt to nominate Roosevelt was staged. This was not expected. John Seibert, an elevator operator in the Capitol building, arose in his seat in the gallery and opened an umbrella revealing a likeness of Roosevelt. A chant began to swell through the house:

"Four - years - more"
"Four - years - more"
"Four - years - more"

The chant flourished, it rose and rose and it stopped the show. For precious minutes nothing could be done. Chairman Henry Cabot Lodge pounded for order, but the convention paid no attention.

In Washington the Taft family, except Robert Alphonso, who was in Chicago, waited in the Secretary's office in the War Department. Mrs. Taft occupied the Secretary's chair. Taft sat on the side of the room, with a half a dozen friends. Their younger son, Charlie, ran in and out from the outer office, bringing bulletins which he handed to his mother. She read these aloud.

The little group had just heaved a sigh of relief at an announcement that the roll call was about to begin, when Charlie brought in a bulletin that described the Roosevelt explosion.

Mrs. Taft sat white and worried in the Secretary's chair. Taft tapped his fingers and whistled.

Charlie came in with another bulletin—the uproar was continuing.

Several more minutes went by. The Secretary's office was quiet as a tomb.

Then Charlie dashed in with another message—Massachusetts had cast twenty-six votes for Taft.

But what had happened to Alabama, Arizona, California, and the rest? They had voted—but no one had heard them. Convention Chairman Lodge, true to a promise that he would stop any Roosevelt stampede, had started a roll call to stop the stampede. But the hall could not be quieted enough even to hear the gavel pounding until Massachusetts had been reached.

Within a few minutes it was over—Taft on the first ballot. Mrs. Taft breathed a sigh of real relief now.

It was Taft 702 on the first ballot, against a field of six, not one of whom got a hundred votes. The Roosevelt machine had done its job.

All that was left to be decided was the vice-presidency. Taft wanted a western man "who has shown himself conservative and at the same time represents the Progressive movement." The liberal Republicans, led by Robert La Follette of Wisconsin, were very leery of Taft and the party platform. Their demands for direct election of senators and government control of railroad rates had been rejected by the conservative platform committee. Samuel Gompers, the labor leader, had tried to persuade the Republicans to adopt an anti-injunction plank, but the National Association of Manufacturers had fiercely opposed the Gompers plan. When Gompers objected to a compromise plank he was told, "Go to Denver," where the Democrats were going to meet in a few weeks. (He did.)

Moderate Republicans, like Idaho's William E. Borah, plumped for Governor A. B. Cummins of Iowa as a candidate who would convince the La Follette wing of the party that the GOP had not wholly fallen into the hands of the conservatives. But the moderates were shouted down. Sunny Jim Sherman, congressman from New York, notable for his nickname and his political loyalty to the party, was chosen to wear the vice-presidential mantle. The La Follette liberals could hardly have been more convinced that the party was going to the dogs.

Roosevelt was well pleased. Strangely enough, so were the movers and shakers of American business.

"Good," said old J. P. Morgan as he got the news on the gangplank of the S.S. *Mauretania*.

A telegram of congratulations came from John D. Rockefeller.

A contribution of $20,000 arrived from Andrew Carnegie.

Mrs. Taft was well pleased, too. Everyone seemed to be, in fact, except William Howard Taft, who wanted to be Chief Justice of the United States Supreme Court. To Taft it was all a nightmare, and as he faced each awful day, he called on Roosevelt for advice and assistance.

Roosevelt stepped in. It is doubtful if he could have been kept out, for he had created the political Taft, in a sense, and now he wanted to be sure to elect him.

Taft was no Roosevelt; he knew it better than Teddy did, and he was discouraged sometimes, by the kind attentions of his mentor, who tried to remake him in the Rooseveltian image. In his acceptance speech Taft laid out for the careful observer the points of political difference that would arise between himself and the progressives of the party. He saw the coming four years as a breathing spell. He promised what Wall Street had been demanding: an end to new legislation that changed the status of business. This was construed by Roosevelt to mean that Roosevelt had made the necessary changes, and Taft planned to keep things in line. It was construed by the business moguls to mean an end to the legislative nibbling at their coattails.

Businessmen were happy with the choice of Taft. Now, to beat that rascal William Jennings Bryan.

The Democratic party's twentieth national convention was to be held in Denver on July 7. There was as little doubt of the outcome of the meeting as there had been at the Republican convention. Bryan was back in control of the party. The conservatives had enjoyed their seizure of party power in 1904, only to be buffeted even more severely than the liberal wing had been in 1896 and 1900. Especially now that the Republicans had chosen Taft, the Democrats moved back to Bryanism, the contrast between the liberal Bryan and Taft was as great as the contrast between Taft and Theodore Roosevelt.

Bryan engaged in open warfare with Colonel James M. Guffey, the Pennsylvania political boss, and tried to have him removed from the Democratic National Committee. The day before the convention the Pennsylvania delegation was to meet in the roof garden of the Adams Hotel in Denver, to resolve their problems. Guffey's men were there. The anti-Guffey delegates came in, asked for a delay until 6 P.M., and marched out.

"Cowards," shouted the Guffey supporters.

"Come down in the alley," called an anti-Guffey man over his shoulder, "and we'll show you whether we're cowards."

There is no record of the Guffey men having taken up the invitation, but they were beaten when the convention credentials committee began meeting the next day.

It was Bryan all the way. The newspapers claimed that every plank in the platform was telephoned to him in Lincoln for approval. At any rate Bryan was running the convention.

Bryan seemed to have learned little from his two previous defeats. In 1907 he had gone to Europe. Just before his return that summer he gave advance warning to the faithful that he would start his campaign for the nomination in Madison Square Garden on August 30. He had discovered a marvelous issue while in Europe, Bryan informed them: government ownership and operation of railroads. That would be the keynote of his campaign.

The conservative Democrats wriggled in agony. They sent a delegation to meet Bryan at ships' quarantine, before the reporters could get hold of him, and talk some sense into that beautiful woolly head.

August 30 came, and a great crowd met at Madison Square Garden. The faithful came to see the hero whose very voice stirred them to the depths of their power-hungry souls. The curious came to see the greatest Democrat of them all. The conservatives came to see if it was really true that Bryan had learned something in the last four years.

The hour of decision approached. Bryan, with the usual flutters in his stomach, rose—the square, manly face pale and the lips a tight line, as always just before he opened his mouth and projected those golden tones. An impressive figure, he looked, as always, every inch the rugged statesman.

Then Bryan began to speak.

". . . I have already reached the conclusion that the railroads partake so much of the nature of a monopoly that they must ultimately become public property and be managed by public officials . . . Public ownership is necessary where competition is impossible."

The shock waves filled the garden. Next day press and politicans attacked bitterly. Soon the statement was recognized as a colossal blunder.

"Poor Bryan," wrote Roosevelt. "I do not know whether I feel more irritated or sympathic with him . . . No private citizen in my time, neither General Grant nor Mr. Blaine, for instance, has been received with such wild enthusiasm on his return from a foreign trip, and in twenty-four hours he made a speech and became an object of indignation and laughter . . ."

Worse than espousing the cause of government ownership, Bryan now tried to back down. Railroad ownership was not an immediate issue, he said lamely, but government might have to take over if regulation proved ineffective.

Conspicuous in restraint of enthusiasm for Bryan were New York, New Jersey, Delaware, Georgia, Minnesota, Maine, and Connecticut. A swaying, shouting Bryan delegate tried to grab the Georgia flag—and was punched in the solar plexus for his trouble. A Tammany bully boy stood guard over the New York standard. He struck two or three Bryan men in the face as they tried to grab the sign. Someone from the crowd wrested the Connecticut sign from the Nutmeggers' hands, but they dived into the mob, elbowed and thrust their way through, and wrenched it back.

At 1:12 A.M. on that second day of the convention Bryan was nominated, prompting the correspondent of the Republican New York *Tribune* to note:

"The most impressive fact of the Democratic National Convention is its absolute unreality. Imagine a thousand delegates and a like number of alternates wildly cheering a candidate whom 75 per cent of them are convinced cannot be elected and at least 30 per cent do not wish to see succeed."

There was more than a grain of truth in those spiteful words.

John W. Kern of Indiana was unanimously chosen for Vice-President. The platform attacked the Republicans for improper use of patronage, arbitrary misuse of executive and legislative power, and imperialism. The Democrats demanded a lower tariff—but so did the Republicans. And the Democrats wanted publicity given to all campaign contributions. The Republicans would agree to publicity only after the election.

The Prohibitionists nominated Eugene W. Chafin of Illinois and A. S. Watkins of Ohio at their convention in Columbus, Ohio, on July 15. They demanded direct election of senators, the imposition of an income tax, stern regulation of corporations, establishment of a tariff commission, a uniform divorce law, child labor laws, universal suffrage, and conservation of natural resources.

Then, along came a new party, formed with the money of William Randolph Hearst, who was totally disaffected with Bryan and the Democratic party. Mr. Hearst's personal organization met in Chicago on July 29, and nominated Thomas Hisgen of Massachusetts (a friend of Hearst) and John Temple Graves of Georgia on an involved and very liberal platform, which included popular election of senators. By now this issue was in every important platform, except the Republican. It had begun, as had many issues, with the minority parties, but public interest had picked up, senatorial election had been adopted by the Democrats. This same pattern of big-party adoption could be traced in many of the platform planks that later became the changes and reforms in governmental processes.

As the campaign began Taft refused to accept a live elephant offered as the symbol of the Republican campaign—possibly because of his own girth and posterior resemblance to the magnificent pachyderm. Bryan gladly took an "educated mule" from the Agricultural Society of Minnesota, particularly since the mule was "said to understand the habits of the elephant."

Taft had hoped to stay at home during the hot summer months. But the big man was to enjoy no such luck. Bryan started off, in his acceptance speech, by asking, "Shall the people rule?"—and indicated that if the Republicans were returned the people would certainly not. A few days later Bryan took to the field, vigorously. He began one trip on August 20, talked tariff in Des Moines on the twenty-first, trusts in Indianapolis on the twenty-fifth, and claimed to be the heir to Roosevelt progressivism in Salem, Illinois, on the twenty-sixth. On the twenty-seventh Bryan called for laws guaranteeing bank deposits.

Bryan made his second trip almost immediately. On August 31 he spoke on Republican extravagance at the Minnesota State Fair in St. Paul. Then he started again on trusts, bank deposits, labor. He was on the road almost continually, speaking at whistle stops, at banquets, at any and all kinds of meetings, back and forth across the country; in New York, which was no longer "enemy country" to him; everywhere, except the Deep South, New England, and the Rocky Mountain states. In Missouri during October, Bryan broke his previous record. He gave twenty-four speeches in one day.

All this activity forced William Howard Taft to lumber forth as the first Republican candidate since Blaine to stump the country. On his first trip the big Republican traveled west to Colorado and returned happy in the feeling that his campaign was moving ahead successfully. Taft was not silver tongued. He read his ponderous speeches, but a pleasant personality served him well, and his infectious grin and chuckle, that started with a wiggling of the stomach, never failed to draw a laugh from the crowd.

Taft was no fighter. He wouldn't wear a roughrider hat, and he wouldn't call names. It was too bad, Roosevelt mused, that Taft didn't have some of the Roosevelt temper, to help him along in the campaign. But to make up for that, Roosevelt campaigned himself, so heartily that he brought forth cries of "foul" from Bryan, who moodily demanded to know why he had to struggle against two Republican candidates.

The Democrats had listened much more sympathetically than the Republicans to Samuel Gompers's plea against the use of the injunction to stop strikes. In his campaign Bryan had charged that Taft was the "father of injunctions in labor cases." Taft answered that he had issued injunctions, but that labor had no more right to disobey the law than the employers. Labor and employers must fight their own battles, without involving the rest of the community, Taft said.

Bryan was delighted when Samuel Gompers stated that Taft represented all the elements opposed to organized labor, and the A. F. of L. leader came out flatly for the Democratic candidate. Gompers had "gone to Denver" with a vengeance, just as the Republicans told him to.

The Democrats smiled happily when Carry Nation called on Taft on September 17 and demanded that he state a position on the menace of alcohol. He refused. Miss Nation flounced out the door, stopping only to proclaim loudly that Taft was an enemy of temperance—and an "infidel." Taft was a Unitarian. Many people thought Unitarians were anti-Christian, and the Democrats were very pleased to let them remain ignorant on this score.

The Democrats were overjoyed when Taft was taken to task for playing golf, described by one critic as a "dude's game." Taft received hundreds of letters protesting this unseemly and unmanly hobby. Roosevelt agreed, warned Taft to soft-pedal the golf stuff as the worst of politics.

The Democrats rubbed their hands when William Randolph Hearst revealed that Senator Joseph Foraker, the Republican leader from Ohio, had been working for the Standard Oil Company while serving as a member of the United States Senate. Foraker had fought Taft, and with this news a planned public reconciliation was dropped like a hot rock.

But Hearst also revealed that Governor Haskell of Oklahoma, Treasurer of the Democratic National Committee, was involved with the gentlemen from Wall Street. Haskell resigned from the committee and dropped out of the campaign. It seemed a standoff, but Teddy Roosevelt stepped in.

Roosevelt had warned the Republican National Committee against accepting any contributions from Harriman, Rockefeller, or any of the "great and moneyed interests" who had opposed the administration with "venomous hostility." He charged that these men were behind Bryan.

Bryan charged that they were behind Taft.

Roosevelt replied that Governor Haskell was a Standard Oil man and that Standard Oil was supporting the Democrats.

Roosevelt and Bryan hurled charge and countercharge. For the moment Taft was forgotten as the two strong men fought it out in the front pages of the newspapers.

The issue was finally settled by John D. Rockefeller, Sr., sitting in his country estate up the Hudson River in New York. Rockefeller was unmindful of the controversy, since he seldom read the newspapers.

With an unerring sense of timing Rockefeller chose this moment to issue a statement in support of Taft and the Republican ticket! The political boomerang struck Roosevelt square in the back of the neck.

T.R. was reduced to helpless spluttering. The country had a good laugh, and the matter was forgotten. It was 1908. Nobody worried much about Standard Oil, the Union Pacific Railroad, or any other big company. Perhaps Bryan could have pushed the big business issue further, but he didn't.

Finally the last words had been said.

Election day was November 3. The weather was clear and cold across the nation. It was, as Chief Willis Moore of the U. S. Weather Bureau wired Taft in Cincinnati, a perfect day "for getting out the Republican country vote." Taft was reassured. The big Republican spent the day quietly at the mansion of his half brother Charles on Pike Street. Finally, at four o'clock in the afternoon, Taft went out to vote.

Bryan had finished off with a half-hour speech to a demonstration in Lincoln. "Our fight is won, and we await the verdict with confidence," Bryan told the press. He had pulled issue after issue out of his bag of tricks. From one end of the country to the other he had worried the Administration as a dog worries a bone. If he had not found one issue that roused the people it was not for lack of trying. But this was not an "issue" year. Bryan closed his last statement with reference to the "tainted" campaign fund of the Republicans. Then he went home to wait.

On election night Bryan sat in the parlor of his home, surrounded by his family and reporters. Taft stayed inside the mansion in Cincinnati. By midnight the result was clear enough. Taft had won, by less than half the lead Roosevelt had amassed four years before, but he had still won by a quarter million votes; 321 electoral votes to Bryan's 162.

In Oyster Bay, a jubilant President watched the telegraphic results with glee. "We have them beaten to a frazzle," he said.

In Lincoln, Bryan came into the sun parlor, where the press

waited. It was the end of a long and weary road for the three-time Democratic candidate.

"I am going to bed, boys," he said. "I am very tired and need rest."

Taft was elected and T.R. made his plans for a well-deserved rest from affairs of state. He would seek the rough-and-tumble life of the outdoors for his rest, naturally.

The automobile was a factor in American life, now. The airplane was still an object of wonder, but the telephone was certainly here to stay, and the electric light.

Explorers were traveling to the darkest and brightest and hottest and coldest corners of the earth, Admiral Robert E. Peary reached the North Pole a few days after Taft took office. Roosevelt, more interested now in adventure than in the political scene, was making his personal plans with the Smithsonian Institution in Washington —for a trip to Africa to hunt big game. Any overflow from T.R.'s bag of trophies would go to the American Museum of Natural History up in New York, a museum T.R.'s father had helped found.

In Europe the Russians and the British and the French had allied themselves in the Triple Entente, and the Germans, who had been living restlessly in the shadow of the British Empire, wanted to expand their colonial possessions.

It was an age of well-being and expansion in almost every way. In the United States reforms and the new force called progressivism were building up steam. . . .

15. That Radical Roosevelt—II
1912

The age of reform continued. Some called it progressivism. Some called it moderate conservatism, but whatever it was called, it was still reform. Big business, which had been lionized in the penny dreadfuls for years, was now whipped up and down the halls of Congress and lesser legislative bodies, while trusts were dissected by the new Interstate Commerce Commission and a few were dissolved by the courts. Magazines and newspapers, sniffing the wind, raked the muck of social and political corruption, and the readers lapped it up and cried for more. Andrew Carnegie and John D. Rockefeller, whose exploitation of available resources had brought them massive wealth, suddenly were overcome with concern for those resources, especially the workingman, and instituted frantic philanthropy to erase the images drawn of them as lustful ogres.

Ragged female and grimy child became objects of deep public concern. The old, the maimed, the widowed, the orphaned were no longer to be scorned or only pitied, but helped. The besotted, boss-ridden laboring man was not just one step above an animal, but had acquired a "dignity," even if he was not always totally equipped to handle it in the local saloon. Poverty, ignorance, disease, and corruption were pronounced curable, and nearly the whole nation was suddenly interested in curing them.

Scores of state governments adopted the referendum, which let the legislature pass the buck to "the people" on controversial legislation; the initiative, which let special-interest groups try to pass laws themselves; the recall, which made elected officers reponsible *all* the time they were in office. A decade before, these had been radical suggestions, offered by splinter parties.

For a time even the Socialists became almost respectable. This atmosphere was fresh sea air to Theodore Roosevelt, who had "bully-ed" and grinned and pounded his way through seven years of storm and sunshine. The atmosphere was confusing to President William Howard Taft, the pleasant giant from Cincinnati, and the change no more suited his slow, deep conservatism than the Chinese robe he sometimes wore as he sat in the presidential chair. Roosevelt the tennis player loved nothing better than to smash the ball into his opponent's court. If he missed the baseline he shrugged. There was always another point coming up. Taft the golfer was deliberate, careful, and ponderously slow on the backswing. Each shot was a matter for individual concern.

Even in the beginning, Roosevelt professed later, he knew that Taft was a mistake. Mistake, hell! He was a disaster, said William Allen White, the Kansas editor, who was even more outspoken than Roosevelt.

Mistake or disaster, it began even during the campaign of 1908. By the time the new President was ready to enter the White House, Roosevelt was still loyal, if leery. He may have had second thoughts now, but this was not the time to say anything. The political Taft was as much a Roosevelt creation as Pinocchio was old Geppetto's.

In making a presidential candidate of Taft, Roosevelt had let the chips scatter far and wide. After the election of 1908 the Republican party was more disunited and bedraggeled than any victorious party ought to be. The progressive wing distrusted Taft and was angry with Roosevelt for foisting the behemoth upon them. More and more Senator Robert La Follette of Wisconsin spoke the thoughts of these liberals. The spittoon-shooting, whisky-drinking, old-line politicos were under the thumb of "Uncle Joe" Cannon, Speaker of the House of Representatives, whose rule was so absolute and so fearsome in Washington that it created a word— Cannonism—a synonym of despotism. The Republicans had a majority of forty-seven in the House of Representatives and a majority of twenty-eight in the Senate, but they had serious differences among themselves too.

This was the legacy Theodore Roosevelt left when he stepped out of the White House in the flaky snow and cold wind of March 4, 1909, such a nasty day the inaugural ceremonies had to be transferred from the Capitol front to the Senate chamber.

Roosevelt had hardly cleared Washington when the story went

around financial circles that Roosevelt was going to Africa—"and Wall Street expects every lion to do his duty." Taft, of course, was pledged to carry out the Roosevelt policies, but he had retained only a pair of the old Roosevelt cabinet members, memory of some general conversations, and what Roosevelt later termed the political coloration of a chameleon. The new men in Cabinet and Congress had ideas of their own, and Taft was a good listener.

If Roosevelt wanted to play the strong, silent adviser (a role for which he was singularly ill cast), bounding off to Africa when the new Administration was scarcely a month old was hardly the way to do it. Taft was described by Senator Jonathan Dolliver of Iowa as "a large body surrounded by men who knew exactly what they wanted." A good many of them—Cannon, Senator Nelson Aldrich of Rhode Island, the right-wing majority leader in the Upper House, not to mention the men of Wall Street and other big contributors to the party—did not want Rooseveltism—which, they said, was almost as bad as Socialism, and maybe even worse, when the ineffable personality of T.R. was thrown into the balance.

Taft was bound to try to follow Roosevelt's policies. Taft tried, but he was not politically adroit, nor did he have the same disrespect for money and power that Roosevelt had. The new President was, in short, a conservative, hardly equipped to carry out a liberal and sometimes rambunctious theory of government.

The first defeat for the Roosevelt program came on the Payne-Aldrich Tariff bill. Taft was committed to revision of the tariff; it had been part of the Republican platform of 1908. The administration bill went into the House hopper whole and came through the Senate deprived of arms, legs, and teeth. Some eight hundred items in the tariff schedule were changed, but the result was a tariff structure a little higher, if anything, than it had been before. The cynical right-wingers defended the new law stoutly. They had said they were going to "revise" the tariff, they grinned. That didn't mean they were going to lower it.

Taft did not bully and push Congress the way Roosevelt would have; Congress was left to fight its own intramural battles, and the public saw confusion in the results. Taft was the scapegoat.

The break with Roosevelt began about a year after Taft took office. Roosevelt's conservation policies had been carried out, to a large extent, by James R. Garfield, Secretary of the Interior. Before inauguration Taft had indicated that he was planning to keep Garfield in the Cabinet, and Roosevelt was satisfied that this would provide continuity of policy. But Taft, instead, appointed Richard Achilles Ballinger, a spoils-system Republican, ardent exponent of free enterprise, who had no sympathy for Roosevelt's policy of maintenance of public lands for public use.

Within a few months Ballinger set out to destroy the Roosevelt conservation plans and there came into open conflict with Gifford Pinchot, a former member of the Roosevelt "tennis cabinet" who was still serving as chief forester in the Department of Agriculture.

The case was well enveloped in mud and personal politics, but the net was that Taft fired Pinchot and kept Ballinger. Pinchot immediately went to Europe to report to his old chief that conservation had been thrown out the window.

When Roosevelt returned to the United States, late in the spring of 1910, the Progressives in the Republican party were disgusted with Taft and were beginning to boom Roosevelt for another term. T.R. wavered. He was still not convinced that Taft was so bad as that, nor was he at all convinced that he wanted to return to the political wars. But how could he stay out? Soon Roosevelt was in a fight for Charles Evans Hughes and the New York governorship against the conservatives. Roosevelt and Hughes lost, but *that* only whetted his appetite for battle.

As the year wore on, Roosevelt accepted more and more speaking engagements. In Denver, in Kansas—wherever he spoke—Roosevelt could not help but speak his mind, and in a column he was now writing for the weekly *Outlook,* a liberal magazine of opinion, the former President took issue with the Administration's departures from Roosevelt Republicanism.

In June 1911, T.R. still pledged himself to Taft. As late as August he said he would not be a candidate for the presidency, although the pressure was increasing. In October, Robert La Follette was proclaimed the candidate of the Progressives in the party, in a meeting of two hundred at Chicago. By this time it seemed extremely doubtful if any Republican could be elected in 1912. Taft and the Republican Congress had caused the voters to change the Republican majority in the House into a Democratic majority of sixty-two in the elections of 1910. In the Senate the Republican majority had been cut to ten. The people had little love for Taft's conservative Republicanism. Taft had little feeling for the political climate of the nation—perhaps because he refused to read newspapers that criticized him.

"I don't care what the other side is doing," Taft once told Mrs. Taft when she took him to task for burying his head in the sand.

It wasn't so much that he didn't care, but that he wanted to—would do almost anything to—avoid unpleasantness.

Early in 1912, Roosevelt made up his mind to run. His old Square Deal—his "New Nationalism"—gave him something to run on. The Progressive-faction leader, Senator La Follette, had given every indication of physical collapse in a speech before a newspaper and magazine publishers' group in Philadelphia. Roosevelt's chances of securing the Republican nomination seemed brighter than they had been. Chances of winning the election were much brighter, if he could count on liberal support.

T.R. announced his candidacy to newspaper reporters in Cleveland, on February 20, 1912, on his way to address the Ohio State Constitutional Convention in Columbus.

A reporter asked the obvious question. Was he going to run for the presidency again?

"My hat's in the ring!" said T.R. "The fight is on and I'm stripped to the buff."

The next night T.R. squared off against all comers. The Ohio convention was shopping among the new reforms for its constitution.

The initiative, the referendum, the recall; all of them were acceptable, if liberal, additions to the body politic. But at the convention Roosevelt now argued the La Follette case. (He had been asked, after La Follette's downfall in Philadelphia, to say something that would give the La Follette men an excuse to come over to him.)

"I believe in pure democracy," T.R. shouted. "Representative government must absolutely represent the people." And among the reforms he advocated was the recall of judicial decisions on constitutional questions, under which the voters after a year could vote down a judicial decision. Only the Supreme Court of the United States could overrule the people.

This was reckless radicalism to the businessmen, the judges, the lawyers, and others of the Republican party who muttered that Roosevelt had now gone radical too.

The Socialists sniffed, as they nominated Eugene Debs again.

Neither Roosevelt nor any of the capitalists, said Debs, had ever spent a day in jail, had ever been hit on the head by a policeman, or had ever produced enough "to feed a gallinipper" (a large mosquito).

The Republican National Convention was scheduled to meet in Chicago on June 18. Ten days before, the national committee began wading through the usual disputes over credentials. It was a conservative national committee, and the outcome was not hard to predict. Senator William Borah of Idaho led the fight for Roosevelt, but it was a losing battle from the beginning. La Follette demanded the loyalty of his men, to the last ditch. If he could not lead the Progressive movement to any kind of victory, then let it die. There were no roll calls in the committee. The Taft men had taken the necessary precautions. It took no less than twenty of the forty-eight members to demand a roll call. Thirty of the forty-eight were committed to Taft.

In the end Senator Borah claimed that fifty-two Roosevelt delegates were unjustly deprived of their seats by a national committee packed for Taft. The deprived ones included Cecil Lyon of Texas, a member of the national committee, who had been so unwise as to support Roosevelt.

Finally, Roosevelt could stand it no longer; so, wearing a new felt hat and a screaming necktie, the old Rough Rider rode into Chicago on June 15 on a Pullman car, jumped off the train, and began shaking hands with everyone in sight.

It was unprecedented for an announced candidate to appear in the city of the convention to plump for himself, but this was an unusual year, and Roosevelt was far from a usual candidate. He had charged across the country shouting that Taft had "stolen" the nomination and had arrived at headquarters to tell his leaders "what they must do to prevent the control of the convention by the thieves, robbers, and highbinders who would steal the people's liberties."

Roosevelt marched off to the Congress Hotel, serenaded by a German band, and up to a suite of rooms overlooking Lake Michigan. The next day one caller was William Jennings Bryan, the lifelong (as his enemies charged) Democratic candidate. Bryan was attending the Republican convention, again ostensibly as a newspaperman, although it was regarded as possible that he had some political interest as well.

On this weekend Taft's campaign managers claimed 590 votes for the incumbent but secretly worried about the Roosevelt raids on the Negro delegates. They had to house, feed, and guard them carefully to keep the Roosevelt men from buying their votes. The Reverend Dr. James W. Shumport, a delegate from the first district of Mississippi, said he had been offered $1000 for his vote. He wouldn't sell. Others were less candid.

The Taft Republicans feared that the Roosevelt Republicans would make a physical attempt to take over the convention. Governor Dineen of Illinois was ready to call out the National Guard to prevent such a coup. The Taft men of the national committee made arrangements for a greatly reinforced police guard. And even the platform of the convention hall was protected. Underneath the bunting, concealed but viciously effective, the railings and posts were wrapped tightly with barbed wire.

Jaunty old ex-Senator Chauncey Depew, now of the New York Central Railroad, was on hand. Newspapermen reported that Taft men said they had a forty majority; Roosevelt men said they had a forty majority. What did it all mean? "That means there are at least eighty liars in the convention," Depew chortled, twitching his heavy white eyebrows and stroking his muttonchop whiskers.

The convention opened on schedule, on June 18. The meeting was somber enough to begin with. The convention was scheduled to begin at twelve, and the chairman, diminutive Victor Rosewater of the national committee, began dutifully banging his gavel on schedule.

It took half an hour to get order, but not for the usual reasons. There were no demonstrations for candidates or potential candidates, there was no applause for any Republican who walked into the hall, no matter how prominent he might be. There was no demonstration for the Californians' gay silk banner, which bore a gold Teddy bear and the motto, "The People Must Rule." Mostly there was the hubbub of a thousand voices, pitched low enough, but talking quickly and earnestly in dead seriousness.

Thirty minutes of gaveling, and Chairman Rosewater got his order. The first business was establishment of a temporary organization. Elihu Root, once Roosevelt's Secretary of War, but now his bitter enemy, was to be temporary chairman, said the Taft men.

Roosevelt men in the contested seats were to be replaced by Taft men, said the national committee.

Not so, said the Roosevelt men. Francis E. McGovern of Wisconsin, a La Follette Progressive, was to be chairman of the convention. Roosevelt delegates were to replace Taft delegates.

It was hardly a contest. The Taft steam roller was already working. Amid cries of "thief," "robber," and "stolen goods," laced with catcalls and stiffened with boos, Root was elected chairman, 558 to 501. The course of the convention was clear.

"Believe me, I appreciate this expression of confidence," said Mr. Root, on ascending to the chair.

"Are you willing to take an election that was stolen?" shouted a Roosevelt boss from Pennsylvania, shaking his fist and the "Thou Shalt Not Steal" badge on his lapel.

Root narrowed on the heckler. For six hours the convention had been arguing, sometimes seemed almost at blows. The delegate would either quiet down, or Root would have the police throw him out of the convention. The silent force of Chicago police stood by, ready to do the chairman's bidding. The Taft machine was really in control.

While the convention steamed, Taft sat quietly in the grandstand at the Washington baseball park, watching the Washington Senators flatten the Philadelphia Athletics, to move into second place in the American League, a game and a half behind the Boston Red Sox. Not a care in the world.

A "moderate progressive," Root called President Taft the next day, as the steamroller whipped the Roosevelt men again in an all-day fight on the convention floor. Taft played eighteen holes at the Chevy Chase Club with his son Robert.

The convention spent three days confirming its temporary roll call, three days without a single inspiring address, three days without unity or purpose, except the determination of the Taft men to nominate their candidate at all costs. Taft felt he was the better man to hold the party together in defeat; he had no real expectation of being elected. Perhaps that—and the preordained outcome of the convention—is why he ate peanuts and played golf as the party divided.

There was a demonstration for Roosevelt on the second day. Mrs. Becky Davis, a lumberman's wife, dressed in a white embroidered gown, big black hat flopping, stood up in the gallery. She put down a big bouquet of sweet peas and unrolled a giant lithograph of Roosevelt, threw kisses at the delegates, and shouted, "Roosevelt! Roosevelt!"

They brought her down from the gallery to the platform, and she dominated the podium for a half hour. Down on the floor the demonstrators did their stuff. Roosevelt's unofficial double, delegate John M. Keyes, from Massachusetts, in his Rough Rider hat, his spectacles, and his big toothy grin, paraded around the floor making Rooseveltian gestures carefully copied from the great man.

But it lacked the old spirit. The outcome was already fixed, and even Keyes was known to all to be a Taft man.

Finally, on the fourth day, the farce ended. Roosevelt refused to let his delegates put his name into the hopper; told them they should not dignify the "theft" by voting at all. When the roll call was taken it was 561 for Taft; 107 for Roosevelt; 349 "present but not voting"; 41 for La Follette; 2 for Charles Evans Hughes of New York.

For the first time in the history of the Republican party there was no motion to make the nomination unanimous. Nobody had the gall to suggest it.

Sunny Jim Sherman was nominated to be Taft's running mate again, and the convention subsided.

But the Roosevelt men did not.

T.R. had no real hope of being nominated when he came to Chicago, although of course there was always an off chance. But Roosevelt wanted to hold the Roosevelt men together. Each day and night, in the big assembly hall in the Congress Hotel, he held forth, regaling his followers with grins and stories, passing good humor and bounce around the room. His delegates went to and from the convention, making demands for an honest roll call but knowing all the while that they were not to get it.

Then, after the Republicans had packed their bags, the Roosevelt Republicans staged a mass meeting on Saturday night, endorsed T.R. for the presidency and Governor Hiram Johnson of California for the vice-presidency. They began, there, to pull together the beginnings of an organization, agreed to go home to rally strength and come back in August to hold a political convention of the third party they had to form to fight the Republicans, and put over Roosevelt's Square Deal.

As those two Chicago meetings ended, the Democracy's William Jennings Bryan took off his reporter's hat and carried his political hat in hand to Baltimore. The way he held the hat, no one quite knew whether he was ready to throw it into the ring again or not.

Norman E. Mack, Chairman of the Democratic National Committee, rubbed his hands when he learned of the split in the Republican party. With Roosevelt in the field, said Mack, the Democrats could elect anyone. So he proposed to name a straight organization man who would recognize his obligation to party workers. Who would it be?

Welllllllllll . . . said Mr. Mack. It looked like Champ Clark, Speaker of the House . . . but then . . . you never can tell.

What about Bryan? He was the big problem, said Mack.

Would Bryan be a candidate?

While life lasts, said Mr. Mack.

Others agreed. Bryan, they said, proposed to support Woodrow Wilson, erudite, bespectacled college professor who had been elected governor of New Jersey in the interest of reform government. Wilson opposed John Beauchamp Clark. That is, Bryan was going to support Wilson long enough to keep Clark out of the job, then turn the convention for Bryan again—for the fourth time.

Reporters asked Bryan the direct question. Would he accept the nomination?

That was like asking a young lady if she would accept a proposal if one came to her, Bryan protested.

The reporters persisted.

Now you get the nomination if you can and bring it to me and see what I do with it, said Bryan.

No one was fooling anyone. Of course Bryan would accept the nomination if it came to him. But did he think he was going to get it? That was another thing, indeed. And as long as he did not declare himself out of the running, Bryan was a more powerful figure in the convention.

The trouble with Bryan, of course, was something like the trouble with Roosevelt at the Republican convention. No one was for him except the party members back home.

Once again, the bosses feared Bryan as death itself. The Nebraskan had hoped to be elected temporary chairman, but that was not to be.

Judge Alton B. Parker, the Democratic nominee of 1904, and now the choice of the conservative wing of the Democratic party for the chairman's job, was elected, 579 votes to Bryan's 508. If things went the way they had at the Republican convention that meant the conservatives were in control, or, as a Texas Democrat put it, it was "Bryan on one side and all Wall Street on the other."

But the Democrats had a tradition, unshared by the Republicans, built for occasions like this: the two-thirds rule. The conservatives were in control, but Bryan had enough power to keep them from getting two thirds. They had to come to some kind of compromise, or plan to sweat in Baltimore all summer.

The move by Tammany boss Murphy to put Parker in as permanent chairman was beaten. To Bryan's delight Ollie M. James of Kentucky was chosen permanent chairman.

There were a number of candidates for the nomination, but it broke down to a fight between the conservatives, backing Champ Clark, and Bryan, backing Wilson.

At three o'clock on the morning of June 27, Charles Bryan burst into his brother's room with news of disaster. He had just learned that Clark's backers had made a deal with Tammany Hall. Somewhere after the first ballot or two Tammany would throw the ninety New York votes to Clark. In exchange, Chairman Mack's pre-convention prophecy would be carried out. Clark would run as an "organization" candidate.

William Jennings doubted it, the whole story. But even at this unseemly hour brother Charles had a plan. He would get one of the progressive leaders to introduce a resolution condemning the Wall Street men. If Clark stood by Wall Street then everyone would know the deal was on.

Before the convention Clark had been regarded as a Progressive. Bryan, in fact, was pledged to vote for him under the unit rule, because the whole Nebraska delegation had been so instructed by the state convention. But several new matters affected voting in this convention of 1912. On Bryan's suggestion it was agreed that the candidate would be chosen before the platform. That call on Roosevelt may not have been so innocent after all. If Bryan were defeated in the convention, said the political experts one could find on every street corner, Bryan would bolt to the Roosevelt party.

While the unit rule bound Bryan to his chosen enemies, the rule had suffered some fractures in recent years. The primary system was replacing the convention system in some parts of the country. Where delegates had been chosen in primary elections they were not bound by the convention to the unit rule.

The relaxation of the unit rule didn't help Bryan, but his brother's idea solved his problem. Bryan introduced the resolution himself, opposing any candidate for the nomination "who is the representative or under obligation to J. Pierpont Morgan, Thomas F. Ryan, August Belmont, or any other member of the privilege-hunting and favor-seeking class." Bryan went further, demanded the withdrawal from the convention of any delegate who represented these interests, in his attempt to show up Champ Clark as a tool of Tammany.

To the embarrassment of all but Tammany, Thomas Ryan had finagled a seat as a delegate from Virginia, and August Belmont was there as a representative of New York.

Eyes focused on them, as delegates jumped to their feet from all sides of the room.

"There is not a delegate in this convention who does not know that an effort is being made right now to sell the Democratic party into bondage to the predatory interest of the nation," Bryan declared. He challenged New York and Virginia to ask their delegates what they thought. If they did not agree with him, Bryan would withdraw the motion.

New York and Virginia were on the spot. If they opposed Bryan's resolution, it was as good as admitting the truth of the charge. Their hope lay in its defeat, for the outright demand for expulsion of Ryan and Belmont annoyed some delegates.

But the ouster half of the resolution was withdrawn, to the intense relief of Bryan, who realized he had gotten in deeper than he had planned. Bryan immediately called for a roll-call vote. Condemnation of the bosses passed. New York boss Murphy instructed his delegation to vote for the resolution, in the belief that without the ouster it was harmless and that New York's "for" vote would make Bryan look foolish.

With a grin Murphy turned to August Belmont and said:

"August, listen and hear yourself vote yourself out of the convention."

On the first ballot Clark had 440½ votes, Wilson 324, and Representative Oscar Underwood, the conservative of Alabama, 117 votes. Governor Judson Harmon of Ohio had 148, 90 of them Tammany's, although Tammany was waiting to move for Clark. On the tenth ballot boss Murphy made his move, stood the convention on end when he cast the state's 90 votes for Clark. This was the signal for a Clark landslide. The convention stopped as the Clark delegates rose in demonstration—singing, shouting, and marching around the hall for almost an hour.

Then the balloting was resumed, and continued. The clerk picked up the roll call:

"North Dakota!!??"

(The convention hushed, to catch every syllable. Would North Dakota catch the trend, switch from Wilson to Clark? If so, it was all over but the victory parade.)

The North Dakota chairman replied flatly.

"Ten for Wilson."

The Wilson supporters let out a yell. It wasn't over yet.

Oklahoma was next. An Oklahoma delegate jumped up, demanded a poll of the delegation, since Clark seemed to be the convention's choice. It was a tense moment, but red-faced Alfalfa Bill Murray held Oklahoma from bolting to Clark. He was damned if he was going to join Tammany in making the nomination. Wilson's forces then began a counterdemonstration that lasted fifty-five minutes and gave their leaders some time to bargain.

On the eleventh ballot Alabama's delegation still stood for Underwood, still hoping for stalemate between Wilson and Clark, and the nomination of their man. By then the Wilson men had bargained well. They had promised that should Wilson be ousted from the race they would throw the Wilson votes to Underwood—if the Alabama men would stand against Clark now. It didn't sound like much of a deal, but Alabama's refusal to stampede delayed the Clark move just long enough.

Wilson, sitting in his old-fashioned frame house at Sea Girt, New Jersey, had almost read himself out of the race. Clark's manager had telegraphed Wilson that it was his duty to recognize a majority vote and withdraw. When Wilson saw the wire he personally agreed, and authorized his manager to withdraw. But the manager did not do it at that moment.

All this maneuvering had taken four days. On the fifth day the balloting began again. On the twelfth ballot, neither Clark nor Wilson gained; as the thirteenth began both gained a bit.

But on that thirteenth ballot when Nebraska was called, Bryan rose and asked for the floor. There were loud cries of "Sit down,"

"Throw him out," but here Clark's managers threw away the convention.

They were feeling grandiloquent, in anticipation of the few more minutes that would end the fight. Their candidate had a majority, and no Democratic hopeful with a majority had ever lost the nomination. Their spokesman asked unanimous consent that Bryan be heard.

Bryan walked to the platform, stood stolidly, enduring fifteen minutes of shouting and abuse, before the chairman could bring the convention to order. The Bryan men were excited; his enemies feared this man more than the devil's advocates.

Bryan stood on his own resolution, announced that he was now refusing to cast his vote for Clark, even though the unit rule demanded otherwise. For Nebraska was a progressive state, he said, and would not participate in the nomination of any man "whose vote depends upon the vote of the New York delegation." Bryan's implication that Clark was a Tammany stooge was unmistakable.

Champ Clark was furious, rushed from Washington to defend himself before the convention, but he arrived too late. The convention had adjourned for the day. The next day the emotional climate had changed. Wilson's star was rising. Bryan's influence came into play when the convention was nearly stalemated. Wilson gained strength after the Bryan speech but not yet enough. If this continued Bryan himself might get the nomination.

The forty-fifth ballot brought matters to a head. Wilson had more than 600 votes, but not yet a two-thirds majority. If he could not get the Underwood support from Alabama on the forty-sixth ballot, Wilson was finished. But he did. On the forty-sixth ballot Senator Bankhead withdrew Underwood's name. At the end of July 2, Wilson was the Democratic nominee and Governor Thomas R. Marshall of Indiana was his running mate.

The Democratic and Republican campaigns were already well begun when the Roosevelt men gathered in Chicago on August 5 for a convention that had many of the overtones of a religious revival.

This was the most progressive movement of all in these progressive times. The day before, when Roosevelt arrived in Chicago, reporters inquired into the state of his health. The colonel grinned, snapped those lovely teeth a few times, and replied:

"I feel as strong as a bull moose."

Roosevelt's party was named.

The next day with fervor the delegates sang "Onward, Christian Soldiers" and the "Doxology," then got down to business.

T.R., of course, was their man. They cheered him and they praised him, they bowed to him and scraped to him, and even let the ladies in. The Republicans and the Democrats had each admitted two female delegates to their councils in 1912; the Progressives let the great Jane Addams of Hull House become the first woman to second a presidential nomination.

Roosevelt led them all in singing "America," "The Battle Hymn of the Republic," and in denying seats to Negro delegates, on the basis that the type of Negro who was in politics "stood for nothing in our political life but selfish office seeking."

The band played, the delegates "mooed" like Bull Moose, and the sandwich men sold "moose ham" sandwiches and "women's suffrage tongue." The platform was written in part by Gifford Pinchot, the forester who had in a sense precipitated the whole crisis by getting himself fired by President Taft.

It was a lollapaloosa of a convention.

The Progressives called for state and national direct primaries, direct election of United States senators, the short ballot, the initiative, the referendum, the recall, and judicial reform. They demanded women's suffrage, limitation of campaign spending and exposure of expenditures before and after both primaries and elections, registration of lobbyists, socialized medicine, a department of labor, agricultural credit, tariff revision (and this meant reduction), inheritance taxes, and income taxes.

The Progressive platform was denounced by both Republicans and and Democrats as "socialistic." The Democratic platform was already full of progressive planks taken from T.R.'s old book; and the Republican platform was a good conservative platform, befitting its conservative candidate, who was more interested in the state of the budget and the support of Congress than in platform or the wave of social reform that was engulfing the nation.

The Progressives were well ahead of their time; the Republicans were well behind the time; and the Democrats were closest of all.

The campaign was fiery; it could hardly be anything else with Roosevelt taking an active part. Wilson, the soft-spoken, high-domed college professor, spoke impersonally and confined himself to the issues. Roosevelt, being himself, lashed out against Taft's "theft" of the Republican nomination, the degradation of the Republican party, and the professorial airs of Woodrow Wilson. Taft sat quietly in the White House.

The Progressives, new and undisciplined, fought among themselves. George W. Perkins, wealthy chairman of the Progressive executive committee, was a tough money raiser, and did his job well, but he was too close to the vested interests to escape attack by Wilson and by the Republicans.

Men took their politics seriously in 1912. In Kansas, Roosevelt visited William Allen White at Emporia, and they talked about the Republican barbed wire they had found in the Chicago coliseum, when the Bull Moosers redecorated the hall.

Roosevelt erupted. He knew about the barbed wire, and the big squads of police. He had heard about them the day of the nomination, and he had felt like taking a pistol and going into the convention himself. If the police had started something . . . He clenched his teeth:

"And by George, I wouldn't have wasted a bullet on a policeman. I would have got Root and got him quick."

Roosevelt was not the only one who talked violence. In Moberly, Missouri, Clark territory, John N. Hamilton, editor of the Huntsville *Herald,* and Van Davis, editor of the Huntsville *Times,* decided to settle their political differences after the Democratic convention in a duel. Hamilton was shot in the right arm. Davis was shot in the hip. Allen Gunn, an innocent bystander, was shot just below the heart.

Roosevelt was shot too, in the chest, while speaking from a platform in Milwaukee. It was a minor wound, but he played it for all it was worth, protected his would-be slayer from the crowd, and insisted on going on with his speech.

Taft knew he could not win. Roosevelt suspected that he could not either, but they fought each other as bitterly as if the contest had been only between them.

In the last moments of the campaign Roosevelt fired his ammunition at Taft, not at Wilson. He referred to Taft's judicial mentality, when he said that the Progressives stood for the Constitution, but would not make the Constitution a "fetish for the protection of fossilized wrong."

Finally it was all over. Wilson won 6,286,314 votes; Roosevelt 4,216,640; Taft 3,483,650. Wilson's vote was a million and a quarter less than that of his combined opponents. He had polled fewer votes than Bryan in the previous election. Even Eugene Debs benefited from the crusading spirit of the day. This election was the Socialist high point; Debs polled 901,873 votes.

Just before the Republican convention an elephantine Taft, bitter at the charges and bullying by his old friend, was reported to have said that whether he won or not was not important; "I am in this fight to perform a public duty—to keep Theodore Roosevelt out of the White House."

He had.

16

Within two years all issues paled before one: war or peace. The European war was ground into the American consciousness day after day. American marines had gone to Vera Cruz in 1914, but their presence on Mexican soil was almost forgotten with the outbreak of war in Europe. By 1916 it was difficult to see how America could stay out of it. Teddy Roosevelt, of course, thought we should not stay out, and was almost psychopathic in his harangues against a President Wilson who spoke quietly in promise of peace.

A Preparedness Day parade was bombed on July 22, 1916, in San Francisco. German saboteurs blew Jersey City's harbor nearly off the map only a week later. . . .

16. And What Did We Do? We Didn't Go to War! 1916

Nineteen-sixteen. The political climate of America had undergone a remarkable change in the two short years following assassination of Franz Ferdinand of Austria. Since political reform is a luxury that only the prosperous, peaceful, and unworried can afford, the Progressive party polled less than two million votes in the congressional contests of 1914, since the elections came after the beginning of war in Europe. War wasn't the only reason, of course. The Progressive party of 1912 had really been the personal vehicle of Bull Moose Theodore Roosevelt—and Roosevelt was not running for any office in 1914. By 1916 the situation and relative positions of the political leaders had changed so much it was almost impossible to assess their strengths.

Wilson had proved an able and popular President, although his way was not Roosevelt's way, and his whole conduct of the presidency was bound to alienate a man like Roosevelt.

William Jennings Bryan was out of it. He had been Secretary of State in the Wilson cabinet but had resigned in 1915 over a strong note Wilson insisted on sending the Germans after the *Lusitania* sinking. Bryan the pacifist would have no part of an act that might lead to war.

William Howard Taft had moved up to New Haven, where he happily occupied a professorial chair at Yale University Law School.

That left President Wilson, the incumbent, ex-President Roosevelt, the beloved gamecock of nearly half the country, and a great flock of Republican hopefuls of all shades of political opinion. This list was led by Charles Evans Hughes, who for six years had been sitting quietly on the Supreme Court of the United States.

By late spring 1916 it was apparent that Wilson would have things all his own way at the Democratic convention. Roosevelt, who had abandoned the Republicans in 1912, was most anxious to secure the Republican presidential nomination this year. The 1914 elections had shown him how things were blowing for the Progressives.

The Republican convention was set for June 7, at Chicago, and the Progressive convention was set for June 7 at Chicago, too. After war began in Europe, and after the Mexican government disintegrated to the point that American troops were dispatched to—and south of—the border, Roosevelt began airing his disgust with the pussyfooting Wilson administration. This heartened the Republican old guard. The old guard had no use for Roosevelt, but hoped to persuade him to support a Republican candidate and destroy the Progressive party.

Roosevelt, ambition in hand, set out on a western stumping tour, just before the separate but simultaneous conventions of the Republicans and Bull Moosers. It was as zestful, cyclonic, and immediately successful as any of T.R.'s tours. At the end of the trip, a typical day, he arrived in St. Louis on the eight forty-five train, was met by a thousand people, and made his way to the Planters' Hotel for breakfast. After a hearty breakfast Teddy jumped onto a couch and gave a short fire-eating speech to the combined leaders of the Republican and Progressive parties.

At lunch at the city's Mercantile Club, Roosevelt threw away a prepared manuscript with a casual comment on the intense heat and delivered an arm-waving speech about business conditions. After lunch, asked if he wanted to rest for a while, he said that was a bully idea, since it would give him time to work over his speech for the evening. And at the City Club, before a thousand admirers, Teddy waved his arms, clenched his fists, and jumped up on the table, to emphasize his strong feelings about the whole concept of "hyphenated Americans."

These were times in which men from the old country were very conscious that they were Italian-Americans, German-Americans, Swedish-Americans; a year in which the Democratic party was to print its campaign literature in eight languages. Characteristically, Teddy was attacking the issue at the source. St. Louis was then the second greatest German-American center in the nation.

Roosevelt also attacked President Wilson. On Memorial Day the President had come out for support of "universal voluntary training." These were "weasel words," said Roosevelt, meaning that a weasel would suck all the meat out of an egg, leaving the empty shell. Wilson advocated military training and no military training, at the same time, T.R. charged.

If Roosevelt were President there would be no such weasel-wording. His audience understood *that*, without a doubt.

Having finished his speech, Teddy bustled off to the railroad station, where he was helped aboard the eastbound train by happy admirers. In Chicago, Senator Reed Smoot had recently put the odds at 10–1 on Justice Hughes's nomination by the Republicans, 20–1 on Roosevelt. But in St. Louis, after that whirlwind visit, the odds were even.

As the magnificent Teddy headed east, to stop off in Newark and shake fighter Bob Fitzsimmons' hand before going home to Oyster Bay, T.R.'s lieutenants joined the political swim to Chicago. George W. Perkins, chairman of the Progressive party executive committee, and Roosevelt's private secretary John W. McGrath, set up shop at the Blackstone Hotel a week before the conventions.

The Republican National Committee was in town, hearing sixty-two contests for seats at the convention. The old-line conservative Republicans were there, learning to their sorrow that their man, Elihu Root, could not gain the support of any but the right wing, but sternly determined that Roosevelt should not have the Republican nomination, no matter what.

Uncle Joe Cannon, the now eviscerated lion of the House, set forth from Washington on a special train made up for congressmen and newspapermen. The clan was gathering. It looked more like two clans—Republican and Progressive—and it was odd that there was so much backslapping and handshaking between them, and such a conscious friendliness toward the Progressives by the crusty old Republicans. The militant Progressives, like Harold L. Ickes, national committeeman from Illinois, wanted no puffs on those Republican peace pipes. They wanted to nominate Roosevelt and go home. Let the Republicans do as they damn pleased. If the GOP wanted to continue the "suicide club," then speed the party's funeral.

Canny old Murray Crane of Massachusetts, one of the most rock-ribbed of the conservative bosses, slipped quietly into the Congress Hotel on June 2 to made his own preparations. Like the other brethren, he could remember back four years and knew that Wilson could not be defeated unless a very large part of the Progressive vote could be converted to Republican. For as of 1912 the Republican party was not second in the land, it was a poor third. The congressional elections of 1914 were proof that the GOP was not finished, but a wrong move at this critical point and the Progressives might be given such a large transfusion of Republican blood that the party of Abe Lincoln would have finished its circle right then.

On June 7 the Republican convention opened at Chicago's Coliseum, and the Progressive convention began at the Auditorium. Both halls had plenty of vacant seats. The Progressives had two completely empty balconies at the Auditorium. But the Republicans made up for their larger attendance in greater gloom. Senator Warren Gamaliel Harding, the temporary chairman of the GOP convention, delivered a speech that was both long and dull. The Progressive meeting across town was wired to Oyster Bay to keep T.R. in contact with the minute-by-minute flow of events. Since T.R.'s secretary, McGrath, was in Chicago, his assistant, Hayes, moved a cot into the little room in the Sagamore Hill house where the telephone sat, and when T.R. wasn't on the phone Hayes was holding the line.

But the Progressives were waiting for something. So were the Republicans.

The first honest emotion of the Republican convention came when Harding announced forthcoming meetings of a joint Republican-Progressive committee, to seek some basis for agreement. This raised a cheer.

Roosevelt hoped to get the Republican nomination. He had no desire to be a perennial third-party candidate, nor did he believe the Progressives, fighting the Republicans, could win over the Democrats. Early in the year, from the West Indies, he had told the New York *Evening Mail* ". . . if the country is not in a heroic mood, they have no need for me." The country was not in a heroic mood. It remained to be seen if it could be aroused.

The Roosevelt strategy was to wait out the Republicans, holding the threat of his nomination over their heads, while the joint committee negotiated. It was not a simple matter, for the western wing of the Progressive party was anxious to nominate Roosevelt, go home and get down to the business of winning an election.

The Republican convention was wide open. Eleven favorite-son candidates were nominated from the floor. On the first ballot a whimsical Texas delegation of twenty-six cast a vote for each of twenty-six separate candidates. Henry Ford got a vote, although he was too busy to attend. He was boomed for the nomination on a peace platform by Michigan Republicans.

The name most damned at the convention was that of Roosevelt, which was also the only name that aroused real enthusiasm. The other name most often mentioned was Justice Charles Evans Hughes, of the Supreme Court, who was not a candidate, who had not indicated his willingness to run, and who had no organization or even spokesman at Chicago.

At home in Washington, Hughes would not talk about the nomination. As the convention opened he stayed in his house at Sixteenth and V streets, studying court cases as usual, and constant in his refusal to talk to the press.

After breakfast on the first day of the convention, Hughes went for his usual morning walk through residential Washington, came back to work with his secretary for a while, and after lunch took a drive in the family's electric runabout.

At the Republican meeting the tension grew. Police kept a sharp eye on the galleries, to make certain no outburst for Roosevelt stamped the convention. In particular the police were watching Becky Davis, the lady who had frightened the life out of Taft's men in 1912. Mrs. Davis was there again, vowing to do "anything for Teddy." If the anti-Roosevelt men running the convention had anything to do with it she would never get a chance.

At the Auditorium the Progressives were whiling away the time, whittling at the party planks, the westerners scheming to nominate Roosevelt quickly, the easterners to stall. As a matter of principle, on the first day, the West managed a demonstration for Roosevelt that lasted 133 minutes, four minutes longer than the record Bryan demonstration in the Democratic convention of 1908—but it got pretty ragged around the edges after a few minutes. Had not a record been involved, the demonstration would have died much, much sooner.

On the third day, June 9, the stalling had to end. Meetings

between the Republicans and Progressives were getting nowhere. At the Coliseum the Republicans could not hold back the nominations of favorite sons, and the political bosses were coming close to agreement that Hughes was their man. He had not been involved in the Roosevelt fight of 1912. Since he had refused to discuss the nomination every delegate could imagine Hughes as his ideal candidate, and Hughes had neither policy nor platform to live down.

That day Senator William E. Borah of Idaho, one of the Republican liberals, visited the Progressive convention "to get inspiration." The Republicans needed a quantity of that spiritual medicine. The "spontaneous demonstrations" in the Coliseum were even less spontaneous than usual. One for former Senator Theodore Burton of Ohio, officially clocked at 33½ minutes, actually lasted 90 seconds. At the end of a minute and a half, 13,000 people sat and talked while a handful of dispirited claque leaders raised a cheer, clanged bells, and shook rattles to fill out the allotted time. When Hughes's name was called some 75 delegates led by an Oregonian in possession of the state standard marched around the room for 18½ minutes, but the rest of the delegates sat quietly in their chairs.

When Elihu Root was named, Mrs. Blanche Root, a short, plump young woman in the gallery, displayed her considerable ability to give the ear-shattering rebel yell during 13 minutes of organized racket.

"Gee," said Chicago Policeman No. 1072, gazing upward in awe. "Her husband had better not try to lick her. He'd get the whole neighborhood down on him."

The suspected Mrs. Davis, pristine in a gray suit, with a wide gray hat, sat quietly in the gallery with a ROOSEVELT streamer across her breast. She clutched a tiny flag, waiting for her big moment. Roosevelt was nominated!

"Watch that woman," warned the Roosevelt haters down below. The police narrowed their eyes as Mrs. Davis threw down her little flag, grabbed a big decorative flag from the wall, and began to wave it rhythmically back and forth.

The policemen moved quietly in on her, talked seriously for a few minutes, and Mrs. Davis subsided.

On Friday, Justice Hughes picked up considerable strength on the GOP's second ballot. He had 328½ of the 494 votes necessary to nominate when the roll call ended that evening. Roosevelt had 81. Root had 98½.

Had the convention not adjourned, Hughes might have fallen completely. There were indications that he was at the top of his strength. If he declined—Roosevelt was a definite threat. The anti-Roosevelt men needed a few hours to work.

That was how Hughes saw it, when he went to bed that night at home in Washington.

"That settles it," he told Mrs. Hughes. "I shall not be nominated. I am going to bed."

At two o'clock on the morning of June 10, Nicholas Murray Butler, the New York Republican, had the unpleasant task of telling Roosevelt he could never be nominated by the Republican convention. A survey showed that of the 987 delegates, 700 of them would never vote for Roosevelt. The regular party bosses had done a good job.

Whom would Roosevelt suggest? After all, the Republicans knew the value of his good will.

Roosevelt suggested General Leonard Wood.

No. It was impossible to nominate a general.

Roosevelt suggested Henry Cabot Lodge.

That prince of reactionaries? The Progressives on the joint committee were stunned. Was Roosevelt out of his mind? (They forgot that Henry Cabot Lodge had been a close personal friend of Roosevelt's.)

At the Progressive convention there were no candidates other than Theodore Roosevelt. The mass of delegates had no idea of the maneuvering that was going on behind the scenes, although such men as William Allen White knew that Roosevelt was extremely leery of accepting the Progressive nomination.

On Saturday morning both conventions forged ahead. George Perkins had successfully held the Progressives in check for three days, had stalled off one attempt to nominate Roosevelt. He could do no more.

The convention was waiting, discussing some parliamentary platitude that no one cared about, when Bainbridge Colby of New York signaled for the floor. As the chairman recognized him, Perkins instinctively knew what was going to happen, rushed to the speakers' stand, so excited, so distraught that no one could understand what he was saying.

The chairman shoved Perkins down in a chair. In seconds, Colby had made the Roosevelt nomination. Governor Hiram Johnson of California seconded it. In a few moments John M. Parker, the former governor of Louisiana, was nominated for Vice-President.

What was Perkins trying to say?

Later Perkins gave the convention a letter from Roosevelt, a letter in which T.R. declined the nomination. Perhaps the party boss wanted to present the letter before the nomination was made, to avoid the bitterness that flowed later.

It made little difference. The convention was determined to nominate Roosevelt. Had he declined in person he still would have been nominated. For the Progressive party, as it stood, was a Roosevelt party.

As far as Roosevelt was concerned, it would have taken the Republican and Progressive nominations to make him run. He had been President for seven years; he had been defeated in election once; and he had declared himself available only in case of a nation bent on heroics.

At the Chicago Coliseum on the tenth of June, Charles Evans Hughes was nominated by the Republicans, Charles Warren Fairbanks of Indiana as Vice-President. In his letter rejecting the Progressive nomination Roosevelt advised the Progressives to wait and see what kind of platform Hughes would run on.

Justice Hughes was at lunch when he learned that he had been nominated. Across the street one of his rich neighbors sent the butler up to the third floor to fly a brace of American flags. Hughes cracked a smile, the first many of the newspapermen had ever seen flit across that granite jaw, and became chummy enough with one of the old hands to remark that he hadn't been seeing as much of the newspaper boys as he wanted to.

There! This sounded a lot more like a presidential candidate.

Knowing what was going on at the Progressive convention, Hughes broke precedent, accepted the nomination by telegram before he was officially nominated, and gladdened Roosevelt's heart by attacking the Wilson administration. That last gave him the support of T.R., and delivered the mercy bullet to the Progressive party.

Immediately, Hughes sat down and wrote a letter.

A little later, at the White House, a man who had considered himself Hughes's friend, read it and looked up, puzzled and annoyed.

To the President:

I hereby resign the office of associate justice of the Supreme Court of the United States.

I am, sir, respectfully yours,
Charles Evans Hughes.

The annoyed man, President Woodrow Wilson, was not puzzled because Hughes had resigned. He did think he might have expected more personal, courteous treatment from a man with whom he had spent a number of social evenings.

But Hughes was a distant and diffident man, much like the President himself. What kind of man was he? Roosevelt clicked his teeth emphatically. He was the kind of man who would vote for Woodrow Wilson in a campaign like this, T.R. said, privately, but publicly supported the GOP ticket.

The Republican politicians worried from the beginning. A few minutes after the nomination Arthur Vorys of Ohio told a pair of friends he was sure to get something from the new President, because he had been against him. The other two—they would get nothing. They had supported Hughes.

That was based on a story about a New York politician who came to Hughes when he was governor of New York to ask for a job, since he had made a great number of speeches for Hughes in the campaign.

Hughes, it is said, stiffened noticably.

"The fact that you have been so actively campaigning in my behalf," he is reported to have said, "precludes the possibility of my appointing you to any office. I cannot have it said that I have distributed offices as a reward for support."

It was obviously a desperate gang of Republican bosses who settled on this man, as the only possible antidote to Roosevelt.

The nomination was made on Saturday. On Sunday, Theodore Roosevelt went to Christ Episcopal Church in the village at Oyster Bay, then home. For the first time since he had marched confidently to New York City Hall to take on the job of police commissioner, the gates of Sagamore Hill were closed to his old friends of the press.

Hughes, as was his fashion, went to the Calvary Baptist Church in Washington, where fifteen hundred persons jammed the church in unseasonable religiousness, and the minister, the Reverend Samuel Greene, pointedly worked into his sermon a quotation from I Cor. 9:24: "So run, that ye may attain."

The President opened his campaign on June 14, the day the Democratic party met in convention at St. Louis. In blue serge coat, white trousers, white shoes, and straw hat, carrying a big American flag like a musket on his shoulder, the President led the Flag Day marchers up Pennsylvania Avenue, then got off at the presidential reviewing stand and watched the five-hour parade pass by. At a ceremonial address that same day he sounded what he thought would be the keynote of the campaign—Americanism.

But at St. Louis, strange things were happening.

There was no question about the name of the presidential nominee as the Democrats assembled. There was no real question about the vice-presidency either. A move had been started by Henry Morgenthau to get rid of Vice-President Thomas Marshall, but it was nipped immediately by Wilson, who declared himself eminently satisfied with his Vice-President.

No, the only question was the campaign.

Wilson was a minority President, and the Democrats faced a serious fight in the coming election. Wilson had polled fewer votes in 1912, although he was elected, than Bryan had in 1900 and 1908, when Bryan was defeated. This year, 1916, there would be no Progressive party to split the Republican vote. The Democrats had to get a good part of that vote or be defeated.

Like the Republican platform of 1916, the Democratic platform was inoffensive to the Progressives. Women's suffrage, long resisted by both major parties, was no longer a serious issue, although the ladies wanted the two parties to come out for a federal law, and both parties wanted the matter handled by the states. But the real issue of the convention, and the campaign, was not to be Wilson's call for Americanism—that fell far too flat.

Governor Martin H. Glynn of New York, the temporary chairman, discovered the real issue of the campaign, quite by accident, in his keynote speech.

Glynn began with all the usual oratorical flourishes. Glynn, setting the note for the convention, pointed with pride to the record of the Democratic administration. The delegates were half asleep. A few roused themselves enough to cheer when William Jennings Bryan entered to take his seat in the press gallery. So far had he fallen by 1916 in party counsels that he was denied election as a delegate from Nebraska. He entered the convention in his guise as newspaper reporter. Bryan could not even address the convention, save by a vote of unanimous consent of all the delegates. Here he was, the strongest, most powerful leader in the history of the Democratic party, the one man who still exerted more influence on the party than any other, apparently powerless to work for good or evil. Yet as he came in the door, his growing paunch preceding him, his wavy locks giving way now to a broader and broader expanse of cranial skin, they cheered him, for what might have been.

Glynn droned on about Wilson:

"No President has displayed a grasp more sure, a statesmanship more profound," he said. There was a short cheer from the front of the hall. Nothing unusual.

But in the corridor outside, this short cheer was mistaken as the cue for a carefully rehearsed spontaneous demonstration for Wilson. In the corridor was a troupe of the Wilson faithful, ready to augment the noise and brighten the proceedings. This troupe possessed, with other accoutrements, a trained jackass, and the script called for this animal to stick his head in the window of the convention hall and bray loudly, on cue.

"No President has displayed a grasp more sure, a statesmanship more profound," said Mr. Glynn.

"Hee-haw," said the donkey.

"Not now, dammit, not now!" shouted somebody.

Governor Glynn was shaken but undismayed. He recovered and began moving even higher up the mountain of peroration. He traced precedents of other presidents who had avoided war; Washington, Adams, Jefferson, Pierce, Van Buren. And as he set up each event, he said: "What did we do? . . . We didn't go to war." It had a beat and the beat caught the galleries, and then the convention. And as it caught them it roused the oratorical soul of Governor Glynn to greater heights.

"And what did we do?" roared the question.

"WE DIDN'T GO TO WAR!" they roared back time and again.

"AND WHAT DID WE DO?"

"WE DIDN'T GO TO WAR!"

At the end the braying of the jackass was forgotten. William Jennings Bryan was crying in his seat in the press gallery. The Democratic party was breathless.

A few glum political second guessers in the crowd were low on Glynn's keynote speech.

"It wasn't a keynote. It was an alibi," growled one. He couldn't have been more wrong. Governor Glynn had discovered the issue that would re-elect Woodrow Wilson.

The next day Senator Ollie James of Kentucky was made permanent chairman of the convention, and he had to speed things up. The delegates had come to endorse Wilson and his handwritten platform. They wanted to do it and be off.

Bryan was called, by special invitation, and he endorsed peace, Wilson, and many of Wilson's works. It was later characterized by Democrats as a great "harmony" speech.

Judge John W. Wescott of New Jersey, who had nominated Wilson at Baltimore in 1912, was selected to repeat the honor in 1916. He did. It was moved that the rules be suspended and Wilson be renominated by acclamation. A single voice from Illinois declared itself opposed to this move.

Chairman James fixed his glaring eye on the owner of the voice.

"I hereby declare Woodrow Wilson nominated for President by the vote of 1092 to 1," he said. Thomas Marshall was nominated a few minutes later for a second term as Vice-President.

In the White House the sixty-year-old President Wilson and his young bride of six months slipped out the door into the rainy night and walked down through the Monument grounds to the Potomac River. Marshall's reactions went unreported as was usual with Vice-Presidents in pre-Eisenhower days.

Marshall's office was a sight-seeing point for almost every visitor to the Capitol.

"I don't see," he once said, "that this room differs much from a monkey cage except that the visitors do not offer me any peanuts."

The Democratic convention adjourned, and a few days later, on June 21, Vance McCormick, the new Democratic national chairman, announced the opening of the campaign.

Wilson was busy in July and August, faced with a crippling railroad strike and an attempt to push a great mass of progressive legislation through Congress before the election. He had no time or inclination to campaign right then.

Hughes, having passed Roosevelt's big test by attacking Wilson, might have expected to reap all the support of the dissolving Progressive party. He had no such luck. On June 26 the national committee of the party met at Chicago and decided by a vote of 32 to 6 to endorse Hughes. Nine members abstained. Altogether, Wilson picked up the support of about a third of the national committee. Roosevelt, of course, went on the stump for Hughes, in his anxiety to defeat Wilson, whom he termed a mollycoddle. But John Parker, the Louisiana Democrat who had been nominated as Progressive vice-presidential candidate, swung to Wilson and took a good percentage of the party with him.

The issue of the campaign was war or peace.

Roosevelt was a war man. Had he been President, the United States would have intervened in Mexico and in Europe long before. Wilson's campaign nicely combined discussion of preparedness and peace. "He kept us out of war" was the magic phrase. It was used everywhere. One campaign pamphlet on social justice ended: "Our country is at peace in a world at war."

An essay on child labor law reminded mothers that Wilson had saved their children from the mines, mills, and sweatshops, and their husbands from "unrighteous battlefields."

Bryan began speaking for Wilson in the West. His anti-war speeches at Pueblo and Colorado Springs, said ex-Governor Alva Adams of Colorado, were "masterpieces in argument and power."

The campaign rolled on as summer ate up the calendar. Hughes and Roosevelt dined on brook trout, squab chicken, and cold asparagus on June 28 at the Astor. This meeting sent Bainbridge Colby and other Progressives into a frenzy against T.R.'s "duplicity," in dealing with the GOP, breaking his pledge to the Progressive convention, and destroying the Progressive party for his own purposes.

In July the Prohibitionists met in St. Paul. The convention went into a wild demonstration when John P. Coffin pledged $50,000 to the campaign fund. It was more money than the drys had ever seen before. Frank Hanly was selected as the nominee after a convention battle with William Sulzer, once Democratic governor of New York, who had been impeached by his own party. Henry Ford got a dry vote, too.

In August, Hughes decided to invade California. He had been on the Supreme Court for so long he felt it important to get out and be seen, across the country. But in California a battle royal was raging between Hiram Johnson and the old-guard Republicans who worked for the Southern Pacific Railroad interests. Hughes had selected William R. Willcox as his campaign chairman, and Willcox didn't like the Hughes trip. But it was Hughes's campaign. He did as he pleased.

He did not do well in California. On August 19, Hughes lunched at the San Francisco Commercial Club. Unfortunately the club was anti-union. The committee on arrangements tried to get the waiter's union to send over sixty-five waiters for this one occasion, but this just rubbed salt in the union's wounds. Union President Hugo Ernst made an issue of it. Certainly Hughes was at the mercy of the arrangers, but the arrangers were all the old-guard Republicans, not the Johnson Republicans and Progressives.

A few days later, in Long Beach, Hughes spent several hours at a hotel, then went on to Los Angeles, without saying hello to Governor Johnson, who happened to be in the same Long Beach hotel at the time. Hughes was apparently unconscious of the error. When he discovered it, he tried to make amends, but Johnson sent back word that Hughes had surrounded himself with all Johnson's enemies, which indeed he had.

In October, Wilson began a belated campaign, from his summer home, Shadow Lawn, in New Jersey.

It was an effective campaign, defending a record that seemed liberal and certainly was treading the narrow line between peace and war in a stricken world. The activities of Congress that spring and summer gave a great deal of ammunition to the President. He had jammed through laws for the farmer, the wage-earner, the poor. He had settled the railroad strike. He could not be attacked as anti-Progressive, and he could attack his enemies as anti-labor and pro-war.

Roosevelt helped Wilson a great deal. His hatred of Wilson was so great and so obvious and his exaggeration so great that it undid all his efforts to help Hughes win the election. Count Bernstorff, the German ambassador, remarked gloomily that if Wilson did win he certainly had Roosevelt to thank for it.

At the end of the campaign the Democrats ran their most effective advertisement. In part, it said:

> You are working, not fighting!
> Alive and happy, not cannon fodder.
>
> Wilson and peace with honor?
> Hughes and Roosevelt, and war?

Even Henry Ford, to the disgust of the Republicans and Prohibitionists, came out strongly in favor of Wilson's election, as a man of peace. Ford didn't go so far, however, as to give the Democrats money.

The Republicans sent a train of women called "The Poodle Dog Special" through the West, to stir up the female vote where it would count. But the women of the West didn't like the idea, since they did not believe they really needed to be told how to vote by any eastern females. Their husbands liked it even less.

Suddenly it was November. The two major candidates wound up in Madison Square Garden within a week of each other, and on election eve Wilson went to Shadow Lawn, Hughes to New York's Astor Hotel, where he and his wife and three daughters rented a suite on the eighth floor.

Betting on Hughes was 10–8 in Brooklyn. Five million dollars had been staked on the election in the big centers of the East. The next day as the polls opened the odds narrowed further; now it was even money.

Hughes got up early on election morning and went to his polling place, a laundry on New York's West Side. He drew ballot No. 13. "A lucky omen," laughed the GOP candidate.

Wilson got up and drove from Shadow Lawn to the firehouse in Princeton where he had voted ever since he was president of the university.

Almost immediately both sides claimed victory. Tammany boss Murphy said he expected a Democratic plurality of 75,000 in New York City.

The Democrats claimed Minnesota, Michigan, New York, Illinois, Kansas, Colorado, Connecticut, Ohio, Indiana, Nebraska, Washington, West Virginia, Oregon, Maryland, North Dakota, and Montana.

Hughes took a nap in the afternoon. He woke after dark, just in time for a family dinner in the hotel suite. While the Hughes family was eating, a telegram arrived from T. R. Dixey of Clinton, New York, congratulating the Republican nominee on his victory. "In twenty-eight years I have never cast a vote for a losing candidate," said Mr. Dixey. Hughes smiled.

A few minutes later Hughes's nine-year-old daughter, Elizabeth, dragged him up from the table to explain the figures on the big New York *Times* bulletin board across the way.

Robert Fuller of the Merchants Association broke in to tell him that he had a 100,000 majority in New York State.

His brother-in-law, Dr. Colin Carter, came in to announce that the New York newspapers had conceded a Hughes victory.

William C. Muschenheim, proprietor of the Astor, brought his granddaughter up to congratulate the President-elect. Mrs. Hughes embraced her husband tenderly and called him "Mr. President." On the roof of the Astor two big American flags were broken out, spotlighted by searchlights and blazing red lights that spelled out HUGHES.

At 1:20 A.M. as Mr. Hughes retired, the moist eyes of the family circle could hardly conceal their jubilation. Hughes wanted to wait until the next morning when the Democrats conceded his election before speaking publicly.

"The indications are that Mr. Hughes is elected," said boss Murphy in his office at Tammany. "The result is a great surprise to me." Then he philosophized. The American people had spoken, and there was nothing to be done. Philosophy came easy for boss Murphy that year, since he and President Wilson were deadly enemies.

Former Governor Sulzer, impeached by the Democrats, spurned even by the drys, was jubilant as he learned the Republicans had won victory in New York. The impeachers were impeached, said he.

The Prohibitionists were in sixth heaven. The states of Michigan, Montana, South Dakota, Utah, and Nebraska had just been dried up. Hurray for John P. Coffin's $50,000!

At Shadow Lawn things didn't look good. Of the states claimed, Michigan, New York, Illinois, Connecticut, Indiana, West Virginia, and Oregon had gone Republican.

But the Democrats did not give up.

By morning things looked better at Shadow Lawn, worse on the eighth floor of the Astor.

That night, November 8, Mr. and Mrs. Hughes went to the theater. The play was called *Nothing but the Truth*, and at one point the heroine offered the hero $10,000 if he could double it. He didn't know whether it was wise to try.

"Is it safe?" asked the girl.

"I don't know. I'm not willing to say until I get the result from California," said the hero.

The audience laughed and looked right at candidate Hughes. For California, the Golden State he had wooed so carelessly, was the key to the election this night. If he carried California, he won. If Wilson carried California, Wilson won.

Hughes got the bad news at 11:20 P.M. Wilson had California. Hiram Johnson, running for senator, had carried the state by 300,000.

Wilson carried it by 3773. But it wasn't that Johnson had not worked for Hughes. He had. Not a single speech had passed without Johnson plumping for the Republican candidate. Hughes, however, had hurt himself in California by dallying with William H. Crocker and the other conservatives. The voters loved Johnson—but not enough to vote for Hughes.

Wilson got the good news aboard the yacht *Mayflower*, on the way to Massachusetts to observe the christening of his first grandchild. He had borne the suspense well. His intimates had never really flagged in their belief that he had won the election, although they admitted some tense moments. It was a narrow victory; Wilson's plurality was less than a half million votes. He had won the woman's suffrage states. In Washington, California, Idaho, Utah, and Arizona, women had carried the day for the man who "kept the country out of war." The Socialists, voting this time for Allan J. Benson, lost more than three hundred thousand votes of their 900,000 of 1912, and most of them went to Wilson.

Wilson was too busy for post-mortems. The Republicans were not. Of all the Republican afterthoughts, most succinct was that of John W. Dwight, an ex-congressman from New York who had learned his politics in the amen corner under Mousy Platt.

Hughes could have been elected for one dollar, said Dwight.

"A man of sense with a dollar would have invited Hughes and Johnson to his room when they were both in the same hotel in California. He would have ordered three scotch whiskies, which would have cost seventy-five cents, and that would have left a tip for the waiter. That's all that would have been necessary. That little scotch would have brought those men together; there would have been mutual understanding and respect, and Hughes would have carried California and been elected."

Wilson did not keep the United States out of war, for long, and he paid the price for it politically in the 1918 congressional elections, which went against the Democrats.

But while the political wars went on, the national effort was well directed toward winning the struggle against the Kaiser. Truthfully, until the fall of 1918, even the Republicans could not have been more docile to President Wilson's guidance, in the national eagerness to make the world safe for democracy.

But disillusion set in on both sides. President Wilson set himself to secure the peace. The Republicans wanted to secure American peace, and they thought the best way to assure non-involvement in war was to refuse to become involved in anything else that concerned other nations. . . .

Of much more concern at home was the struggle for prohibition. The Prohibitionists had gained strength in the wave of morality that washed across the nation, and somehow it was tied in with woman's rights, sanctity of the home, mother, and honesty in government and politics. Carry Nation had gone to her reward in 1911, but her spiritual descendants kept chopping away at saloons, literally and figuratively.

Finally, in 1917, the Eighteenth Amendment to the Constitution, prohibiting sale of alcoholic beverages, was submitted to the states for ratification. The first state, Mississippi, ratified it on January 8, 1918. The thirty-sixth state—all that was needed—ratified it on January 16, 1919. It never was ratified by Connecticut and Rhode Island, but that did not keep prohibition from becoming the law of of Land.

*Late in 1919, the Volstead Act, which enforced the amendment,
was passed by Congress over President Wilson's veto. Now, the
drys rubbed their hands in glee, but not as happily as the bootleggers,
whose fortunes had just been assured by federal fiat. . . .*

17. Mr. Wilson's Mistake 1918-20

Just after the turn of the year 1920, the politicians began snapping their cuffs and shifting their neckwear in anticipation of the coming presidential campaign. The gargantuan Boies Penrose of Pennsylvania surveyed the situation from his seat in the United States Senate and found it very good. Nineteen-twenty would be a Republican year, if he had ever seen one. And since it was bound to be a Republican year, it didn't make much difference who was picked to run. The Republican candidate would win. Why not keep it all in the family? That, of course, meant keeping power in the hands of the old guard, of which Penrose was one of the largest members, in every sense of the word.

A flock of Republicans wanted to be President that year—and not a statesman in the bunch. Strangely, Charles Evans Hughes, who had lost by such a narrow margin in 1916, was not seriously considered by the political bosses for the nomination. Part of the cause was Hughes's stern and austere personality. He was never a favorite of the gentlemen in plug hats.

But a greater consideration was Hughes's corollary inflexibility in matters of political favor and patronage. In 1916 the party bosses had chosen Hughes, not with any great pleasure, to match a strong and vigorous President Wilson. Besides, the GOP bosses were not completely masters of their own house that year. They faced the ever-present threat of an indefatigable Teddy Roosevelt.

In 1920, Roosevelt was dead. Wilson was desperately ill after the stroke suffered in Colorado in September of the previous year. It was openly rumored that Mrs. Wilson and the White House staff were carrying on any presidential work that was done at all. Wilson was out of the picture.

Since no strong man sought the GOP presidential nomination the old guard could afford to relax and let the convention take its course, until they saw the best combination to unlock the White House door. If, as happened, the same combination unlocked the Treasury and opened the federal coffers, it must not be inferred that the entire leadership of the Republican party was dedicated to venality.

The Republican convention was scheduled for June 8 at Chicago's Coliseum. By early spring a number of hats were in the ring, most prominently those of General Leonard Wood, Governor Lowden of Illinois, Senator Hiram Johnson of California, Senator Warren G. Harding of Ohio, Governor Calvin Coolidge of Massachusetts, and a mining engineer named Herbert Hoover, who was then administering the program of relief for a struggling postwar Europe from an office in New York City.

Until late spring, interestingly enough, Hoover was an unknown political quantity. Louis B. Wehle, a prominent Democrat, had suggested to Colonel House, Wilson's old confidant, that an unbeatable Democratic combination would be Hoover for President and the young Assistant Secretary of the Navy, Franklin Delano Roosevelt, for Vice-President. As postwar chief for Europe, Hoover was a well-known figure, but so far unsullied by a known political opinion —or enemy. Wehle sensed that the Democrats could use a non-controversial candidate after eight years of the Wilson administration. Roosevelt was rich, young, handsome, and he had that wonderful name. Wehle had gone down to Hoover's Broadway office to suggest this. Hoover listened in silence, doodling on the blotter in front of him. He didn't want to get mixed up with a bunch of political bosses, he said. Wehle shrugged. Politics was politics. If a man wanted to fish in presidential waters, he had to get a license. Before the end of the conversation Hoover had agreed to call Colonel House and discuss the matter. But in April, Wehle read in the newspapers that Hoover declared he would not accept a Democratic nomination or run as an independent. He was a Republican, the administrator announced, and he would accept only the Republican nomination.

Congress was late in session that year. It was a Republican Congress, damned by Wilson as a do-nothing legislature.

The mid-term elections of 1918, which elected the Republican Congress, had been the second most important in history. In 1866 the election of a Radical Republican Congress had unleashed harsh reconstruction on the South in punishment for the Civil War as demanded by Senator Charles Sumner. Fifty-two years later, in 1918, the election issues were progressivism, internationalism, tariff, prohibition, government regulation of business and taxation. The Republican victory in the 1918 congressional election put an end to progressivism and established isolationism as national policy.

In February 1918, Will Hays of Indiana was chosen chairman of the Republican National Committee. Hays was a good-looking, foppish man of slender build, but broad ideas. He was prowar and anti-Wilson, as any good Republican should have been. One of Hays's first promises was that a Republican victory would assure business of treatment "with an appreciation of its fundamental importance."

Wilsonism, said Chairman Hays, was not far from socialism. One of these "near-Socialists," Henry Ford, decided to run for the Senate at the President's request. The Republicans would spend almost $200,000 in Michigan to defeat him. To Republicans in the border state of Kentucky, always tenuous for both parties, Hays promised to send two dollars for every Republican dollar raised.

After the American war declaration in 1917 party lines had become vague. Wilson got the generous support of Republicans to wage the war. But by 1918 sentiment had changed. So this campaign was marked by two important events. First, Samuel Gompers threw the weight of the American Federation of Labor to the Democrats, charging that the Republicans were the party of big business.

Second, Woodrow Wilson took his case "to the people" against the advice of practically everyone he consulted. The President asked Americans to elect Democrats who would support him in his attempt to negotiate a just and lasting peace at the end of the war. It was a mistake. Republican leaders lost no time in crying that the President was interfering in local elections, trying to dictate to the American people. Teddy Roosevelt devoted most of a three-hour speech in Carnegie Hall to castigation of Wilson for this affront to public intelligence. The Republicans won those elections of 1918 very handily.

The Republican Congress that assembled in March 1919 would have opposed the President even if he had been the most warm and congenial politician in the land. Since Wilson surrounded himself with secrecy and seldom let his left hand know what his right was doing, there was soon open enmity between legislative and executive authority. Wilson was always autocratic and professional in his approach to Congress, and now the Congress was not disposed to back down. No one denied that the President was brilliant and inspired, but Congress was heartily aware of its own powers and was tired of brilliant, irascible leaders who told the legislature what to do. The elections of 1918 indicated to the Republican leadership that the voters were becoming tired of Wilson.

After the war and the negotiations at Versailles, when Wilson proposed that the United States enter the League of Nations, Congress bridled. Wilson's cause was not served by the personal enmity between the President and wiry Senator Henry Cabot Lodge, whose white goatee bristled at the very name of Wilson; yet it was hardly politic for the Chief Executive to feud with the chairman of the Senate Foreign Relations Committee.

Basically, the United States was still isolationist. Americans had dipped their toes into the Atlantic and found it cold and wet. The war won, most Americans wanted to stay home and mind their own business, which was business. Congress so emasculated the Versailles Treaty that Wilson refused to sign the law when it came to him. Instead, he took to the stump to campaign for the treaty and United States membership in the League. Then came the Wilson collapse.

It left a pretty kettle of fish; technically the United States was still at war with Germany, and the country was virtually leaderless.

In the spring, as Congress stalled, the White House fever of two GOP candidates broke into a rash that could not be concealed from the public. Ugly rumors went around that General Leonard Wood and Governor Lowden were trying to buy the Republican nomination outright. Investigation showed that General Wood's backers had spent a million and a half dollars, Governor Lowden's supporters over $400,000; while the campaign expenditures for Hiram Johnson of California, Warren Harding, Herbert Hoover, and Calvin Coolidge were around $200,000 each.

Before the Senate adjourned in June, they authorized investigation of the postconvention expenditures of all parties. The old-guard Republicans fought the investigation to the last, called for points of order, suggested absence of a quorum, and pulled out all the parliamentary stops, without success.

They might have succeeded, but the clincher was the discovery of the participation of Colonel Procter, the Ivory Soap king, in General Wood's campaign. The colonel had put up $521,000. Later, he signed more notes that brought the Wood men another $200,000.

When these facts were revealed, an outraged Senate authorized the investigation.

Senator William E. Borah of Idaho, a maverick Republican for many years, warned the Republicans to clean house "by next Saturday night." He had set that date in the assumption that the Republican convention would be over by then. It was unlikely that any candidate would command enough attention to force delegates to pay for an extra weekend of hotel space. In addition, since the whole country was officially dry, the usual liquid lubricators and pacifiers of political conventions were available only surreptitiously, if at all.

Heading for Chicago, the Massachusetts delegation ran afoul of the Volstead Act in Detroit when their train was stopped and searched by a stern and inflexible government agent. Notwithstanding the loud cries, agents confiscated all the whisky that could be found. This was certainly no help to the candidacy of Massachusetts Governor Calvin Coolidge, yet perhaps the dry and colorless Coolidge seemed to many best viewed through the bottom of a glass.

As the convention opening drew near there was no heavy favorite. Hiram Johnson was undoubtedly the most popular candidate of all, but he was detested by the professionals who would never forget his Bull Moosism of 1912. Now they blamed him, for having single-handedly engineered the defeat of Charles Evans Hughes in 1916 when California was lost.

Johnson, General Wood, and Governor Lowden each claimed more than 100 pledged delegates, but there were 982 votes in the convention, 509 of them not yet instructed for any candidate. In the scurry for delegates no early trend emerged. Among the dark horses Governor Sproul of Pennsylvania was most prominent with 76 pledged Pennsylvania votes. Governor Sproul's influence was enhanced because Senator Boies Penrose, the Pennsylvania boss, was being kept home in Philadelphia by his doctors this year. Ohio's Warren Harding fretted, although his manager, Harry Daugherty, had all the confidence in the world. This was the week Harding had to file for re-election as United States senator or he could not run. But if Harding was to be nominated for the presidency, it would be suicidal to file for the Senate, too.

Harding's backing, aside from Daugherty, came largely from eastern business interests, who had been given to understand that Harding would be pliable.

By June 6, two days before the convention, nineteen names were mentioned prominently for the nomination, but Hughes was only the avowed candidate of the Anti-Saloon League, which had come to Chicago in force to be sure no wet plank found its way into the Republican platform.

General Wood and Governor Lowden were still hopeful, although they had been sorely injured by the disclosure of their financial efforts to secure the nomination. They were determined to keep Hiram Johnson out of the race, and their managers agreed to co-operate at least *that* far. From that point on, it was anybody's guess.

General Wood's suite at the Congress Hotel was opulence itself. His adherents had taken over the Elizabethan Room and erected a number of eight-foot partitions to serve as private offices. "The stable," the delegates called it, as they came dutifully to pay their respects and pick up the varicolored Wood feathers offered by handsome young ladies at the door. As they came in delegates passed by an impressive suit of armor tastefully decorated with a sign: "Leonard Wood for President."

The crowds were heavy there, and at Governor Lowden's $1000-a-day headquarters located appropriately in the Gold Room. As a Democratic senator had remarked in the investigations, the governor had personally spent some $400,000 before the convention to secure the nomination for a job that paid only $75,000 a year.

In the houses of the dark horses, there was neither light nor gaiety. Harding's headquarters in the Florentine Room was a "vast vacancy." Nicholas Murray Butler, the New York educator and politician, maintained another room that was nearly as deserted. But most magnificent in its loneliness was the suite of Calvin Coolidge. Perhaps the word had gone round that the refreshments of the Massachusetts delegation had been lifted by the revenuers.

There was much jostling and bustling around the Congress Hotel in those pre-convention days as delegates swapped lies and the tense managers did their best to corral votes.

Close by, important work was afoot at the more sedate Blackstone Hotel, whose atmosphere was an equal compound of richness and quiet toleration of convention shenanigans. Here, the General Electric Company's Charles Pierce talked Harding day and night. Ambrose Monell, a king of the metals industry, Samuel Vauclain of Baldwin locomotives, Cornelius Vanderbilt, and four of the J. P. Morgan partners were all *in situ*. Many met at night to discuss the presidential possibilities, meeting with men like Daugherty and Chairman Will Hays, who shared a suite at the Blackstone with George Harvey, editor of the powerful *North American Review.*

When the convention opened on June 8, keynote speaker Henry Cabot Lodge attacked the Versailles Treaty and defended the Senate's rejection of the League of Nations.

"We make the issue; we ask approbation for what we have done. The people will now tell us what they think of Mr. Wilson's League and the sacrifice of America," said Senator Lodge.

The League—prime issue of the election—was an issue within the party, too. Senators Johnson and Borah were opposed to the League of Nations in any form. A less isolationist group in the party wanted only to castrate the League. The more moderate wing won. The platform paid lip-service to the League, but it was only lip-service.

Then came the question of the candidate.

Leonard Wood's men had jettisoned the suit of armor as too militaristic by Friday, June 11, when the nominations were to be made. A few more delegates had trickled into the dried-up Coolidge headquarters. The theme song of the convention, "How Dry I Am," was played with great and nostalgic frequency by the brass band in the Coliseum, to the dismay of every thirsty delegate in the house.

On Friday seventeen candidates were nominated. After four ballots it became apparent that it was not going to be an easy job to choose among them. General Wood led with 314½ votes. Governor Lowden was next with 289. But it took 493 votes to nominate. The best Wood and Lowden could do was prevent anyone else from being nominated. Each had reached the top of his strength.

Harding sweated. He had already let his senatorial filing deadline pass despite Mrs. Harding's urgings to drop his absurd presidential aspirations.

"I can't see why anyone should want to be President during the next four years," she told the newspapers.

Harding went to Daugherty for advice. Sit tight, he was told, and stop worrying. Hadn't Daugherty said in February that he didn't expect Harding to be nominated on the first or second ballot, but that on Friday morning at about eleven minutes after 2 A.M. fifteen or twenty men around a table would be trying to break a deadlock—and then he would suggest Harding?

Harding, rumpled and wearing a scrubby beard, went back to his poker game and illegal whisky.

There had to be a compromise. The delegates were restless. They wanted to go home.

The story is that the senatorial bloc met in the Hays-Harvey suite at the Blackstone that Friday night, with other powerful Republican leaders. Philander C. Knox wouldn't do. He had voted against the Eighteenth and Nineteenth amendments. Wood and Lowden were both tainted. And the Prohibitionists and suffragettes were important. The GOP needed an ordinary, simple candidate. At one in the morning editor Harvey came out of the Blackstone suite for a moment and told reporters that "this man Harding is no world-beater, but we think he is the best of the bunch."

And as smoke from the expensive Havana cigars seeped under the door, Warren Gamaliel Harding went in. It was a little after 2 A.M. At four, he came out. The next day, on the eighth ballot, Lowden and Wood's supporters forced an adjournment, to see if one would take second place. But neither would give in. When the convention came back Warren G. Harding was selected on the tenth ballot as standard bearer. Calvin Coolidge was nominated as Vice-President, because he represented opposition to the forces of organized labor.

Coolidge's one great claim to fame was stopping the great Boston police strike by a call for the national guard, and a wire to Samuel Gompers that no police force had the right to strike at any time.

Coolidge wanted the presidential nomination, but he was satisfied to take the vice-presidential job. The convention was eager to confer the honor and get away from torrid, dry Chicago. But no sooner had it done so than the charge was leveled that Harding was nominated by a handful of men in a "smoke-filled room," a charge denied by many but not by all. Jake Hamon, the Republican national committeeman from Oklahoma, told a friend before it happened that Harding would be nominated on Saturday, and that it had cost a million dollars.

Hamon was not an unimpeachable source. He was mixed up with the oil interests that wanted so desperately to "develop" the U. S. Navy's oil reserves. Later, Hamon was shot to death by his mistress. But unimpeachable or not, the facts seem to support much of Mr. Hamon's contention. Harding had spent twenty years as an Ohio politician, at first as fixer for Senator Foraker's machine, then as a member of the legislature, as lieutenant governor, governor, and finally as senator. He was mentally undistinguished. Strangely his very lack of distinction turned out to be one of his greatest political assets.

The "puppet candidate," said his opponents. "Weak and colorless and mediocre," said others. True, but these same facts endeared Harding to the Republican machine and to a public that wanted to forget that there was anything in the world but apple-pie normalcy and plain old American prosperity.

The Democratic nomination of 1920 was as unsettled as the Republican when it convened on June 28 at San Francisco. As President and leader of his party Wilson might have been expected to designate an heir apparent or at least to tell the convention that he had no candidate in mind. But Wilson in no way released the convention, although everyone who wanted the job tried to curry favor with him.

The front-running candidates were William Gibbs McAdoo, cabinet member and Wilson's son-in-law; A. Mitchell Palmer, Attorney General; and James M. Cox, governor of Ohio and newspaper publisher.

Both McAdoo and Palmer claimed the officeholder vote. Franklin Delano Roosevelt, Assistant Secretary of the Navy and delegate from New York, was for McAdoo. So were some fifty-six postmasters, assembled along with other officers of the government to lend importance to the McAdoo campaign. But there were as many officeholders cheering for Palmer, and among his prominent supporters was Cordell Hull, national committeeman from Tennessee.

Altogether there were fourteen Democrats in the race for the presidential nomination. The invalid Wilson was not among them. He had served two terms, of course, but his strange silence from the White House indicated a desire that he be offered the nomination, at least.

On the convention floor there was little serious thought of offering the nomination to Wilson. The professional bosses—Tammany's Murphy, Nugent of New Jersey, Taggart of Indiana, and Brennan of Illinois—wanted no part of Wilson. They held him responsible for the defeat of the Democrats in 1918.

The convention opened musically. The United States Marine Band played "The Star-Spangled Banner"; the biggest American flag in the world was unrolled behind Connecticut's temporary chairman Homer Cummings, who stood and defended the war effort of 1917–18 as "the cleanest war" ever fought. On the second day, when the band broke into "Hail to the Chief," the convention went wild for Wilson. Men and women began parading around the floor, snatching state standards as they went.

Franklin D. Roosevelt grabbed the New York standard, but Judge Jeremiah Mahoney, a Tammany stalwart, held on tight, and the big, husky Roosevelt had to tear it away from him, while the Tammanyites sat in their seats and sulked.

The League of Nations, again, was recognized as the big issue of the campaign. The drys were there to keep a wet plank out of the Democratic platform. William Jennings Bryan, a confirmed dry and this year back in the good graces of the party, went even further than the Anti-Saloon League would have dared go. He proposed a supporting prohibition plank in the platform.

"If you can't get alcohol enough to make you drunk," said Bryan, "why do you want alcohol at all?"

Bryan was referring to the hopes of Tammany and the California delegates that a light-wine and beer plank could be put in the platform.

The prohibition issue seemed strange since the Eighteenth Amendment had been ratified and was law. The Volstead Act, which enforced prohibition of the production and sale of spiritus frumenti, was the law of the land, piously enforced sometimes but frankly and vigorously disobeyed by all drinking men everywhere. The Republicans had refused to acknowledge any issue in prohibition, but the Republican candidate kept a plentiful supply of liquor on hand for consumption by his friends.

In the Democratic camp it was different. The lean McAdoo joined Bryan in his demand for a bone-dry plank.

"There will be no compromise," said Bryan nervously, the sweat running down his face as he spoke under the arc lights. "Either this convention will be turned over body and soul to the brewers, or the liquor interests will be put out of business so they never again will bother another Democratic convention."

Despite his queer aberration, Bryan got an overwhelming demonstration of love and loyalty. He was cheered and huzzaed in a twenty-minute demonstration—before all five of the platform planks he wanted were chopped up.

Governor Al Smith was the Tammany candidate that year—but not seriously. Tammany had no hopes that a Catholic could be nominated and elected. They had already made a deal to give their votes to James M. Cox, but first Governor Smith was to be honored. And so he was, by a forty-five minute demonstration in which the band inaugurated his political theme song, "The Sidewalks of New York."

The fourteen names soon boiled down to four: McAdoo, Palmer, Cox, and John Davis of West Virginia. The former Miss Izetta Jewel, once an actress but now a Virginia matron, spoke up to second the nomination of Davis. When she finished, the band played "Oh, You Beautiful Doll," and the delegates all sang the chorus. Other lady delegates were on hand, raring to make speeches. One, when she learned that her candidate had already been spoken for by another lady, cheerfully changed the name in her speech and delivered it in behalf of another candidate.

The ladies were going to vote this year. Some nineteen million were still unfranchised, despite passage of the Nineteenth Amendment, but some seven million could vote, and both the sons of the jackass and the spawn of the elephant were afraid to stand up against the feminine might any longer. The Democrats announced that from this year on there would be a national committeeman and a national committeewoman from each state.

For the nomination McAdoo, the "Crown Prince," fought it out with Cox and Palmer. On the first ballot it was McAdoo 266, Cox 134, Palmer 256. On the twenty-second ballot it was McAdoo 372½, Cox 430, Palmer 166½. Just before the twenty-ninth ballot one delegate suggested that the lowest candidate on each ballot be dropped, until finally, one was "nominated by exhaustion." The convention retired, until Monday morning, July 5.

Meanwhile the Hardings, having cleaned up their affairs in the Senate Office Building and at their senatorial residence, set off with a box lunch to motor to Marion, Ohio, where the senator maintained his little newspaper and planned to conduct his low-pressure, McKinley-type front-porch campaign, seeing visitors and speaking out on the issues he felt like speaking out on, under conditions he could control.

William Randolph Hearst, disgusted as usual with the way the Democratic convention was going, was trying to get Hiram Johnson to run for President on an independent ticket. Herbert Hoover, with his gift for misinterpretation of the political scene, was telling the people there would be no third party this year. And Hearst's American Constitutional Party, the American Labor Party, the midwestern Non-Partisan League, the farmer's alliance, and the World War Veterans were making plans to meet in Chicago on July 10.

On Sunday, Warren Harding, now in Marion, issued a statement that was to typify the campaign.

"Government," the candidate intoned in all seriousness, "is a very natural thing."

"That man," said a Democrat, "is just like five million other men." (Harding took this as a great compliment.)

At the Palace Hotel, anticipating a long fight and willing to wait it out for a while, Attorney General Palmer's wife bought a small stove to cook her candidate-husband's eggs the way he liked them. Undoubtedly an insult to the proud chefs of the Palace, this was necessary because Palmer was very fussy about eggs. He hadn't been so fussy when he stepped on a few strike situations, particularly in the coal fields, acquiring an anti-labor reputation that was to eliminate him in this campaign.

The Cox men went visiting over the weekend. By Monday they had convinced enough delegates that "Fighting Jimmie" was the man for the job. They hadn't convinced Carter Glass of Virginia, who now let it be known that Cox was not acceptable to Wilson.

The Cox men got on the telephone to Washington and spoke to presidential secretary Joseph Tumulty. The Cox men explained the problem. Tumulty promised to do what he could, and in a few hours Wilson announced that he had no preferences among the candidates. Cox was the man. He was nominated at 1:39 A.M. on July 6.

Franklin D. Roosevelt got the vice-presidential nomination, since the politicians figured the Roosevelt name should be worth 30,000 votes in upstate New York. Tammany was happy enough with this, for Roosevelt was a thorn in boss Murphy's aching side, and if he were elected he would be buried as Vice-President. If defeated he would be buried anyhow.

When it was all over, the newspaper boys asked William Jennings Bryan what he thought of it. Bryan paused sadly, recalling his defeat on the prohibition amendment.

"My heart is in the grave with our hopes," he said. "And I must pause till it comes back to me."

Others were not so gentle. Harding would win in a walk if the issue was to be the Wilson administration, they claimed, because Harding stood for the great commonness of the unpretentious small-town American. "Back to normalcy" was the campaign, and every American wanted just as much normalcy as the law allowed, even if he didn't know quite what it meant.

On July 10 a third party stole the scene for a few days in meetings in the Cameo Room of Chicago's Morrison Hotel. Here met clean-cut young clergymen of the English-vicar type, sleek ladies from Fifth Avenue, bespectacled and flat-heeled young women from Greenwich Village, red-handed Dakota farmers, visionary book-keepers and tough-eyed professional left-wingers.

Out of all this on July 14 was formed the Farmer Labor Party, hammered out in fist fights on the floor and verbal fights in the committee rooms.

R. N. Buck, a representative of labor's left wing wanted to read the majority report. La Follette's delegates told him to shut up.

Thereupon Abraham Lofkowitz of New York took off his coat.

"Nobody's going to read the platform except the platform committee," Lofkowitz warned.

Things quieted down, but in St. Paul boss Townley of the Non-Partisan League said flatly that nobody from the League was officially representing the body at that love feast.

Then matters flared again. Lester Barlow of the World War Veterans tangled with the physical Mr. Lofkowitz, and there was more confusion. La Follette refused the nomination. Finally Parley P. Christensen of Salt Lake City, a dissident Mormon, was nominated for the presidency, and Max S. Hayes of Cleveland, old third-party hand, for Vice-President.

The young hopefuls, the vicars and bobbed girls and dudes and debs from Fifth Avenue who had engineered the meeting, deserted in droves. If there was to be an emblem for their committee, some of them said, it ought to be a goat.

The Democrats, that year, had made an unofficial attempt to change their emblem. The wild jackass, stamped upon them by cartoonist Thomas Nast, as the elephant was wished on the Republicans and the mangy tiger on Tammany Hall, was to be exchanged for a rooster, crowing the dawn of a new era. Buttonholes of both men and women began to sport roosters for Cox.

The campaign was one-sided. Publisher Cox conferred with President Wilson and went out about the countryside, supporting the League of Nations. Franklin Roosevelt stumped the country too, energetically, if not always profitably. Despite the complaints of Boies Penrose and some of the other Republican bosses, Warren Harding stayed on his front porch, delivering long and short speeches. "Don't let them cheat 'em" was his own campaign phrase, meaning, apparently, that the public should not be shortchanged on campaign rhetoric. Senator Harding was an ideal candidate for a nation that wanted to forget itself.

There were other candidates, of course. The Socialist party nominated Eugene Debs again. The Socialist Labor nominated William W. Cox of Missouri. But these were protests. At least they were effective in getting votes cast, unlike the abortive Farmer Labor coalition that had tried to put itself together in Chicago. That group, struggling in its own lather, dissolved quietly and ineffectually in a few weeks, leaving only a pattern for the future.

Cox rattled about the country, supporting the Wilson administration and the League of Nations. Harding sat on his front porch. Roosevelt followed Cox. Calvin Coolidge spent a good deal of the campaign on his father's farm at Plymouth Notch, Vermont, chopping wood.

The nation evidently preferred porch sitters and wood choppers to internationalists. Harding polled 16,152,200 votes, Cox 9,147,353. Socialist Eugene Debs polled nearly a million, quite a record for a man who was sitting in federal prison for his anti-war activities. Socialist Laborite Cox polled 31,175 votes, a tribute to the American political system, if anything.

Harding won 404 electoral votes to Cox's 127. It was a telling victory for reaction and conservatism over progressivism and internationalism. Americans wanted things the way they were. They did not want to be bothered, for the moment, with any newfangled ideas.

18

Teddy Roosevelt died at Oyster Bay in 1919, aged sixty; his old enemy Wilson sat, half crippled, in a little house in Washington; and the Republicans made hay in Congress, the White House, and the executive offices.

Sacco and Vanzetti, a pair of anarchists, had been convicted by 1921, and the endless round of appeals had begun to make their case a cause célèbre in the history of American civil liberties. The Washington disarmament conference brought temporary limitation of arms, the high point of statesmanship in the Harding administration.

In Europe, Lenin died, and the occupation of Germany was ended. A young agitator named Adolf Hitler was jailed after an abortive attempt to seize control of the government in Germany. And a woman was elected governor of Wyoming, another elected governor of Texas.

—Strange times. . . .

18. Prosperity and Pork Barrel
1924

"I can see but one word written over the head of my husband if he is elected, and that word is tragedy," Mrs. Warren G. Harding had said in those indecisive hours at Chicago in 1920 after her handsome husband passed up the chance to run again for the Senate.

Mrs. Harding was an oracle. Harding's election brought both personal and political tragedy. As a country editor in Marion, Harding had been a Rotarian, a Chamber of Commerce committeeman, a hail-fellow.

He was always a lion with the ladies, an indefatigable poker player, and a two-fisted drinker. He first entered politics as a henchman of Senator Foraker, when that gentleman was fighting Mark Hanna for control of the Ohio Republican organization. Harding did all the things henchmen are thought to do. He fixed things, made appointments, paved ways, and cleaned up political debris. There is a story that at one time the young Harding was thrown out of Mark Hanna's office on delivering some suggestion from Foraker to which Hanna took particular exception.

Harding's careers as state legislator, lieutenant governor, governor, and United States senator were not marked by any acts of statesmanship. But, except for such personal peccadilloes as fathering Nan Britton's child (that came back later to haunt him), those cipher years were also free from any political errors.

Harding was a crony among cronies until he got to the White House. There the loneliness and awesome responsibility of the nation's highest office began to affect him, to some degree as they had affected the better men who preceded him. But the tradition was not enough. Harding had neither the character nor the inclination to be anything but what he was.

For two years, from inauguration day, 1921, until the summer of 1923, the clock of progress was turned backward. It was almost as if the Roosevelt, Taft, and Wilson administrations had never been. An untamed gang of old-school capitalists rode into Washington with Warren Harding, squatted there, and began drilling for oil. Jess Smith, an Ohio crony, went to live with Harry Daugherty, now Attorney General. Smith held no official position, but he was the man to see if you wanted something out of jail. Smith killed himself mysteriously on May 30 in Daugherty's apartment at the Wardman Park Hotel just after he learned that his name had been removed from the White House social list.

Charles R. Forbes, another Harding crony, put in charge of the Veterans Bureau, began to sell new government property as surplus, pad veterans' dental bills, and pocket large sums of the proceeds. After it all ended, some $200,000,000 in goods and money never was accounted for. Forbes went to Europe when even the gullible Harding could no longer be convinced that all was well. Forbes sent back his resignation. Later, he returned confidently to face charges and investigation, but after Harding's death, the confidence was ill founded. Forbes was sent to Leavenworth Prison. The Bureau's legal advisor, Charles F. Cramer, was made of weaker stuff. He shot himself one day in his bathroom.

Albert B. Fall was a poor man with a tumble-down ranch in New Mexico when he was appointed Secretary of the Interior. Miraculously, Fall's fortunes took a sweeping turn for the better a few months later. Harry Sinclair, a kindhearted oil magnate, gave Fall tips on the stock market that enabled him to make several killings. Sinclair found the lease on the naval oil-reserve lands at Teapot Dome, Wyoming, worth every tip. Later, he said the lease was worth $100,000,000 to him.

Then there was Edward L. Doheny, another oil man, who proposed that Fall lease him the Elk Hills naval oil reserve in California. Fall listened, borrowed $100,000 in cash from Doheny. Then Fall accepted the Doheny proposal.

Fall resigned shortly afterward, but the raw smell of oil had permeated the Administration.

President Harding aged rapidly in his two years in the White House. His hair turned gray, his face grew drawn and lined. Harding had been ill in January, and had sworn off liquor, telling the newspaper boys he did not think it fitting for a President to drink when it was against the law. But abstinence did not improve his appearance through that busy spring when a stream of officials were shooting themselves or departing from government.

By 1923 the country had come "back to normalcy" with a vengeance, if normalcy meant the untrammeled right of those in power to mulct the public of its tax revenues, to sell off public property, to hand out favors and to circumvent the laws.

By June, as the Hardings prepared for a two-month tour of Alaska, all Washington was talking, and even President Harding knew he had been victim of a gigantic confidence game.

On June 10 the Hardings traveled to Milford, Delaware, so the President could be initiated into the Tall Cedars of Lebanon, the highly advanced, secret order of third-degree Masonry. Then it was back to Washington, after a few hours on the presidential yacht *Mayflower*, back to the prisonlike grind.

Those last few days in Washington were harder than usual for a man much more at ease addressing a golf tee or drawing to a pair than worrying over problems of state. Luckily for the nation, to match Fall, Daugherty, Forbes, and Smith there were the unimpeachable Charles Evans Hughes, Secretary of State, who conducted foreign relations with considerable skill; Herbert Hoover, the quiet, competent Secretary of Commerce; and William Howard Taft, who was displaying far more talent as Chief Justice of the United States Supreme Court than he had ever shown around the White House.

Hughes was to "sit on the lid" while the President was away. Vice-President Calvin Coolidge was planning to spend the summer months in the coolness of his native New England.

President Harding worked hard on those last few nights. He had to prepare nineteen set speeches for the two-month trip across the country and Alaska. By June 19, the day before departure, he finished seven of them, and on that last night dealt with an onerous stack of requests for pardons. President Harding commuted the terms of twenty-seven political prisoners left over from the war, refused to take action in the cases of another twenty-four. Then, wearily, he went to bed.

The next day was the hottest of the year in Washington. By two o'clock, thoroughly fretful, Harding joined his wife on the steps of the White House and got into the car that would take them to the Union Station.

Harding stopped off to make major speeches at St. Louis, at Kansas City, and on across the country. They were well received. The nation was still unaware of the rottenness eating at the federal government. But as Harding went across the country he heard more and more scandal. At Kansas City he was closeted for an hour with the wife of Secretary Fall. It was after this meeting that he told a casual acquaintance he wasn't worried about his enemies, but his friends.

At Tacoma, just before leaving for Alaska, he received a long telegram in code. It upset him so much that intimates wondered if he could continue. He asked Secretary Hoover what a President should do when betrayed by his friends.

Then, on the return trip, en route to San Francisco, the President became seriously ill. The remainder of the schedule was canceled, and he was rushed to the Palace Hotel in San Francisco.

On the night of August 2 the President seemed improved. Mrs. Harding was reading aloud an article about him from *The Saturday Evening Post.* Suddenly, Harding was unusually quiet. She called the doctors. In a few minutes the President was dead.

Vice-President Coolidge was found at his father's house at Plymouth Notch, Vermont. Routed out of bed by the old man, he scurried around to find the Constitutional requirements for qualifying himself as President. The presidential oath was typed up in the house, and Colonel John Coolidge, for many years a notary public, administered the oath to his son in the family sitting room by the light of a kerosene lamp.

Within a few minutes the new President had caught a special train at Springfield, Massachusetts, and rushed to Washington to face a strong Congress, accustomed to having its own way.

The little New Englander did not get on well with the senatorial cabal from the beginning. As Vice-President, he had been a practiced nonentity. Few members of the Senate were aware of his principles or of anything else about him, except his quiescence and frugality. It was a common joke around Washington that the Vice-President banked most of his take-home pay.

Congress was riding on the crest of a tremendous swell of conspicuous consumption. Prices were high and growing higher. More and more citizens were discovering that they could make profits, even killings, by speculation in the stock market. The whole nation was bullish except one small bear: Calvin Coolidge.

But as the rottenness of the Harding administration began to out, the firm-jawed little man from Massachusetts became, overnight, a symbol of clean government. He swept out the Daughertys and the lesser evils of the Harding administration, and began to remake the executive branch of government in his own image.

There was not much time. Coolidge had less than a year in which to prove himself as an administrator, and he faced a Congress that held him in little respect. Senator Henry Cabot Lodge, the Republican majority leader, secured passage of the soldiers' bonus against Coolidge's objections and then second passage of the bill over the President's veto. Lodge joined Idaho's Borah to defeat the World Court bill Coolidge wanted, opposed the President on immigration policy. So it went, almost down to the day of the Republican convention in Cleveland. In fact, even as the senators prepared to move out for the festivities, Coolidge was vetoing a postal pay raise bill, squarely on the grounds that it would cost the government $68,000,000, that the postal employees had already had three recent pay increases, in excess of the rise in cost of living. "Government extravagance must stop," said the little man.

In a very short time Coolidge had become extremely popular. He stood against tax increases and against big government. He had no cronies, he did not play poker, and there was not the slightest smell of the back room about him.

This public endorsement made it possible for Coolidge to wrest control of the Republican party from the hands of the senators. While Lodge was winning all the publicized victories in Congress, the Coolidge managers, Frank Stearns and William M. Butler, quietly outmaneuvered him in party affairs. By convention time it was obvious that there would be no opposition to Coolidge's renomination. "Keep Cool With Coolidge" was the slogan as the Republicans assembled in a drenched and drizzly Cleveland on June 10.

Usually the politicking at national conventions starts at least a week before the banging of the opening gavel. This was not so in Cleveland in 1924, much to the disgust of the city's businessmen, who had paid the Republican National Committee $125,000 to bring the convention to their city. As late as June 8 there were no expensive headquarters in operation at the big hotels. The city was almost uncluttered with signs. A few lithographed portraits of Coolidge were to be found, but little else. The casual visitor would hardly have known that Cleveland was about to house a national political convention at all.

If there was an issue to come before the convention it was the need for tax reduction. A tax cut was so heartily backed by the cold and hard-boiled businessmen that no one need show up early at Cleveland to debate it.

The only thing the convention had to do was select a Vice-President. Coolidge refused to get involved. He would have backed Senator Borah, had the latter consented to run, but Borah was opposed to presidential support of the League of Nations and the World Court and would not let his name be used.

The senators wanted Governor Lowden, who had so narrowly missed the Republican nomination in 1920. Two days before the convention Colonel Edward Clifford of Chicago set up a small shop to plumb for the candidacy of Charles G. Dawes, Harding's first director of the budget, a profane, pithy, retired general.

All around, it was to be a quick, if dispirited, convention. The order had gone out that Cleveland was to be bone-dry during convention week. The state government ordered thirty-four extra prohibition officers to town. The federal government sent in a large force to supplement the regular fourteen-man anti-alcohol unit. First blood was drawn when officers lurked outside one of the city's most exclusive golf clubs and stopped all visitors to see if their cars carried any liquor.

On June 7 the Coolidge headquarters at the Hollenden Hotel was empty. It was not until two days later that reporters in town had much to do except interview one another, or speculate on the vice-presidency or the efforts of Tris Speaker's Indians to pull themselves out of the American League cellar in the forthcoming series with the Washington Senators.

As the convention began, it was apparent that Coolidge was completely in charge. His single show of force was a display of personal vengeance against Senator Henry Cabot Lodge. It particularly rankled Coolidge that Lodge had pushed the soldier bonus bill over his veto. To Coolidge's well-ordered mind Lodge, as majority leader, had the responsibility of supporting the Administration's program. Since Lodge did not support that program he was to be punished.

The punishment was awesome. As the Massachusetts delegation moved into town the Coolidge men let it be known that Lodge was to have no place in their counsels. He was to be only another delegate to the convention, this bristly bearded old party war horse who had been keynoter, committee chairman, and permanent convention chairman in years past.

Many doubted if the Coolidge forces could get away with it. Lodge himself scarcely believed it. But when the Massachusetts delegation caucused at the Hollenden on June 9, Lodge was deprived of his chairmanship of the delegation, removed as the state's representative on the convention resolutions committee. He was given a hotel room so demeaning that one of his former secretaries, there as a spectator, traded with him to improve the senator's lot. Lodge was allowed to sit in the front row at the convention, since Massachusetts and Vermont claimed those front positions as the President's home state and birthplace. But his grandson, Henry Cabot Lodge, Jr., there as a Boston *Transcript* reporter, probably exerted as much influence on the proceedings as did the old man. A wag suggested that Lodge might be made the Massachusetts representative on the official convention committee of notification that would call on his enemy Coolidge, but the old man was spared this indignity.

Representative Theodore E. Burton rang the keynote of the convention—economy in government. It surprised no one, nor did the nomination of Coolidge, although one wild gambler had staked $200 to $3000 that Coolidge would not be nominated. Perhaps the odds were so good he couldn't turn the bet down. There could have been no other reason.

For the first time, a radio hookup was arranged to cover almost all states as far west as Kansas City. And modern telephone transmission had made it possible for newspapers on both coasts to print pictures of the goings on within a few hours after they were taken.

Usually, the national committee's rooms at the convention were the center of activity, but in this strange year, the unofficial headquarters was Coolidge manager William Butler's suite on the ninth floor of the Cleveland Hotel. From this suite came all official information. Such proceedings irked the senate group, for while it was generally known that Butler would assume the chairmanship of the national committee after the convention, the Coolidge men were pouring it on.

Then they rubbed it in. They selected Representative Burton as temporary chairman of the convention as planned. They elected former Representative Frank Mondell as permanent chairman as planned. The plans were made without any consideration for the wishes of the senators. In the days of Murray Crane and Boies Penrose, this would not have gone unfought, but both were gone in 1924, and the rest were stunned by the almost offhand punishment of Senator Lodge.

It rained constantly, but Cleveland made every attempt of recoup financially. Drugstores advertised a "Keep Cool with Coolidge Highball," ice, pineapple juice, grape juice, and a raw egg. One burlesque house featured The Republican Girls' Parade, and another The Keep Cool Kuties. Generally it was, as one writer said, a chilly convention in a chilly city to nominate a chilly man.

Few high jinks pepped up the proceedings. The Hometown Coolidge Club of Plymouth, Vermont, dressed up in the kind of smock Coolidge wore on the farm, then sang "Keep Cool and Keep Coolidge." The singers distributed some 5000 copies of the song and made available, for $10 each, 2000 rustic canes of birch, maple, and willow cut from the cow pasture of the John Coolidge farm. The Red-Headed Legion of America, meeting in Long Island, announced that it was going to support Coolidge in the campaign, for the obvious reason. Wellesley College alumnae appeared in the convention hall and at the hotels selling stuffed elephants, but there were few buyers.

It was not a good convention for men: political men or married men. From the opening, when keynoter Burton attacked the record of Congress and was greeted by a healthy cheer, it was apparent that the senate bloc's power had been broken. Next most discomfited, perhaps, were the husbands of the lady delegates, some fifty in number, who formed an association called "The Consorts" (their motto, "Give me the check"). The ladies had finally come into their own, politically speaking. It had taken some twoscore years of agitation, but this year Mrs. Elizabeth P. Martin was chosen chairman of the committee on permanent organization of the convention, a most important job.

Even before the convention opened, former Governor Lowden had said he would not be candidate for the vice-presidency, but the convention nominated him anyhow. He turned the offer down in no uncertain terms, so the convention turned to Charles G. Dawes. Then, the business done, the delegates left the dripping but dry Cleveland for home.

This year while neither party was willing to make an issue of prohibition, the great experiment was not working very well. The Association Against the Prohibition Amendment, Inc., recalled the findings of congressional investigations, which showed the bootleggers in one state paid $1,800,000 in graft, allowing them to do $25,000,000 in business. One wholesale druggist had paid $250,000 in a month for illegal whisky permits. In one big city $4,000,000 changed hands in ninety days in the sale of whisky permits, enabling a buyer to purchase legal whisky for "medical use." A member of Congress had gone to prison for violating the prohibition law he had helped pass; the first director of prohibition enforcement, handpicked by the Anti-Saloon League, had escaped federal indictment under the Volstead Act only by turning state's evidence against others. A superintendent of the Anti-Saloon League had been exposed as a bootlegger. And throughout the land Americans were making bathtub gin, home-brew, and soaking up the poisonous wares of local bootleggers.

The drys, unhappy in the open violation of the prohibition laws by a great many Americans, sought aridity for the nation in fact as well as in theory.

This year the Democratic convention was to be held in the wettest city in the country—New York. Herbert Bayard Swope of the New York *World* had been instrumental in getting the convention for the big city; he had managed to raise $205,000 to pay the Democratic National Committee, and that was $5000 better than the bid of any other city. It was a high price, but the city's hotelkeepers and speak-easy operators thought it would be worth it in increased revenue.

The Republicans had not yet left Cleveland when the Democrats were massing their forces in New York, although their meeting was not scheduled for another two weeks. The two outstanding contenders for the Democratic nomination were William Gibbs McAdoo, Wilson's Secretary of the Treasury, and Governor Al Smith of New York. It was going to be a hot fight. No one had any doubt about that. McAdoo had been an attorney for oilman Doheny in the Teapot Dome affair. And while he had nothing to do with the oil speculations, some of the smell of oil was on him. McAdoo was as dry as a bone, too, and Smith was as wet as any Tammany politician who ever staggered out of a saloon after a winning election night.

Smith was a Catholic, and thus a target for the Ku Klux Klan which had raised its sheets in the South and Middle West and was riding into the political arena on a wagonload of 150 per cent Americanism. In Indiana the Klan had captured the Republican organization and would control the governorship and state offices in the coming election. The Klan was also to have a brief and disgraceful orgy of triumph in Colorado.

The Democrats' natural issue was the corruption of the Harding administration. That did not mean a Democratic victory was a foregone conclusion. It would take a strong campaign and a unified party to defeat the Republicans, for Coolidge was popular, and it was no easy matter to hold him responsible for the sins of his predecessor.

On July 7, anticipating a bloody battle for nomination, but secure in the belief that their man had 614 of the 732 votes needed to control the convention, William G. McAdoo's men moved into the Hotel Vanderbilt. In New York the Smith forces were led by the crippled Franklin Delano Roosevelt, who was just now recovering enough from his bout with polio to get back into the political picture. Roosevelt's workers were carrying on an extensive campaign of direct mail to all potential voters.

In between the Republican and Democratic conventions attention turned to St. Paul where the Farmer Labor party began meetings on June 17. There, it became quickly apparent that William Z. Foster, chief American communist, was in charge. The La Follette Progressives, who were watching the two big parties before deciding their course, immediately condemned the Farmer Laborites.

The newspapers quickly refocused on New York, where the city's Democrats had planned a gay round of social events for the delegates and their wives.

There would be a tea at the Metropolitan Museum of Art, a reception at the Brooklyn Institute of Arts and Sciences, a tea at Mrs. Frank Vanderlip's house at Scarboro-on-Hudson. Other events were planned by the Museum of the City of New York, the Museum of Natural History. Franklin Roosevelt's house was to be thrown open to visitors. And two weeks before the convention the police began rounding up pickpockets and putting them away for the season.

Governor Smith came down to the Biltmore Hotel from Albany on June 12. McAdoo arrived by private rail car on the eighteenth and was met by a cheering crowd of 3000 and a brass band. That same day at Hornell, New York, William Jennings Bryan stepped off an Erie Railroad train to keep a Chautauqua speaking engagement. Smith would never be nominated, the great commoner told the porters. Of course, the prohibitionist Bryan didn't like Smith, who was an avowed wet. So sensitive were dry palates that year that when McAdoo ate cake flavored with sherry wine, he had to explain.

On convention eve the gaiety continued, as the delegates enjoyed the wicked big city. At the Shubert Theatre, Bonnie Glass and a fellow named Clifton Webb danced during a huge fashion show, to music furnished by bandleader Irving Berlin.

Great American flags hid the roof of Madison Square Garden as the convention was called to order on June 24. Senator Tom Walsh of Montana, the man who had uncovered the Teapot Dome scandal, presided over the meeting. The keynote attack on the Republican scandals was sounded by Senator Pat Harrison of Mississippi. As usual in Democratic conventions, the platform weighed heavily on those who built it. The Ku Klux Klan caused bitter committee fighting. The resolutions committee never did mention the Klan by name in its plank on religious tolerance.

But everyone knew the platform committee would have trouble; the convention decided to go ahead with the nominations while waiting.

Alabama's Fordney Johnson nominated Senator Oscar Underwood and asked for a platform plank "reaffirming the party's position against the Know-Nothing policy of proscribing from public office members of certain races and creeds, as is now proposed by the Ku Klux Klan."

Half the audience and many delegates rose to show their approval.

California nominated William Gibbs McAdoo, and then Connecticut yielded to New York. Wearing braces on his paralyzed legs, Franklin Delano Roosevelt was helped to the platform to nominate Governor Al Smith.

Other candidates were mentioned: James M. Cox again; John W. Davis of West Virginia, white-haired former ambassador to the British court; United States Senator Samuel M. Ralston of Indiana; Bryan's brother Charles, now governor of Nebraska, and nine others.

Smith's chances were hampered by his Catholicism and the death of Charles Murphy, the Tammany boss, a few weeks before the convention.

For four days in committee and then on the floor the convention struggled over the issue of religious liberty. Speakers were long-winded and eloquent. Most long-winded and most eloquent of all was William Jennings Bryan, trying to pacify every side, but this year he was interrupted by hisses and boos from both floor and gallery.

In the early hours of Saturday morning, June 28, the vote was finally taken. The proposal to single out the Klan was defeated, 546.15 to 541.85. The issue was not settled in the platform, it would have to be settled in selection of the candidate. And there the choice was between the fair-haired prohibitionist Protestant American, slightly tarnished by his Doheny association, and the urbane anti-prohibitionist Catholic, a product of New York's Lower East Side, a self-styled graduate of the Fulton Fish Market.

As in 1920, McAdoo received the highest vote on the first ballot; 431½ to Smith's 241, Cox's 59. Underwood, sixth, got 46½. John Davis, eighth, polled 31, and Ralston 30.

That first day of balloting the convention held 15 roll calls, the next day 15 more. On the thirtieth ballot McAdoo polled 415½, Smith 323½, Davis 126½, Underwood 39½, Cox 57.

The sixtieth ballot broke all records of balloting for Democratic national conventions. The sixty-first made it quite plain that the convention was deadlocked. It was now July 3, and the squirming Democrats were well into their second week. Dispositions were so frayed that Chairman Walsh several times threatened to adjourn the convention and move to another city, if order could not be maintained in New York.

Suddenly it was the Fourth of July, and the Democrats adjourned thankfully for the holiday.

On July 4 the La Follette Progressives assembled at Cleveland, tired of waiting. Senator La Follette had stayed away from the Republican convention, to see whether or not he could support that party. He had watched carefully the Democratic debates in New York. And he had decided, as nearly everyone knew all along, that he could support neither party.

La Follette had no illusions about winning an election, but he allowed himself to be nominated anyhow. Burton K. Wheeler, a Democratic senator from Montana, was the bipartisan vice-presidential choice of the Progressives.

Coolidge was at the White House, politics out of his mind because young Calvin, Jr., was running a high temperature. An infected blister on his toe had brought blood poisoning. In New York the Democrats were still indulging in a binge of emotions.

In Long Branch, New Jersey, on the Fourth of July, some two thousand Ku Klux Klansmen, women, and their offspring rallied and picnicked. It was the state Klorero, to demonstrate political strength of the Klan in New Jersey, eastern Pennsylvania, and Delaware. Resplendent in his ghostly finery was John A. Baker, Supreme Dragon of the Royal Riders of the Red Robe of New York and New Jersey. The elders erected an effigy of Al Smith clutching a bottle of scotch whisky. They bought baseball throws (three a nickle) to assault the bogeyman. A hooded wedding was performed by a hooded bride and hooded groom, hooded attendants, hooded minister, and hooded Red Bank Klan band, which serenaded the happy couple through bedsheet and purple cape.

Since Indiana was the brightest star in the Klan's crown, Judge C. J. Orbison of the Hoosier State made the principal address of the day. "I have just come from Jew York," the judicious one told his eager listeners, "and have been to the Democratic Klonvention. No matter what they do there will not be anybody but a Protestant as President or Vice-President. If the Democrats are foolish enough to nominate Al Smith they won't carry six states in the Union."

In Clinton, Missouri, Herman P. Faris, the candidate of the National Prohibition party, promised that when he was elected the White House would be white—"not splotched with either oil or booze." He asked Americans why they wanted to adopt a dry law, and then elect a wet nurse for it.

Next day, holiday over, the Klansmen again became private citizens, Calvin Coolidge watched sorrowfully at the bedside of his dying son, and the Democrats went back to their suicide attempt.

The seventy-first ballot was McAdoo's apex. He polled 528 votes, 200 short of the two thirds necessary. On the eighty-sixth ballot Al Smith passed the "Crown Prince." On the ninety-fourth ballot McAdoo rose again, to 395 votes, but it was a last gasp.

On July 8, Governor Smith called McAdoo for a meeting at the Ritz-Carlton Hotel. Smith said he was willing to withdraw if McAdoo would. McAdoo would consider withdrawing only in favor of Senator Ralston of Indiana. Smith demanded unconditional withdrawal by both. The deadlock continued.

McAdoo walked back into the Vanderbilt Hotel, where he was corralled by two women.

"You will not desert us?" one of them breathed.

"No."

She dropped to her knees in prayer.

The next day Franklin Roosevelt reported that Governor Smith was willing to withdraw if McAdoo would step down. Now McAdoo had to step down, or take sole responsibility for what might happen to the party. Reluctantly, on the ninety-ninth ballot, when he was exactly tied with Smith at 353 votes, Wilson's heir apparent told his delegates to use their own judgment. Smith then withdrew.

McAdoo's was an equivocal statement, but it did the job. The convention recessed until evening that Wednesday. On the hundred and first ballot McAdoo dropped to 52 votes, Smith to 121, John W. Davis rose to 316, Senator Underwood to 229½. Senator Walsh, the chairman, received 98, former Secretary of Agriculture Meredith of Iowa, 130.

But on the hundred and third ballot Davis was nominated by an exhausted, embittered convention. The nomination was made "unanimous" over the voluble objections of delegates from Oregon and Arizona.

Senator Walsh refused the vice-presidential nomination. Meredith was nominated. He withdrew. Finally, Governor Charles W. Bryan of Nebraska was nominated, in a chorus of shouting from disaffected delegates. At 2:25 A.M., Thursday, July 10, the national Democratic convention adjourned, sine die.

It had talked longer than any other Democratic convention. It had held more roll-call votes than any other convention. And it had split the Democratic party more seriously than ever before in peacetime. The Democrats had gone into convention on June 24 clutching the Harding scandals high, sure that a Democratic victory was theirs for the taking. They emerged on July 10, after the press had set a new telegraphy record, 9,705,603, words, telling in precious detail the story of dissension and abuse and enmity that was to make Calvin Coolidge's victory certain.

The presidential campaign of 1924 was late in starting, uneventful in execution, and just plain dull. The death of Calvin, Jr., had taken much of the heart out of his father.

But gradually life at the White House returned to the old routine, even if it never again seemed the same to Calvin Coolidge. The President rose at six-thirty or so, shaved with his straight razor, walked with one of the secret servicemen for company, and returned to breakfast with Mrs. Coolidge in their apartment. By eight the President was dictating letters or a speech in the library, and an hour or so later he began to receive his daily callers.

On one occasion Coolidge shook hands with nineteen hundred people in thirty-four minutes. He liked this part of his job. It was a simple pleasure to meet people that way.

And the people liked Coolidge. The country was prospering, the "little fellow" got a good press because he was always willing to appear in funny hats or woolly chaps for the newsreelmen. His cold poise and dry monosyllables fitted the national stereotype of the New Englander. After Harding, the nation was ready for the rock-bound.

Coolidge made only one speech for himself in 1924. He needed to do no more. The Democrats had knocked themselves out at Madison Square Garden in the fight over Catholicism and the Ku Klux Klan. Republican Chairman Butler, recalling the Bull Moose vote of 1912, concentrated the Republican fire on the La Follette Progressives, warning that La Follette meant social revolution. Republican indifference to the Democrats angered Democratic candidate Davis, who was speaking three and four times a day, mostly on Republican corruption and mismanagement. But while many heard, few listened.

In the November 4 election, Coolidge polled 15,725,003 votes to Davis's 8,385,586 and La Follette's 4,822,856. The Socialists had not put up a candidate this year; from his bed in a midwestern sanitarium Eugene Debs had asked the party to support La Follette. The Communists, labor party, and other fringe groups polled just over 100,000 votes altogether, and the strongest of these was the Prohibitionist party with 56,289.

It was the greatest Republican victory in history.

Davis carried only the 136 electoral votes of the solid South and Oklahoma; La Follette carried Wisconsin's 13 and Coolidge got all the rest, 382. Yet in the peculiar American system, in which a candidate must win a majority in each state to win *all* the electoral votes of that state, an aroused and united Democratic party might have won the election of 1924, for Coolidge ran behind the combined total of the Democrats and Progressives in 27 states that had 248 electoral votes.

19

By 1924 the gin mills were grinding furiously. The flapper and the raccoon coat and the model-T Ford were all animated symbols of a gay society. College boys were lionized and their peccadilloes cheered. It was a time of flinging about, of scattering a few harmless wild oats.

The country was prosperous, and if a pair of men's shoes cost twenty dollars, well there were more men in the country with twenty dollars to spend for shoes than ever before. The nation felt righteous enough just looking at Calvin Coolidge's stern picture, and if Coolidge could be kept in office, it was obvious that all would be right with the world. . . .

19. Rum, Romanism, and Socialism: The Campaign of 1928

Coolidge, of course, could have had the nomination in 1928 just for the asking. He did not ask. On August 2, 1927, at his vacation camp in the Black Hills of South Dakota, "Silent Cal" has issued a cryptic statement in response to questions about the 1928 campaign. "I do not choose to run for President in 1928," he told the press, in a release he distributed himself to reporters.

No one could understand it, the cynics looked for the political angle, and the faithful continued to work for Coolidge anyhow. He would not amplify, nor would he discuss the issue. But part of the answer must have been that the blister still ached; the "power and glory" of the presidency had flickered out with a sixteen-year-old life in the summer of 1924.

"I do not choose to run" is not the kind of statement that ends political speculation. Herbert Hoover went to the dictionary to look up the word "choose" and to study its peculiar colloquial meanings and insinuations in New England American. Senator Charles Curtis of Kansas, another Republican hopeful, asked the President for amplification. He did not get it.

Hoover, now badly afflicted with the presidential itch, asked the same. He got no answer.

If any man in Washington could have gotten Coolidge to answer, it should have been Herbert Hoover, his Secretary of Commerce. Hoover was the only member of the Cabinet who supported the President's opposition to the McNary-Haugen bill, which would have created farm price supports and government purchasing commodities. But Coolidge kept his own counsel. He attacked the Republican National Committee in Washington on December 5 and told the committeemen that his statement stood. But always there seemed to be something unsaid. The business leaders of the country kept hoping Coolidge would change his mind.

Hoover was the heir apparent to the Coolidge mantle. Vice-President Dawes, beloved by the party old guard, opposed the President on the farm issue and earned Coolidge's bitter enmity. Most other politicians in the capital opposed Coolidge here too, for they could recall the five million votes La Follette had polled in 1924, most of them in the plowed furrows of the Middle West. But Coolidge stood on his principle, against expenditure, government interference, and all political advice. Hoover alone supported him.

So Hoover got Coolidge's support too, although it came in a traditionally sidelong and unspoken way. In February, Hoover asked Coolidge if he intended to file in the Ohio primary. Calvin Coolidge looked at him.

"No."

The moonfaced Hoover then asked what the President thought about Hoover's own case.

"Why not?" asked the President.

In the middle of the spring Hoover had secured the pledges of some 400 delegates of the 1089 who would attend the Republican convention in Kansas City on June 12. Still nervous about Coolidge's behavior, he went again to the President and offered his support.

"If you have 400 delegates," the President told him, "you'd better keep them."

By now it was Hoover against a field that included Curtis, Dawes, Senator Watson of Indiana, and former Governor Frank Lowden of Illinois, who had so nearly won the nomination in 1920 and had declined second place in 1924.

Unlike the convention of 1924 the politicians began arriving early in Kansas City for the political festivities. On June 3, with the meeting still nine days away, a story seemed to be shaping up. Political correspondents were already predicting a party fight like that of 1912, and a bolt of the anti-Hoover forces.

"Stop Hoover" was the battle cry of the early arrivals. Coolidge had just vetoed, for the second time, the McNary-Haugen bill. Since Hoover represented the Coolidge record, the spleen of the farmers of the Middle West was directed against the big man from California. Secretary of the Interior Hubert Work, one of the Hoover generals, was already in Kansas City, directing the activities of his forces. But the big noise came from the enemy.

Within a few days that enemy had united, for a last-ditch stand. Hoover now claimed 531 votes of the 545 necessary, but 73 were involved in contests to be taken before the credentials committee. Slim as it was, there seemed still a chance to defeat the big mining engineer.

On June 7 the twenty-five anti-Hoover leaders met to plan their strategy in the Lowden headquarters in Kansas City's Hotel Baltimore. Louis Emmerson, Republican candidate for governor of Illinois, was elected head of the executive committee to lead the fight. Equally important was Mrs. Ruth Hanna McCormick, widow of Senator Medill McCormick and daughter of Mark Hanna. But most important was the presence and tentative adherence of Charles D. Hilles of New York, vice-chairman of the national committee and a leader of the "Draft Coolidge" group.

The most effective anti-Hoover noise was coming from the farmers, and the farmers were already being urged to make a march on Kansas City, to push "anyone but Hoover." The anti-Hoover group got squarely behind the farm movement.

Hoover's candidacy got an important boost that pre-convention week from William Randolph Hearst, the usually undaunted Democrat, who noted that while Hoover was a bit too conservative for his personal taste, these were conservative times and that Hoover was the best man for the job.

On June 8 the anti-Hoover coalition decided to concentrate on unseating sixty-six Hoover delegates whom the national committee had seated temporarily. In high spirits, Mark Hanna's daughter proclaimed the end in sight.

"Hoover is done. That much is certain," she said.

It was far from certain. All Hoover needed was the Pennsylvania delegation, and he was sure of the nomination on the first ballot. The Pennsylvanians had promised one another in May that they would vote as a unit; and they would not make any decisions until they got to Kansas City. Most influential of the Pennsylvanians was Andrew Mellon, Coolidge's Secretary of the Treasury, a member of the "Draft Coolidge" claque.

By June 10, even though the first-ballot question had not been settled, Hoover had enough second-choice commitments now to assure nomination on the second ballot, unless the roof somehow fell in. Even National Chairman William Butler was now resigned to giving Hoover the support of Massachusetts, although he desperately hoped President Coolidge could be persuaded to run.

Kansas City really looked like a convention town. The streets were alive with bunting; Republicans from every corner of the nation clapped each other on the back and asked what was new, although there was very little new. Prohibition was four years older, and so was the determination of a great body of Americans to ignore it. On Sunday night the authorities raided four bootlegging establishments in Kansas City.

President William Green of the American Federation of Labor, determined to keep his segment of organized labor out of politics, called for 2.75% beer for the workingman, the five-day week, and guarantees against conscription for the armed forces.

Michael Williams, editor of *The Commonweal*, the influential Catholic magazine, told the world that the religious issue was hardly likely to play an important role in the coming campaign, for the bugaboo of religious bigotry was dead.

On the night of June 11 the Republicans staged a grand pre-convention parade. By torchlight, stimulated by twenty-six different bands, some five thousand marchers started south on Grand Avenue, and out to Penn Valley Park, among them an elephant with a Shriner jouncing along in a howdah on his back. Floats recalling Abraham Lincoln and Alexander Hamilton drew cheers, but Teddy Roosevelt's float drew the biggest cheers of all—bigger by far than those for the large red bandwagon labeled Hoover.

Then the struggle for first place on the ticket was all over. William S. Vare, the Philadelphia political boss, broke the Pennsylvania pledge, announced he would throw his support to Hoover. From Vare's vantage point this was a good day to put one over on Secretary Mellon, and to assure himself of consideration in the division of spoils. Mellon and Butler conferred with Everett Sanders, Coolidge's secretary, and were convinced that President Coolidge would not change his mind. Sadly, they acknowledged the death of the "Draft Coolidge" movement.

The next day the Republican National Convention met, bent on ratifying Hoover's victory, to hedge as much as possible on the important issues of farm relief and prohibition, and to choose a Vice-President. The last job was left to the delegates, because neither Hoover nor Coolidge would interfere.

National Chairman Butler opened the convention just after ten o'clock. Already the news of Hoover's coming victory had wafted back to Wall Street. The long-standing bull market promptly collapsed in disappointment. Many Wall Street men regarded Hoover as a dangerous internationalist with radical leanings.

Hoover was also the butt of a last-minute protest by the farm bloc. Three hundred farmers, led by Governor Adam McMullen of Nebraska, marched to Eagle Hall to demand a plank for strong farm support. Feeling ran high. Governor A. G. Sorlie of North Dakota was supposed to be one of the protest leaders, but when someone asked him whom he favored in the campaign, he said he was first for Lowden, but second for Hoover.

"Traitor," shouted one of the farmer bystanders, amid the hisses and catcalls.

"You'll never be governor again," yelled another.

The next day five hundred of these farmers marched down to the convention hall, determined to air their views before the highest body of the Republican party. They almost made it. About twenty pushed through the lines, but the police rallied and threw the husky farmers out onto the street, where after some mumbling they decided against trying further to storm the convention.

That same day President Coolidge departed serenely by private car for his summer encampment in Wisconsin's Brule River country. Coolidge had done everything he would for Hoover.

The anti-Hooverites hadn't quit yet. Governor Lowden flatly refused to withdraw his name so Hoover could be nominated by acclamation. Someone invoked the name of General John J. Pershing, the hero of World War I, but Pershing was not having any of that. All Mrs. McCormick and the others could do now was squirm.

Hoover was nominated by John L. McNab of California. Then came the nominating of Senator James E. Watson of Indiana, Charles Curtis of Kansas, George W. Norris of Nebraska, and Guy D. Goff of West Virginia.

That day, June 14, the issue was so little in doubt that the American Legion notified the Hoover men that any one of five World War veterans would be acceptable to them for Vice-President.

The next day Hoover was nominated on the first ballot, with 837 votes against the field. Almost immediately Senator Curtis called Hoover, who was in Washington, to pledge his support. It was a wise move if he wanted any influence with the Administration, for he sided with the "Stop Hoover" movement, had argued in favor of the farm relief program, and could have become extremely popular with the Hoover men at the flick of another eyelash.

Governor Lowden made no such overtures. He had run out his string and, knowing it, departed silently that night for his home in Oregon, Illinois.

Charles G. Dawes could have had the vice-presidency again, if he would accept the Hoover forces' demand and make a public statement that the GOP platform had disposed of the farm issue. But Dawes did not believe that Hoover's call for "voluntary" co-operation on the farm issue was the answer. He would make no such statement.

That night the organization decided Curtis was the man to placate the farmers. The next day it took the convention just an hour and five minutes to ratify the decision. Curtis gave the Republican ticket two firsts: he was the first Indian candidate for such high office; and he and Hoover made up the first and only western ticket in history.

Wall Street had rallied considerably, for Hoover looked pleasantly conservative. The alternative, Wall Street guessed, would be Democrat Al Smith. He had won re-election in 1926 as governor of New York against a strong Republican candidate by more than a quarter of a million votes. As the Democrats moved in on Houston, Texas, to hold their first southern convention since the Civil War, there was very little chance that anyone else would be nominated. But unlike Hoover, Al Smith had not campaigned for votes, because he did not have to. He was obviously the best Democratic vote getter in the party.

Smith stayed in Albany, while Mrs. Smith and other members of the family happily went South to join the fun. This year they were sure it would be fun, for no one expected the kind of religious and radical tensions that had made a nightmare of 1924. The power of the Ku Klux Klan had waned.

On Friday, June 22, New York City Mayor Jimmy Walker set off in a borrowed private railroad car for Houston, and the Texas city began rolling out the red carpet for "The American Prince of Wales." Houston's special efforts for the convention included a hall built in sixty-four days and a Coney Island atmosphere, with one genuine Coney Island showman ready to exhibit "the largest ape ever captured" at fifteen cents a look.

Already the Woman's Christian Temperance Union was on hand, determined to secure a dry plank and a dry candidate, and holding noonday prayer meetings for any delegate who wanted to sit in.

Senator James A. Reed of Missouri was lodged at the Rice Hotel, an earnest candidate without a ghost of a chance. Smith floor leader Franklin D. Roosevelt had heard Graham McNamee of the National Broadcasting Company and J. Andrew White of CBS describe the Republican convention and didn't want the Smith nomination to sound as though it, too, had been laid out by a steam roller, so Smith supporters did nothing at all to gain support for their man.

Sometimes, as in 1924, when listeners could hear the profanity and behind-the-scenes maneuvers, the broadcasts were more revealing than the reporting in the newspapers. The Smith men wanted to guard against mistakes. They hired no band and employed no spontaneous demonstrators to hang around hotel corridors.

The Democrats had their "Stop Smith" movement, but it was not so well organized or so vocal as the anti-Hoover force had been at Kansas City. The prohibitionist Democrats, who detested Smith's wetness, made a last-ditch stand to rally around Senator Reed—also an avowed wet. Their parade on June 24 featured forty-eight donkeys ridden by Boy Scouts. But this good deed had little noticeable affect on the wet temper of the pre-convention proceedings.

On June 25 the drys enjoyed only sparse attendance at breakfast, noon, and evening meetings, but Tammany Hall, the hated Tammany, was greeted with cheers and pretty girls and happy laughter when its three trains pulled into town! The braves of Tammany must have been overwhelmed, for they were more familiar with jeers, black looks, and extra police protection.

Now that Tammany was there, Houston could erupt in joy. The Tammany men had hardly lit when the pretty girls led bands and marches down Main Street; a hundred cowboys on sorrels, pintos, big bays, and lean ponies erupted along on sidewalks, giving the rebel yell and yells of their very own. They uncoiled lariats and roped the pretty girls and dudes.

The cowboys gone, down Main Street marched a grim-visaged army of women, many in black, walking eyes straight ahead, in that dedicated fierceness that only women on parade can achieve.

"A Dry Platform and a Dry Candidate—Nothing Else Will Do,"

proclaimed the sash of a seventy-year-old, as she hobbled along, aided by a younger friend.

The Democratic convention began the next day, June 26, in the new hall. The northerners new to the ways of the South noticed the segregated gallery for Negroes and that the Negroes stayed away in droves.

There was only one open issue in the convention of 1928—prohibition, since the Democrats straddled the farm issue right along with the Republicans. Like the Republicans, the Democrats wanted to play both ends of the prohibition issue, too. After heated debate the platform committee came up with a plank that called for enforcement of the prohibition law, but indicated the states had a right to try to change the law. The drys were extremely angry.

On the second day, a pink-cheeked, healthy-looking Franklin Delano Roosevelt, despite braced legs and heavy cane, made his way to the platform and nominated Al Smith, whom he christened "the Happy Warrior." Others nominated Senator Reed, Walter George of Georgia, Evans Woollen of Indiana, Representative William Ayres of Kansas, Representative Cordell Hull of Tennessee, Jesse Jones of Texas, Huston Thompson of Colorado, Gilbert M. Hitchcock of Nebraska, and Atlee Pomerene of Ohio.

Coolidge was in Wisconsin taking a canoe lesson from an Indian guide.

Next day, on the first roll call, Smith received 724⅔ votes, whereupon Ohio changed its vote and added more than the ten needed to nominate.

Then, many of the Democrats erupted in glee, for the party had nominated a proven vote getter. But some, especially from the South, sank down in their seats in silent gloom. They were not forgetting 1924, nor could they wipe out the hidden Catholic or liquor issues.

In an effort to cheer the South, the Democrats took Smith's own choice for Vice-President, Senator Joseph Robinson of Arkansas. It was the first nomination of a man from below the Mason-Dixon line since 1860, but even this was not enough to heal the Democratic wounds of 1924. Many southerners openly growled their intention of voting Republican. Southern dry leaders issued a call to Asheville, North Carolina, to mull over local candidates and to work for the defeat of Smith, the "Tammany wet." Selection of John J. Raskob as national chairman didn't help any. Raskob was chosen because he was former chairman of the General Motors Corporation. This was the Democratic answer to "Coolidge Prosperity." But Raskob, too, was a confirmed wet.

The drys were not Smith's only opponents in the sullen southland. The Ku Klux Klan, weakened as it had been in the past four years, still exerted every effort to defeat the Democratic candidate. There began one of the most bigoted political campaigns in history, probably no more vicious than others, except that much of the viciousness came from the "nice" people of the nation.

Unfortunately, it was not confined to whispering against Smith's Catholicism. Ministers from pulpits urged their flocks to vote Republican. Assistant Attorney General Mabel Walker Willebrandt urged Methodists everywhere to vote for the Republican party. The Klan's Imperial Wizard in Atlanta and the Grand Dragons all over the map warned their followers to "Keep the Pope Out of the White House." An Oklahoma preacher roared from his pulpit, "If you vote for Al Smith you're voting against Christ, and you'll all be damned." Lutheran editors condemned Catholicism in the White House because of the supposed conflict between allegiance to the state and to Rome.

Not all church opposition was on religious grounds. Some was prohibitionist. Governor Smith had pledged himself to uphold and enforce the Volstead Act, but he also said he believed that states should be allowed to vote on the question of light wines and beer. Had he chased them with an asp he could not have more infuriated the drys.

Dr. Hugh K. Walker, moderator of the General Assembly of the Presbyterian Church wrote in *The Presbyterian* magazine that it was the plain duty of every churchman to work and pray and vote for the election of Herbert Hoover.

The campaign was further marred by slanderous whisperings. Smith was a drunkard, said many, careful to note they had this on unimpeachable evidence from a reliable source, but also careful not to identify the source. The obscene charge grew so serious that Senator Robinson denied it publicly in a campaign speech in Texas. There were some in the Democratic camp who thought the denial a mistake, but Robinson's ire had been aroused by the constant snip-snip-snip of bigotry's shears at the reputation of the New York governor.

Nor was Hoover immune from attack. "The Perfect Hypocrite,"

Heywood Broun called him in newspaper and magazine articles.
But that was mild stuff, delivered across the top of the table. Hoover's
reputation had been first besmirched by members of his own
party in the bitter "Stop Hoover" drive before the Republican convention. He was pro-British and anti-American, said his enemies.
He had once cheated a Chinese out of a fortune, it was said, behind
a half-closed hand.

> O 'Erbert lived over the h'ocean.
> O 'Erbert lived over the sea;
> O 'oo will go down to the h'ocean,
> And drown 'Erbert 'Oover for me?

Thus sang the Democrats. While Hoover, the solemn, unwinking
Hoover was to complain bitterly about his lot, he took far less punishment than his Democratic opponent.

Both were men of good will, and both tried to put an end to the
evils of the campaign, but to no avail.

As election day came near, it became apparent that Hoover would
win. The farmers were against him, but they were so stirred up,
these conservative dry farmers of the Middle West, that mortgages
meant less to them than the Devil. The Chicago *Tribune* reported
that Catholicism, Tammany bossism, plus the innuendoes about
Smith's drinking and the question of prohibition would keep the
Corn Belt Republican. To help things along, some of the anti-Smith
forces said that Al Smith was really a friend of prostitution. Farm
relief? Who cared?

Hoover campaigned on Coolidge prosperity, and in truth the prospect of the boom seemed unending. Hoover did not like crowds
and he did not like politicians and he cordially detested political
speeches. He made only seven in the campaign, in contrast to the
scores of major addresses, lingering meetings, and train-platform
talks of Al Smith, who clutched his ever present cigar, spat amiably,
and waved his brown derby at the crowds.

Hoover was not quite so clawless as he seemed, however. Just
before the close of the campaign he charged flatly that the Democratic program would bring state socialism to America. But even
this, while political demagoguery, was well within the framework
of the political house rules. Norman Thomas, the Socialist candidate, was indignant to have his party's honor besmirched by com-

parison to the Democrats. He had as much amiable contempt for Smith as for the Republicans.

The campaign of 1928 produced strange bedfellows and flirtations. Vance McCormick, Democratic national chairman in 1916, went over to the Republicans on the prohibition issue, and a number of prominent Republicans voted Democratic that year. Governor Lowden announced almost grudgingly that he would remain loyal to the Republicans. William Gibbs McAdoo, on the lip of the election, announced that while he disagreed totally with Smith on the prohibition issue, he would still vote Democratic.

Election day was November 6, Mrs. Smith's birthday. Smith spent the day in that cloud inhabitable only by men running for office and after dinner went to the Sixty-ninth Regiment Armory in New York City, where the members of the Tammany society were gathered to receive the election returns. Defeat was apparent early in the evening, for Hoover even bit into the solid South to snatch Virginia, North Carolina, Florida, and Texas for the first time since the carpetbaggers had been thrown out. The border states went to Hoover, too. But worst of all, New York, in which Smith had been four times elected governor, went into the enemy camp.

Hoover spent election night at his home in Palo Alto, silently puffing a pipe and watching a blackboard, on which the returns were jotted as they trickled in. His family grew excited as it became a landslide victory, but Hoover went on posting the returns.

He had won, squarely, if not altogether fairly. And could the candidate be blamed for the temper of the times?

Hoover, himself, had conducted an honest and decent campaign. He had prosperity going for him, and equally important, he had Smith's Catholicism, wetness, and Tammany connections going for him too. A great many people voted for Hoover and the status quo —and many more voted against Alfred E. Smith.

Altogether 21,393,190 voted to put Hoover in office, 15,016,443 for Smith, 267,420 cast for Norman Thomas, 48,770 for William Z. Foster and the communist Workers Party, and 20,106 for Prohibition candidate William F. Varney.

Feelings ran so strongly even after the election that the Democratic candidate went on the radio to reassure the nation that it was all right. Al Smith was wiping the soap from his window.

Hoover, now elected President, could contemplate his victory in satisfaction, and look forward to March 4, when he would begin stuffing a chicken in every American pot, and two cars in every American garage. All certainly did seem right with the Republican world.

20

The scandals of the Harding administration finally came home to rest, and on November 1, 1929, Albert B. Fall, the Secretary of the Interior who had sold off the nation's oil reserves, was convicted of accepting a bribe. But Fall's conviction was a matter of no more than passing interest, for the nation had a great deal on its mind.

Three days before, on what is known as Black Friday, the stock market collapsed. The collapse of October 29, 1929, was no three-day panic, but triggered a depression that cut stock values fifteen billion dollars in two months, wiped out the savings of widows and orphans, put countless men and women on the dole, and began a rash of suicides by men whose fortunes were destroyed overnight. A month after the crash Commander Richard E. Byrd and Bernt Balchen flew over the South Pole, but even this notable event did not receive the attention that was bestowed on the stream of suicides and ruined speculators.

Yet in those halcyon days between Hoover's election victory and inauguration, the Republicans seemed to have acquired a new stranglehold on their traditional adversaries. . . .

20. A New Deal or a New Bolshevism? 1932

John J. Raskob walked away from the Democratic disaster of 1928 an angry but more thoughtful man than before. The Democratic national chairman was sure of one thing: presidential politics had now become a full-time job. If the Democrats expected to win in 1932, they must begin working in 1929, not in the spring of election year, as had so often been the habit in the past. It was a view worthy of a man who had been chairman of the board of General Motors.

Raskob argued, pleaded, and in the end paid a good deal of the cost himself, to establish a permanent executive and publicity office for the Democratic National Committee. Jouett Shouse became chairman of the executive committee of the party, and Charles Michelson, a bright and trenchant journalist, took on the publicity function, both at salaries around $25,000 a year.

Their mission was to keep the issues of the day alive, to build up the Democratic position, and at all times to question the activeness and politics of the Republicans and the Republican President. "Coolidge prosperity" was at its height, and the Republicans controlled both houses of Congress. All the more reason for year-round activity.

The Republicans felt the same need for expansion. Radio had brought the national government into every living room. Competition had sharpened the search for information and for "news" stories that would lure listeners and sell newspapers. The day after President Hoover's inauguration in 1929 Republican National Chairman Hubert Work recommended that the committee also maintain a permanent organization, to keep the party mechanism oiled between elections. It would save the party money in the long run, Work claimed. In 1928 the Republicans had spent $3,500,000 to elect Hoover and Curtis. If the organization were kept together, victory shouldn't cost half that in 1932.

The committee listened and approved. National party politics now became a full-time paid activity for the first time in the history of the two major parties.

But even with full-time party activity, Hoover's administration was like the man: high forehead and no visible heart. In the beginning that was enough, for Hoover was elected as the caretaker of Coolidge prosperity. He was to make sure there was the chicken in the pot, the cars in the garage. On March 4, 1929, it seemed a reasonable task, requiring neither forensic skill nor personal charm. Business was good, and the less people were bothered with government, the better they felt.

On March 4, as Hoover sat alone at breakfast in his house on Washington's S Street, the day's inauguration ceremonies held no dread, nor did the prospect of four years in the catbird seat of American government.

The President-elect retired to his library that morning and worked until time to don morning coat and formal trousers. The work fascinated his incisive mind as much as the frills annoyed. At the inaugural ceremony he conformed in the outward trappings, but balked at the traditional velvet-collared overcoat, wing collar, and stovepipe topper favored by his friend and mentor, the retiring Coolidge. Hoover appeared in a plain overcoat, and his own high, rounded collar, topped by the heavily crushed felt hat that became a trademark.

It was a day of triumph for the Republicans. Twenty-six governors attended the inauguration. Even the rain-drenched paraders could not dampen the victor's spirits.

But almost eight months later a torrent of stocks and bonds thrown on an unwilling market washed away the Republican prosperity. As the months wore on, the crash became a depression, then the worst depression in history.

In March 1932, an anti-administration humorist in the House noted, "Three years of Hoover's term have expired, and nearly everything else in the country as well." And in June 1932, twenty-eight mayors gathered tensely in Detroit, to ask the federal government to declare a "war situation" and grant five billion dollars in loans to finance public works and get men, women, and children off the bread lines.

Very few Americans had been aware of the impending disaster. Democratic Chairman Raskob had been unfortunate enough to state his belief in the boom in a national magazine that was published in August. As Hoover noted, Governor Franklin D. Roosevelt of New York did nothing to cinch up the regulation of the New York Stock Exchange, although he could have, nor did Roosevelt issue any warnings about speculation.

President Hoover did worry. He did warn both bankers and businessmen about the danger. He did try to use his influence to check speculation. But he did it all as a matter of persuasion, guided by his inherent conservative feeling for the responsibilities of local government.

When the crash came few Americans were aware that it presaged the greatest depression the nation had ever known. President Hoover knew what was happening, but in an effort to restore confidence to the nation, Hoover confined himself to optimistic statements. Governor Roosevelt apparently did not know what was going on. He expressed the belief that the nation's business was fundamentally sound.

From that point on, any similarity between the Republican and Democratic positions on the national economy was almost purely coincidental.

As the country wallowed in distress, Hoover bent his every effort. He saw the depression's causes in the postwar distress of Europe, and its impact on American banking and industry. He worked from the top. The President called for increases in public spending programs, to employ those displaced by industry. But in retrospect, it is apparent that the small increases he asked could not possibly have kept up with the displacement even enough to give a hungry and disillusioned public the feeling that anything was being done for them.

Roosevelt was largely concerned with affairs in New York State. Then, as his eye fell more and more on Washington, he expanded his concerns.

The elections of 1930 made major changes in the political standings for 1932. The Republicans lost control of the House of Representatives, which meant that Hoover now had to play politics as well as to try healing the wounded nation. He was ill equipped, for he had no taste at all for politicians, compromise, or maneuvering.

Roosevelt, running for re-election in New York, won by 725,000 votes. More important, from a national standpoint, this Democratic governor carried the upstate vote by 167,000. Apparently a large number of Republican voters split off to go Prohibitionist in this campaign, but the electric impact of the Roosevelt landslide allowed none of the professional analysts to worry with that. Reference to Roosevelt's greatest handicap, his health, was carefully guarded. Any references to his illness were quickly and angrily minimized. In truth, above the knees, Roosevelt's legs were strong enough that he rode horseback. His upper torso was stronger than Jack Dempsey's.

In 1932 it was obvious that the Republican candidate would again be Herbert Hoover, who, even if he had personal desires to retire, as he indicated, had no choice but to run again and defend his record. It was almost equally certain that the Democratic candidate would be Franklin D. Roosevelt, although there was no enthusiasm for him in the party councils. John Raskob, who held the party together in the lean years, was definitely a Smith man, and Smith, while he had said he was *not* a candidate for the nomination, most definitely *was* a candidate.

Roosevelt formally declared his hat in the ring on January 22, 1932, and at that time assembled the now famous "brain trust" of professors and experts on government to help him plan an election campaign. Almost immediately he began to pick up pledged delegates . . . the first from Alaska. By late spring Roosevelt had 532 pledges. The movement in the opposite direction was not an Al Smith movement or a surge for Senator James A. Reed or Speaker John Nance Garner but a "Stop Roosevelt" drive.

There was no similar movement against President Hoover in the Republican camp. The closest to party rebellion was a movement to draft Calvin Coolidge again. But it was no more than just an idle thought, as the Republicans prepared for the meeting of the clan, at Chicago.

A few days before the convention, John D. Rockefeller, Jr., raised the liquor issue as a serious campaign matter. Rockefeller and his father were reported to have donated $350,000 to further the campaign for the Eighteenth Amendment at the end of World

War I, and the Rockefellers had been big contributors to the Anti-Saloon League. On June 6, 1932, John D. Jr., deserted the dry fold, and publicly declared for repeal of the prohibition amendment. Over the past decade enforcement of the law had proved practically impossible. It was common to talk of a man who "voted dry but drank wet." The nation was rolling uneasily on a sea of booze, most of it bad, all of it expensive. Bad scotch sold for ten dollars a quart, bad bourbon for almost as much. In Manhattan alone, the beleaguered commissioner who was charged with enforcing this law knew of 3844 speak-easies and gin mills.

While somber Republicans poured into Chicago, wild, and even revolutionary groups of Americans were gathering in the bigger cities, and some of them were moving on to Washington. These were the bonus marchers, veterans of World War I who saw in a congressional bonus bill some relief, temporary as it might be, for their personal miseries. The bonus marchers were undoubtedly whipped up and spurred on by Communists, as the police and the Hoover administration so carefully and so often pointed out. But the bonus army was *with* the Communists on this issue, and the entire country was experiencing an uncomfortably revolutionary tension.

On June 3, bonus marchers in Cleveland seized the Pennsylvania Railroad yards, forced thirty shop men to quit working, and yelled that they would stop all railroad activity in the yard until their demands were met.

On June 6, in Detroit, 3000 men trying to demonstrate in front of the Mack Avenue plant of the Briggs Manufacturing Company were driven away by policemen shooting tear gas. The demonstrators were led by John Schmies, one-time Communist party candidate for mayor of Detroit. But not all of the shouting men were communists.

On June 7, a bonus army of 7000 paraded in the streets of Washington. In New York that day, General James G. Harbord, former president of the National Republican Club, called for an end to the bonus march as "ominous and nasty." But 100,000 Americans lined the streets of Washington and cheered the marchers as they passed.

On June 9, in New York, in suburban Hartsdale, and in Chicago, two former company presidents and a board chairman committed suicide, two of them dedicating their last words to warnings against the stock market. That day a seventeen-year-old in Manhattan was fined twenty-five dollars for leading blind beggars through the New York subways and taking ten per cent of their gross.

In Chicago the two open questions of the Republican convention were shaping up. Prohibition was one. The vice-presidency was the other. Hoover's private secretary, Lawrence P. Richey, arrived in a light tan suit and a Panama hat on the eleventh, saw to it that a special telephone circuit was properly hooked to the White House, and plunged into a series of mysterious conferences with another Hoover secretary and Postmaster General Brown.

The Republican wets, led by the Association Against the Prohibition Amendment, chartered a string of buses, draped them with anti-prohibition placards, festooned them with loud-speakers, and denounced the evils of prohibition from one end of Michigan Avenue to the other. The wets staged a yacht show past the naval pier, a six-mile parade of anti-prohibition floats, and an aerial circus over Lake Michigan in which "Old Man Prohibition" was thrown from a plane, after which two parachutists made a fine show of trying to rescue the submerged dummy.

The drys were led by E. C. Dinwiddie, secretary of the National Prohibition Board of Strategy. The fire-eating Methodist bishop, James Cannon, was on hand to denounce drink rousingly at a mass meeting.

The Reverend Daniel A. Poling preached against alcohol at the Third Presbyterian Church, two blocks east of the Chicago stadium where the convention would soon open. A wet heckler interrupted the sermon, but was thrown out. On the steps the wet was joined by a half dozen cohorts. They erupted in bravado, and nearly fifty drys descended on them. Police emerged to drown the cacophony and break up what was left of the meeting.

On the other end of the private line, President Herbert Hoover was trying to reach some compromise on the prohibition issue. Senator William E. Borah, the legislative kingpin of the drys, indicated he would support a plank that would send the issue back to the people. So Hoover sat down to put it together.

The convention opened on June 14, with mention of neither prohibition nor Calvin Coolidge in the keynote address. On the floor there was a marked absence of enthusiasm for Herbert Hoover.

There was no talk now about "Coolidge prosperity." A band of three hundred Communists tried to storm the convention but were promptly chased down the alley by police, dropping signs that

said "Down with Evictions" and "The Hoover Government Is Starving Millions of Workers."

Inside the hall the theme of the wets—"How Dry I Am"—was
accompanied in demonstrations by miniature casks, ale mugs, and
those shining tin pails known in earlier days as "growlers." The
Illinois and New York delegations had their own placards, proclaiming "We Want Repeal. No Bunk." And Democrat Al Smith's
"Sidewalks of New York" was cheered more loudly than Hoover's
"California, Here I Come."

Illinois and New York didn't get a repeal plank. They got the
bunk they didn't want, instead. Against mighty opposition, Hoover
forced through a prohibition straddle. The issue was to be joined,
he said, in a new amendment that would send prohibition back to
the people in the form of local option.

The white-haired and distinguished Senator Hiram Bingham of
Connecticut, leader of the wets in the convention and a member
of the resolutions committee, was excluded from the sub-committee
that wrote the plank. He prepared a minority report and took the
fight to the floor against the "sham" plank. The crowd cheered
Bingham as he pleaded for repeal, and booed the Administration's
leaders, Ogden L. Mills, Secretary of the Treasury, and James R.
Garfield, son of the assassinated President, but in the end, the
Hoover steam roller won. The entire party platform was adopted
by a voice vote without a roll call.

At one time a move seemed afoot against the renomination of
Vice-President Curtis, who by now was aged and doddering and
whose bone-dryness did not appeal to the wets. But their alternative,
Charles G. Dawes, refused flatly and unequivocally to leave his
bank and stand for another term. So Curtis was to have the job
again.

Just before the balloting for President former Senator Joseph I.
France of Maryland, an announced candidate for the presidency,
rushed to the front of the room. He plotted to seize the platform,
and then start a stampede for Calvin Coolidge.

Poor France! He got to the platform all right, but that was all.
The Administration's sharp-eyed lookouts were on him in a moment,
and before he could speak he was overwhelmed by policemen and
hustled off the floor.

In the apathetic balloting that followed, Herbert Hoover was nominated by 1126½ of the 1154 votes. Coolidge, France, Dawes, John J. Blaine of Wisconsin, and former Senator Wadsworth of New York shared the pitiful remainder.

In Washington, Hoover was sitting in the study of the White House with Mrs. Hoover and several other persons. When the balloting ended he got up from his desk, noted that the result was not wholly unexpected, and walked off to his office with all the emotion of a barn owl.

A number of Republicans managed to work themselves into a belief that they would win the 1932 elections. Hoover was not among them. He knew he was going to be defeated, and by this time he must have been pretty sure of the name of the man who was going to beat him. Franklin Roosevelt's ambitious crew of young upcountry politicians, intellectuals, and theoretical experts had been working hard, right up to the opening gun of their party's convention. It assembled in Chicago on June 27. The brain trust had trampled on many toes and alienated many of the party's well-known figures. Learning that Jouett Shouse was tapped by the national committee for the permanent chairmanship, and knowing that Shouse was for Al Smith, Roosevelt's campaign strategists decided to pick an open fight with Chairman Raskob, Shouse, and Smith. They were feeling their oats so much that they then announced an attack on the ancient and revered two-thirds rule of the Democratic party that made any Democratic candidate the choice of a coalition of interests. A month before the convention James A. Farley, Roosevelt's campaign manager, announced confidently that the nomination was in the bag. But he didn't count on the vehemence of his opposition or the reaction of a great number of Democrats to an attempt to destroy the two-thirds rule. The 532 votes pledged to Roosevelt looked good to Farley, who even warned the restless, pro-Smith Tammany Hall that F.D.R. didn't need New York's votes to be nominated, a twisting of the tiger's tail not calculated to make friends in the Ancient Society of St. Tammany.

On June 19, Farley, the ex-newspaperman and long-time Roosevelt adviser Louis Howe, and the rest of the Roosevelt convention contingent arrived in Chicago and set up in a large block of rooms on the eleventh floor of the Congress Hotel. Farley announced cheerfully that it would be Roosevelt on the first ballot.

Two days later, the beleaguered John J. Raskob arrived, to snort contemptuously and advise reporters it was better than even money that Roosevelt would be stopped by the convention. Al Smith started from New York that day, June 21, in a blue suit, straw hat with a blue band, and a word of contempt for "Jim Farley's ballyhoo." A contest was underway before the national committee concerning the seating of the twenty-man Louisiana delegation. One contingent, headed by three former governors of the state, claimed that the group headed by Senator Huey Long, a Roosevelt supporter, was "hand-picked." Long retorted that the handful of defeated office seekers opposing him "couldn't be elected constable in any town in Louisiana from the Gulf to the Arkansas line."

That same day, as the contestants began warming up in Chicago, Big Bill Thompson, former mayor of the city, a Republican whose hands had been slapped at the Hoover convention, arrived in New York to see the Sharkey-Schmeling fight, and was asked to deliver a prediction on the outcome of the election:

"The history of American politics shows that the people don't vote for continued depression. When depression is upon the nation, the party in power is removed."

The wily Thompson left himself an out, but Nicholas Murray Butler, sailing off for Europe so he would not have to watch the carnage, washed his hands of the Hoover administration, disgusted with the weasel-worded prohibition plank. Butler said the Republican plank had offended millions of Republican voters.

Four days before the convention, the "Stop Roosevelt" movement was the busiest in Chicago. Al Smith and William Gibbs McAdoo met and shook hands at the Congress Hotel. This was hailed as a healing session, and after it was over, the "Stop Roosevelt" men let it be known that it had worked. Mayor Frank Hague of Jersey City, the Democratic national committeeman from New Jersey, told the world that Roosevelt could not possibly win. He was the weakest candidate whose name was before the convention, said boss Hague.

The day before the convention opened, Philip Hornbein, a delegate from Colorado and member of the resolutions committee, revealed a plot to deluge the convention with a flood of 100,000 telegrams protesting Roosevelt's nomination and demanding votes for Al Smith. This statement was backed by Oscar A. Whitenack of Denver, chairman of the Citizens' Forum of that city.

"The press, the radio, and the telegraph and telephone companies are all allied against us," said Roosevelt supporter Whitenack.

Left-handedly, perhaps, the issues before the Democratic convention were summed up in a popular chant of the day:

> Who do we want—we want Smith!
> What do we want—we want beer!

So sang the anti-Roosevelt delegates as they moved from room to room in search of liquids and followers. Dr. F. Scott McBride, superintendent of the Anti-Saloon League, disagreed violently. Neither Smith nor Roosevelt would be an acceptable candidate, he said.

On June 27, as the convention opened, Roosevelt, sitting in his office in Albany, learned that the two-thirds rule fight was abandoned as quickly and painlessly as possible. After a complicated committee battle it became apparent that the fight was lost. His little army had overplayed its strength, and might even have weakened its cause. Roosevelt ordered the fight stopped immediately before the matter ever got to the convention floor.

Roosevelt recouped the next day. His candidate for permanent chairman of the convention, Senator Thomas J. Walsh of Montana, was elected over Jouett Shouse by a vote of 626 to 528. Two of three contested Roosevelt delegations, Louisiana and Minnesota, were seated by the convention. Roosevelt did not have two thirds of the convention with him, but he had a majority. After the Walsh victory, Tammany Hall, which had scheduled a caucus of the New York delegation, abruptly canceled their caucus and decided to sit on the fence for a while longer.

The prohibition issue kept the Democrats on the edges of their seats from the first moment. Most of the scores of fist fights and wrestling bouts that enlivened the proceedings over prohibition were given an added assist by weather so hot that the immaculate Grover Whalen removed his morning coat and top hat and settled down in his shirt sleeves.

During one demonstration on the first day by the wets, the Texas delegation's standard was misappropriated and a fight followed. A policeman, helpfully inquiring if he could be of some assistance, got only a snarl.

"This is a private fight," shouted one of the protagonists. "Get out!"

Later in the day delegates craned in their seats to see what was going on over in the Iowa delegation. One eagle-eyed minion of the law saw clearly that delegates were poking each other in the chin.

On the platform Senator Alben Barkley, the keynoter, explained that it wasn't a fight at all. Just a few of the Iowa delegates taking a friendly poll, said the Kentucky senator.

It was the third day before the prohibition issue had been fought and refought sufficiently in committee to bring the remains before the delegates. When Resolutions Committee Chairman Gilbert Hitchcock read, "We favor the repeal of the Eighteenth Amendment . . ." the hall exploded in the greatest demonstration of the convention. Tennessee's somber Senator Cordell Hull was booed as he presented a contrary minority report.

Al Smith received a great ovation as he rose to speak for the majority report. Part of the way through his speech an attendant tried to hand him a glass of water.

"Drinking water is not in the plank," cracked candidate Smith. The convention roared.

On June 30 the convention adopted the rest of the platform without breaking stride and moved on to the presidential nominations. Smith's backers thought they had stopped Roosevelt. Smith had only about 200 votes, but Frank Hague claimed he could count 500 anti-Roosevelt votes now. Jim Farley and the others were hard at it, doing their best to sway the votes of Cactus Jack Garner's Texas and William G. McAdoo's California delegations, solid for Garner.

Unless Roosevelt won the nomination on the first or second ballot, said Hague, he was sunk.

Roosevelt polled 666¼ on the first ballot to Smith's 201¾ and Garner's 90¼. It was a shock to the Roosevelt men, who had forced the convention to sit all night—since they believed they could develop the 770 needed votes. On the second ballot Roosevelt picked up 11¼ votes. Now his men wanted to adjourn. But the anti-Roosevelt forces smelled victory and forced a third ballot. Roosevelt picked up another five votes. Deadlock. California's McAdoo asked for adjournment until evening. Then the fun began.

Roosevelt's key lay in the Garner vote, and it was to the secret meetings of California and Texas at the Sherman Hotel that all eyes turned.

At nine o'clock the convention reassembled. Boss Hague had been wrong. Roosevelt wasn't nominated on the first or second ballot, and his goose was not cooked. McAdoo, the man who had held the hatchet-burying ceremony to which the anti-Roosevelt forces had pointed with pride, now buried the hatchet, right in Al Smith's head. When California was called on the fourth ballot, McAdoo climbed to the rostrum and announced his state's forty-four votes for Roosevelt. Garner, afraid of another deadlock like that of Madison Square Garden in 1924, had released his votes.

The bandwagon rush was on, and soon Roosevelt had 945 of the convention's votes, without those of his own state. He was nominated.

Nominated, yes. Loved, no. The convention was marked by what New York *Times* reporter Elmer Davis called "wholesome apathy." Davis put these words in the mouth of one Godfrey G. Gloom, an old-fashioned and fictional Jeffersonian Democrat from Amity, Indiana, with whom Mr. Davis had innumerable conversations during the various political conventions. The apathy of the various delegates who demonstrated for Roosevelt in the nominating speeches was "wholesome," Senator Gloom had insisted, because it showed they knew he was going to win. That was why they marched for him, not because they liked him.

Garner, of course, was nominated Vice-President. That was part of the deal that had put those forty-four California votes in Roosevelt's pocket.

Roosevelt notified the convention that he would come in person to be formally notified and accept the nomination. It was a well-timed breach of tradition. In a day when radio flashed the proceedings of the political conventions into living rooms across the nation, and airplanes could fly halfway across the continent in a matter of hours, the weeks of wait between the nomination of a candidate and formal acceptance had lost all meaning.

Americans were ready for this change, and by and large they respected the man who had the courage and good sense to effect it.

Physically it wasn't as easy as it sounds. Roosevelt had to be wheeled into the big silver trimotor, and the pilot had to fight headwinds all the way from Albany, while the convention stalled and dawdled away the hours, waiting for the candidate.

Finally, the plane arrived, letting out a cold and worn group of passengers, except the candidate, who was as chipper and alert as an eagle.

Down through the town he rode in the motorcade, grinning at the crowds and flipping the pages of his speech; reconciling, a little at least, the acceptance words written by loyal, conservative Louis Howe, with the quite different challenging views beaten out by his brain trust. At the arena Roosevelt opened with Howe, then switched to the Brains.

He pledged to the American people a new deal. Headline writers blew it up that next day, and it was a New Deal vs. a Hoover administration that had grown more and more conservative.

The depression had passed its depths that summer, and the economy was beginning to take a turn for the better. That was Hoover's view. (It was supported by facts compiled years later but suppressed in the Roosevelt administration.) But with 10,000,000 Americans out of work, with bread lines still defacing the public streets, and with a Hoover who was incapable of a personal campaign, nobody believed the Republican claim in 1932.

Roosevelt contradicted himself on farm policy and on economic policy. He started with the traditional Democratic view of tariff for revenue only, ended with a position very much like Hoover's. Hoover and his assistant campaigners pointed this out, Hoover in the nine long, dull, and uninspired addresses he consented to make, his helpers in publicity. But Hoover's words got scant attention from the voting public. There was no chicken—and there were too few pots. There was no second car; the garage would go with the rest of the house when the mortgage was foreclosed. The "noble experiment" of prohibition was no longer noble, or an experiment. There was no Santa Claus.

Roosevelt might be dangerous, as Hoover and the predominantly Republican press often said he was. Roosevelt might be a "face liberal" as Socialist Norman Thomas said, equally bitter. But he had confidence in the future, and people could feel it.

Both Roosevelt and Hoover talked about balancing the budget. Hoover had threatened to keep Congress in session all summer if it didn't do his bidding. Roosevelt went further. He promised economy and a twenty-five per cent reduction in the federal budget.

Publicity chief Michelson had done a good job in pointing up the issues for the Democrats during the years after 1928. The night of Roosevelt's nomination, John J. Raskob was replaced as chairman of the Democratic National Committee by James A. Farley. Jouett Shouse was eliminated from the party scene, but Michelson stayed on. Hoover became "That Man in the White House," who had never done anything for the American people.

Roosevelt stumped the country, from coast to coast, riding in motorcades, sticking out his chin and his black cigarette holder, and above all, grinning, cheering, waving at the crowds, and convincing them, with that magnificent presence, that somehow everything was going to be all right.

The Republicanism of most metropolitan newspapers turned out to be a blessing, albeit an expensive one, for the Democrats. Farley put Roosevelt on the radio, and through the one speaker's timbrous, cultured, strong voice, with overtones of both bravery and gaiety, tamed millions of wild votes.

Hoover wrote his own speeches. When he delivered them, it would have made no difference if they had been written by Carl Sandburg. Hoover was meant to be read in the newspapers, not seen or heard.

In the end the President became more frantic in his attacks, as the name-calling of the public and the frustration overwhelmed him. He compared Roosevelt to Hitler, he warned against abandonment of the traditional American way, he pleaded the case of his administration. The people's laugh was part sneer, part sob.

". . . Unless I mistake its temper, the country demands bold, persistent experimentation," Roosevelt wrote on May 22. That is what he promised. And that is what Americans voted for on election day.

There was little doubt about the result, even before the polls closed. Hoover, who carried all but six states in 1928, carried six states in 1932.

Roosevelt polled 27,821,000 votes to Hoover's 15,761,000. The Democratic candidate won 472 electoral votes, Hoover 59.

Louis Howe, who ran the Democratic election headquarters at the Biltmore Hotel in New York, waited anxiously on election night for Hoover to concede. Until that happened, he could not rest. At 2 A.M. Hoover's telegram arrived, and Howe could then walk off happily to his couch. The New Deal was on.

21

The world saw several New Deals at work. In Soviet Russia the communist government pushed forward to control of the country, conducted purge after purge, and worked on a five-year plan. It was called the Great Experiment, and it attracted the idealistic and the professional followers in America as well as Europe.

Another deal was in the doctrines Adolf Hitler proclaimed for a National Socialist Germany. Hitler's socialism was a kind of state capitalism, he said, and all the more to be admired because it would produce a race of supermen.

In southern Europe the dramatic Benito Mussolini dreamed of the glory that was Rome, as he exercised in his private gymnasium and swam in his private pool, or watched visitors tramp down the long empty space to his impressive desk for an audience.

All three programs had admirers in the United States, admirers who would have transposed the systems to this country. But Franklin Delano Roosevelt's great innovations in the body politic kept almost everyone off guard, and kept his political enemies so far off balance that it was had for any of the "isms" to gain a strong foothold. Communism, promising the most to the greatest number, seemed for a time to have an opportunity. Yet even communism could hardly thrive on the decline of bread lines, the movement of apple sellers to WPA projects, and the slow but growing belief that the nation was finally beginning to pull out of economic paralysis.

The "great experiment" in control of drinking had ended now. In 1933 the voters realized they had made a dreadful mistake, and if they were to rid themselves of the tentacles of organized crime, to say nothing of abolishing wholesale poisoning, they ought to regulate consumption of alcohol, not ban it and wink at it. So they dealt prohibition a deathblow despite the pleas of the drys, except, of course, in a few states like Kansas. . . .

21. The New Deal Endorsed
1936

In the election campaign of 1932, while Franklin Delano Roosevelt
crisscrossed the country in special train and motorcade, waving a
cigarette holder, a friendly little man in laced boots, knee breeches,
and heavy jacket slogged his way across the fields of Kansas, bum-
ming cigarettes and chinning with the natives.

Both men captured Kansas. Roosevelt carried the Sunflower
State that year by 75,000 votes. Republican Alf M. Landon won
the Kansas governorship from two other candidates, a registered
Democratic incumbent and a goat-gland doctor.

Landon's victory was narrow; he led both opponents by 6000 votes.
But in 1932, Alf Landon was one of the few successful Republican
candidates in the whole United States, a fact that did not fail to
impress large numbers of the Republican party. Landon followed
the victory with a down-to-earth administration that aped the New
Deal in many ways, but surpassed it in one—Alf Landon balanced
the Kansas budget while the federal budget went heavily into the
red.

Governor Landon's office door was always open. He knew a great
many people in his state, and encouraged them to drop in. He was
an earthy, friendly small-town politician who could win elections.
When it came time for the nominations of the Republican party
in the summer of 1936, this meant a great deal, for the party was
bankrupt of ideas and personalities. Furthermore, Alf Landon had
been re-elected in 1934, when even fewer Republicans were managing to hold onto their political heads. There were only eight Republican governors in all the United States. The House and Senate
were both three-fourths Democratic.

The pre-nomination campaign for Alf Landon started at the American Legion convention in the fall of 1935. John D. M. Hamilton, Kansas national committeeman and Landon's pre-campaign manager, raised money quickly, going up and down a Roosevelt-hating Wall Street, while Landon remained in Topeka, with his door open, making middle-of-the-road speeches.

But Landon was still not a national figure. Nor was he the only candidate. Michigan's Senator Arthur Vandenberg held high hopes for the nomination in the spring of 1936. Vandenberg, in those days, belonged to the "give 'em hell" school of anti-New Dealers. "What America needs," he said on May 31, "is a dose of confidence and a release from political terrorism." This was a call for Democrats to unite with Republicans against what he called the Roosevelt "third party." Vandenberg had counted that Democratic vote of 1932 and knew that the Republicans would have to win Democratic votes in 1936 if they were to carry the election.

But "third party"? In 1936 there was no enthusiasm for a third party. It was true that the Farmer-Labor party of Minnesota called a conference of third-party advocates in Chicago at the end of May. Eighty-three delegates came from twenty-two states, but they voted down a motion to call an organizing convention, even though the Communist party pushed hard for such a move.

At the other end of the political spectrum sat the American Liberty League, talking "third party." The League had been formed in 1934 by John J. Raskob, Jouett Shouse, Al Smith, John W. Davis, and other conservative Democrats who had fallen out with Roosevelt. Its one common denominator was hatred for the man in the White House, and its Democratic leaders were so blind with rage that they had even asked Republican Herbert Hoover to join, apparently not recognizing the cancer that ate him caused him to snarl at any who had supported his enemy Roosevelt in the campaign of 1932.

But even Democrats who had never liked Roosevelt in the first place or who disagreed with his New Deal were not so foolish as to talk "third party" with another victory in the air.

The Republicans, despairing after the Democratic congressional victories of 1934, took heart in 1935, when Republican candidates won local elections in scattered areas. When they wrested control of the New York legislature from the Democrats, the GOP gained even more confidence. The optimists in the party read in this a waning of enthusiasm for the New Deal.

Besides Vandenberg and Landon, serious candidates included Frank Knox of Illinois, an old Rough Rider who had, like Landon, gone with Teddy Roosevelt to found the Bull Moose in 1912. Senator William Borah was a candidate. He had entered several primaries to confound the old guard, but no one really knew how serious he was. Former President Hoover, still the titular leader of the Republican party, could easily have been coaxed, had anyone been of a mind to coax him.

The old-guard leaders from the big cities of the East maneuvered to keep key state delegations either unpledged or pledged to favorite-son candidates. That way, when the convention met on June 9 at Cleveland, they could maneuver to their hearts' content, and no matter who got the nomination, the spoils of the election would be protected.

In the rank and file of the party, even by the first of June, Alf Landon was the favorite. On June 6, as the convention delegates assembled in Cleveland, Landon was estimated to have 400 of the 503 delegates needed for nomination. Manager Hamilton and the Wall Street money had done their work, but more, the rank and file of the party seemed to recognize better than their leaders how desperate the Republican situation was, and in their revulsion turned to a political unknown who was also very definitely a moderate. The whole Republican world was upside down. The party was morally bankrupt. It had no program but "Stop Roosevelt." And all around it was the evidence of the New Deal. Even as the convention workers went into Cleveland's public auditorium to put up the bunting, they encountered the 600 WPA workers who were reconditioning the auditorium to extend its life for such public functions, provide work for the unemployed at $93.50 a month, and cause Republicans to foam at the mouth in the contemplation of "socialism" and unbalanced budgets.

Cleveland was ill equipped to handle the convention that year. The national committee's Marian Lang somehow found housing for the fifteen thousand who had asked for help, but she was not able to fit them all into hotels, or even private accommodations. Two lake steamers, the *Seeandbee* and the *Greater Buffalo*, were turned into floating hotels for the week.

Delegates and spectators were pouring into the city by the

thousands, now, but they were a sobersided group, not given to the drinking and whooping it up of years past. The party's leaders consoled themselves with the happy thought that this year there were no great vacant expanses in the galleries. At least there were Republicans around, even if they were not as enthusiastic as they might be.

Oregon's Senator Frederick Steiwer tried to rouse the convention in a keynote speech that called for an end to inflation, tax cuts, and a balanced budget.

The convention went like clockwork.

In the perennial fight between the "black and tan" and "lily white" delegations from the southern states, the Negroes took a beating this year. In fact, it turned out to be another push for the Negroes toward the Democratic party. In 1932, Hoover had tried to unseat several Negro delegations from the South but had given up the fight when the Negroes threatened to go to the public. This year, Negro claims in contests were thrown out by the national committee except in Mississippi and Tennessee, and the convention seated the "black and tan" delegates from South Carolina. A "lily-white delegation" from Florida was seated.

The next day Herbert Hoover arrived to address the convention, and received a greater ovation than he had in 1932 when he was running for a second term. Republicans pushed through the aisles and stood cheering on top of their seats, sang hymns, and wept as the big prune-faced man walked to the podium to denounce the New Deal as "fascist," Roosevelt as a dictator, and call for a "Holy Crusade for Freedom."

Hoover, this time, was setting himself up in comparison to the middle of the roaders, specifically to Landon. If the Republican party wanted to fight the campaign on the issues as Hoover saw them—the good old system as opposed to this New Deal apostasy—then Hoover was their man. Smiling, but noncommittal, the ex-President departed for New York, leaving the implication that he was open for a draft, even though he had said in May that he was not a candidate.

There was no draft. The next day, after candidate Landon had telegraphed demands for a gold-standard plank and wages and bonus protection to the convention, and had been mollified by their acceptance, the Kansan was nominated on the first ballot, to join U. S. Grant and William McKinley in the small list of immortals to achieve such honor. The five unsuccessful candidates all seconded the nomination: Frank Knox, Senator Vandenberg, Senator Dickinson of Iowa, Governor Nice of Maryland, and Robert A. Taft of Ohio, who had come into the convention as a favorite son.

A disappointed Knox left the convention hall. That night the scrubwomen voted Kansas the delegation that chewed the most gum. The next day Knox was on the road when he heard the convention planned to get "Off the Rocks, with Landon and Knox."

With no argument over the convention platform, because it had to accept much of the New Deal, the convention still managed to generate some enthusiasm. The newspapers saw the end of bossed conventions, as Landon, led by his manager Hamilton and a strange combination of old guardsmen, and a gang of amateurs planned a campaign. Evil-minded observers suggested that the pros saw how the wind was blowing, and turned the whole mess over to the Landon men, to get rid of them in 1936's certain defeat so they wouldn't hamper Republican chances of victory in 1940. Perhaps. But the Landon crew had no sense of predestined defeat. Everyone of them, from Landon right down the line, was confident that Landon would walk off with the election.

On June 15, Landon took his first campaign trip, including a visit to his birthplace in Mercer County, Pennsylvania, and to Chautauqua, New York, where he had spent a good deal of time as a young man. This gave him an adequate excuse to invade the East.

"Jim Farley knows he has lost the East," said a cocky Hamilton, who was also positive that Landon could not fail to carry the whole western bloc.

But Jim Farley was a stubborn man. He remarked the next day that he would not concede a single one of the forty-eight states to Landon, continued to seek the $2,000,000 he wanted for the campaign fund, and continued to round up the fifty seconding speeches that would show Roosevelt to be the darling of every segment of the Democratic party.

Squinting, glass-eyed Representative William Lemke of North Dakota announced that he would be a candidate for the presidency, since he could stomach neither Landon nor Roosevelt, and the Reverend Father Charles E. Coughlin, the radio priest of Royal Oak, Michigan, announced immediately that he was going to support Lemke with his National Union for Social Justice. So did Dr. Francis E. Townsend, who had achieved a remarkably vociferous support for his move to give pensions of $200 a month to everyone past sixty, and Gerald L. K. Smith, who operated a "share the wealth" movement to raise wages and give everyone a free college education.

Much of the lunatic fringe was taken care of. The Communists and Socialists and the bitter-enders of one kind and another nominated their own candidates and set out to convert as many of the masses as they could. But many left-wingers had found a new home in the New Deal.

There was no controversial public issue at the Democratic convention on June 23. The Democrats knew the New Deal would be the target of the Republican campaign, and Roosevelt was ready to run on his record.

Al Smith and a group of respected conservative Democrats wired the assembling convention that they would bolt unless the Democrats changed their New Dealing ways and did something to throttle Roosevelt. Somehow that telegram got lost and never did receive official consideration on the floor.

"Cotton Ed" Smith, the senator from South Carolina, walked out of the convention on June 24, when a Negro minister from Philadelphia was asked to introduce the afternoon session. Smith was annoyed anyhow. He hadn't been given a ticket or a badge when he arrived, he had been twenty-seven years in the Senate, and he felt he was being treated miserably by his own party. Governor Olin D. Johnson didn't help matters along any by telling the press that his fellow South Carolinian "better be thankful he got here as a delegate."

Smith was annoyed about many aspects of the Roosevelt group, not the least of them the abrogation of the two-thirds rule, which Farley had tried to force through the 1932 convention. Now, with no conceivable opposition to the incumbent Roosevelt, the two-thirds rule was simply a matter of principle, and as such it was a good deal easier to whip than it had been when the principle was backed by the desires of a half dozen candidates for the presidential office. On June 25 the convention voted out this rule that had served the party both well and ill for so long.

Al Smith's American Liberty League friends did not appear at the convention, as some thought they might, but on the twenty-fifth Smith banners suddenly appeared in the upper balcony. This was not in the program, and the program committee set out to investigate.

Joe Marinelli, Deputy Attorney General of Pennsylvania, started up the aisle, reached the little claque of noisy Smith rooters, and seized a handful of their banners, which he trampled underfoot. One of the angry young men rose, landed a neat left hook on Marinelli's jaw, and sent him tumbling down three rows of seats before he could catch himself. But Marinelli's apostle of law and order was undaunted. He came back and, joined by two gentlemen from Georgia, began slugging it out with the offenders. The state highway patrol and city policemen came in quickly to break it up, rounded up the claque of fifty Smith rooters, and hustled them off to the basement through an angry crowd of New Deal Democrats.

"Al Smith," shouted the miscreants. "We want Al Smith."

Down to the basement they were taken, and out of the hall.

Later that day they were identified by Pittsburgh boss David Lawrence as rowdies from the Republican Second Ward of Philadelphia.

Having very little to do and really nothing to decide, including the vice-presidential question, since Cactus Jack Garner would again be Roosevelt's running mate, the Democrats gave themselves up to having a good time.

Large quantities of alcohol were consumed, and light sleepers were awakened by revelry in many hotel rooms. A lady Democrat, trying to feed a donkey sugar in one hotel lobby, made the mistake of putting her index finger in the animal's mouth along with a piece of sugar.

W. E. Kelly of the Pennsylvania delegation amused himself by riding around the convention hall on another donkey during the first day's warmup. Other Democrats, some normally dignified legislators and judicial personages, joined in snake dances, song fests, and the general festivity. There were several bands. Jovial Jim Farley, the party chairman, was pleased with the evidences of harmony, both political and musical. Vladimir Romm, correspondent of *Izvestia*, and a newcomer to the American scene, was less so.

"Music with your meals is bad enough," growled the dyspeptic Russian, "but music when you are forming a government is terrible."

Sir Wilmot Lewis of the London *Times* called the convention a "debauch."

The harmony was rudely shattered when Cotton Ed Smith walked out again, this time after Representative Arthur W. Mitchell, the only Negro in Congress, had addressed the convention. "I'm through," the Carolina senator yelled. The death of the hundred-year-old two-thirds rule and acceptance of the political equality of Negroes had disenchanted him with this administration, and maybe the Democratic party.

He was not alone. Senator Donahey of Ohio left the convention too, albeit much more quietly, when Farley kept after him to second the Roosevelt nomination. Donahey didn't want to second, and the only course seemed to be to disappear. He did.

Just about everything else went off as planned. On June 27, President Roosevelt came to Philadelphia's Franklin Field to make his acceptance speech in his own new tradition, to denounce the "economic royalists," before a crowd of 100,000 who cheered and wept and prayed for him. His campaign was begun.

The Republican convention was the high point of Alf Landon's campaign. Shortly afterward, the Gallup poll showed 52 per cent of the voters attracted to Roosevelt, 48 per cent to Landon. But from that point, Landon began to slide.

The Kansas governor was a great campaigner, when he could stop off at a country store or on a small-town street and chat with people for a while. The trouble with Landon, as a presidential campaigner, was that he had no more color than a white rabbit and his toneless voice took a bit of getting used to. In the campaign for the White House there was no such time.

Landon's backers tried to prepare the public. He was a terrible speaker, so in his radio broadcasts he was almost invariably introduced as one who was "no silver-tongued orator" before he picked up the script and began drugging the listeners with an almost unbelievable monotone.

Landon had certain advantages in the campaign. He had almost an unlimited supply of money. The "economic royalists" castigated by Roosevelt outdid themselves to get the New Deal off their backs, and raised more money than ever before for the Republicans. Sunflowers, Landon's pictures at desk and in his oilman's boots, Landon and Knox buttons, all ringed the land. Small boys passed out handbills in Portland, Oregon, and stuck Landon leaflets under windshields in Portland, Maine, proclaiming the need for salvation from the Roosevelt administration.

Landon had the press with him, too, or a substantial majority of it. Roy Roberts, editor of the Kansas City *Star*, and Oscar Stauffer, who owned a chain of newspapers centered in Kansas, were guiding lights in the campaign to take permanent leadership of the Republican party away from the eastern bosses. Most Republican newspapers favored the candidate with such glowing characterizations that he could not possibly have lived up to his billings. The Hearst press, in particular, adopted Landon, so wholeheartedly that he was made to possess all the virtues of every past President, including Roosevelt, and none of the faults of any.

When the voters read about this knight in shining boots, it was one thing. When they saw him or heard him, it was another.

But more than that, there were still ten million unemployed workers in the United States, and the lower-income groups were quite sure that Roosevelt would help them. They had no such confidence in the Republican party. Their confidence was not increased by the personal attacks against Roosevelt. Hamilton, who had been selected chairman of the Republican National Committee, now that his candidate was the nominee, chose to take the issue with James Farley, his Democratic counterpart. Hamilton spent a good deal of his time baiting and attacking Farley, and Hoover could always be counted on for a speech against Roosevelt and the New Deal.

Landon spent the first few weeks of the summer in semi-seclusion at a ranch he had rented in Estes Park, Colorado, and then set out on the first of four campaign trips across country. He worked hard and confidently through most of the campaign. When the "superman" approach fell flat he was painted by his well-wishers as a "plain, average" man, in the hope that this would influence Roosevelt. But Landon was so very average, in appearance and speech, that the emphasis on his lack of color must have hurt, both personally and politically.

Landon was presented to the voters as "Frugal Alf" and the "Cash and Carry Governor." Frugality, obviously, was a virtue to the middle class and the upper strata of American society, but to the lower strata it was a virtue not so highly prized. And here is where the Republican party and a usually accurate political poll made a vital error. The *Literary Digest,* the only report in the nation that showed Landon consistently running ahead of Roosevelt in 1936, depended on telephone listings and automobile registrations for its polling. In 1936 the balance hung with people who had neither.

The campaign wore on from summer into fall. Roosevelt did not answer Landon directly, did not even reply to the bitter attacks made on him by the Republican party machinery. In the beginning Landon wisely confined himself to issues; it was only in the end of the campaign that he began to speak desperately of totalitarianism if Roosevelt were re-elected.

On the last of his four tours Landon lost his temper, and called the trip "a battle to save our American system."

With the Republicans in control of most of the nation's press, the Democrats again turned to radio to be sure of getting their message across. But of course the vast difference in the aural personalities of Roosevelt and Landon made this use of radio an undeniable asset.

Roosevelt, too, had a great facility for using the press, willy-nilly. Even during the Republican National Convention the President of the United States was not crowded off the front pages of the nation's newspapers—Republican or Democratic—because he was out of Washington, in the Southwest, making a series of important policy speeches that could not be ignored.

Jim Farley was not inclined to believe the *Literary Digest*, or any poll but his own. During the campaign he polled some twenty-five hundred Democratic leaders three times to learn that Landon's peak was reached just before his acceptance speech, and that the Republican candidate had been traveling steadily in the opposite direction since.

Roosevelt did not really begin to campaign until September 29, when he spoke at the New York state Democratic convention in Syracuse. He made a few other speeches, after his return to Washington, then set out on October 8, on his major campaign effort.

The Roosevelt theme was simple enough. He asked for a vote of confidence for the administration. The recovery program would be scuttled if the Republicans were elected, continued if Roosevelt were returned to office. Alfred Mossman Landon's name was not mentioned once, at whistle stop or in major address. The Republicans were attacked as a party, not as individuals, and even as a party the President attacked their principles. This was good politics for the champion, running against a challenger. And it paid off, as Landon lost control in the last month. "It is the essence of the New Deal that the Constitution must go," Landon said heatedly at Baltimore. "Franklin D. Roosevelt proposed to destroy the right to elect your own representatives," he said at Albuquerque.

The eleven-car Roosevelt train rolled on through the countryside, without a harsh word for the Republican candidate but with many harsh words for economic royalists, now characterized as the "forces of reaction." In Madison Square Garden the President repeated his pledges to the farmers, consumers, unemployed, home owners, slum dwellers. Whom did he leave out? No one but big business, and the big-business men of the country wanted no part of F.D.R. or his programs. But business now did not have the power or the prestige it had enjoyed in previous administrations.

The campaign week wound up in a flurry of charges against Roosevelt, but he went to Hyde Park prepared to vote and await the returns. Jim Farley may have had more qualms than he showed when he jotted down Maine and Vermont for his office-pool prediction of the Republicans' electoral strength, but Farley was supremely confident of victory at this late hour.

Roosevelt spent Monday before election day traveling up and down the Hudson near his home. He campaigned a little, but spent more time renewing a tradition. F.D.R. visited the same areas in which he had opened his political career for the New York legislature a quarter century before, by whizzing around the district in a snappy red roadster.

On election night some fifty of Roosevelt's Dutchess County neighbors were invited to dinner in the big house at Hyde Park. They listened to the radio in the library. Roosevelt retired to the dining room, with a few stalwarts like Samuel Rosenman, and kept tabs on the election returns.

Early in the evening a report came in that Roosevelt had carried Republican New Haven by fifteen thousand. He didn't believe it and ordered a telephone check. When the figure was confirmed, Rosenman said, the President leaned back, blew a smoke ring, and said "Wow."

In Topeka, the yellow brick executive mansion was lit up like a Christmas tree. The shades were up as usual, so the people on the big lawn could see in. The Landon family listened to the returns, as a garage full of reporters sat and waited. In late afternoon the first results, especially that fifteen thousand from New Haven, indicated a Democratic landslide. The Landons served coffee and doughnuts to a small party of friends, and listened to the bad news, as it swept from east to west. Finally, at nine o'clock the reporters were asked in to join the meager feast.

Roosevelt had won the greatest majority in history, with 27,750,-

778 votes to Landon's 16,680,259 and Lemke's 893,747. Roosevelt had 523 electoral votes in 46 states, Landon eight electoral votes. Jim Farley's prediction was so exactly right that newspaper columnists could not believe he had made it or that he had made it seriously.

And not only had Roosevelt won re-election, but the Democrats had gained five seats in the Senate and twenty in the House.

Why? Because millions of people in the United States had faith in Roosevelt and were able to develop none in Landon or his party. And where the Republican party was not morally bankrupt, it was amateur. One young man, just out of college and working in New York as a soda jerker during the campaign, heard two Republican officials discussing a Landon campaign speech. He scoffed at the speech, said he could write a better one himself. He was promptly hired by the Republican National Committee, wrote speeches all summer and fall praising Landon and the Republicans and damning Roosevelt and the Democrats. Then, on November 5, he went to his polling place and voted for Roosevelt.

At eleven o'clock on the night of November 5 it was decided. The telegram of concession and congratulations was on its way east. At twelve o'clock the lights of the Kansas executive mansion winked out, one by one. A few minutes later Alf Landon was sound asleep.

The federal relief program ended on November 29, 1935. The depression, it seemed, was whipped. Jobs still were not plentiful, of course, but the national economy was picking up.

Across the ocean, Italy was entering bravely into a period of imperialism. The victim was the little kingdom of Ethiopia in East Africa, a land of mud huts and barefoot soldiers carrying muzzle-loading rifles to fight the dive bombers and tanks of the brave Il Duce.

But Ethiopia was a long way from New York or Des Moines.

We cared more when the Spanish Civil War broke out, and quickly became a proving ground for the weapons and tactics of the Nazis, who supported Francisco Franco, and the Soviet Communists, who supported the popular-front Republican government of Spain. But America was not ready to take sides in the war, even though a handful of young idealists went to Spain to fight in the International Brigade, and to be lionized in American literature.

Communism, by now, was becoming more suspect in the United States, for there were serious fears that the Communists had begun to undermine the American government and penetrate its innermost secrets. Whittaker Chambers had already gone to Washington to try to stir up interest in Soviet espionage. He was unsuccessful.

Organized labor had developed into a political power after John L. Lewis resigned from the A. F. of L. to form the Congress of Industrial Organizations. The CIO organized big steel, and then moved on to the automobile industry. With those battles won, the CIO had real strength and could show it.

But now, 1937, the economy seemed to be taking a tumble! Factories began to close, and little knots of people began to recall the cold frightening days of 1930 and 1931. . . .

22. Don't Rock the Boat
1940

One by one the precedents fell into the trough of history. On January 20, 1937, Franklin Delano Roosevelt began his second term as President of the United States. The Twentieth Amendment had eliminated lame-duck government this year. In another break with the past, Vice-President Garner was sworn in on the inaugural stand outside the Capitol, rather than in the traditional ceremony inside the Senate Chamber. John Garner took the vice-presidential oath, then Franklin Roosevelt stepped forward, and after Chief Justice Charles Evans Hughes had read the binding words the President, his jaw out, repeated them syllable for syllable.

Somehow it was a symbol of Roosevelt's determination, to forego the simple affirmation. Now, in his second term, Roosevelt faced multiple economic problems. A new labor weapon, the sit-down strike, plagued American industry, just as it begun to revive after the depths of the great depression. The recession of 1937 was on!

Democrats dominated both houses of Congress by majorities of four to one that year, but Democratic majority did not mean the New Deal would have an easy road in Roosevelt's second term. Deep cracks had already split the uneasy alliance between the New Dealers and the conservatives of the Democratic party. The schism was to deepen, as the stubborn, tireless Roosevelt hammered out his program of drastic change.

In the first hundred days of his first administration Roosevelt had created the deal he promised in the acceptance speech at the 1932 Democratic convention. Congress had passed the Agricultural Adjustment Act, establishd the NRA to control industrial output, established the Civilian Conservation Corps, the Works Progress Administration. Two years afterward, a conservative U. S. Supreme

Court began showing reaction. The average age of the nine justices was sixty-eight years, and if the eldest, Justice Louis Brandeis, was the most liberal, still when the Court granted sixteen hundred injunctions in two years to restrain federal officers from carrying out acts of Congress, the New Dealers dubbed them the Nine Old Men. The implication was clear that these were thorns in the foot of Progress.

Thus began the Roosevelt struggle with the Supreme Court.

Roosevelt had talked once about major changes in the Constitution. But before the end of the 1936 campaign he backtracked and said it was not so much a need for constitutional change, as a need for a new attitude on the part of the law's interpreters. Roosevelt's answer was a proposal that he be allowed to appoint a new Supreme Court justice to match each of those over seventy years of age. This plan was tied to a bill to overhaul the whole federal court system, but the whole package was immediately labeled a "Supreme Court packing plan."

The plan was balked by a combination of conservative Democrats now allied with the Republicans, who had remained silent but watchful under the Senate leadership of Charles L. McNary, senior senator from Oregon.

In 1937, Roosevelt announced he had no intention of seeking a third term, but that same year Jim Farley, the Democratic national chairman, detected signs of wishfulness for 1940. Farley was sensitive to the signs, apparently, because he had some hopes himself.

The next year the President took cognizance of the deepening split in the party. Roosevelt declared for candidates he wanted reelected in the congressional primaries and against a number of Democratic incumbents who had opposed him, including Senator "Cotton Ed" Smith of South Carolina and Senator Walter George of Georgia.

The conservative Democrats had rebelled. Senator Joseph T. Robinson of Arkansas had died in office, leaving vacant the majority leader's chair. Roosevelt's candidate for the job was Alben Barkley of Kentucky, but in the waspish campaign, Barkley defeated the Dixie bloc's Pat Harrison of Mississippi by only one vote.

The struggle left a residue of alkali that was not to wash away. Harry Hopkins, now as close to Roosevelt as any man, told Iowa Democrats that he, and presumably Roosevelt, would prefer that another man occupy Senator Guy Gillette's seat in the Seventy-sixth Congress.

Roosevelt supported Governor Olin Johnson of South Carolina in a bid against "Cotton Ed" Smith, opposed Millard Tydings of Maryland, and George of Georgia. Roosevelt also spoke for Claude Pepper in Florida, Senator Bulkley in Ohio, Barkley in Kentucky, Caraway in Arkansas, and Thomas in Oklahoma. Those incumbents he supported won, but those he opposed won also, and the Republicans and the press made a great deal of the presidential interference in congressional elections.

The 1938 elections certainly showed a revolt as well as the normal attrition Presidents had come to expect in off-year elections. In the House the Republicans increased their strength from 89 to 170, and in the Senate from 17 to 23.

That same year a young Republican "gangbuster" in Manhattan named Thomas E. Dewey ran for governor of New York. He lost, but along the way rolled up a most impressive vote. Dewey was defeated by less than 100,000 votes; he would have been elected had it not been for the vote of the local left-wing American Labor party, which went almost solidly for his opponent, Herbert Lehman.

When the Republican convention of 1940 rolled around, New York's Dewey was a very definite candidate for the nomination. So was Senator Robert A. Taft of Ohio, whose wife, when asked why her husband should be elected President, briskly gave a reporter three sensible reasons: brains, character, and experience. Opposing these party pros was an amateur candidate, the president of the Commonwealth and Southern Corp., a utilities holding company, Wendell Willkie.

As the advance Republicans began to get together in Philadelphia toward the first of June, the splotlight was on the European war. The "phony war" had ended. By the end of May the Germans were racing through France and Belgium. On May 31, as trains carrying delegates hooted peacefully through the Alleghenys, German dive bombers blasted the beach and breakers of a little-known place called Dunkirk, trying to pulverize the remainder of a British expeditionary force waiting for rescue to come from across the channel.

It was not America's war. Roosevelt asked Congress for a billion dollars extra for preparedness, and for authority to call out the National Guard and army reserves—but only in case such drastic action was necessary to preserve American neutrality.

The Republicans began painting itself as the "peace party." The GOP numbered among themselves the midwestern isolationists, vehemently opposed to war at almost any cost.

A week before the convention the Republican National Committee, as usual, assembled to begin thrashing out problems in the seating of delegates and manufacture of the party platform. John L. Lewis, president of the Congress of Industrial Organizations, appeared before the group working over the platform, to state his organization's demands. Dr. Glenn Frank, the political scientist from the Middle West, told Lewis he could put those demands into the GOP platform. Frank had officiated in that strangest of all seminars, the drafting of a mid-term platform. For in 1938 the Republicans had felt it necessary to revive the party, and, after rejecting the idea of a mid-term national convention, had settled on a giant committee of some two hundred to try drawing up a modern statement of party principle. Dr. Frank's committee accepted, with only slight camouflage, the irreversable changes made by the New Deal. But the GOP remained an anti-New Deal party, with very little indication of a program of their own.

Other early arrivals in Philadelphia were campaign managers for the various presidential hopefuls. Thomas E. Dewey's group, led by Mrs. Ruth Hanna McCormick Simms, took seventy-eight rooms in the Hotel Walnut and hung a banner outside the hotel proclaiming it headquarters. "Delegates pledged to Dewey," said Mrs. Simms confidently, "will be Dewey delegates when the final vote is taken."

Senator Taft's supporters were even stronger in number. They hired a hundred and two hotel rooms at the Benjamin Franklin. Candidate Frank E. Gannett, a New York newspaper publisher, held forth at the Harvard Club and in forty-eight rooms at the Benjamin Franklin. Senator Vandenberg's forces, not so well organized, managed to find space in several hotels, while tucked off in two rooms in the Benjamin Franklin was a committee called "Willkie for President."

Willkie was a dark horse but by no means coal black. Newspaper columnists had been pointing to him for several months as a logical choice for the presidency, since he was: midwestern, Indiana, liberal; a lawyer; not hated by Wall Street (his offices were just around the corner); a corporation president; and an attractive man, characteristically rumpled and cowlicked in the best little-boy-grown-up tradition. Besides, Willkie wore long underwear.

A week before the convention Willkie's chances were strong enough that a Dewey-Taft coalition was started against this six-month wonder. It was strange, since Dewey's men claimed more than 400 votes and Taft's some 300 for their man, while Willkie's organization, when pinned down, laid claim to only 50 or 60 votes.

The Willkie movement was new, and inexperienced. It was stirred up, originally in 1939, by newspapers, speculating on candidates. Willkie had proved himself an able attorney, in arguments before the Supreme Court and in negotiating a favorable deal with the government's Tennessee Valley Authority for his private power company. He was much in demand as a speaker on utility problems. In May 1939 he shared a Connecticut podium with Governor Raymond E. Baldwin, impressing both the governor and liberal businessmen, who were searching for a candidate outside the lichenose Republican mold—one who would appeal to the general public, and one who could win.

Early in 1940, Oren Root, Jr., grandnephew of old Elihu Root, sent a thousand petitions for Willkie to the Ivy League college alumni. The petitions returned hale and hearty, and caused inquiries in such droves as to swamp the switchboard of young Root's law firm for two days. Root decided to go into the political business, with Willkie as his stock in trade. He opened an office on New York's Madison Avenue, called it the Associated Willkie Clubs of America, and began putting ads in newspapers to raise money. By the time the convention began seven hundred clubs had been organized.

Willkie arrived in Philadelphia with a straw hat tilted over one eye. Immediately he began a low-pressure, but continuous campaign of buttonholing, in a city festooned with elephants of all kinds, even hanging from lamppost and street sign. Willkie stopped in bars to drink whisky and soda and shake hands with the grinning, waving delegates. He engaged in debates on street corners and in hotel lobbies, and bearded former Senator James Watson, the tough old Indiana political mogul, in the lobby of the Bellevue-Stratford.

But Watson, an old-guard Republican, could see no virtue in Wendell Willkie. After all, the disapproving ex-senator reminded the candidate, Willkie had been a Democrat up until a very, very short time before. And while Watson had no objection to the church's converting ladies of the evening, he was not going to invite one of them to lead the choir. In 1935, Wendell Willkie sat with Jim Farley and Bernard Baruch as a member of the New York County Democratic Committee. After the New York *Times'* Arthur Krock had started the Willkie speculations in 1939, a story leaked out to the newspapers that Willkie had voted for Landon in 1936. Perhaps he had, although the story dated Willkie's new-found Republicanism a bit early. As late as 1938 Willkie was still a registered Democrat, and on December 1 of that year Jim Farley reported Willkie had lunched with him and declared his loyalty to the cause of the wild jackass.

In Philadelphia, Willkie continued in his effective, naïve way, drawing support from every side. Connecticut Governor Baldwin turned his delegates over to Willkie before the convention began, and other Republicans who had no enthusiasm for the old formulas began to work for the big tousled fellow from New York and Indiana.

In Washington, President Roosevelt, in a gesture that started out as a slap on the back but wound up as a blow to the solar plexus, appointed Henry L. Stimson Secretary of War and Frank Knox Secretary of the Navy. Both men were Republicans. Partly, of course, the appointments were made to emphasize the bipartisan nature of national defense. But more to the point, the Republican party was making noises like a "peace party," and trying to create an image of the Democrats as a "war party." A pair of Republicans in the top defense posts could hardly have a deleterious effect on the Democratic position.

The Republican party chiefs were furious. John D. M. Hamilton, Landon's campaign manager in 1936 and still Republican National Chairman, read Knox and Stimson out of the party.

When the convention opened on June 24, Hamilton called on handsome young Harold Stassen, the governor of Minnesota, to give the keynote address, whereupon the young governor set the tone of the convention in terms that fitted Wendell Willkie very well. Stassen spoke grandly of liberty, freedom, and individualism. After Stassen handed the chairman's gavel to Permanent Chairman Joseph Martin of Massachusetts, the Minnesotan stepped down to become floor leader of the Willkie movement.

Now the Willkie band wagon was rolling. Day and night delegates from every state visited the puny headquarters. Willkie, sustained on cigarettes, whisky, and black coffee, saw them at his rooms, visited around, and even buttonholed delegates on the floor of the convention, in breach of the tradition that the candidate is above horse trading.

Willkie had the society women, the Wall Streeters, and the taxi drivers with him; for he appealed to something different in each group. But he didn't appeal to the old pros in the Republican party. The dire threats and predictions began.

Senator Thomas of Idaho said he wouldn't even run for re-election if Willkie were nominated. Senator McNary of Oregon predicted defeat in the West if Willkie was a reciprocal trader, in whom they saw all the earmarks of a Democrat and interventionist.

Herbert Hoover, invited back to the same old stand to present the same old ideas, received a tremendous ovation. The implication of his speech was clear enough again. If the Republicans wanted to really make a fight of it, then they might look at Hoover, but of course he was not seeking any nomination.

Nor was he seriously sought. Dewey was the first nominated, a cocky young Dewey who predicted that he would be nominated on the second or third ballot. Senator Taft's name came next. Then, Representative Charles A. Halleck of Indiana nominated Wendell Willkie, and the galleries raised their voices in cheers and boos. But the floor was silent. What had happened? The Willkie men had simply forgotten to make arrangements for a spontaneous demonstration. When he was nominated there was nobody ready to start yelling. But finally a member of the New York delegation tore the state standard away from the Dewey men and started around the floor. He picked up support as he went, and in the end the demonstration really *was* spontaneous, all twenty minutes of it, to the amazement of a jaded convention and the delight of the press and galleries.

There were fourteen candidates in all, including Hoover and Fiorello La Guardia, the fierce little mayor of New York. But only four were really in the running: Dewey, Taft, Senator Vandenberg, and Willkie.

Stassen was a good Willkie general, and he had a candidate who could pull pledges for secondary ballot support. Even from the beginning, Stassen followed the rule: he could not show all his strength on the first ballot, for the pyschological strength of a declining vote would sink the Willkie ship. Besides, many of the commitments Willkie was now getting precluded first-ballot support, already committed elsewhere.

Dewey was in the unfortunate spot of a front runner without overwhelming strength. The Dewey generals put his whole strength forward on the first ballot. It was impressive. Dewey led with 360 votes. But there were 1000 in the convention, which meant that 501 would nominate. On the second ballot Dewey dropped to 338, and never came back. Vandenberg, with 76 votes on the first ballot, declined slowly but consistently. Taft made constant small gains, and a real show of strength on the fifth ballot, when he picked up more than a hundred delegates, most of them from Dewey. But Willkie picked up more. And on the sixth ballot, Willkie had it, with 659 votes.

It had been an odd convention. The unusual pressures brought to bear for Willkie had been unprecedented. Western Union's superintendent said he had delivered 40,000 telegrams to delegates on Thursday night alone, and those telegrams, on the eve of the nominations, were overwhelmingly for Willkie. A Dewey supporter in the New York delegation said he had received 22,500 letters and wires asking him to support Willkie. (He didn't.)

Senator George Norris, the maverick Nebraskan who kept deserting the party fold to support Roosevelt, called Willkie "Insull the second," after the infamous utilities magnate. Norris charged that the "power trust" had bought the nomination for Willkie. But even such cynical observers as the daily newspapermen who covered the convention were sure in their own minds that, for once, they had seen a grass-roots movement. Certainly the Willkie forces, in Wall Street and in politically knowledgeable circles had taken every advantage of the popular demand for Willkie. But the proof of popular support was there. When the Willkie workers sent out petitions for Willkie, the petitions were returned, signed by the thousands. If Willkie's men asked a laundryman to put flyers in the delegates' wash, he was delighted to do so. Just about everybody, it seemed, really *did* like Willkie's bright, fresh face.

Willkie had already won, but in a few minutes the vote was 998 for Willkie on that sixth ballot, as the delegates began switching for appearances' sake. It was 998 and unanimous.

Then the Republicans chose as vice-presidential candidate Senator Charles McNary. The fact that he had opposed Willkie made no difference at all. McNary was the concession to the West, to high tariff, to the isolationists, to the party machinery, and to the farm bloc. Willkie was committed to Governor Baldwin but was persuaded to jettison him, and Baldwin took it like a man. McNary accepted the nomination, yoking together two men who weren't even acquainted, whose philosophies were as different as day and night, but healing, both hoped, the breaches in the party. Joe Martin, whom no one ever called a raving liberal, was chosen to run the Willkie campaign not long afterward. Another concession to unity.

Willkie, exhausted, set off immediately after the convention for a few days' rest on the yacht of newspaper publisher Roy Howard. Recovered, he returned to New York to resign his $75,000 a year as president of Commonwealth and Southern, and headed for Elwood, Indiana, where in the tradition of soft shirt and flowing tie, plain country food, and, of course, long underwear, he would make his formal acceptance speech.

It was a flop. Norman Thomas, an incisive commentator as well as perennial Socialist candidate for President, characterized the speech as "a synthesis of *McGuffey's Readers*, the speeches of Tom Girdler, and the *New Republic*." Thomas said Willkie had at first agreed with Roosevelt's entire program and then warned it was taking the United States straight into disaster.

Harold Ickes added a dash of acid. Ickes answered Willkie's speech, called him a "simple barefoot Wall Street lawyer." That one stuck. "The Barefoot Boy from Wall Street" was to become a specter of the campaign. Styles Bridges, replying for the Republicans, called Ickes a "Hitler in short pants," and while that drew guffaws from the press gallery it had no particular effect because Ickes was running at the mouth but not for office.

In a big red-brick house borrowed for the summer Willkie established himself as a citizen of Rushville, Indiana, where he owned several operating farms. The newspapers now carried pictures of the Republican candidate, bucolically attired, looking over cattle or leaning on the fence of one of his Rush County farms. In later years other candidates struck the same pose.

It got so bad, his farm manager remarked, that whenever the hogs saw a photographer they immediately ran out to strike a pose.

Willkie chewed straw and waited for his erstwhile friends and political companions to select their nominee at Chicago. Select, perhaps, is not the proper word, for by the opening of the Republican convention the appointment of Republicans Stimson and Knox to the Cabinet was a clear public indication of a third-term try by President Franklin D. Roosevelt.

Roosevelt had made it almost impossible for any other candidate to get started. The President had been asked, countless times, about his political plans, but had not made them clear. Consequently almost all the Democratic hopefuls were candidates with a big IF —because they knew that if Roosevelt wanted the job again, he would have it.

That's the way it was. A few Democrats spoke out against the third term. Big Ed Johnson of Colorado said Burton K. Wheeler of Montana was the only man who could defeat Willkie at the polls. But the Gallup poll indicated nine out of ten Democrats wanted Roosevelt to run again.

Jim Farley announced his retirement, to put it delicately, as Postmaster General and Democratic national chairman. Farley felt strongly against the third term and had his own hat in the ring. Yet, despite this opposition, three quarters of the delegates to the Democratic National Convention were instructed for Roosevelt.

Cactus Jack Garner, maintained a campaign office at the Sherman Hotel, to be sure, complete with cowboy trappings, a bar, and free lunch. But Tammany Hall's men were talking about the fourth-term drive, "since the third term is already in the bag."

Roosevelt did everything he could to persuade Farley, still national chairman, to get himself and all the other hopefuls out of the race in the interests of party unity and the clear-cut "draft" Roosevelt wanted. But Farley was a staunch opponent of the third term, and, full-well knowing he couldn't win, he stuck it out to the last, despite the blandishments of Harry Hopkins, at the convention as Roosevelt's personal envoy, and James F. Byrnes, who led the draft-Roosevelt forces.

On July 16, just after the convention opened, Roosevelt released his pledged delegates. With a statement that he had no desire to run for the presidency again, he told them to vote their own choice.

The platform, again, was the Democratic record, but refurbished with a pledge against war, with Roosevelt's promise that American soldiers would not be sent abroad to fight unless the United States was attacked. On July 18 the delegates chose Roosevelt on the first ballot, with 946 13/30 votes to Farley's 72 27/30, Garner's 61, Senator Tydings 9 1/2, and Cordell Hull's 5 2/3. (Some delegations had split their authorized votes to the nth degree, to satisfy all factions of the state party organizations.) Then, in a generous and politic gesture, Jim Farley moved to have the nomination made unanimous. He had made his point, and he was as happy as one might expect under the circumstances. The pressure had been intense, but he had held up. Among his 72 votes was one from a young delegate from Massachusetts, John Kennedy, son of the ambassador to London. Roosevelt's men, trying to dissolve the anti-Roosevelt sentiment, had even telephoned Kennedy's father, to put pressure on the young man, but Ambassador Kennedy had refused to interfere.

Then came the fight for the vice-presidential nomination.

A number of men wanted the job this year, for the mathematical chances against a third-term President surviving in office were just that much better than those of a second termer. Paul McNutt, former governor of Indiana, was one man anxiously seeking the job. Byrnes wanted it, and so did Speaker William Bankhead of the House of Representatives, the Texas banker Jesse Jones, and Henry Agard Wallace, the New Deal philosopher and Secretary of Agriculture. It was a wild year. Someone even suggested Bascom Timmons, a Washington correspondent, for the vice-presidency. Roosevelt said it was to be Wallace. Immediately the protests flowed to the White House from Harry Hopkins's purple-trimmed room at the Blackstone Hotel, and from Jim Farley's suite. They were going to have trouble, said Hopkins. Wallace was a mystic and a left-winger, complained Farley. The party teetered for a moment, as the fight resolved itself to a struggle between Bankhead, supported by the anti-Roosevelt men, and Wallace, supported by the Roosevelt faithful. In Washington, Roosevelt would accept nothing but a total victory. He prepared a statement declining the nomination, as he listened beside his radio to the speeches of his enemies in the party. If the party did not accept his choice of Wallace, he would decline.

But playing it as the political genius he was, Roosevelt had put the pressure straight on the convention. He would not accept the nomination until the vice-presidency had been settled. Finally, the convention balloted. It was Wallace 627 7/10, Bankhead 327 4/15. Roosevelt made his acceptance speech. Wallace, primed to go proudly before the convention to accept his lesser honor, was restrained. It was better not to try the ragged tempers.

Willkie's campaign was conducted aboard a special train, called the Squirrel Cage by the men and women who rode it. A lady Republican orator fell off the back of the train and was nearly run over when Willkie pulled the emergency cord and the train engineer began to back up. Princeton students cried "hoax" when they tried to get Willkie to come out in the wee hours and got brother Ed Willkie instead. But the campaign was not humorous; it was marred by violence reminiscent of the attempt to assassinate Roosevelt in Florida just after he began his first term, when Mayor Anton Cermak of Chicago was killed by a bullet intended for F.D.R. Willkie's train was stoned outside Grand Rapids, Michigan, and he was the target of Democratic abuse as well as Democratic vegetable throwers. Willkie took it all and tried to steer a campaign course that would lead to victory, if not general popularity. It was difficult, since Willkie basically was not so different from Roosevelt in his political approach. Joe Martin could attack the Democrats baldly; could say that it wouldn't be a Republican victory but an American victory. It was harder for Willkie, but he mastered the art. Soon he talked about clearing out communists and fellow travelers from the government, and he charged Roosevelt with playing politics with defense. Senator Taft in Chicago charged that the New Deal was leading the United States to a greater depression than 1929, which would result in national socialism. Senator McNary flayed the Democrats for spending too much money. Publisher David Lawrence ran full-page newspaper ads condemning the Administration for everything from the third term to waste of federal funds.

The Gallup polls still gave F.D.R. a healthy lead, but by the middle of October, Roosevelt, who had first indicated he would not campaign actively, was deep in the campaign for re-election.

And as election day grew closer Willkie lost more of his restraint. On October 18, in Springfield, Illinois, he charged that the main issue was Roosevelt's state socialism.

Fiorello La Guardia answered this one. He called Willkie a promoter and "ballyhoo artist." "If Wendell Willkie is a businessman," said New York's Little Flower, "I am Mercury."

Almost at the end of the campaign, John L. Lewis bristled his eyebrows, pursed his lips, and endorsed Willkie. It split the CIO from stem to stern. "Benedict Arnold," shouted the local unioneers as they made haste to jump into the Roosevelt camp. The American Federation of Labor's William Green predicted mildly that organized labor would resent Lewis's actions, and in Albany, New York, Henry Wallace compared Lewis to Joseph Goebbels.

Willkie was a nervous, energetic campaigner. Early in the game his voice began to fail. Robert Montgomery, the actor, secured the services of one of Hollywood's doctors-to-the-stars, who kept Willkie going until the end.

Both candidates wound up in Madison Square Garden. On October 28, Roosevelt's train pulled into Pennsylvania Station for the big push. Steve Early, his press secretary, got into a fight with a Negro policeman who tried to bar him from a train. The Willkie men were properly "shocked" by this terrible affair, particularly since Early had kneed the policeman in the belly and put him out of action. It looked like a serious incident, but the policeman resolved it by declaring that he still intended to vote for F.D.R.

Not all attempts to capitalize on incidents were so unsuccessful. The campaign was marked by smear propaganda on both sides. The Republican National Committee, seeking the Negro vote, said that F.D.R. had done the Negroes wrong, and would not stop lynching. The Democratic National Committee indicated that Willkie was anti-Negro, and linked him indirectly to Hitlerism, because of his German grandparents. Then, in good demagogue fashion, the campaign literature quoted Adolph Hitler's statement, "Negroes are apes," and tried to indicate that Willkie subscribed to that slander.

The Republican National Committee countered: it put out literature showing Roosevelt pulling into Washington a Trojan horse, over which hung a hammer and sickle.

On November 2, Willkie appeared at Madison Square Garden to get an ovation that was, if anything, larger than the one enjoyed by the President a few nights before. The Republican Garden party had everything. Joan Crawford was on the platform. She spent most of her time signing autographs; her presence was most decorative. The single sobering note was the seizure of a man with a gun just a few feet from the platform and the Republican candidate.

Outside, Clare Booth, the playwright, appeared before the giant street rally where 90,000 who could not get into the Garden were showing their Willkieism. Miss Booth rushed hatless from the meeting to read a speech she had just given inside, and the crowd booed Roosevelt, all New Dealers, Mayor La Guardia, Elliott Roosevelt, Dorothy Thompson, Stephen T. Early (the kneer), and even started to hiss Jack Dempsey who had come out for Roosevelt. It was, as Willkie had said, a "crusade."

Then the waiting began.

Election day was November 5. Willkie did not stay in his Fifth Avenue home, but set up shop at the Commodore Hotel in New York. When the returns started to come in, they showed a narrowed margin for Roosevelt, but still a Roosevelt victory. Early in the game, vice-presidential candidate McNary conceded and went to bed, far off in Oregon. But Willkie could not concede, could not believe he had not won the race. At 1:30 A.M. he still refused to give up and kept glued to the television set that so fascinated him in his fourteenth-floor suite.

The next morning the results were unmistakable. Franklin D. Roosevelt was still President of the United States of America.

At Hyde Park the old champion laid the cornerstone for a new post office, talked briefly about its architecture, which copied that of an original farm building in the area, and discoursed at bit about neighborhood spots of historic interest. Then he went back to Washington.

Indochina was dismembered by Japan and Thailand, the war in Europe was no longer "phony" but a terrible slaughter. It was evident, even before the January 1941 inauguration of Franklin Delano Roosevelt for his third term that we could not stay out indefinitely.

The United States lent destroyers to Britain in exchange for bases in Bermuda; we promised a billion dollars worth of aid to the Russians to help them save themselves; we kept the pipelines open to Britain and the rest; boys from Iowa and New York flew under the Chinese flag in a strictly extra-legal arrangement, at which the military and State Department both winked casually. War was on our doorstep in 1941, even as Saburo Kurusu and Admiral Nomura arrived to "negotiate" our differences in the brisk days of November.

Then—Pearl Harbor—and all F.D.R.'s promises about keeping the country out of war were set aside as it became obvious that the war had been brought to us. Even the Republicans forgot them, for the moment, in that happy and marvelous ability of wars to help people forget political differences in the greater need of the hour.

World War II was conducted in deadly earnest. At first it took every ounce of American energy just to catch up. The Japanese and Germans and Italians had been preparing for years. America's military might was a paper tiger, as the Chinese say, although America's military potential was not.

And catch up we did. By 1943, given time, we had caught up a great deal. Ugly, squat but effective Liberty ships were waddling down the ways of a shipyard in port cities. Airplanes were riveted together by well-paid housewives and college students home on holiday. Civilian youths went into khaki one day, and a few months later came out tough and sinewy.

Perhaps they were not finished fighting men—but they were getting there.

Nineteen forty-four. The war moved more our way, and it was obvious now that victory was a matter of time. We had ringed our enemies. We had cut their supply lines. We had pushed back their best fighting men . . . we: the Americans and the Russians and the British and the French and all the international components of our armies, and, by courtesy, the Chinese, who had to be congratulated on their long struggle against Japan, even if their military might was little, and that fragmented by civil war.

With the turn of the military tide, the Republicans, rightly enough, felt they could afford to show their political independence once again. . . .

23. He Who Changes Horses . . . 1944

In the summer of 1943, Harrison Spangler, new GOP national chairman, called a "postwar advisory council" to meet at Michigan's Mackinac Island, and ostentatiously refrained from inviting either Willkie or Herbert Hoover. (Someone thought they canceled each other out.)

By 1944 the Republican party had accepted a great deal of the philosophy of Wendell Willkie. Yet it was more apparent, than in 1940, that the party had not accepted the man himself, even though as the candidate of 1940 he was titular head of the GOP.

The Mackinac conference included both congressional and gubernatorial leaders of the party. From the beginning the governors took control and pushed through the Willkie program, including the discovery that all nations lived in one world. Governor Thomas Dewey of New York was one of the chief promoters of this victory for modern man over the pterodactyls of the old guard.

Dewey, at forty-one, was a far more accomplished politician than he had been at the Republican convention of 1940 when he had been so soundly trounced by Willkie. In 1942, while the Democrats barely kept control of the House of Representatives, and while Roosevelt supporters like Nebraska's George Norris were defeated for the Senate, the Republicans for the first time in twenty-two years elected a governor of New York. Such an impressive victory could not go unnoticed by the Republican professionals, who wanted, above all else, to be on the winning side for a change. So while Wendell Willkie was making good-will missions for Roosevelt in the interests of a united war effort, Tom Dewey was making hay in the Republican pasture and gathering up the regular party machinery.

Willkie was never one to pay much attention to party machinery.

He gathered a group of men around him because he respected them, and consulted them on political problems. In 1943, Willkie held his own political conference, a sort of front-porch affair, at the symbolic, bucolic, Rushville, Indiana, homestead.

Then Willkie made the great blunder of a political career that had been gilt-edged with luck. On a trip across the country he announced—almost a year before the election—that he would go into the Republican convention of 1944 with 400 votes pledged of the total 1059. Further, Willkie named the states and his position within each state.

When John D. M. Hamilton, the old-guard leader, read this amazing story in the newspapers he made a few calls and decided to take a seventeen-state swing in the interests of sinking Willkie. Hamilton wandered from state to state, bearing in hand the newspaper that carried Willkie's damning words and questioning the party leaders, to see who had pledged himself to Willkie. Hamilton found little Willkie support.

Willkie was no professional politician. In all probability he did not realize the depth of the Midwest's isolationist and anti-liberal sentiment. Instead of placating, wheedling, and half lying to the politicos of the midwestern states, Willkie told them to go straight to hell if they did not like him or what he stood for.

The "sink Willkie" move went into operation. And there, of course, the Republicans made *their* great error of the 1944 campaign. They began to believe that the party was greater than Willkie. While it might have been true historically, it was certainly not true in the minds of the independent voters whom the Republicans would have to attract to win the election.

Willkie's more liberal advisers decided he ought to enter the Wisconsin primary. Convention time was drawing irrevocably closer, and the votes were not materializing as they ought to. On balance, Wisconsin seems to have been the worst possible choice. It was located in the heart of the isolationist belt, was still reverberating with the waves of La Folletteism, and Willkie had already managed to antagonize the bigwigs of organized labor in the state. Further, his campaign was run by men not well known in Wisconsin and whose political views were not widely shared . . . such men as Ralph Cake, the banker who was national committeeman from Oregon and a member of the Willkie fraternity.

Willkie had broken with Harold Stassen, his floor manager at the

convention of 1940, partly over the latter's review of Willkie's book
One World in the New York *Times*. Stassen had chided Willkie for
underestimating the dangers of communism and overestimating the
evils of colonialism. Willkie, characteristically, was offended, as he
had been offended by an earlier Stassen remark that Willkie had no
monopoly on internationalism. When the Wisconsin primary rolled
around, Willkie had to face Governor Dewey, who now controlled the
mechanism of the party, and General Douglas MacArthur, an ultra-
conservative who was not averse to having his name used, although
he did not stir a finger in his own behalf—or even leave his post as
occupation commander in Japan. Willkie had to face Stassen as well.

Willkie campaigned. A Willkie campaign on a county level was
always a potential disaster, for Willkie could not refrain from being
himself and would not use a diplomatic phrase where a frank word
served truth. So while he campaigned and the others did not, Willkie's
campaign may have helped to beat him.

When primary day came, April 1, the small-town politicians stood
their safe distance from the polls, collaring all comers and asking
them to vote for anyone but Willkie. The Republicans of Wisconsin,
in majority obliged. It was Willkie against the Republican party,
and the party won, hands down. Dewey won fifteen convention votes,
Stassen won four, and MacArthur won three. Willkie won none.

When the news came to him, he was campaigning in Nebraska.
On April 5 he brought a major political address in Omaha to a
startling climax. Wendell Willkie announced his withdrawal from the
campaign.

Tom Dewey was delighted. Now there was nothing between him
and the nomination except time. Willkie, retired from the field,
devoted his time to writing on political subjects, hoping that his
views would seep through a backward, disunited Republican party
that seemed to be verging on the brink of a return to know-nothing-
ness. Several times, before the Republican National Convention met,
Willkie arranged appointments with Governor Dewey, who apparently had no desire for Willkie advice and who had not then
sufficient prescience to understand the value of the Willkie
imprimatur, for the election if not the nomination.

It is probable, too, that the little governor and his advisers were
afraid that Willkie at the convention might become Willkie the
nominee, even though he had withdrawn from the race. They could
remember 1940 only too well. So Dewey and the Republican

organization of New York kept Willkie from a seat as a delegate from New York. Almost insultingly, he was offered a seat on the platform by Chairman Spangler, but had he accepted he could not have participated in the convention. Willkie was not asked to address the convention. Because he was still the most popular non-Democrat in the land, the Republican politicians were frightened to death.

Until the meeting itself several of Willkie's friends urged him to come to Chicago, but others warned that his presence might mean a victory for John Bricker, the ultra-conservative governor of Ohio. To Willkie, Bricker was an even less desirable candidate than Dewey, for while Dewey was opportunist, Bricker was openly isolationist.

Bricker seemed to have some chance for the nomination, if the Dewey steam roller could be sidetracked by one of those rare political miracles. In 1940, Bricker had made a deal with Taft: he would support Taft's candidacy if Taft would step aside for him in 1944.

In Chicago, Ruth Hanna McCormick Simms was again in charge of the Dewey headquarters, at the Blackstone Hotel. She bravely claimed 750 delegates, while Bricker's men claimed 174 and gave Dewey credit for only 72. Everyone knew the Bricker claim was nonsense. The convention was due to open on Monday, June 26, but on Saturday it was conceded that it was cut and dried for Dewey. There were only two possible openings for drama: 1) Willkie might make a whirlwind entrance and demand an internationalist platform; 2) Governor Earl Warren of California, the Vice-President designated by the steam roller, might refuse the nomination.

Willkie received an advance copy of the platform, not from the Republicans but from a newspaperman. He found the foreign policy planks sadly lacking. He released the platform to the press, before Chicago did, with some caustic comment. The Republicans (Willkie hardly seemed one of their number now), immediately yelled "foul."

Robert Alphonso Taft, the senator from Ohio, was chairman of the platform committee. When he picked up the afternoon Chicago papers on June 26 and saw his handiwork attacked, he was angry. Willkie had compared the platform to the Republican platform of 1920, which also paid lip service to "internationalism" but which was so general that when President Warren Harding declared the League of Nations dead after his election, none could say he was reneging.

It was not hard for Taft to inflame the others of the old guard against this corn-fed will-o'-the-wisp who had seized control of their party four short years ago. Taft challenged any Willkie supporter to press his protest against the platform. Sixteen governors took Taft up on his challenge and did press the protest. They were lucky to escape with their political lives as the old-guard steam roller ran over them.

The governors were trying to take control of the Republican convention of 1944. They had drawn the mid-term platform at Mackinac in 1943. The governors felt that the rejuvenation of the Republican party was beginning at the state level. They had little use for the ultra-conservative bloc of Republicans who dominated the congressional section of the party—who were seriously talking about nominating as Vice-President Senator Harry F. Byrd, the budget-guarding Democrat orchardist from Virginia.

It was apparent from the opening day that while the governors' bloc would control the nomination, making Dewey the nominee, the old-fashioned congressional bloc would control party policy. Dewey's men invited Senator Taft to consult them about the formation of the platform, but Taft ignored them as he went his majestic way.

On the second day, the convention accepted the resolutions committee's platform without a whimper. Many, no doubt, were as enraged as was Taft at Willkie's violation of the faith. Some, led by the dissident governors, felt that Dewey, who had already announced for a program of international co-operation after the war, would show the nation a more liberal policy than the platform indicated.

The troglodytes, meanwhile, were up to their old tricks. House leader Joseph Martin, the congressman from Massachusetts and permanent chairman of the convention, labeled the New Deal "fascism," and the Republican platform makers talked about "a fair protective tariff," which could mean either higher or lower import duties.

The platform was nebulous enough to appease even its detractors, who, after all, were more concerned with a Republican presidential victory than anything else. The convention hurried it out of the way.

The next day, June 28, without a flurry, Thomas E. Dewey was nominated for the presidency, 1056 to 1—the one die-hard vote cast by a supporter of General MacArthur.

Dewey estimated that he would get the nomination by three o'clock that afternoon, so he could arrive conveniently by airplane, more speedily, but in the tradition of Franklin D. Roosevelt in

1932. The Republicans did much better for him. The convention was opened by Chairman Martin at 10:49 A.M. Not only Dewey, but vice-presidential hopeful John Bricker was nominated by 1:43 P.M. (Warren had refused the nomination after all.) Dewey arrived at Chicago by 7 P.M. and was on the platform at nine-thirteen, ready to proclaim his surprise at this "draft," after the gentlemen on the platform had found him a box to stand on.

"Today we bring Sir Galahad in quest of the Holy Grail, the knight in shining armor who will burst the biggest gang that has ever infested the United States," joyfully shouted Chicago Municipal Judge Patrick P. Prescott. "New York now gives Thomas E. Dewey to the limitless ages."

Governor Dewey expressed his pleased surprise at the unexpected honor in a twenty-six-minute acceptance address. When Dewey stopped, his sartorial elegance marred only by the perspiration wriggling along his cheeks, the nominee showed his teeth to the yelling crowd, shook hands with running mate Bricker, and at 9:42 P.M. Chairman Martin recognized a delegate from Pennsylvania. At 9:42½ P.M. the 1944 Republican convention was ended.

Two days later no one was shocked when Herbert Brownell, Jr., a New York lawyer who was the chief of the young kingmakers around Dewey, was elected to run the party's 1944 campaign. Wendell Willkie had sent his telegram of congratulations to Dewey, with a significant omission of any words of support for the Republican candidate. Dewey declared himself opposed to an international police force, and the 1944 Republican campaign was on.

Dewey did not know it, but he was running against a sick man. Not many of Roosevelt's political supporters knew it either. In fact, by this time Franklin Roosevelt did not even discuss such matters with his wife; but Eleanor Roosevelt knew her husband was far from well. She also knew that he planned to run again if the war was still on, and that there was no use trying to tell him anything different.

During the winter of 1943–44, the President ran a low fever and suffered generally from an undetermined malaise. Just after the first of April he went down to Bernard Baruch's plantation in South Carolina for a month, to try to get a little rest, in the hope that the sun would take away the fever. It seemed to help.

A fourth term was no issue, as the third had been. The men who had quit in disgust on the third-term issue were gone, and the others were not concerned with the matter. Jim Farley, who had already given up the postmastership and resigned as national chairman, now also resigned as New York state chairman, but it created scarcely a stir. As far as the Democrats were concerned, Roosevelt could have a fourth term, and a fifth, if he could live that long, and wanted it.

The fight in the party of the donkey, this year again, concerned the vice-presidency. Henry Wallace was still suspect, as a mystic, as a violent left-winger, and as a muzzle-headed idiot who could ruin the country if it were ever placed in his hand. In the South, particularly, the opposition to Wallace was virulent. Eleanor Roosevelt had been stirring up the South with all her talk about equality of the races. The Democrats' leaders of the South couldn't do anything about *that*, but their violent feeling came out against Wallace, who agreed with her.

Wallace had been fighting with Jesse Jones, the conservative from Houston, who had brought a banker's sense and banker's ties to the New Deal.

But Wallace was valuable to Roosevelt, just because of his intensely strong radical support, and it would be no easy job to dislodge him.

Robert E. Hannegan, the Democratic party national chairman, took a trip around the country, with his ear to the ground and his finger on the pulse of his party. He returned to announce that he could find no grass-roots sentiment for Wallace, and that everyone he talked to was conscious of the renewed importance of the vice-presidential nomination, in the event of a fourth-term President.

In June, Hannegan gave these facts to Roosevelt, with the expected information that most of the delegates to the Chicago convention were already pledged to him. Hannegan was blunt. If Roosevelt was to support Wallace, he might or might not see the issue through the convention again, as in 1940, but it would surely split the party so wide open this year that the Democratic ticket might lose.

Roosevelt decided to jettison Wallace, if need be. He asked Samuel Rosenman to inform the Vice-President, and Rosenman and Harold Ickes had breakfast with Wallace just after his return from his mission to China. Wallace paid no attention, but that same day saw Roosevelt and secured a promise that Roosevelt at least would not actively oppose him at the convention.

Rosenman said later that the nomination of Senator Harry Truman was settled at the White House at least two weeks before the Democratic convention in Chicago. Perhaps it was. But Truman, who was not seeking the job, did not know about it; neither did Wallace, nor James Byrnes, who wanted the vice-presidency very badly, nor were any number of other prominent Democrats let in on the secret.

And when the national chairman, Mr. Hannegan, appeared in Chicago on July 15, he avoided the assemblage of reporters like the very plague. This alone, coming from an old pro like Hannegan, who had always found the press very useful, was enough to let the newspapermen know that something unusual was up.

Wallace had secured a letter from Roosevelt to Senator Samuel Jackson of Indiana, which endorsed the Vice-President for renomination, although hardly in unequivocal terms. What it said, in effect, was that if Roosevelt were a delegate he would vote for Wallace, but that didn't mean the convention had to. This was a quite different attitude than Roosevelt had exhibited in 1940—when he had laid down the name Wallace and, when the convention threatened to balk, had prepared his own letter refusing the nomination.

Byrnes had persuaded Harry Truman to nominate him. Alben Barkley, the Senate majority leader, was also after the vice-presidency. It was no secret that Roosevelt found Barkley too old, and Byrnes too unsatisfactory to labor. The labor vote was important, particularly since the wild old goat of the labor movement, John L. Lewis, had just come out in support of Tom Dewey and the Republican labor plank. Byrnes was also unsatisfactory to the NAACP, whose Walter White was on hand to point out that in the four largest states, with 135 electoral votes, the Negro vote was larger than Roosevelt's majorities in 1940.

Obviously, Byrnes was not the man, and when it came out that he was Catholic born, Episcopal bred, he was through.

Philip Murray and Sidney Hillman of the CIO were in Chicago to plump for Wallace, and before the convention they advised him to get to Chicago as quickly as he could to fight for his own interests. As the Vice-President rushed West the cocktail-party circuit was already mumbling that Wallace had been sacrificed for Harry Truman, and the press knew Hannegan had some kind of letter from the President. The chairman denied everything.

Two days before the convention a delegate turned to Senator Carl Hatch of New Mexico in the elevator of a hotel and said,

"Senator, wouldn't you call this the nicest vice-presidential convention you ever attended?"

But as the convention opened on July 19, it was anything but nice. Roosevelt's acceptance speech was already arranged for the night of July 20; the fight could only last two days. Those two days were to be full of strife, although Byrnes, after conversation with Roosevelt, quit the race "in deference to the President's wishes" and told the South Carolina delegation not to put his name in nomination. Roosevelt wanted Truman. It was out now, although still not official. Truman was a compromise; quiet, unassuming, loyal to the party. He came from a state on the edge of the South and was not offensive to labor.

Now the rush was on to Truman's band wagon, but Wallace was still committed to the finish.

Self-consciously, Wallace walked into the convention. The band struck up "Iowa, Iowa, That's Where the Tall Corn Grows," and the organist, off in the far corner of the convention hall, chimed in. Then they played "My Hero," although a number of members of the convention would have disputed the fitness of the selection.

Wallace and his backers denied the existence of any letter from F.D.R. to Hannegan, but others, who claimed to be in the know, said they had seen the letter and that Roosevelt had told Hannegan either Truman or William O. Douglas, Associate Justice of the Supreme Court, would be quite acceptable as a running mate. The only letter, the Wallace men said, was the one which had been sent to Senator Jackson. Wallace suggested that Harry Truman's machine-politics background would made him unacceptable to labor, that Dewey would make an issue of Truman's link with Tom Pendergast's Kansas City machine.

But even off in Washington the Republicans' Senator Taft could read the Roosevelt handwriting. Wallace had been jettisoned, said Mr. Republican.

"In this solemn hour, as representatives of the common people of every state and territory in this nation . . ." boomed genial, big Bob Kerr, the oil-rich Oklahoma governor, in his stentorian keynote speech on the first day. The festivities were beginning, deceptively quiet.

Foreign policy was no issue. The Democrats had built a stronger plank on international co-operation than the Republicans, still without endorsing that international army that would take away most of the national sovereign right to start wars. The only threat to unity, as usual, was the racial plank in the civil rights section of the platform. The South was determined now, with the inroads made by Mrs. Roosevelt and others, to maintain white supremacy, and would have no part of any plank that attacked the segregated way of life. The North and West were demanding a strong statement against racial discrimination.

On July 20, as Adolph Hitler narrowly escaped violent death by a bomb in Berlin, Franklin Roosevelt was nominated for a fourth term as President of the United States, by a vote of 1086 to 89 for Senator Byrd, and 1 for Jim Farley, representing, but not respectively, southern and conservative opposition to the New Deal. Shortly thereafter, Chairman Hannegan made public his letter from F.D.R. about Truman and Douglas, effectively deflating the Wallace balloon.

The letter was dated July 19, although Samuel Rosenman said it had been written and given to Hannegan long before the convention. Whatever the truth, its appearance at that particular moment probably kept Wallace from being renominated. For on that second day of the convention Hannegan did not have the votes to put Truman over, and he sought adjournment for an evening of wheeling and dealing. The Wallace men felt that adjournment meant disaster to their candidate.

Truman, who had worked first for Byrnes, was finally convinced that he must be the candidate, and in good humor he told his friends now that it was all over, that he was going to be nominated the next day.

The Wallace men knew it was now or never. They jammed the aisles in demonstration, but the chair recognized David Lawrence, the Pittsburgh political boss. Lawrence moved for adjournment for the night, demanded a voice vote, and the chair announced it carried, although it was hard to hear him through the thunder of "no" that shook the house.

In the fifth session the next day, Wallace led on the first ballot 429½ to 319½ for Truman. The rest of the votes were scattered among fourteen favorite sons. There were many who wanted the job, obviously. But after the compulsory favorite-son votes were out on that first ballot, the real pledges of the delegates were to show up. On the second ballot it was all over. Wallace got only 66 votes. Truman was sitting on the platform eating a sandwich when the result was announced. It was a victory of the big-city political bosses over Sidney Hillman's CIO Political Action Committee, which wanted Wallace and had jammed the galleries with shouters.

The next day, at the La Salle Street Station, a lonely Henry Wallace walked to the train, without being recognized by a soul in the station, save a lone newspaper reporter.

Wallace forced a smile. "I'm glad you came down to see me off," he said ruefully. Just then a trainman stepped down from one of the cars and looked at him.

"Your name Wallace?" he grunted, and the Vice-President of the United States nodded. "Couple ladies back there said to tell you where they were." He turned and walked off as Wallace got slowly on the train.

The minority parties were not important in this election. In fact, the minorities had ceased to be of great importance except to show the protest of various segments of American society. Socialism had never gotten started in America, and while Norman Thomas campaigned bravely and regularly—again in 1944, as he had so many times before—his party had nothing new to offer.

Other minority groups put up candidates: the Prohibitionists ran Claude A. Watson for President, the Socialist Labor party ran Edward A. Teichert. There was an attempt to revive the Greenback party, made by a small group that nominated Leo C. Donnelly. The America First party nominated Gerald L. K. Smith, a man who had already made reputation as a right-winger and racist. The Communists did not run a candidate at all, but supported Roosevelt. Since the United States and Russia were now allies the Adminstration was temporarily acceptable.

If minority parties were to become important again—it would have to be new minority parties. The Prohibitionists had had their little fling, and the rest were simply dwindling, depending on one's point of view. But the fact was that none of them had anything to offer that Americans wanted, and most of them polled votes in such insignificant number that they were not counted by any but the most meticulous students of political affairs.

The Republicans pulled out all the stops in this campaign, linking Roosevelt and the Democratic party with treason and with communism. Thirteen Republican members of Congress got together and used their franking privilege to send out three million copies of such a speech, by Representative Fred E. Busbey of Illinois, a fact that did not go unnoticed in the campaign, particularly when the Republicans talked of economy in government.

The Democrats ran scared, and while Roosevelt did not campaign strenuously, he made his addresses on the state of the nation at war do double duty. The Democratic theme—don't change horses in midstream—was played in every conceivable way.

Dewey, now that he had captured the nomination, would very much have liked to have the active support of Wendell Willkie. But he had gone too far to get it easily. Roosevelt wanted that Willkie name, too, and made several gambits to get it. He asked Willkie to come and see him, but Willkie, sensing that this was a political move in a political year, answered that he would be most anxious to do so, right after the election. Some of Roosevelt's intimates said later that the President was looking forward, and would have proposed that Willkie join him in formation of a new, liberal party, to embody the principles of the New Deal and jettison the southern autocrats and conservative nabobs of the East. Perhaps, but Roosevelt wanted to do this before the election, and it seemed to Willkie that there was a price tag attached, particularly when Roosevelt kept leaking news of his invitations to the press.

At any rate, Willkie's support became a rhetorical question long before election day. On October 7, following an infection and several heart attacks, Wendell Willkie died in a New York hospital. The "conscience of the Republicans" was no more.

Without conscience, the Republicans campaigned. They charged that Roosevelt had bungled the depression, had failed to prepare for war, that his whole administration was dominated by the left wing where it was not actually communist, and that these left-wingers and communists were tired old men, unfit by senility to operate the government.

The Democrats countered that Herbert Hoover had just about destroyed the American system by neglect; that the Republicans in 1940 had done everything they could to keep the nation from being prepared for war, that the communist charge was an outright lie, and that Democratic experience in government was of more use to the American people than Republican eagerness.

In their eagerness the Republicans pulled one frightful political blooper. Roosevelt had gone off to the Pacific during the summer on an inspection tour that was hardly free from political overtones.

Somehow the rumor got started that his little Scotty, Fala, had been left behind in the Aleutians and that a U. S. Navy destroyer had turned around in mid-ocean, at astronomical cost, to bring the dog to his master's side.

This annoyed Roosevelt. In a speech in the Midwest in the middle of his campaign he denied it flatly—and poured ridicule on the heads of the Republicans for trying to attack him through his little dog. The country laughed at the ridiculous charge, the President's amused superiority breathed confidence, and the Republicans were no better off for the whole exchange.

Infuriatingly, Roosevelt never gave an opponent a chance to get at him. Again, he blithely ignored the candidate, and this roused Dewey to the fury that only the overlooked can muster. In one speech, he imitated Roosevelt's voice and mannerisms, sarcastically attacking the Roosevelt pledge of peace. The sarcasm and the strong charges did not help.

In the last week of the campaign Senator Joseph H. Ball of Minnesota, the chief internationalist of the Republican party, struck a terrible blow at the party's protestations that it was now liberal in its overseas policies. He switched horses, announced that he was going to support Roosevelt, simply on the international issue.

Roosevelt spent election day in his traditional fashion, at Hyde Park, and election night in the dining room of the big house, playing at his big bulletin board with the election figures as they came in.

The old champ won again, this time by 3,600,000 votes and 33 electoral votes, and the Democrats gained seats in the House, strengthening their control.

Strangely, Henry Wallace turned out to be the best seer of all that election night. He called the shot at nine-thirty, although it could not have been a sure thing until 11 P.M.

There was another who showed a sort of extrasensory perception in that election. Tom Dewey, when he registered at New York's Hotel Roosevelt on election day, carefully wrote after his name his occupation—"lawyer."

24

The great year 1945 brought victory in Europe, but it also brought tragedy in America, with the sudden death of Franklin Delano Roosevelt. He had been a controversial figure, but few would deny that the news was shocking.

The course of the European war could not be changed by this event, for the Germans and the Italians in complete rout, and what remained in the spring of 1945 was a cleanup operation. The cleanup took time, lives, and much matériel, but the outcome was never in doubt.

The war in the Far East was almost the same. Japan knew all was lost in that spring of 1945. Few men in Japan were under any illusion about the final outcome of the struggle. But when? Under what conditions? And how . . . ? These were all questions unanswered about the ending of the war.

Harry S. Truman answered those questions, when he made the brave, fateful decision to drop the atomic bomb. The first, dropped on Hiroshima on August 6, showed the Japanese (and ourselves) that we had at our disposal the most terrible weapon of all time. The second, dropped on Nagasaki on August 9, showed the Japanese that we had control of the weapon and could use it again and again, devastatingly.

The war ended.

Within a few months, traditionally, mothers and wives and sweethearts were clamoring that their boys be brought home from foreign shores. The clamor was heard in the halls of Congress, and answered, on a non-partisan basis, by loud and prolonged demand for the dismemberment of the American military machinery.

The machine was dismantled, as slowly as the military and foreign service experts dared dismantle it in the face of overbearing public demand.

A war economy ended—rationing and butterless days and meatless meals, deferred vacations and rattling old cars and shoes that made do.

It was time for a change. November 1946 rolled around, and with it rolled the heads of Democratic senators and representatives. When the ballots and heads were counted, the Eightieth Congress of the United States was found to be Republican, for the first time since 1928.

Now, the elephant was riding high. . . .

24. The Fair Deal
1948

If there is one single image of the 1948 presidential campaign, it is a lonely little man on the observation platform of a railway car, steaming across a vast country, fighting almost singlehandedly for his Fair Deal and a party that had lost its nerve.

By 1948 such Democratic stalwarts as Colonel Jake Arvey of Chicago had been ready to ditch the little man. In Los Angeles, National Committeeman James Roosevelt was conducting a boomlet for General Dwight D. Eisenhower. Leaders of the battered and fractured Democratic party were spending as much time fighting one another as trying to put together a combination to beat the Republicans.

Nineteen forty-eight had all the earmarks of a Republican year. In 1946 the voters had returned a Republican Congress for the first time in twenty years. That Eightieth Congress immediately began to ride roughshod over the plain man who had been catapulted into the presidency on Franklin Roosevelt's death in 1945. In 1944, President Harry S. Truman had neither sought the vice-presidency nor dreamed of having the presidency thrust upon him. In one way, his background seemed woefully inadequate. He had grown up in Missouri, had gone to war with the AEF in 1917, and come home from France a captain of artillery. He had taken a flier in the haberdashery business, but had soon found that he was not suited for the American business world. Harry Truman went into politics. For a while he was a county judge, and he liked the job just fine. But there were bigger things in store, and Harry Truman ended up being elected to the United States Senate as a scion of the Pendergast Democratic machine of Kansas City. Senator Truman's record was distinguished by his conduct of a war investigating committee that did a great deal to stop waste and profiteering after the United States entered World War II. The Truman committee was well known and well respected.

Little of this background seemed to fit him for such high office, but Harry Truman showed a remarkable adaptability, once the mantle of state had fallen on his unwilling shoulders. One thing stood him in good stead: his avid interest in the history of American government. He might not have had the advantages of an eastern prep school and Ivy League education, but Truman could reach back into memory for precedents, and from the past derived strength to meet the frightening problems he had to face as Chief Executive of the United States.

Truman had, in fact, been left a spoiled kettle of fish by Franklin Roosevelt. Whether Roosevelt was ill, whether he underestimated the wiliness of Joseph Stalin, or whether the Soviet-American clash was inevitable, by 1946 it became apparent that the interests of the two greatest powers were not the same. From the icy waters of Korea to the clear blue Mediterranean of Greece, the two worlds were in conflict. Soviet Russia was straining to expand, in a pattern of imperialism almost like that espoused by the czars. The United States was determined to limit Soviet expansion.

At home, Americans were sick of the outside world, even though they were quite sure by now they had to live in it. At least, however, they wanted change in matters like rationing and price fixing and production control. The United States had won the war, hadn't it?

The boys were coming back from overseas. They wanted blueberry pie and ice cream, but they also wanted new suits, new cars, education, wives, jobs, and houses to live in. It was time, the nation felt, for a return to something like normalcy.

The Republican Eightieth Congress tried to give Americans all these things, starting in 1947 when, for the first time since Herbert Hoover, the GOP controlled both houses of Congress. But the Republican theory, the Democrats said, was that if you left everything in the hands of business, it would turn out all right. And the Republicans were anxious to make a record that would endear them to the voting public as the party of free enterprise and sensible government. That, they believed, was what Americans wanted above all.

President and Congress clashed over farm policy, labor policy, removal of price controls, and a score of other national matters. In the international field, the differences were more restrained, due largely to the forbearance and supreme efforts of Michigan's Senator Arthur Vandenberg. This Republican senator had become an ardent internationalist and advocate of bipartisan foreign policy, and while he was sometimes rebuffed by the Administration, he did preserve bipartisanship.

The Democrats could scarcely keep their house together. President Truman made a strong statement about civil rights. It so angered the South that a delegation of southern governors descended on the Democratic National Committee.

The South sought Senator J. Howard McGrath's assurances that the rights issue would be soft-pedaled in the forthcoming platform and campaign. McGrath was loyal to Truman. He turned the southerners down, and they went home spouting dire imprecations.

Henry Agard Wallace had quarreled with Truman early. But for his discard by the convention of 1944, Wallace would have been President himself. After the 1944 election Roosevelt appointed Wallace Secretary of Commerce. When Truman took office, he kept the Roosevelt cabinet, but Wallace interfered with Truman's conduct of foreign policy until finally they parted company. By 1948, Wallace had announced his intention of forming a third party to seek the presidency. He was an open advocate of a soft policy toward the Soviet Union, so he attracted the pacifists, kindhearted but softheaded liberals, and many of the young. Equally important, as it was to turn out, Wallace attracted the communists, who decided to take him over.

By late spring, then, the Republicans were chuckling with glee and estimating the majorities by which they would win control of the presidency and of Congress. Since the Democrats had decided early in the game that Senator Robert A. Taft would be the most difficult candidate to beat, the Democratic National Committee began a campaign of vilification against the Republican Senate majority leader. Democratic press releases invented new words, such as "Tafter" to describe any Republican who yielded to lobby pressure, "Taft-wits" to describe anyone who agreed with the Ohio senator. None of the barbs stuck in the American language, but they got under Taft's skin. Finally Truman personally ordered the name-calling halted. But the charges against Taft went on.

The press was labeled by the Democrats as 90 per cent pro-Republican, though some six hundred papers regularly printed the

Democratic National Committee's sprightly newsletter "Capitol Comment" as a political column. Yet the national committee was worried about getting its whole message across, this year, and suggested that Truman get out and meet the people personally, in the style of Mark Hanna, Teddy Roosevelt, and the politicians of the pre-radio and television days.

On June 3, President Truman embarked on a ten-thousand-mile, eighteen-day, cross-country tour to test the political winds. He was pleasantly surprised to see vast crowds of citizens turn out. Truman had discovered a new way of speaking. Early in the game he had been a reader, and his twangy, even voice was deadly. But speaking to the newspaper editors meeting in Washington in the spring, Truman had extemporized and realized instantly that his own natural style was far better than anything that could be prepared for him.

On the cross-country tour Truman spoke his mind, often without a note. He gave the Republicans no quarter, and the crowds seemed to love every minute of his speeches.

In Omaha, Truman stopped long enough to offer a four-plank farm program that promised permanent price supports, and to march in the parade of his old 35th Division veterans. Truman started out riding in the parade in Nebraska Governor Val Peterson's car, but the President's old buddies began taunting him, along the route. "Why the hell can't Harry walk?" one asked. The President grinned, got out of the car, and marched alongside Frank Spina, the old barber of Battery D. Truman wore the battery's red brassard on the arm of his gabardine suit and tipped his hat right and left to the admiring parade watchers.

Carroll Reece, Republican national chairman, registered a loud yelp about the payment for this political trip out of federal funds, but the Democrats shrugged him off.

Sensitive to the southern Democrats' fear of the Truman civil rights stand, Senator Taft invaded the South, on a three-day campaign tour. Taft spoke at Lenoir, North Carolina, the day Truman was parading in Omaha. The theme of Taft's speech was "states' rights," a speech delivered on a platform under spreading shade trees, facing directly into the Confederate Army memorial shaft in the public square. It was a strange place and a strange speech for a member of Mr. Lincoln's party, but times had changed, and there was an election to be fought.

There was no question after the trip that Truman would receive the Democratic nomination, no matter how official Washington and the Democratic leaders might wring their hands in anticipation of defeat. Truman had 618 pledged votes of the 1234 of the convention. Only 94 votes were definitely committed against the President, although some Alabama and Florida delegates were pledged to bolt if Truman insisted on a strong civil rights plank.

Glen H. Taylor, the singing cowboy senator from Idaho, had already bolted the party to join the Wallace-for-President movement, and on June 8, Taylor spoke in Brooklyn, as a warmup for the Wallacite convention. The Wallace party still did not have a name, but it planned to meet in Philadelphia, just as did the Republicans and Democrats, but the new group would assemble after the two major parties had concluded their business.

The Republican convention, which would be held first, was anything but cut and dried this year. Although Governor Dewey was expected to poll 325 votes on the first ballot, with some in reserve, Senator Taft claimed 306 votes. Senator Arthur Vandenberg was a grass-roots candidate. Harold Stassen, who encountered Dewey in Baltimore in the frantic search for delegates, predicted that he would have 340. Three hundred and sixty were pledged to favorite sons. Altogether, with 1094 delegates to attend the convention, someone seemed to be oversubscribed, but it was difficult to tell who it was.

Just before the Republican convention Truman characterized the Eightieth Congress as "the worst in history." Speaker Joseph Martin of the House of Representatives cracked back that Truman was the worst President in history, but the countercharges of the Republicans lacked Truman's fire. Even when Senator Taft said Congress should adjourn and await election of a new President since Truman's attitude toward Congress was so bad, it sounded somehow false and fiesty. And Carroll Reece charged that Truman was wooing the communist vote, then suggested that Wallace sue Truman for infringement of copyright.

On the eve of the Republican convention the vast majority of a poll of 815 newspaper editors picked Senator Vandenberg as the Republican nominee, a Vandenberg who had shown himself a statesman in his co-operation with the Democratic administration on foreign policy.

The convention was to prove them as inaccurate as the public-opinion polls they trusted so well.

In Philadelphia, Herbert Brownell, Jr., one of three Dewey managers, set up shop at the Bellevue-Stratford Hotel. Senator Taft's headquarters was at the Benjamin Franklin and Harold Stassen's on Walnut Street. Each headquarters predicted victory. It was a foregone conclusion that the Republican nomination this year meant the presidency, for the public-opinion polls showed Truman's popularity far below its previous levels. Even the Democrats were concerned. The only politician who had real hope of a sure Truman victory was Harry Truman. "If I felt better I couldn't stand it," said the jaunty President, still on his lay-of-the-land inspection tour.

In Philadelphia, Harold Stassen cheerily predicted his nomination on the ninth ballot, and served visitors nine hundred pounds of cheese. Dewey-man Herbert Brownell predicted Dewey on the second ballot, and served nothing. Governor Warren of California stayed in his room quietly but hopefully.

Reporters spotted Big Jim Farley of New York, who was in Philadelphia on personal business. Still impressed by his awesome prediction of Roosevelt's 1936 landslide, reporters collared Farley for opinion. Dewey had the lead, Farley replied, but he would have to secure the nomination on an early ballot if he was to win.

When the twenty-fourth Republican convention opened, its theme was set by Dwight Green, governor of Illinois. The keynote of 1948 was a blistering attack on sixteen years of Democratic "misrule."

On June 21, the convention in session, Colonel Robert McCormick of the Chicago *Tribune,* a would-be kingmaker, came out for a combination ticket of Taft and Stassen, likening it to the McKinley-Teddy Roosevelt ticket of 1900. Stassen said it was no deal. He was too close to the prize this time, he felt, and there was every chance that Dewey and Taft would cancel each other out, as U. S. Grant and James G. Blaine had in 1880, to force the nomination of James Garfield.

The Republican platform committee of 1948 labored manfully, but few really cared. The convention was only interested in a candidate—in choosing the man who would occupy the White House in January 1949. Herbert Hoover received a tremendous ovation when he appeared on June 22. He smiled his rueful smile, contemplating, perhaps, his unfortunate role as political house-mother ever since the debacle of 1932. But the business of the convention whizzed on right around him. Taft and Stassen, loosely combined for the moment to try to stop Dewey, lost a round when the Georgia delegation of Dewey supporters was seated by the credentials committee, rather than the Taft delegation. The next day, strength waning, the Taft men abandoned the brave floor fight they had planned. Senator Edward Martin of Pennsylvania announced he would second Dewey's nomination. This meant he had thrown Pennsylvania's vote to Dewey, and Martin's move meant that the struggle was all over to everyone but Harold Stassen, who said Dewey was "desperate," and to Senator Taft, who said Dewey was stopped.

On the third day—really at 2 A.M. on the fourth day—Stassen's forces staged a great rally, even greater than the demonstration for Wendell Willkie in 1940. One reporter claimed that for sound and sheer theater this Stassen war dance was the greatest political demonstration in history. Scores of balloons were released to ascend ninety feet to the convention hall's ceiling. Men and women tooting musical instruments paraded up and down the aisles, leading other men and women who bore thirty-two state standards and, on stalwart shoulders, a girl in a canoe. An Indian chief in full war bonnet paraded with the other citizens. The Dewey, Taft, and Warren demonstrations were much less spectacular. George Murphy, the dancing actor from Hollywood, led the "We Want Warren" chant from the podium. He was joined by Irene Dunne, until Miss Dunne fled the harsh and unflattering lights of the rostrum. Taft's men loosed scores of balloons and rang cowbells and sang "Four-Leaf Clover," which had become a Taft trademark. It was all spontaneous and combustible. Observers, though, noted that the same demonstrators appeared again and again in different parades on the floor.

When the fun was over, and the candidates for nomination listed, the convention settled down to the serious business of trading votes and balloting. It was Dewey on the third ballot, after leading Taft almost 2–1 all the way. Governor Dewey thus became the first candidate to be chosen after once having been defeated in a presidential election. California's Earl Warren was chosen by acclamation for the second spot.

Governor Dewey expressed his gratification at the Republican nomination. So did President Harry Truman. In view of the efforts by James Roosevelt and others to draft General Eisenhower for the Democratic ticket, President Truman was particularly pleased by

Eisenhower's flat refusal to be a candidate. Ike then believed a general should not accept high office except in a compelling emergency. Said Texan Sam Rayburn of Soldier Eisenhower: "Good man, wrong business."

The sometimes visionary Senator Claude Pepper of Florida wanted to draft Ike as a non-partisan President, let him write his own platform and pick his own Vice-President, and adjourn politics for four years. But then, said the Democrats as they lowered their eyebrows, Claude Pepper always was a queer one.

The South wanted to be sure the Democratic party had no specific plank on civil rights this year; Harry Truman meant to make sure that the civil rights plank was clean and hard. As the Democrats began assembling in Philadelphia for their innings it was obvious that Truman would be in control. The California delegation was uneasy about James Roosevelt's attempt to jettison the President. In their caucus just before the convention began, John P. McEnery, vice-chairman of the state committee, moved to oust Roosevelt as national committeeman. While this was proposed Roosevelt lounged against a radiator near an open window, but said nothing. Finally, in the interest of party harmony, the ouster motion was tabled.

Two days later that old bluegrass orator, Senator Alben W. Barkley, spoke for sixty-eight minutes (from memory), flogging the Republicans up one side of their platform and down the other in gusty paragraphs interlaced with stories and quotations.

The South was fulminating, even as Barkley spoke, and the next day the men from Dixie tried to reinstate the two-thirds rule, to revive their life-or-death power over the convention. They failed. On July 14 it was apparent there would be no states' rights plank, and there *would be* a strong civil rights plank, calling for abolition of poll taxes, a national anti-lynch law, and a Fair Employment Practices Commission with power of enforcing its rulings against discrimination, throughout the land. Thirty-five Democrats from the Deep South took the long walk out of the convention. The Alabama delegation voted to meet the following Saturday in Birmingham to decide what course to follow.

In Philadelphia southerners who had not left the Democratic convention put up Senator Richard Russell for President. Former Indiana Governor Paul McNutt got ½ vote, Russell 263. President

Truman received 947½ votes, to win nomination on the first ballot.

Mr. Truman had come up from Washington early on the night of his nomination, but he was forced to sit in party chairman McGrath's convention-hall office for three hours, while the delegates fought out the issue of the vice-presidency, and the southern bolt.

At the end Alben Barkley was chosen Vice-President. Truman had picked Barkley, largely because the Kentucky senator wanted the job, and because Justice William O. Douglas had turned it down to stay in the Supreme Court.

At one-thirty on the morning of July 15, Truman and Barkley made their appearance in the convention hall. The planned demonstration included a covey of pigeons, scheduled to fly up gracefully to the ceiling, and create an awesome effect. Two of the birds died from the heat before they could be released, frightening the party's publicity chairman half to death. He could see the SPCA descending on him fang and claw. When the pigeons were released one flew up to the top of an immense electric fan and seemed in danger of being chopped to pieces at any moment. Another landed squarely on convention chairman Sam Rayburn's polished bald dome —a marvelous sight indeed.

Then Harry Truman spoke. The President had something important to say.

The Republicans had promised to solve the problems of prices, agriculture, civil rights, business, housing—all the worries that beset the nation. All right, said Harry Truman. Let the Republican Eightieth Congress solve them, and live up to the GOP platform. The President then and there called a special session of Congress for July 26 (Turnip Day in Missouri), and Truman promised the Democrats that he and Barkley would win the election for them. For the first time during the convention a flare of honest enthusiasm had been loosed. Some of the delegates almost believed the man from Missouri.

The South did not. In Birmingham's Municipal Auditorium on July 17, some six thousand spectators gathered to watch the southerners, in shirt sleeves and broad-brimmed planters' hats, name J. Strom Thurmond, governor of South Carolina, and Fielding L. Wright, governor of Mississippi, to run on a states'-rights ticket. Dixiecrats, they were named. Rule or ruin was their aim. If the Democratic party would ignore the demands of the South, said these men, in the tradition of Alabama's William Yancey, then the South would wreck the Democratic party.

A portrait of Robert E. Lee was raised high in the air, the ear-splitting rebel yell rattled in the heads of all and sundry, and the convention denounced Truman and a civil rights program that threatened "to make southerners into a mongrel, inferior race by forced intermingling with Negroes."

Thurmond drew heavy applause when he claimed the FEPC was the closest the United States had yet come to communism, and when he accused Truman of betraying the South. Representatives of the still-unnamed Wallace party picketed the convention, but departed in a flurry of catcalls and boos when representatives of the thirteen states in the convention approached threateningly.

Now the Wallace men began to convene in Philadelphia. C. B. Baldwin, Wallace's campaign manager, said twenty-five hundred delegates would come to demonstrate their loyalty and to help form the party of the future.

On July 22, James Loeb, Jr., executive secretary of the Americans for Democratic Action, called on Wallace to throw the communists out of his party. This infuriated the communists who were running the party. The party platform was to include peace, which at this point in history could be achieved and assured only by adopting a soft policy toward Russia. The party also wanted public owner-ship of a large segment of American industry, direct election of the President and Vice-President, and defeat of the Mundt-Nixon subversive control bill that was such anathema to the communists.

Wallace, stubborn and perhaps feeling a bit trapped, refused to denounce the communists. He rode down from New York on the day coach to Philadelphia's Broad Street Station, where he was met by a group of ardent admirers, chanting "Jim Crow Must Go," "Wallace or War," and similar slogans of good will to all. At a press conference Wallace refused to discuss the attacks of columnist Westbrook Pegler. Wallace did suggest that the Allies should give up their rights in Berlin to secure better relations with the Russians over Germany.

Eventually, they nominated him, and called themselves the Pro-gressive party. They thought they were going someplace. The communists were now in absolute control, even blocked a motion to deny that the party endorsed the Soviet Union's foreign policy. The Progressive platform contained every specific recommendation listed two months before in the proposed platform of the Communist party—except one. A quick switch in the communist international line had made the American communist plank calling for a homeland for Macedonians less than desirable to the reds. Russia was now feuding with Tito, who had sovereignty over a number of Macedonians himself. Dutifully, the Macedonian question was excised from the Progressive party platform.

President Truman had a real job now. He expected to take a dispirited, half-whipped Democratic party that had lost its extreme left to the communists and its extreme right to the racists, and with what was left whip the Republicans. There was a way to do it, he was sure of that. No one else gave him a Chinaman's chance.

As Truman ordered, Congress was called back into session, and as he predicted, Congress did little but twiddle its Republican thumbs, cursing Truman all the while for the "cheap political fakery" that had led him to call a special session. The Republican Congress, said Dewey campaign manager Brownell, could not be expected to enact the Republican platform. And a few small voices asked: why?

When Congress adjourned without doing what Truman wanted, the President charged the Republicans with reneging on their platform. Meanwhile, the housing shortage grew worse. Some citizens were reduced to eating horse meat by the price of all other meats. Living costs rose to an all-time high—thirty per cent more than in 1946.

"Gluttons of privilege," "economic tapeworms," "bloodsuckers." These were the phrases Harry Truman used to describe his opponents in the 31,000 miles he traveled by train, in the 550 speeches he made to audiences, great and small, across the nation.

The crowds yelled, and grinned, and waved at him.

"That's the stuff, Harry," they shouted. "Give 'em hell."

Mr. Truman gave them hell, selling what he called the "Fair Deal." And in promising the Fair Deal, Truman began to revitalize a sloppy defeated Democratic party. In New Jersey, Truman found that state leaders did not even arrange a statewide radio hookup for him. But he spoke strongly and positively. Bad management in Michigan cut his audiences to nothing. Yet he made himself heard, through press and whistle stops and radio. The same thing happened across the plains, and in the Southwest. On one occasion, some five hundred words were cut off the end of a national radio address, because the Democratic National Committee did not want to pay for an additional half hour of radio time. Still, Harry Truman got the message across. His election would mean four years of concern for the national good, he said. Election of a Republican would not.

The Democratic party started a radio program on the American Broadcasting Company network. They called it the "Democratic Record Show," aimed it at housewives. The program opened and closed with the "Missouri Waltz," Truman's tune. On the first show the Democrats awarded a prize to Republican Senator Kenneth Wherry of Nebraska, the man who knocked out meat price controls. The prize: a personally conducted tour through the nearest butcher shop. Harold Ickes, the old irrepressible, referred to Dewey as "elusive Dewey, the candidate in sneakers." The program occasionally featured an interval of absolute, dead silence—described as Dewey speaking up on important issues.

Republican candidate Dewey ran an eminently correct and quiet campaign, following the rule book for front runners. From the beginning the opinion polls showed that Dewey would win in a walk. There was nothing the Democrats could do about it. All Dewey had to do was be sure he did not kick the election out the window —by losing too many votes. If you didn't do anything, you weren't likely to lose votes. So Dewey did nothing, handsomely. He mouthed platitudes, smirked, and tendered a limp right hand. Dewey's public image was hardly prepossessing, but, secure in the contemplation of the polls, his advisers did not extend themselves to change it. In Denver, for example, after Republicans had arranged a cocktail party for press, radio, and local dignitaries to meet Dewey, the governor did not make an appearance at all. Dewey was tired, from the bruising schedule of traveling (half as far as Truman traveled) and speaking (slightly more than half as many speeches as Truman made).

"There isn't any more I could say to you," Governor Dewey told an audience at Buffalo when his Victory Special stopped there en route to New York from Michigan. "You are all going to vote for me anyway, or I couldn't persuade you."

In the last days of October, Governor Dewey accused Truman of softness on communism. The governor pledged national unity. He promised international peace.

Truman accused Dewey of nonfeasance in failing to meet and address the issues of the day.

Dewey accused Truman of conducting a fight campaign.

The campaign ended. An almost exhausted Harry Truman returned to Independence, voted, went to the Kansas City's Hotel Muehlebach to wait, and then quietly sneaked off to the resort hotel at the little town of Excelsior Springs on election night, for he wanted a good night's sleep. He was awakened, two or three times during the night, to listen to the predictions of commentators. But he slept well.

Dewey's election day was more formal. The governor spent the weekend on his farm at Pawling (where not long before he had posed with Governor Warren for a pastoral picture, only to have the Democrats chortle that the fence gate he leaned on was upside down). On election day Governor Dewey drove to New York, registered at the Roosevelt Hotel, and dined at the home of a friend, following an eleven-year custom that began when he first ran for district attorney. The governor was offered consommé, roast duck, and blueberry pie. Then Dewey, too, sat down to wait.

The polls had already elected Thomas Dewey President of the United States. George Gallup, the Boston *Herald*, the New York *Daily News*, the Chicago *Tribune*, the Denver *Post*, and scores of others—all predicted a Dewey victory, some of them by as much as 6 to 2. Radio and television commentators began the evening ho-humming. Then the returns began to come in.

The New York *Times* predicted that the Republicans would carry 345 electoral votes, the Democrats 105. The *Times* also predicted that the Republicans would control both the House of Representatives and the Senate, the latter by 47 to 46.

At New York's Democratic headquarters in the Biltmore Hotel a handful of reporters had gathered.

The networks concentrated all their big guns at the Roosevelt, Republican headquarters. Who wanted to waste expensive talent reporting a wake?

Jim Farley, at the Biltmore, excited as always by an election night, was interviewed by one broadcaster, took cognizance of a Truman lead in New York, but predicted the victory of Thomas Dewey.

The Dewey victory did not materialize as rapidly as many had thought. It was not going to be a landslide, after all, just a comfortable victory.

But the comfortable victory began to evaporate as the evening passed. Connecticut went Republican, but Rhode Island went Democratic. So did Massachusetts, so did Illinois, although New York, where Wallace counted, went for Dewey, and the South, where Thurmond had waged his war, was split wide open.

One grizzled old man on the street told a political reporter how it looked to him:

"These political experts, they're like the weather man. The weather man predicted rain tonight and the political experts picked Dewey. There's no rain, and it looks like it might not even be dewey."

It came to be a question of Ohio and California, and finally it was over. The commentators were stunned, the newspapers shocked, the political experts confounded, and the Republicans beaten. It was the closest election in eight campaigns. Truman carried 28 states, 304 electoral votes and almost exactly 50 per cent of the popular vote. Dewey carried 16 states, 189 electoral votes, and 45½ per cent of the vote. Thurmond polled less than a million votes, although he won 38 electors. Wallace polled just over a million votes, but did not win a state. And to top it, the Democrats won comfortable control of both House and Senate, with 150 new faces to enter the House, most of them young and liberal.

Jim Farley's reputation as a political seer was tarnished, but he was in excellent company, joined by almost all the newspaper editors, political writers, and pundits in the United States. Cecil B. De Mille, the movie mogul, had predicted that five million persons would vote for Wallace, because there were five million Americans who would vote the communist line. He missed by eighty per cent. That didn't cost the movies anything, but it would cost something to redub the sound track on the movie *June Bride,* which had a line of dialogue that read "from McKinley to Dewey."

In his victory celebration President Truman held up a copy of the Chicago *Tribune*—high enough so the newsreel and television audiences could see it well. DEWEY DEFEATS TRUMAN said the awful, big, black headline. And a man from Missouri, elected President in his own right, by his own efforts, stood there and grinned and grinned and grinned.

The *Tribune* would never be quite the same again. Nor would the nation.

As President, Harry S. Truman proved strong and able in the field of foreign affairs, moderate, though mildly liberal, in his approach to national problems, and sometime waspish in politics and personal affairs.

The nation took his great good sense in stride and accepted most of his national program as reasonable—though Congress balked at the farm program as it has balked at nearly every planned farm program.

The reaction to four elections of Franklin D. Roosevelt had now set in. Congress proposed a constitutional amendment that would limit the tenure of a President to two four-year terms. In characteristic fashion, Harry Truman denounced this legislation as foolhardy and vituperative. But it passed anyway, and it was not long before the required two thirds of the states had ratified in the traditional American horror at the thought of dynastic rule.

Harry Truman was specifically exempted from the new constitutional amendment, but Harry Truman didn't want to be President again anyhow. He stepped down. And with him, an era of American politics drew to a close—for while H.S.T. was an extension of Rooseveltian democracy, without being a carbon copy, any Democrat after that would necessarily be his own man, and would necessarily change the pattern of Democratic party politics, no matter how much prima facie control Harry Truman might retain.

It was apparent, even in the early months of 1952, that the Democratic party was in the throes of indecision. But for that matter, so were the Republicans. Neither organization was sure of itself in January 1952. . . .

25. "Twenty Years of Treason" 1952

Americans have always reserved a strange combination of ecstasy and torture for their national heroes. They shower the hero with gifts and adoration. They examine his history, habits, and morals with a microscope. They tax him with constant demands. If he balks irrevocably, he loses heroic status. If he fails in some impossible task, he is scorned. His only release is disability or death.

So it was with Ulysses Simpson Grant in 1865. So it was all over again with Dwight David Eisenhower four score years later. Before the war ended, General Eisenhower was pestered by a stream of reporters and politicians. In 1945 on his way to Potsdam, President Harry Truman offered to support Eisenhower for the presidency in 1948. The general laughed and said that he would not be Mr. Truman's opponent. In 1946 and 1947 a trickle of visitors to Army Chief of Staff Eisenhower's Pentagon office urged him to seek the presidency. But the general foreswore political ambition.

In 1948 anti-Truman Democrats tried to draft Eisenhower for the nomination. So did some Republicans for their party. This dual pressure brought the strongest statement yet. Eisenhower, then laboring as president of Columbia University, said he thought professional soldiers ought to stay out of politics, "in the absence of some high and overriding reason." At any rate, Ike said, his decision to remove himself from the political scene was definite and positive.

But not irrevocable. Four years later the pressure had become too great. The Gallup poll sought public sentiment on the presidency in a survey in June 1951. Eisenhower's name led all the rest among both Republicans and Democrats. Senator John J. Sparkman came back from Eisenhower's North Atlantic Treaty Organization headquarters near Paris to plump for the General's nomination as a Democrat. Representative Hugh Scott pressed Eisenhower to run as a Republican. Senator Henry Cabot Lodge, Jr., took charge of an Eisenhower campaign that must first persuade the candidate to run for the Republican nomination, then win it for him.

Finally Eisenhower was half convinced. On January 6, 1952, Lodge told the Washington press corps Eisenhower's name would be entered in the New Hampshire primary in March. Eisenhower confirmed Lodge's statement. The general would allow his name to be used. If the Republicans wanted to give him the nomination he would accept. General Eisenhower thought then that the nomination would come to him, as it had to General Grant—a national gift. Eisenhower had every reason to think so. His availability announcement electrified the nation. Within two days the New York *Times* and the Chicago *Sun-Times* (both nominally Democratic) had endorsed the Eisenhower candidacy. So had some twenty other major newspapers in the United States.

But not Senator Robert A. Taft of Ohio, the balding, blank-faced mixture of blind reaction, innate conservatism, and surprising liberalism who stood first in his party.

Taft was, as far as anyone knew, the most intelligent man in the United States Senate, and one of the most intelligent men who had ever occupied a Senate seat. He was Mr. Republican, from the dome of his shiny cranium to the instep of his conservative shoe. *He* was the logical candidate of the Republican party in 1952, for who else had shaped that party's congressional policy? Who else had nurtured the party back to health after its many defeats? Who else could be shown to combine character, brains, courage, and Republicanism to such a high degree?

In 1952 few Republicans would have been eager to lock horns with Senator Taft in his fight for the nomination. He had worked for that nomination and believed that he had deserved the support of his party in seeking the highest office in the nation.

On the basis of the record few could disagree with him. But there were liberals in the party who did not like Taft, and there were conservatives who did not believe a conservative could win. These groups tended to turn their eyes to Eisenhower.

Taft began to refer to Eisenhower as "the phantom candidate," and then to redouble his efforts to sew up the nomination. For even at this early date, Taft could see that he was in for a battle.

Eisenhower's Republicanism, at this point, was as shadowy as

Grant's in 1868. The simple fact is that politics is anathema to a military career, and neither man had any real partisanship. The general had told Roy Roberts of the Kansas City *Star* in 1947 that he was an old Kansas Republican. But that was just a social pleasantry. Eisenhower's real political decision was made within the confines of a conscience that had been exposed to the Republicanism of two brothers, many newspaper publishers, and business friends, and the ugly sounds of Democratic scandal from the "five-percenter" investigations of the Truman administration in Washington.

The grass-roots Republicans wanted Eisenhower from the beginning. The professional politicians did not. The conservative old guard had taken control of the Republican National Committee and the Republican organizations in most states after Dewey's second defeat in 1948. Until Eisenhower came along the old guard had nearly convinced the Republican party that the White House could be reached only by tearing down the works of the Democratic administration. The old guard's candidate was Senator Taft.

Taft met the Eisenhower challenge squarely. He campaigned in New Hampshire, but when March came, and brought the Republican primary to that state, Eisenhower polled more votes than Taft and Harold Stassen combined. In Minnesota, Eisenhower's name was not even on the primary ballot. Harold Stassen won in his own state, but Eisenhower (or Iznhaur was written in on 106,000 ballots, Taft's name on 24,000.

Taft's organization kept working and piling up delegate commitments. Eisenhower's backers organized a Citizens for Eisenhower movement, to appeal to independents and Democrats.

The Eisenhower movement did appeal to disillusioned Democrats. This was to become a vital issue in the campaign for the nomination. The movement of Democrats into the Republican ranks again disturbed the old guard, as it had in the Willkie campaign of 1940. The "regular" Republicans had worked for the party year in and year out. They had suffered twenty lean years. Now, with another chance, should they give it up to a gang of upstarts who had never done anything for the party?

This philosophical matter came to a head in Texas. There the Taft Republicans controlled the party organization but were outvoted by new Republicans at precinct and county meetings. The Taft men left the convention, then elected their own rump delegates, supported by the Taft-dominated state executive committee. At the

state convention in Mineral Wells that spring, thirty-one local delegations were in contest, involving more than half of the 1060 votes
of the convention. The Taft state organization decided twenty-six
contests in favor of Taft men. Now the ousted Eisenhower delegates
walked out, bearing banners that said "Rob with Bob" and "Graft
with Taft." The Eisenhower forces moved into a separate hall and
held their own convention. Each sent a delegation to the national
convention in Chicago.

"Stealing a man's vote," declared Eisenhower campaign manager
Lodge, "is just as wrong as burglarizing his home."

Eisenhower, now, was in France, commanding NATO with headquarters near Paris. He had gone back to active army duty when
called by President Truman as the most likely candidate to weld
together the shaky forces of the Western alliance. Many suspected
that Eisenhower had gone back gladly to a military job, after his
experience as the head of a great civilian university.

On May 31, General Eisenhower was ready to leave his military
command in France, to come home for the political wars. Several
hundred men, women, and children from Paris and its suburbs came
to see him off at Orly Field. In the final ceremonial moments
Eisenhower spoke quietly of the growing glory of France, in a warm,
friendly, but really a political address. Then the general and Mrs.
Eisenhower got into the big four-motored transport plane. The
general waved his cap from the doorway, and took off to become
a civilian candidate for President.

In America the Eisenhower backers faced some serious difficulties.
Taft was showing great strength. The problem was to make the
delegates aware of Eisenhower before they were irrevocably committed to Taft. As the big transport droned steadily across the Atlantic, convention delegates were being invited to come to visit
Eisenhower after his return home, with all expenses paid. Senator
Taft's managers objected strenuously. John D. M. Hamilton, who
had returned to prominence in party counsels after Dewey's defeat,
said these pilgrimages would cost somebody a half million dollars.
"Everyone knows that the local Eisenhower funds are scooped up
from the deep vaults of Wall Street international bankers," Hamilton
charged.

New York's Senator Irving Ives, an Eisenhower man, retorted that
such carping showed the Taft forces were "desperate."

The Eisenhower managers felt it was vital for their man to meet the delegates, since the Taft forces boasted control of the executive and credentials committees of the national committee. If Eisenhower was to win the nomination he would first have to defeat the party machine. It would be possible only if Eisenhower could develop overwhelming support on the floor of the convention from the delegates themselves.

On June 1, when General Eisenhower landed in Washington to report to the President and the Pentagon before retirement, Taft led in pledged delegates, 420 to 387. General MacArthur came out for Taft in a message to South Dakota Republicans, on the eve of their primary. Senator James H. Duff of Pennsylvania, an early Eisenhower man, said it was "going to be close" not only in South Dakota but also in California, the District of Columbia, and Indiana

Eisenhower arrived to face a political barrage even before he could unpack his civilian clothes. Taft charged that the deterioration of United States air power had started when Eisenhower was chief of staff. In the same voice Taft eulogized MacArthur as "our greatest soldier." B. Carroll Reece, former national chairman, and now Taft's southern campaign manager, said Eisenhower's silence on corruption and the foreign policy failures of the Truman administration indicated the general was too closely associated with Truman, and could not make a strong campaign for the Republicans. David Ingalls national Taft campaign manager, accused Eisenhower backers of having taken trips to Paris at taxpayer expense to confer with the general.

Four days after his homecoming, Eisenhower made his first political move, when he returned to Abilene, Kansas, to touch home plate. The Abilene affair was a carefully planned celebration, including a kickoff political speech and dedication of an Eisenhower Museum, all in a carnival atmosphere of bunting, photographs, and foot-long hot dogs. A pair of mangy elephants had been trucked four hundred miles from Kelly's Circus in Colorado to be staked on Cedar Street, north of the Santa Fe tracks, mute reminders of the real reason for the whole celebration.

The Eisenhowers flew in from Washington to the Kansas City airport, where they were met by a small welcoming committee. As the general stepped off the plane, reported New York *Times* correspondent James Reston, he was grabbed by Dan Thornton, the cowboy-booted governor of Colorado.

"Hi, podner," boomed Thornton.

For a moment General Eisenhower looked as though a drunken army private had suddenly embraced him. Then he grinned, put his arm around Thornton, and turned to his wife. "Here's Mamie. You remember Dan, Mamie." Ike Eisenhower, politician, was born.

Ike did equally well when he got to Abilene, only to find rain. Ike calmly donned a raincoat and broad-brimmed hat to attack the Democrats and assail Truman for his mistakes at home and abroad. Several thousand persons in the stands and standing in the mud gave the program the atmosphere of a revival meeting.

By now, Taft claimed 588 of the 604 delegates he would need for nomination. Ike had planned to go to Denver for the summer. He did not want to attend the Republican convention, since he still believed the presidency ought to come to him, not he to it. In Denver the Ike men explained the political facts of life to their leader. If he wanted the nomination, Ike had to go to Chicago. He had to fight for every delegate. So Eisenhower reluctantly gave in, agreed to do battle.

Eisenhower men redoubled their cries of "theft" and evil dealing against Taft over the delegate question. The Taft men attacked Eisenhower equally bitterly. In a way, the clock of history seemed turned back to 1912, when another Taft and Teddy Roosevelt were throwing charges at one another.

Taft did offer a compromise on disputed delegates, but Senator Lodge knew Ike needed every one of those votes, not just half, so it was easy for the Eisenhower men to take a high moral tone.

The Republican convention was still a month away. On June 10, the Taft group, who owned and operated the national committee announced that General MacArthur, already committed to Taft, would be the keynote speaker. National committeeman Ralph Cake of Oregon, the old Willkie man, now an Eisenhower sympathizer, moved to bar candidates or active partisans from convention posts. Cake was squelched. The Eisenhower men put up a howl, but it did not help. Since MacArthur at seventy-two was frail and not accustomed to running civilian political circuses, Walter Hallanan, a Taft leader from West Virginia, was to be temporary chairman. The committee worked hard to set its convention lineup. When the work was ended, and the result announced, the roster of right-wing convention officials was enough to freeze the blood of an Eisenhower supporter:

Keynoter: General MacArthur
Temporary Chairman: Walter Hallanan
Permanent Chairman: Joseph Martin of Massachusetts, House
    Republican leader
Resolutions Committee Chairman: Senator Eugene Millikin, of
    Colorado

These men, plus the parliamentarian, sergeant at arms, and assistant doorkeepers, were Taft supporters. Herbert Hoover, not yet
a flaming liberal, was to make the principal address the second
night. There was only one exception to the conservative trend: Mrs.
Charles P. Howard of Massachusetts, an Eisenhower supporter, was
elected temporary secretary of the convention. Even this was more
of a fluke than a concession. The Taft machine tried to oust her,
but here the conservatives ran afoul of the solidarity of woman-
kind—their own pro-Taft lady members voted for Mrs. Howard.
When Senator Lodge saw the list of convention officials he snorted.
The Taft people were trying to turn the convention into a kangaroo
court.

Clearly, if Lodge was to secure the nomination for Eisenhower,
his work would have to be done before the convention, outside it,
and on the floor itself. Eisenhower would get no comfort from the
GOP management.

Both Taft and Eisenhower were anxious to sew up the votes of
uncommitted Pennsylvania, where Governor John Fine was playing his cards very close to the chest. Ike was becoming convinced
that he was in a fight, now. The general went to his Gettysburg
farm, casually enough, but used the trip to meet with sixty delegates
of the Keystone State. A few days later, in Dallas, Ike accused Taft
of deliberately disenfranchising the Eisenhower Texas delegates.
He was learning the harsh language of American politics.

A week before the convention Taft claimed 603 of the 604 delegates needed for nomination. Now the fight was over 75 delegates;
the issue was whether Democrats could join the Republican party
and participate in the GOP's deliberations. On July 2, the national
committee seated the pro-Taft Georgia delegation, after first refusing
radio and television reporters the right to transmit the actual proceedings to the eager nation. The committee was obviously playing
with a deck stacked for Taft, but the public was made aware of
the action, both by the press and by the offended electronic

journalists. The public did not like it, it seemed from the growls in the papers. Even Senator Richard M. Nixon of California, who was generally regarded as quite friendly to the Taft group, said this whole proceeding threatened the survival of the party.

Eisenhower was installed at the Blackstone. His presence had been necessary, to show his interest in the nomination, for the Taft men had done a good job of selling the story that Eisenhower wanted the nomination on a platter. Had this not been so, Eisenhower might almost as well have remained in Denver, but under the circumstances, staying in Denver would have cost him his chance.

Now, all the candidates were getting into gear at Chicago. California Governor Earl Warren's headquarters, on the fifteenth floor of the Conrad Hilton, was buzzing with activity. A pair of scurrying, if not entirely realistic, Oklahomans were trying to line up delegates for MacArthur. Harold Stassen was on hand again. There was a smattering of support for every candidate, but all knew the struggle was between Taft and Eisenhower. If another became the nominee, it would be only in case of deadlock.

The convention opened Monday, July 7, Taft predicting his victory on the first ballot. The first order of business was establishment of the rules under which the convention would work until the permanent organization could be installed. Senator Bricker moved that the convention adopt the 1948 rules, but the Eisenhower men had persuaded twenty-three governors to sign a manifesto calling for "fair play." By this the governors meant that the contested delegations from Georgia, Texas, and thirteen contested seats from Louisiana should all be kept vacant until the contests had been decided by a majority of the convention. A Taft substitute was defeated, and the Eisenhower "fair play" proposal was adopted by a voice vote. This maneuver completely overshadowed General MacArthur's oratorical attack on the Truman administration and his call for conservatism. The convention was in no mood for an old soldier's histrionics.

The next day, Tuesday, the credentials committee—Taft stacked —seated the pro-Taft Georgia contingent. Lodge protested. Even Taft's managers could feel the blast of heat that rushed through the convention.

On Wednesday, Taft offered Eisenhower the thirteen contested Louisiana seats and a split on the Texas seats. But Eisenhower still needed *all* the contested seats. Lodge again stood on high principle and refused the offer. It would be all or nothing!

That night the full convention listened to debate on Georgia's seats for nearly two hours, then voted 607 to 531 to seat the Eisenhower men. There was debate, but Taft made no contest on Texas, knowing he was defeated in numbers. The Eisenhower delegation was seated, as Taft's men glumbly sat back for the fight on nomination.

Senator Everett Dirksen of Illinois, a Taft supporter, emphasized the bitterness of the contest when he pointed a finger at Thomas Dewey, whom the Taft men accused of engineering the Eisenhower campaign.

Amid a chorus of boos, Dirkson said, "we followed you before. You took us down to defeat." The boos thundered out for Dirksen from the liberal wing, for Dewey from the old guard, that remembered too well the defeats of 1944 and 1948.

The old guard was losing its carefully established control. Governor Fine declared for Eisenhower, taking fifty-one of Pennsylvania's seventy delegates to the side that promised "least risk of failure."

There was no clash on the platform. The strong foreign policy plank was written by John Foster Dulles. Dulles had been candidate Dewey's foreign minister, and later the Republican showpiece of bipartisanship in the Democratic State Department. In all probability John Foster Dulles would have been Secretary of State no matter which Republican was nominated. Dulles's greatest ambition was to run the State Department, in which so many of his ancestors had served.

On July 11, the Eisenhower-Taft struggle ended on the first ballot, as Taft had predicted, but the candidate was Dwight David Eisenhower. Ike received 595 of the needed 604 votes on the first roll call to Taft's 500. Minnesota called for the floor immediately after the last tally, switched to Eisenhower because the Minnesota commitment to Stassen ended when he failed to poll 10 per cent of the votes. Before the switches were complete, his 595 votes had become 845 and the general was nominated.

Eisenhower went to Senator Taft's rooms at the Hilton; victor and loser posed there for photographers and the electronic journalists. The breach was not healed enough to offer Taft the vice-presidential nomination; however, it is doubtful if he would have accepted, but his supporters wanted him to have the opportunity to turn it down.

Senator Richard Nixon had won election over Helen Gahagan Douglas in 1950 by the largest majority of any Republican senatorial candidate. He was right-wing, young, and he was a comer. He was sitting with a ham-and-cheese sandwich at the Stockyards Inn across from the convention hall when he was summoned to the Eisenhower presence. Nixon lost no time in accepting the bid for Vice-President. He was only thirty-nine.

The next day Taft's hold on the national committee was broken in the election of Arthur C. Summerfield, an Eisenhower supporter, as national chairman. The committee was enlarged, too, on a kind of promotional representation basis; this slashed the importance of the South.

Eisenhower motored out the following day to Fifth Army Headquarters at Fort Sheridan, Illinois, where his son was staying before embarkation for Korea; thus the Republican nominee escaped the feverish descent of Democratic combatants on Chicago.

Senator Richard B. Russell's headquarters at the Conrad Hilton was open a full week before anything else at the convention. Hardly had the Republicans gotten the Taft debris cleaned up than Russell moved into the same rooms. Senator John J. Sparkman of Alabama arrived to say that Russell was not just a southern candidate, but a man of national stature. Before his nomination as Vice-President, Richard Nixon had said he thought Russell would be the strongest Democrat, hardest for the Republicans to beat. Representative Brooks Hays, the great compromiser from Arkansas, arrived with a modified civil rights plank that he hoped would heal the sores left from 1948's festering Dixiecratism.

Hays's plan called for repeal of the poll tax by constitutional amendment, a federal anti-lynching statute, and establishment of an FEPC with powers of persuasion but not enforcement.

Altogether there were seven announced Democratic candidates in 1952; Senator Barkley; Governor Averell Harriman of New York; Senator Estes Kefauver of Tennessee; Senator Robert Kerr of Oklahoma; Senator and Brigadier General Herbert C. Holdridge, an Illinois candidate backed by the American Rally of Peace, Abundance and Constitution; Senator Russell, and Senator Brien McMahon of Connecticut. There was one favorite son, Hubert Humphrey of Minnesota; and there were two undeclared candidates, representative Samuel Rayburn, the convention's permanent chairman from Texas, and Governor Adlai Stevenson of Illinois. Stevenson had been offered Truman's support for the nomination earlier. Truman did not choose to run for the presidency. Neither, Truman discovered, to his chagrin, did Adlai Stevenson.

All the active candidates began predicting their own nomination. But this year the platform had to be dealt with first, for it contained the seed of controversy: civil rights. In the spirit of 1860 the southerners had recessed their state conventions until after the national Democratic meeting. The threat of another season of Dixiecratism hung behind the façade of the convention.

If anyone had the edge for the nomination, it seemed to be Kefauver. The Tennessean had been campaigning hard in his Davy Crockett 'coon-skin cap. Already, two labor conventions had endorsed Kefauver, and the AFL and CIO would have a strong hand in the convention, both in drafting the platform and because the CIO alone counted one hundred delegates and alternates selected by local party organizations.

Gael Sullivan, the stormy petrel of Democratic politics, was running the Kefauver campaign. He hit first at wealthy Bob Kerr. Sullivan said Kerr's men were trying to bribe California delegates pledged to Kefauver. John Anson Ford, the Los Angeles national committeeman just elected, told Sullivan that one delegate had been offered $300 to get three other delegates to switch to Kerr after voting for Kefauver on the first ballot. Ford also reported eight California delegates had been offered free transportation to Chicago if they would switch from Kefauver to other candidates.

Senator Kerr said that Senator Kefauver was desperate.

Then Sullivan said some Democrats opposed because the Kefauver Crime Investigating Committee had exposed ties between criminals and Democratic politicians in a number of states.

This talk did not make Kefauver any more popular.

On July 15 the "Draft Stevenson" headquarters had been opened in room 1500 of the Conrad Hilton. Stevenson had been very much opposed to his own nomination, but the pressure few men could resist was on him, too. He was wavering. Someone had explained to the Illinois governor that if the Republicans won, Joe Martin would be Speaker of the House and Robert Taft would be majority leader of the Senate. This alarmed him enough, he said, to consider a draft, if the convention were deadlocked over other candidates.

Governor Averell Harriman, whose unimaginative slogan was "the man for the job," had campaigned hard for the nomination, in his own soft way. Among other suggestions, Harriman proposed establishment of a permanent anti-graft commission in answer to charges that "five per centers" in the Truman administration were bleeding the nation.

Managers for all the candidates were working overtime now, handing out buttons, booze, and ballpoint pens. Kefauver's Sullivan took over what had been the Taft Literature Bar, and turned it into the Kefauver Delegate Service Bureau, dispensing such items as campaign songs ("The Long Tall Guy in the 'Coon-skin Cap"), sheet music, match books, and pictures of Kefauver with old men, with little girls, or by himself.

Barkley's men were handing out badges that showed a red bolt of lightning. "It means we're going to shock the hell out of 'em," a Barkophile interpolated. Gael Sullivan decked out the main lobby of the Conrad Hilton with more Kefauver material. This caused the management to descend on the whole crowd. There couldn't be any more of this, said the management of the world's largest hotel. So a truce was negotiated, and the campaigners agreed to keep their exuberance within bounds.

Stevenson backers brought Ralph Newman, proprietor of Chicago's Abraham Lincoln Bookshop and a historian of more than a little note, to sit around all day in the "Draft Stevenson" rooms, exploding the theory that no reluctant candidate had ever been nominated. (Remember Horatio Seymour, the kidnaped Democrat?)

Stevenson continued to resist nomination, even though the Illinois delegation calmly ignored his appeal that they not vote for him. "I just don't want to be nominated," Stevenson said. To illustrate, he told the story of the man who was asked whether he wanted to go to heaven or hell.

"I don't want to go to either place," the man said. "I want to stay right here."

But a great number of delegates to the thirty-first convention of Democrats wanted Stevenson to go elsewhere—to the White House. He was harassed from all sides. Even when he went to services at the Fourth Presbyterian Church, Dr. Harrison Ray Anderson preached a sermon on indecision.

One fight developed in the credentials committee over demands that the southerners take a "loyalty" oath. The South was still suspect. Who knew how many incipient cases of Dixiecratism still existed? Governor Harriman, who saw his chance in amalgamating everybody else against the South, spent several days trying to organize a coalition to take the loyalty question to the floor, after the national committee seated southern delegates who would give only qualified pledges of party loyalty.

Maury Maverick, former congressman from San Antonio and leader of the "loyal," non-Dixiecrat Texas delegation, turned down an offer for a 50–50 split on the Texas contest. "Kick us out like dogs," Maverick said, "or seat us as the only legal delegation from Texas."

As the convention itself opened on July 22, Stevenson gave a fifteen-minute welcoming speech that sounded more like a keynote or an acceptance speech than a simple address of hello from the governor of the host state. When Stevenson finished, a five-minute demonstration called for his reappearance, but Stevenson had left the platform and the hall.

Stevenson had moved ahead. Kefauver and Harriman talked about combining to stop him. Even an educated mule in the lobby, when asked which of the candidates was going to win, pawed out "Stevenson on the fourth ballot."

The following day, July 24, South Carolina, Virginia, and Louisiana delegates refused to sign loyalty pledges. Sixty-four were disqualified from voting, but they did not walk out of the convention.

Chairman Sam Rayburn's fast gavel solved the platform problem, when the 1948 civil rights plank was reincorporated in the 1952 platform. During the voting, after the ayes had responded, Georgia's Herman Talmadge jumped up to protest. But Rayburn said the platform had just been adopted by voice vote. It was too bad, he said, but that was the way it was.

Now the nominations began. Alben Barkley was madder than a wet hen, because he learned his old friends in organized labor had turned thumbs down on him. He withdrew his name in a fit of pique. Finally Barkley's old friend Philip Murray, long-time president of the CIO, dispatched a long and laudatory telegram to assuage his feelings.

Estes Kefauver acted pleasantly surprised when he arrived on the convention floor at the moment of a carefully planned demonstration in his behalf. During Kefauver's demonstration when the band was playing "The Tennessee Waltz," the crowd was amazed when a woman suddenly screamed and slapped the man behind her. It might have been a scene from a Mack Sennett comedy.

Stevenson supporters were now so confident of their man that they increased the Stevenson headquarters from two rooms to seven.

The chastised southern states were unrepentant. If the convention did not want to seat them without a loyalty oath, they would stay out.

But now the convention, as a whole, was concerned about unity. The lesson of 1948 had been well learned by all. The South knew it could not make a break from the party, successfully. The northern delegates could see that Dwight Eisenhower would be a very difficult man to beat. They needed harmony, not intra-party bickering. So, quietly, the southern states were given back their full voting rights and retook their seats in the convention.

On the first ballot for the presidential nomination Kefauver led, but as the votes were being counted the word was out on the floor that he had passed his peak of strength.

On the second ballot it became obvious that Kefauver would not win. Neither would Russell or Harriman. They did not have the appeal. Stevenson, who ran second to Kefauver, did have the appeal. On the third ballot he was nominated, and in a quick follow-up gesture Senator John J. Sparkman of Alabama was chosen for the vice-presidency, unanimously. Every effort was being made to bury the hatchet of North-South strife, in preparation for the coming campaign.

As usual, the campaign was rough and tough on all concerned. The right wing of the Republican party talked of "twenty years of treason" when they spoke of the Democrats. Republicans sneeringly refused to refer to the Democratic party, but talked of the Democrat party.

Eisenhower was more restrained. He spoke of "a scandal a day" in the Administration. Stevenson talked of Republican "reactionaries." He would have preferred to run without reference to the Truman record, but Truman hired a special train and set off about the country to speak his mind about the issues. Truman speaking for Truman in 1948 was one thing. Truman in 1952 speaking for Stevenson was something else again. The Republicans sent a "truth squad" of senators along Truman's trail. They caught him up from time to time, and what they missed in truth they made up in charges against the Administration and the Democratic party.

Truman, said Republican Chairman Summerfield, was the hachet-man of the Democrats.

Nixon, as it turned out, was the hachetman of the Republicans until he almost cut off his own toe. Nixon had accepted a special expense fund of $18,235, a fund made up by some seventy-five sup-porters in California. Nixon's rough, tough campaign talk had begun to get under the Democratic skin, and the fund became a major issue for the Democrats. Nixon was not the first to take money thus. But the others had not been carrying on a "crusade" for clean govern-ment. For a time it seemed that Nixon might be dropped from the Republican ticket, but the vice-presidential candidate made a mar-velous recovery. In a histrionic telecast on September 21, Nixon praised his furless wife, revealed his bank balances, and spoke lov-ingly of his little dog. For the second time a candidate's dog proved to be his best friend. Eisenhower pondered, held a fatherly conversation with his erring running mate, pronounced him "clean as a hound's tooth" and fit to participate in the great crusade. All was right again in the Republican world.

The campaign rocked back and forth, both sides running scared. Eisenhower was plagued with decisions to be made about men like Wisconsin's Senator Joseph McCarthy and Indiana's Homer Cape-hart, who wanted envelopment in the Eisenhower coattails but no part of the candidate's program. Ike endorsed them, anyhow, on the basis that a bad Republican was still better than a good Democrat.

Stevenson, after hearing rumours about his tax situation, re-vealed his financial statement, and Eisenhower, after his first balking, revealed something about his earnings. This had some of the earmarks of the Tilden campaign of 1876.

Eisenhower campaigned on corruption, communism in govern-ment, and the Korean War. Some of his oratory did not represent the highest of statesmanship. At one point he endorsed a suggestion that the brunt of the fighting in Korea be turned over to Koreans.

As Ike learned the political game his speeches gained in polish, and lost in vigor. He yielded some of his spontaneous bad grammar and good humor to the slickness of canned addresses written by speech writers who were more interested in acceptable content than the over-all impression on the public of one man's views.

Stevenson conducted an erudite campaign, but drew nothing like the tremendous audiences that turned out to see Ike. It was a case of an intellectual, brittle and brilliant, campaigning against a national hero, a folksy, un-intellectual, small-town American.

Stevenson said that the Republicans had a "me too candidate" running on a "yes but" platform, advised by a "has been" staff (Dewey's leftovers). These were bright words, but at Fort Dodge, where Stevenson used them, a farmer remarked that while Stevenson was "a nice, intelligent man," he thought he'd vote for Eisenhower this time. So did voters in California and Colorado and Connecticut. Labor supported Stevenson overwhelmingly. John L. Lewis returned to the Democratic party for the first time in sixteen years. But labor's members, some of the battles won, were not as receptive to organizational efforts as they had once been.

Less than two weeks before the end of the campaigning, Eisenhower found his crowning issue. He had been talking about Korea and criticizing Truman's conduct of the war. Truman challenged him to come up with a plan. Two of his speech writers did.

"I shall go to Korea," Ike proclaimed grandly in Detroit. He would go after elected to study conditions and find a solution to the fruitless, dragging war.

Go to Korea? Truman grimaced. Eisenhower had gone to Korea as chief of staff, in 1947, he said, and had returned to recommend that American occupation forces be withdrawn. Would Ike's judgment be any better a second time?

But Americans were sick of the Korea stalemate, and President Truman was sputtering by this time. It was reminiscent of the precedent of bitterness and inaccuracy established by President Herbert Hoover in 1932. The people heard Eisenhower, and ignored the President. Neither statement, of course, was much more than grandiloquent campaign oratory, but Eisenhower's, at least, was positive.

Eisenhower wound up his campaign in Boston on Monday, November 3, and went back to New York to vote. Stevenson finished in Chicago.

As the returns came in it was soon apparent that an Eisenhower landslide was in the making. It tumbled down the political mountain, burying the Democratic candidate. When the dust settled, Eisenhower had 422 electoral votes to 89 for Stevenson, and had polled 6,000,000 votes more than Stevenson in a total of 57,000,000 votes.

Ike's party did not do so well. The Republicans won control of the House, by a handful of votes.

In the Senate the balance was held by Wayne Morse of Oregon, who had bolted the Republican party after Eisenhower's nomination and was listed as an independent at the time. Morse had been educated in the Wisconsin of Robert La Follette, and now certain affinities with the old Progressive leader seemed to appear in his political portrait. Morse was to vote with the Democrats more than the Republicans in the Senate, and finally to declare himself a Democrat.

The campaign over, Stevenson began to pick up the wreckage in Springfield. He would, of course, have to move out of the governor's mansion, for in seeking bigger game he had given up almost certain re-election as governor.

What was he going to do? asked the reporters. Did he plan to run again for the presidency in 1956?

"Fifty-six"? exclaimed Stevenson with a grin. "Examine that man's head."

The nation was hunting communists and peering nervously under administrative and political beds in 1952. A strange dark-bearded man named Joseph McCarthy led the chase of communist ghosts, turning up dentists, generals, clergymen; and a neophyte politician, President Eisenhower, stood silently by and let McCarthy run out his string.

McCarthy finally tripped in the halls of the United States Senate, where members of his own party tired of the constant catcalls and outrageous character assassination. McCarthy was censured by the United States Senate. His power was broken—not because anything had changed particularly in the United States—but because he had gone too far, for too long.

There were other differences in the Republican administration's approach to national affairs than the Democrats before Eisenhower. Ike did not favor public power of the big power-irrigation projects that had dotted the West during the Roosevelt and Truman years. Eisenhower paid lip service to a program of power partnership between government and industry, but the government, if a partner, was a most silent one.

Nor did Eisenhower favor extension of government effort in any field. He wanted less government, and more private initiative. Consequently, educational needs were not met, public health needs were not met, but even so the federal government continued to grow, despite the reluctance of its Chief Executive. Soon the federal government employed more men and women than at any other time of peace in history.

Foreign policy was marked by intensive travel, no major programs, and a few serious miscalculations—i.e., bluff and bluster, such as Secretary of State Dulles's announced policy of "massive retaliation" that was supposed to stop brush-fire wars the communists arranged in the Near and Far East.

The Eisenhower administration, as it swung into stride, was a far different animal from the Truman administration before it, and it boasted that there would be no "mink coat," "deep freeze," or influence-peddling scandals under Republican rule.

26. They Still Loved Ike 1956

While Ulysses S. Grant had tried to bring the military command system into the White House and failed, Dwight David Eisenhower succeeded admirably. President Grant had attempted to make politicians out of generals. In so doing, he subjected them to temptations and pressures they were ill equipped to resist. President Eisenhower brought the military system to political Washington, but not military men. He organized his administration on a command basis, with New Hampshire's ex-Governor Sherman Adams as chief of staff. If Eisenhower was not always aware of the factors that went into command decisions, at least the government operated with admirable efficiency.

So efficient was the Administration, in reality, that in 1955 when the President was stricken with a heart attack on a Denver vacation there was scarcely a stir in the function of government. The Cabinet and public were shocked by the news, of course. Vice-President Richard Nixon, at home in Washington, was besieged by the press, but wisely finished off in the face of leading questions about the conditions under which he would "take over."

A complication in the crisis was the absence of Sherman Adams, the "assistant president," who was vacationing in the British Isles. Had Adams been on hand, perhaps the President's staff would have been a bit more candid with the press. As it was, the press secretary told reporters that Eisenhower had suffered an upset stomach, and stayed with that story long after the reporters were aware that the illness was something much more serious. But in a remarkably short time Sherman Adams was back at his post, affairs were brought under control, and the function of government went on.

Nixon conducted cabinet meetings and the sessions of the

important National Security Council. Nixon was on the spot, and had to move more carefully than would a less patently ambitious Vice-President. His every word and action were examined microscopically. Nixon's enemies waited for that one slip that would enable them to claim "Tricky Dick" was looking for an excuse to seize power. In a political career that began only after World War II, Nixon had managed to make more enemies and arouse more distrust than many politicians did in a lifetime. In part, it could be attributed to his methods of campaigning. The Vice-President was a tough campaigner. He attacked his opponents where it hurt. If that was below the belt, so be it; his opponents attacked him below the belt, too. In the contest with President Harry Truman in 1952, Nixon came out with a reputation for vicious mud-slinging; Truman was simply chided for exaggeration and misdirected energies.

Perhaps it was Nixon's obvious lack of humor, his tremendous drive, and the gleam in his eye when the word presidency was mentioned. But during the President's illness, Nixon's ambition was reined in tightly. Through the long months, he never sat in the President's chair, figuratively or literally. If he had to go to the White House, he worked in an obscure corner. If he had to counsel with a cabinet officer, they met in the secretary's office, not in Nixon's. When he conducted a cabinet meeting, he acted as moderator, not leader.

Nixon's was an incredibly skillful performance under the most difficult conditions. His perseverance while the country watched Eisenhower's temperature served Nixon well, for it quickened the respect of the President. When the weakened Chief Executive returned to his duties, finally, he delegated more authority to the Vice-President. Later, this respect made it possible for Nixon to sew up his own renomination with scarcely a whimper from his many enemies within the Republican party.

Eisenhower did not seem at all sure that Nixon ought to be the vice-presidential candidate. Early in 1956 when the President announced his own candidacy, he suggested a cabinet post for Nixon, but the Vice-President did not leap at it. He wanted to think it over. The President said that was all right, Nixon ought to chart his own political course for the future. But Nixon ought to remember, Eisenhower added, that no man had been elected President directly from the vice-presidency since Martin Van Buren, and that only because Andrew Jackson had absolutely insisted on it. Even then

Jackson had to invent the political convention to place his men in the job.

While Nixon was pondering his future, the Democrats were engaged in a knock-down, drag-out fight to see who would ride the Democratic donkey in the 1956 campaign. The pre-convention campaign boiled down to a struggle between Estes Kefauver, the 'coon-skin-capped senator from Tennessee, Governor Averell Harriman, the hundred-per-cent Truman Fair Dealer, and Adlai Stevenson, who had been unable to shake the presidential itch in three years of private life.

Both Kefauver and Stevenson conducted strenuous campaigns for support by delegates who would be elected in state primaries. The balance seesawed back and forth, and the charges began to heat up. Stevenson was the product of Colonel Jake Arvey's Chicago bossism, said the senator. Kefauver was the senator who did not appear on the floor of the Senate often enough to vote on key issues, rejoined the former Illinois governor.

In April, Vice-President Nixon announced that he had examined the waters minutely, and had charted his course for the vice-presidency again. Eisenhower grinned, and told the press he would be delighted to have Nixon on the ticket with him.

What about somebody else? asked the press.

Of course, the door was open, said the President. He wasn't going to try to dictate the course of the Republican convention. He had the highest respect for Vice-President Nixon, but certainly there were other acceptable men in the party.

Would the President name some of them?

Well, no, he would not. But Mr. Eisenhower would be receptive to any of the candidates that he thought would be qualified—that is, have the qualifications—for the job.

The President thus created a difficult situation for Nixon, but an absolutely impossible situation for any other vice-presidential hopeful. In the face of Eisenhower's bland refusal to open or close the issue, anyone who sought the vice-presidential nomination was courting political disaster. The pros of the party, led by jolly Chairman Leonard Hall, were gentlemen of the old school. Plug hats and black cigars had gone out of style, but not the old-fashioned thought process. A ticket that won in 1952 still ought to win in 1956, and was at least twice as good as any other. Besides, Nixon was a reasonable fellow, the pros knew, and if something tragic happened and he were catapulted into the presidency, he might turn out to be even more reasonable than Eisenhower.

That "something tragic" seemed other than remote in the spring of 1956. Eisenhower came down in June with an intestinal block, a disease called ileitis. Once again the White House talked about mild stomach upset, but this time the cynical reporters scarcely believed them. (The Washington press corps' capacity for disbelief grew year by year, as the Administration displayed its proclivity for concealing information on matters privileged and otherwise.)

The President was taken to Walter Reed Hospital for surgery. After recuperation he was pronounced fit and healthy by the doctors. Some of his political doctors went further. Eisenhower, they said, was fitter and healthier than anyone else, because he *had* suffered the heart attack, and *had* suffered from the ileitis. Eisenhower didn't have those problems to face, which a lesser, not-yet-stricken man might have. This bit of Alice-in-Wonderland reasoning was thrown out into the public air with a straight face but created so many astounded guffaws that it was quickly brushed over. Yet the Republican political doctors were not quite so sanquine as they seemed, and within many an elephantine breast beat the scarlet doubt that Eisenhower would survive a second term.

That possibility, however, could not be discussed or even hinted by the faithful.

The only man brave enough or foolhardy enough to disturb the calm of Republican family unity was Harold Stassen. Stassen was a sometime Republican presidential hopeful, and minister without portfolio or authority in charge of disarmament discussion. He was also an author of the famous "I shall go to Korea" speech that did so much to win the 1952 election for Eisenhower. To the surprise and distaste of nearly all the Administration, Stassen took the President's "open convention" talk seriously. If the Republican convention at San Francisco was to be "open," then it was about time that some other candidates for the vice-presidency be unearthed. Stassen appeared one day at the White House with such a revolutionary proposal.

Eisenhower was not pleased, but, having declared the season open, he could hardly declare it closed. If Mr. Stassen was so anxious to murder his own future, there was no way to stop him. Stassen announced his advocacy of Christian Herter, governor of Massachusetts, on the grounds that Richard Nixon was a definite detriment to the Republican ticket.

Stassen tried to see Nixon. He had promised the President he would talk the matter over with Republican leaders before moving. But Nixon did not see Stassen. Neither did Leonard Hall. Stassen went ahead on his own. He called a press conference, where he produced a poll that showed Nixon would drag the ticket down.

Governor Herter was panicked. There was little question but that Herter would have liked the vice-presidential nomination, but the whole political machinery was locked against change. Herter called the White House, to protect his innocence of traitorous intent. Sherman Adams assured Herter that they knew all about it, and quieted him down with discussion of a future commitment for Herter's services within the State Department.

It was arranged, then and there, that Herter would nominate Nixon at San Francisco. *That* would certainly put an end to any disloyal shilly-shallying.

"How silly can you get?" asked Leslie C. Arends, Republican whip in the House of Representatives. And an Associated Press poll showed that Nixon was the overwhelming choice of Republicans everywhere.

Seemingly undaunted, Stassen continued his efforts to dump Nixon, with a statement that Nixon would cost the Republicans "millions of votes." Stassen took a month's leave from his disarmament job to conduct this campaign, since it must never be said that there was dissension within the "team" that ran the Administration. Stassen was asked to talk to a National Press Club luncheon in Washington. Club President Frank Holeman introduced Stassen as "the only man who ever got a license from the President of the United States to go hunting for the Vice-President for thirty days." Mr. Holeman, of course, was in no position to know that the hunting preserve had just been cleared of game.

The Democrats watched all this Republican maneuvering with glee. In truth, the donkey needed diversion. Senator Kefauver and Governor Stevenson had fought almost to a standstill. In the Florida primary election the two men had made severe charges against one another. The charges had been repeated in the California primary. When Stevenson won both, Kefauver withdrew from the race on July 31, in favor of Stevenson. Kefauver wanted to continue as a leader of the Democratic party. New York's Governor Harriman claimed half the 200 votes that had been pledged to the Tennessean, but everyone knew that Harriman's chances for the nomination were very slim. Just before the Democratic convention reporters in Chicago estimated that Stevenson had 404½ of the 686½ votes needed for nomination. Kefauver's 200 votes, if they went solidly for Stevenson, would do a great deal to sew up the matter. Harriman claimed only 141 committed votes of the 303 votes pledged to a number of favorite sons. At his headquarters in the Continental Illinois Bank Building in Chicago's Loop, Adlai Stevenson was relaxed and confident.

Few Democrats had any such assurance about the fate of the party platform in 1956. The South was distressed over the Supreme Court's 1954 decision that ordered integration of the nation's public schools. Subsequent court decisions on Jim Crow railroad practices and other racial matters made it quite plain that the school ruling would not be reversed. The court had appeared sympathetic, in ordering integration with reasonable speed. The Eisenhower administration had appeared sympathetic in trying to stay out of the picture as much as possible. But now the race issue was hotter in the South than it had ever been. This time, the National Association for the Advancement of Colored People had forces, funds, and organization to press its fight for civil rights. The NAACP was proceeding slowly but inexorably. Consequently, southern Democratic leaders called a pre-convention conference in Atlanta at the very end of July. Eleven states sent 366 convention delegates, roughly 20 per cent of the 1372 who would soon meet in Chicago. In Atlanta, on August 1, thirty-seven of the party's prominent leaders met in private caucus to plan an attack.

Adlai Stevenson let it be known that he was holding out for full acceptance of the Supreme Court decision, for equal voting rights and equality in public transportation of Negroes; for equality in public education, in job opportunities, and in housing. The southern Democrats let it be known that they would demand a compromise civil rights plank if they were not to leave the party again.

Senator Sam J. Ervin of North Carolina said that Stevenson's civil rights stand might cost him the election. The South would accept the 1948 and 1952 platform planks on civil rights without a whimper, but not this greater danger. The Supreme Court ruling would make integration a part of daily life.

On August 11 former President Truman came out flatly for the

nomination of Governor Harriman, apparently much to the relief of
Adlai Stevenson, who had found Truman's assistance in the 1952
campaign almost more than he could bear. Stevenson, said the tough
little Truman, had no stomach for a hard fight. Truman also
announced his stand for a strong civil rights plank, and to prove
it, went off to Chicago's South Side that day to lead a parade
commemorating the feast day of Bud Billiken, mythical heroic
godfather to all Chicago Negro children.

On August 13 the Democratic convention opened. Governor Frank
Clement of Tennessee assailed the Republicans mightily in an
oratorical masterpiece that somehow seemed passé in 1956. Clement
invoked the ghost of William Jennings Bryan when he challenged
the Republicans: "You will not crucify the American farmer on a
Republican cross of gold." Somehow, it didn't quite fit—although
the speech did set some speculators to talking of him as a future
candidate.

The civil rights struggle began, but ended with scarcely a blow
struck. The Mississippi and South Carolina party "regulars" were the
cause of conflict. In the fight over party loyalty a move had been
made in the national committee against seating these delegates, but
the convention was in no mood for anything but conciliation and
harmony, no matter what the cost. There had been too little harmony,
too much name-calling already. Monroe Sweetland, national committeeman from Oregon, claimed, for example, that keeping Senator
James Eastland of Mississippi out of the convention would add a
million votes to the Democratic ticket. Sweetland was squelched
and Senator Eastland brought his prejudices onto the convention
floor.

The civil rights plank of the platform was compromised. The
Democrats did not give specific support to the Supreme Court
decision on schools.

The remainder of the platform was standard. The Democrats
attacked the Republicans for fostering monopoly, giving away
natural resources, and scandalous behaviour in the Dixon-Yates
private-power contract that would have undermined the Tennessee
Valley Authority, by giving preference to a private-power project.
They asked for repeal of the Taft-Hartley Act Law, as in 1948 and
1952, full-knowing they would not get it; restoration of 90 per cent
farm-price supports; extension of civil service to more government
jobs, and a tax cut for the "little man."

Stevenson was nominated on the first ballot, with 905½ votes to 210 for Harriman, 45½ for Senator Stuart Symington, 80 for Senator Lyndon Johnson, and 131 for assorted others.

Former President Truman expressed surprise at the outcome, but wished Stevenson luck and announced his support. Truman had opposed Stevenson, and had lost some face in so doing.

Stevenson wanted to make his acceptance speech on Thursday night, August 16, so he would not have to share the platform with Harry Truman, who was scheduled to address the convention on Friday. But Chairman Paul Butler balked. The party was so badly divided that it must be unified. The best road to unity was a make-up session between Stevenson and Truman.

Stevenson yielded, grumpily. He did insist on appearing before the convention Thursday night. He had something to say. Chairman Butler balked again, but this time Stevenson had his way.

That night Stevenson took a dramatic slap at the Republicans, who were so obviously lined up for Richard Nixon and no other. He had no preference for any running mate, Stevenson said. The vice-presidency was entirely up to the convention. Let the Democrats show the Republicans the meaning of the words "free and open convention."

There was no shortage of candidates for the vice-presidential nomination. The candidates most prominently tooted were Senator John Kennedy of Massachusetts, Senator Hubert H. Humphrey of Minnesota, Senator Kefauver, Governor Frank Clement, and Mayor Robert Wagner of New York.

It narrowed down to a choice between Kennedy and Kefauver. The young Massachusetts senator was the choice of the party professionals. Kefauver, who had antagonized the South with a strong stand on civil rights, was the overwhelming favorite of the party faithful out in TV-land.

On the second ballot Kefauver led, but Kennedy crept past him and was within 38½ votes of the nomination. Then Senator Albert Gore, who held the Tennessee vote, withdrew and threw his delegates to Kefauver. This belated support from Kefauver's own state persuaded other states to switch. Kefauver was named on that second ballot. The band played "The Tennessee Waltz," again.

"I sure am tired," yawned the big Tennessee senator, when he wandered, late as usual, into the convention hall to accept his moment of glory. The unfortunate vendors who had stocked

Kennedy buttons were forced to dispose of them. The next day Harry Truman decided Stevenson was a real fighter and Stevenson welcomed Truman's support in the campaign, hoping it wouldn't sink the ship.

Chairman Paul Butler benefited by the harmony spirit more than anyone except the segregationists of the South. Stevenson was quite angry with Butler's foot-dragging on the Thursday night speech, and had several other small bones in his craw. He first announced that Butler would have to quit as national chairman, with the obvious implication that Stevenson Campaign Manager Richard Finnegan would take over. Butler was resigned to it, for the national chairmanship had always depended on the good will of the presidential candidate. At ten o'clock on the morning of August 18, when the national committee met to settle its unfinished business, Butler was prepared to throw in his resignation. But the national committee, with a single dissent, voted that Butler should not resign. The dissenter was George Rock, national committeeman from Colorado.

"Did you vote no?" they asked him.

"I sure as hell did," said Mr. Rock, not an admirer of Butler's.

Despite Mr. Rock and candidate Stevenson, the committee sat firm. Stevenson then had to make a public issue of the matter, or back down. He backed down, but put the real power of running the campaign in manager Finnegan's hands.

By this time, the Democrats were exhausted, and the Republicans were kicking up their heels in the restaurants and bars of San Francisco, waiting for their convention to begin at the Cow Palace.

Unlike Chicago, San Francisco was full of apparent harmony. The fissures did not appear on the surface, though occasionally the ground shifted beneath somebody's feet. California's delegation seethed with discontent. Vice-President Nixon, Senator Joseph Knowland, and Governor Goodwin J. Knight all possessed long-term, gnawing ambition. Within the seventy-man California delegation they had all their supporters. In this instance Knowland and Nixon combined forces, and it was sure that the seventy votes of the delegation would go for Nixon under the unit rule. But all was not serene. On August 18, Nixon, Knowland, and Knight met at the governor's eighth floor suite in the old-fashioned Sheraton Palace Hotel. Seventy minutes later the three emerged, grim. They had reached no agreement. Some of Knight's supporters still threatened to nominate him from the floor for the vice-presidency.

But if the ground in California was shaky, the very rug had been pulled out from under Harold Stassen. His hunting license was about to expire. On the eighteenth Stassen called a press conference in the Nob Hill Room of the Fairmont Hotel. There he released a new poll that showed eight per cent of the Eisenhower vote would be lost if Nixon ran on the Republican ticket.

As soon as the Republican high command heard what Stassen was up to they rallied to find an antidote. Senator Styles Bridges marched up to the podium of Nob Hill as Stassen marched down. Bridges presented another poll, taken by a New Hampshire newspaper which used only ex-FBI agents to do the polling. The retired guardians had discovered that fifty-four per cent of the voters favored an Eisenhower-Nixon ticket, compared to only twenty-five per cent who favored an Eisenhower-Herter ticket.

Stassen's secret weapon, Governor Christian Herter, arrived bearing a letter for convention Chairman Joseph W. Martin, in which he withdrew his name, in case of nomination.

President Eisenhower was to arrive at the convention a day before he had planned—some said because he was angry with the Democrats for charging him with do-nothingism, some said because he wanted to spike the anti-Nixon campaign quickly; Ike said it was because he was excited by the convention.

If Eisenhower was excited he was just about the only Republican who was. It was, as one delegate put it, "an open convention, secretly arrived at." National Chairman Leonard Hall told reporters, as he had been telling them for weeks, that it would be Eisenhower and Nixon, and they could stick that in their hats.

On Sunday the Very Reverend Julian Bartlett preached the sermon at Grace Episcopal Cathedral, and Governor Knight and Sherman Adams read the scripture lessons to the congregation. Dean Bartlett was very pointed in condemning the politicos—of both parties—who claimed that God was on their side in the campaign. This partisan piety had been increasing in the past few years, particularly since Eisenhower began his "crusade" for clean government in 1952. By 1956 the official American pledge of allegiance had even been changed to include the words "this nation, under God." The Reverend Mr. Bartlett reminded the congregation that, any Republican ideas to the contrary notwithstanding, this phrase, if it meant anything, meant that America was under the judgment of God.

That day Tom Dewey aired another favorite Republican topic—Eisenhower's health.

"I saw him last Wednesday," the diminutive lawyer told reporters, "and I never saw a man with more vigor, more bounce, and more clarity of mind."

Eisenhower arrived in San Francisco on Tuesday, when the convention was engaged in session. He did not stop at the convention in the Cow Palace on his way from the international airport into the city, but drove straight to the St. Francis Hotel, then opened the presidential suite and invited any who might want to discuss the possibility of becoming Vice-President to come for inspection.

Nobody came. The fate of Harold Stassen was object lesson enough. Stassen could hardly negotiate the corridors of the Fairmont Hotel without being booed. Elroy W. Bronwich, chairman of the Missouri delegation and a Stassen-Herter man, was roughed up by a Nixon admirer. Bronwich and his wife were minding their own business, they reported, when the Nixon man came up and started pushing Mrs. Bronwich. Mr. Bronwich tried to intervene but was slugged in the face by a rolled-up newspaper. "There is that—— Herter supporter," the attacker mumbled.

Washington's Governor Arthur B. Langlie had devoted his Republican keynote speech to promises of peace and prosperity and four more years of the quasi-religious crusade for a better America. The convention applauded Langlie, but in the tepid fashion of delegates who were more interested in what restaurant they would try that night.

Even the platform contained little to excite anyone. If a platform could have been written with the word "Ike," quipped one newspaper wag, it would have been. Since it could not be so written, the platform confined itself to praising the Republican record and promising more. The Republicans favored the Supreme Court decision, but also said "use of force or violence by any group or agency will tend only to worsen the many problems inherent in the situation." The words could not conceal the implied promise of the federal government not to interfere in southern affairs.

On August 22, Eisenhower indicated that no rival to Richard Nixon had raised his head. Small wonder. Harold Stassen's "dump Nixon" campaign had failed miserably. If there were any other candidates they wouldn't admit it. After a short interview with the President, Stassen announced defeat and asked to be allowed to second the nomination of the man he had tried to remove as a wart on the elephant's trunk.

Nixon was magnanimous. He was willing to let Stassen second the nomination, as long as Stassen did not displace any of the other half-dozen seconders, and as long as Stassen didn't exceed the two minutes of seconding time Chairman Joe Martin was allowing for the rites.

Stassen listened politely. He delivered an eleven-minute speech seconding Nixon.

One small bit of byplay exemplified the wide-open nature of the proceedings.

A delegate from Nebraska, Terry Carpenter, had written Chairman Martin a note about his wish to make another vice-presidential nomination when the delegation was called. Martin learned that Carpenter planned to nominate Fred Seaton, Secretary of Interior.

Seaton didn't want to commit political suicide any more than the next cabinet officer. He refused to let his name be used.

When Nebraska was called Martin explained these facts to the large, bespectacled Carpenter. Carpenter listened, then mumbled that he still wanted to nominate somebody. The name? He thought for a moment. Joe Smith.

"Joe who?" rasped Chairman Martin.

"Joe Smith," said Mrs. George P. Abel, chairman of the Nebraska delegation.

Martin grunted and passed on to the next delegation. The reporters, lulled by the predictable events ahead, suddenly smelled a story. They converged on Terry Carpenter, disrupting Mr. Martin's well-laid plans.

Martin glared down at the swarm around the Nebraska delegation. "Take your Joe Smith," Martin shouted at delegate Carpenter, "and get out of here."

Carpenter and the reporters adjourned to the hallway, where GOP doorkeepers tried to keep Carpenter from saying anything.

Joe Smith, as it turned out, was an apocryphal character, dreamed up by former Democrat Terry Carpenter just because the Republican convention was too tame for his taste.

Delegate Carpenter was used to the rough-and-tumble disagreement that characterized almost all Democratic conventions.

In the end, complete harmony prevailed. Even Terry Carpenter was persuaded to cast his vote for Nixon so the unanimity would not be shattered. The Republican convention broke up into little bands of delegates heading back to the views and San Francisco's famous food.

The short 1956 campaign was not as vicious as 1952, although it was vigorous enough. Stevenson campaigned against the Eisenhower record, and in the middle of the campaign brought out the issue of nuclear testing. He demanded that nuclear testing be ended, that we seek agreement with the Soviet Union to stop contamination of the atmosphere.

But the nation was not ready to admit that nuclear testing was dangerous, and this plea fell on deaf ears. Stevenson found himself allied with Albert Schweitzer, with a handful of other thoughtful men and women, and a large variety of pacifists, whose views were given small credence.

Further, world events worked against Stevenson this year.

First came the Suez crisis, with the implied threat of World War III. Then Hungary exploded in a blaze of Molotov cocktails and rattling machine-gun fire in the empty streets of Budapest. Both events strengthened the "ins." On November 6, when Americans entered their polling booths, they returned Dwight David Eisenhower to the White House in a landslide, by 457 electoral votes to Stevenson's 74. But they did not show so much faith in Eisenhower's party. As in 1954, the Democrats won control of both the House of Representatives and the Senate.

27

The Republicans suffered a bad break in the summer of 1958, when Sherman Adams was implicated in a case of influence in Congress.

As such things go, it was nothing serious. The fact was that all Adams got out of it was an occasional free hotel stay, a rug for his Washington house, and a few minor favors. He was not even using his influence very strongly, and in any case the public weal seemed hardly in danger from the few telephone calls he made on behalf of industrialist Bernard Goldfine.

But Sherman Adams, the thin-lipped white-haired, and tough New Englander, had been the leader of the Eisenhower crusade for honest government. If there was ever a politician who gave other politicians an inferiority complex, it was Sherman Adams. "Holier than thou," he was hated up one side of Pennsylvania Avenue and down the other, and on both sides of the Senate and House.

This was certainly a blow to the hound's-tooth cleanliness of the Eisenhower administration, and it could not help but influence the coming congressional elections. . . .

27. Who Now?

Two years after the 1956 presidential election, despite the efforts of President Eisenhower, the Republican administration suffered a crushing defeat in the congressional elections.

Vice-President Nixon conducted his usual brisk campaign against the Democratic congressional hopefuls, but this time it did not work. Eisenhower himself went on the stump to speak against the "radicals" who would control American federal affairs if the Democrats won. Even so, the important states of Connecticut, Maryland, Vermont, and Delaware turned up after election day without a single Republican member in the House of Representatives. Since at least three of these states were sometime Republican strongholds, it was not hard to see that the elephant was in trouble. His head might be healthier than ever, but his body was weak and creaking at the joints. In the party's defeat, President Eisenhower consoled himself with the belief that the people did not understand the danger of reckless federal spending, i.e., Democratic spending. Seers began to speculate on the future of an Eisenhower-less Republican party, which seemed much more to the point.

As they cast their eyes around the forty-eight states to see what had actually happened in the 1958 election, the pundits discovered one blossom in the GOP crown of thorns. In the state of New York a newcomer to politics (but not to headlines) had won the governorship by more than a half million votes—twice what his most optimistic supporters claimed before election day. Nelson Rockefeller's was a victory in the tradition of Teddy Roosevelt.

Eisenhower's position within the Republican party was weaker than that of any previous President in one respect. He could not succeed himself: he was the first American President to be bound by the Twenty-second Amendment to the Constitution, which prohibited any man from serving three terms in the administrative factory on Pennsylvania Avenue.

The White House, where the Teddy Roosevelt family had overflowed into the basement—this White House could no longer accommodate any but the most intimate personal friends as guests

The public, which had nearly torn the White House apart in Andrew Jackson's time, which had wandered in and out of the White House to visit and scorn Abraham Lincoln—this public was no longer permitted run of the mansion. Since William McKinley's murder the President was a guarded, sequestered man. A tight-lipped President Coolidge had enjoyed his most serene moments in greeting line after line of awed White House visitors in public reception. Neither Eisenhower, nor any later President, could indulge in such informality.

The office had become too demanding, the responsibility too great The President, in reality, was prisoner of his job. Despite Dwight Eisenhower's concern with federal spending, the executive branch of government had never been so large, nor, in time of peace, had it ever spent so much money.

Nor had any President of the United States ever run so far ahead of his party for so long as had Dwight David Eisenhower. When his stern words about "radicalism" had gone unheeded in 1958, and a heavily Democratic Congress greeted him on the morning after election, the President squirmed uncomfortably in contemplation of his pre-election prediction of a cold war between Congress and the White House, if the Democrats won. But the Democrats were not inclined to gloat, or to attack the father image Eisenhower cast across the nation. They rested secure in a new-found fact: Eisenhower's personal popularity was not transferable to any other Republican. So far no Republican presidential hopeful had shown Ike's popularity with the voters. Nelson Rockefeller was too new at the game to count.

Nixon? He was still a great unknown quantity. To be sure, Richard Nixon had mopped up the ballroom with two formidable Democratic opponents—Representative Jerry Voorhis in 1946 and Representative Helen Gahagan Douglas in a titanic battle for the United States Senate in 1950. But in both instances the issue was left to the voters of California, a state that many considered slightly wacky, at that. Besides, while the Nixon tactics of 1946 and 1950 had won elections, they had given him an extremely bad reputation as master of the low blow. Vice-President Nixon had been trying, with only modest success, to live down his congressional campaigns ever since 1952. Eisenhower had pulled Nixon to victory in 1952 and 1956. No one was particularly concerned with Harold Stassen's charges in 1956 that Nixon would drag the Republican ticket. It was obvious that Eisenhower did not believe them and did not care. If Ike did not particularly want Richard Nixon for a running mate, he did not particularly want anyone else either. In Eisenhower's studied impartiality the influence of party Chairman Leonard Hall carried the day for Nixon, and the real chance to discover Nixon's personal strength within his own party was lost. Twice elected Vice-President, Richard Milhous Nixon was emerging as an affable, serious student of public affairs with restrained smile and carefully controlled gesture. He did all the things Eisenhower did not care to do, from speaking to dentists' conventions to facing hurled vegetables and foul abuse on a good-will tour of Latin America. He did all things equally with hardly a change of pace or expression. In some ways, Nixon seemed almost a mechanical man, striding with measured beat toward the White House goal. But Nixon on his own still remained an X quantity with the voters. His national strength had never really been tested. The closest approach to a test came that night on television in 1952 when he exposed his frantic, beating heart in answer to the charge that he had been corrupted by easy money. As the nation was turned for a moment into a kind of continental revival meeting, Nixon was absolved by Eisenhower of wrongdoing. But the American people had never voted on that charge. They had never voted on anything that indicated how they felt about Richard Nixon. Some said he had been defeated, in a sense, when one of his friends lost in a California race in 1958, or that Nixon had suffered a defeat because his speeches did not elect Republican hopefuls in other parts of the United States that year. That same test of popularity, or lack of it, applied to Eisenhower as well as to Nixon. Auras, whatever they might be, are blown away in transfer.

As Nixon looked to the 1960 election it was obvious that he would be the candidate of the party old guard. He was close to the Republican machinery. He had always done the party's bidding. He could expect the payoff in 1960. But already certain small facts were becoming clear. Although the national chairman, Thruston B. Morton, Republican senator from Kentucky, declared his personal support of Nixon, he had also declared for fair play. If he meant it, he would not exercise that support to stack the convention for Nixon. Eisenhower, the one man in the party with enough influence to sway sizable numbers of Republicans, independents, and even Democrats indicated that he would not interfere in the selection of a Republican presidential candidate.

The Eisenhower accolade, if bestowed handsomely on Richard Nixon, would put him across. The party machinery, if allowed to function naturally, would work for Nixon in 1960 as it had for Robert Taft in 1952. Barring the emergence of a whirlwind candidate from political outer space, another Eisenhower, as it were, Nixon would have the nomination.

The candidate from outer space existed, in embryo, at least, in Nelson Rockefeller. This likeable man with the Dick Tracy jaw, scion of the Standard Oil fortune, had every attribute the name and wealth imply: the best education, the frugality of upbringing disposed by his elders to build character, quiet competence in management of vast affairs. Better, he had come to national prominence in the Democratic years of President Roosevelt, in a politically innocuous but respectable job, as "co-ordinator of inter-American affairs." He was known and liked by Latin Americans who spat on Richard Nixon. Unimportant in itself, this comparison still didn't hurt.

Amateur politican though he was in 1958, Rockefeller quickly showed his ability to sow a friendly personality and reap votes. He campaigned on the boardwalks of Coney Island and in the beatness of Greenwich Village's Father Demo Square. He spoke Spanish to the Puerto Rican voters of Harlem and spoke faultless boarding-school American among the furs and gray-flannel suits of the silk-stocking district. He spoke conservatism to upstate New York voters whose strength is so important to election of Republicans since the big city runs Democratic; and he talked liberalism in Manhattan.

Almost immediately after arrival in Albany, Rockefeller began to feel the pressure to run for the Republican presidential nomination in 1960. As in a good handshake, he returned the pressure. It was apparent in less than a year that Rockefeller was an unannounced candidate. The thing that could stop him was some indication of Richard Nixon's overwhelming popularity or a Nixon endorsement by Eisenhower. The latter situation would hardly arise. The President, basically apolitical, was more concerned with maintenance of his own image than with any future effect on the Republican party.

All other Republican candidates were relegated, automatically, to the dark-horse role. They would become important only if the support for Nixon and Rockefeller evened out by convention time and the two fought to a standstill in the manner of Al Smith and William Gibbs McAdoo at the Democratic convention of 1924. Rockefeller's candidacy was apparent early and important in the East, where he appealed to independents and even Democrats, but in the West he was virtually unknown as a political figure. An early tour convinced Rockefeller that GOP leaders in the West were organized for Nixon. His fate so uncertain, Rockefeller withdrew, officially, at the beginning of the political year. The field seemed to belong to Richard Nixon, barring death or disaster. After the New Hampshire primary, where he ran better than Eisenhower had run before, Nixon appeared to be the undisputed candidate of his party.

The roll of Democratic candidates for 1960 began to emerge early after the 1958 elections, but none of these Democratic possiblities, save Adlai Stevenson, seemed to have all the historical attributes of presidential timber.

John Kennedy, the front-running and early-running young senator from Massachusetts, was a Catholic. None of his boyish appeal, his intelligence, not even his big happy grin and his unruly shock of sandy hair could change that. And a boyish candidate has appeal, to be sure, but boyishness is not exactly the attribute most demanded by a nation searching for a Chief Executive to operate a multi-billion-dollar business in human welfare on an irrevocable four-year contract.

Kennedy's Back Bay Boston family came about as close as one might get in American politics to holding a princely cartouche. But (again) princehood is not an unmixed blessing in a country that still honored the bumptious crowd of revolutionaries who had founded the nation.

President Eisenhower said that Catholicism was no bar to election as President. In the early New Hampshire primary, Kennedy, like Nixon, ran very strong.

The Gallup poll indicated the same strength. But polls ask people to cast their public opinion, not their private vote. And polls have been known to be as wrong as public opinion. In 1924 religious bigotry destroyed Democratic chances for victory when Al Smith and W. G.

McAdoo wrested for the Democratic nomination. In 1928, although responsible religious leaders the nation over said bigotry was dead, it cost Democratic candidate Smith uncounted votes, and possibly the election. The trouble in 1928 was that nobody consulted the bigots. Nor were they likely to consult them in 1960.

Senator Hubert Humphrey, a dark horse in 1952, was an appealing candidate for the liberal wing of the party. Humphrey had some farm following, and he attracted heavy labor support. But labor support, with the merger of the AFL and the CIO could not mean to any candidate in 1960 what it had meant in the halcyon days of big labor. Traditionally, the American Federation of Labor stays out of national politics. Since the earliest days of the labor movement, when the printers' union and then Samuel Gompers had burned their fingers, the AFL had confined itself to issues and local candidates. The CIO, born in depression and raised in strife, had suckled on national politics and grown strong. But when the two organizations merged, the AFL demanded the presidency. George Meany, conservative president of the older organization, became chief officer of the new. Walter Reuther, president of the CIO, stepped down to a secondary post. As long as Meany continued to be president, the conservatism of the AFL would dominate big labor, and the value of its support would be diminished. Humphrey had more support than his frenetic race would seem to attract, but in 1960 that support was more questionable than before.

Another labor favorite, Democratic Governor G. Mennen Williams of Michigan, had already decided he had been governor too long. No one else could conceivably be blamed, by outsiders, for Michigan's near bankrupt economy. Senator Stuart Symington was a strong advocate of national defense. If it seemed to be a one plank platform, still Symington's Missouri background gave him a chance as a compromise candidate, and Harry Truman liked Symington, for what that might be worth.

Senator Lyndon Johnson, the majority leader, unfortunately hailed from the South.

Governor Robert Meyner of New Jersey was a very quiet candidate.

Adlai Stevenson didn't think he would be nominated a third time.

The issues of the campaign of 1960 were much easier to predict, even a year before the election. Within the Republican party there were no real issues, except the traditional struggle for party control.

Between the Republicans and the Democrats there would be several vital issues. The record of the Democratic Eighty-sixth Congress was one. It was dubbed the "won't do" Congress by Republican leaders in a campaign reminiscent of Harry Truman's deprecation of the "worst" Eightieth Congress of 1948. Other issues would be farm policy, housing, education, foreign policy, and—the visceral quarrel —civil rights, an issue that harked back a hundred years.

The Republicans would have to run on President Eisenhower's record, a good record, as such things go, in a period of international strain. Foreign policy would be vital only as it could be translated into big issues that could be shown directly to affect world peace. If Eisenhower reached a modus vivendi with the Russians it would work to the advantage of the Republicans.

On schools, housing, and the rest, neither the Republicans nor the Democrats could show an outstanding record.

Civil rights affected other issues: foreign policy, in American relations with the uncommitted nations, most of them "colored"; housing; education; and labor.

And on civil rights the Democrats found themselves uncomfortably close to their position of 1860, in attitude, if not in fact.

A year before the elections Democrats in the deep South were hardly solid. In some states preparations were under way to remove a restriction that presidential electors had to vote for the Democratic candidate. Integration of schools, ordered by the United States Supreme Court in 1954, was proceeding at a snail's pace. After two years of racial tension in Little Rock, Arkansas, token integration had been accomplished in the high schools. Then someone raised the specter of segregated classrooms within integrated schools. The inch-by-inch struggle for civil rights seemed never ending. Throughout the South the battle was fought, in Virginia, Alabama, and Georgia.

Perhaps the Democrats could unite on civil rights, as Senate majority leader Lyndon Johnson hoped. If they could it would mean establishment of a civil rights platform plank. But Democratic candidates outside the extreme liberal mold were showing a tendency to straddle the issue. In 1956, had the Democrats carried all the Negro precincts in America's big cities, the outcome of the presidential election might have been different. In 1960, Democrats could be sure of one thing: unless they satisfied the Negroes, the Negro vote would go more solidly against them than it had four years before, for in the four years the southern Democrats had proved recalcitrant to a degree that could be compared only to the period a hundred years before.

One negative factor softened the issue for the Democrats. After 1956 the Republican party showed none of the decision that the Republicans had shown between 1856 and 1860 on the same subject.

There were plenty of present-day compromisers, similar to Stephen A. Douglas in the Democratic ranks, and plenty of fervid states'-righters like Alabama's William Yancey.

But no Abraham Lincoln or even William Seward spoke out for the Republicans with determination to solve the racial issue. A century before there had been scores of outraged Republicans to speak out from high places.

The Democrats, in their usual divided house, no longer had a two-thirds rule that would protect the South against an unwanted candidate. The Negro has assumed more importance than before as a voter. There are more Negroes voting than before, and the Negro vote in the North, concentrated in city areas, is the potent force.

Only one thing could be certain for the presidential election year of 1960: Nothing would be certain, nor could any prediction be more than a wild guess until that fateful moment on the convention floor when a candidate is nominated.

The history of both parties shows the strange things that can, and do, happen, as in brilliant strategic victories of Lincoln's political general David Davis in 1860 or of Eisenhower's Henry Cabot Lodge in 1952. Or consider the weeping reluctance of Horatio Seymour in 1868, the narrow escape from nomination by William McKinley in the obviously Democratic year of 1892, the long and fruitless struggle of James G. Blaine in 1888, when he was defeated by his own physical collapse on the eve of the convention. Had he not collapsed, he would have been nominated. Had he been nominated, he would almost certainly have been elected.

History shows the years in which it was apparent from the start who would be the nominee of one party or the other. Grant was obviously the Republican choice in 1868; no other need apply. Cleveland had the Democratic nomination sewed up in 1892, despite all Tammany's scheming against him. Such a situation exists for 1960 in party only.

But, in 1960, there is no national hero who stands above all other men. There is no Eisenhower or Grant or Cleveland, Washington or Lincoln or Teddy Roosevelt to command the overwhelming respect or love of party and people. Neither party has a great figure to put forth. Adlai Stevenson, a two-time loser, faces the future weakened by overexposure without visible success. For the rest, the Democrats have a stable of anxious front-runners and cautious dark horses, with one or two thoroughbreds and not a few jackasses.

It is certain that no non-political or dual-political messiah will arise from the multitudes, as did Wendell Willkie in 1940, to lead either party in the elections of 1960.

The Democrats, for all their collection of minorities, are the largest party of the two. They control Congress, and while the Eighty-sixth Congress was not brilliant, pottering along with small laws, it did nothing shocking.

The staleness of twenty years of Democratic rule was wiped out in eight years of Republican rule. In those eight years the Republicans failed to create a new, slimmer, streamlined pachyderm, as many liberal Republicans had hoped. A good look showed that under the spangled blanket of Eisenhowerism the Republican party was still the gray, wrinkled party of business and conservatism, the party of economic reaction. The American people had their moment of reaction to war, tension, and fourteen years of Democrats which resulted in election of the Republican Eightieth Congress in 1946.

That much of the picture favored the Democrats for 1960.

But the Democratic donkey, though grown slimmer by eight years removed from the political feasting, is not as sleek and healthy as might be.

It is sorely riven by old conflicts. If the elephant is the symbol of economic reaction, now the donkey threatens to be labeled, immemorially, as the symbol of social reaction.

The struggle between the northern and southern wings of the party is the key to Democratic prospects in 1960. If the party can resolve the conflict to the satisfaction of white southerners and northern Negroes, it will win the presidency in 1960. If it cannot, and the Republicans take a strong civil rights stand, the GOP will win. In a century, the political wheel has come full circle. The Democrats face the same problem that split their party in 1860; never having resolved the issue, it is likely to split them again, or at least make it impossible for the party to win victory on a national basis. This is the political dilemma of 1960. If the Democrats fail to resolve their overriding issue, the Republicans will win the White House by default.

In the absence of issues or their even partial resolution before election, Americans vote for the man, not the party. So it has been for more than a century. Of vital issues that stood above the men running for office, there have really been only four in this century of two-party politics: slavery, money, depression, and war. Money was the issue in the day of Cleveland and Harrison. Then it was the question of the tax on goods imported from foreign lands—the tariff. The Republicans claimed that salvation lay in high import taxes, in supporting American industry. The Democrats claimed salvation lay in low import taxes—heavy foreign trade. The nation tried it both ways, and never did resolve the issue to its complete satisfaction. Finally, the Eisenhower administration committed the Republicans to the low tariff, called now reciprocal trade. But within the Republican party beat many stern high-tariff hearts waiting only to get their hands on the party's platform or, better still, on legislation.

Money, of course, was an issue in the Bryan campaigns for free silver coinage—cheap money. Bryan was never able to make it so great an issue as to win election for him, nor were the Greenback or Populist parties. But, under Franklin Roosevelt, the nation turned to cheap money, and has never turned back to the days when store-keepers gnawed on twenty-dollar gold pieces. Even Eisenhower has not tried to turn back the clock.

Depression defeats Presidents and parties in power. It elects the opposition, on the public's principle that nothing can be worse than the status quo. Prosperity elects incumbent office holders and the party in ascendancy at the moment.

Slavery defeated Stephen Douglas in the South in 1860, and elected Abraham Lincoln in the North. Slavery, the resulting Civil War, and civil rights disagreement colored and controlled every presidential election for a quarter of a century. The issue lay quiescent for nearly seventy-five years. But now slavery's quadroon descendant, racial equality, *will* color and will probably control every future election until the equality is achieved.

War has been an issue, not so much in itself—except in the protest of early 1864 over the war's conduct—but because the existence of a stab of war favored the incumbent, both in 1916 and in 1944. War made it almost impossible to dislodge the President in office. In the face of this, the phenomenon of greatest interest for the long haul is the renewed resilience of the two-party system in the

United States. As Norman Thomas has said wryly on a number of occasions, the big parties have stolen the issues from radical parties such as Thomas's own Socialists. Never has that been better illustrated than now, when, practically speaking, no third party exists outside the lunatic fringe. Even the communists have destroyed themselves. In 1956 the communists squirmed in the revelations of Stalin's crimes. Stalinism died, as ordained by comrade Nikita Khrushchev in Moscow. The American party tore itself apart, trying to prove that it was home-grown, omniscient, and not following a Kremlin line. Beyond peradventure, the American communists have lost *all* support they ever had in labor, intellectual circles, and among minorities, the lunatic fringe again excepted.

The two major parties—great coalitions of different and often conflicting economic and social interests—are stronger than ever before. A hundred years ago a dissatisfied Democratic South had no hesitation in splitting its party squarely in two. Even a scant dozen years ago the states'-rights Democrats essayed a split, which became a rump action and then backfired in the election of a Democratic president without the help of the radical South.

There will be third parties in the future. There will be third parties on the ballot in 1960. But the fact remains that the Republican and Democratic parties continue their great tradition of embracing almost all shades of political thought. In each party one finds advocates of individualism. The weighting of the middle creates the difference, and if non-Americans find it difficult to understand that there is any difference, it is because they regard political parties as advocates of specific doctrine. In Europe, if a man ceases to believe the doctrine of his party, he changes parties. In America, a man changes parties if he moves from a Republican to a Democratic region, or if he has political ambition. (It is usually much easier to work your way up in the minority party than the majority.) Seldom does a man change from Republican to Democrat as a matter of deep principle. Why should he? He can be just about anything he wants in either one. The two-party system, the system of compromise, slow achievement, balloons, brickbats, bumble and brilliance, is here to stay.

Appendix

Election of 1860
(Chapters 1 & 2)

PRESIDENTIAL AND VICE-PRESIDENTIAL CANDIDATES

Republican Abraham Lincoln, Illinois
     Hannibal Hamlin, Maine

Democratic Stephen A. Douglas, Illinois
     Herschel V. Johnson, Georgia

National
Democratic John C. Breckinridge, Kentucky
     Joseph Lane, Oregon

Constitu-
tional
Union John Bell, Tennessee
     Edward Everett, Massachusetts

ELECTION STATISTICS

Popular vote Lincoln   1,866,452
     Breckinridge 847,953
     Douglas   1,375,157
     Bell   590,631

Electoral vote Lincoln   180
     Breckinridge   72
     Douglas   12
     Bell   39

States carried   (In 1860 there were 33 states in the Union.)

Lincoln: Maine, New Hampshire, Vermont, Massachusetts, Rhode Island, Connecticut, New York, Ohio, Indiana, Illinois, New Jersey (4), Pennsylvania, Michigan, Wisconsin, Oregon, California, Minnesota, Iowa

Breckinridge: Delaware, Maryland, North Carolina, South Carolina, Georgia, Alabama, Mississippi, Louisiana, Arkansas, Texas, Florida

Bell: Virginia, Tennessee, Kentucky

Douglas: New Jersey (3), Missouri

37th Congress	Senate	31 Republicans
		10 Democrats
		8 other
	House	105 Republicans
		43 Democrats
		30 other

Election of 1862

38th Congress	Senate	36 Republicans
		9 Democrats
		5 Unionists
	House	102 Republicans
		75 Democrats
		9 Unionists

Election of 1864
(Chapter 3)

PRESIDENTIAL AND VICE-PRESIDENTIAL CANDIDATES

Unionist   Abraham Lincoln, Illinois
        Andrew Johnson, Tennessee

Democrat   George B. McClellan, New Jersey
              George H. Pendleton, Ohio

Radical   John C. Frémont, California
Democrat   John Cochrane, New York

(The Radical Democratic party existed only between May 31 and September 22, 1864, when Frémont was persuaded to withdraw.)

ELECTION STATISTICS

Popular vote   Lincoln   2,213,665
                  McClellan   1,805,237

Electoral vote Lincoln   212
                  McClellan   21

States carried (In 1864 there were 11 states in secession, 36 in the Union, but only 25 voting.)

Lincoln: California, Connecticut, Illinois, Indiana, Iowa, Kansas, Maine, Maryland, Massachusetts, Michigan, Minnesota, Missouri, Nevada, New Hampshire, New York, Ohio, Oregon, Pennsylvania, Rhode Island, Vermont, West Virginia, Wisconsin

McClellan: Delaware, Kentucky, New Jersey

39th Congress   Senate   42 Union
                              10 Democrats

                   House   149 Union
                              42 Democrats

Election of 1866

40th Congress   Senate   42 Republicans (Union Party)
                              11 Democrats

                   House   143 Republicans (Union Party)
                              49 Democrats

Election of 1868
(Chapter 4)

PRESIDENTIAL AND VICE-PRESIDENTIAL CANDIDATES

Republican Ulysses S. Grant, Illinois
Schuyler Colfax, Indiana

Democratic Horatio Seymour, New York
Francis P. Blair, Missouri

ELECTION STATISTICS

Popular vote Grant 3,012,833
Seymour 2,703,247

Electoral vote Grant 214
Seymour 80

States carried (In 1868, 37 states voted.)
Grant: Maine, New Hampshire, Vermont, Massachusetts, Rhode Island, Connecticut, Pennsylvania, West Virginia, North Carolina, South Carolina, Florida, Alabama, Arkansas, Missouri, Tennessee, Ohio, Michigan, Indiana, Illinois, Wisconsin, Minnesota, Iowa, Nebraska, Kansas, Nevada, California

Seymour: New York, New Jersey, Delaware, Maryland, Georgia, Louisiana, Kentucky, Oregon

(Mississippi, Texas, and Virginia were unreconstructed, so their votes were not counted. Eight electoral votes from Louisiana and six from Arkansas were not counted.)

41st Congress Senate 56 Republicans
11 Democrats

House 149 Republicans
63 Democrats

Election of 1870

42nd Congress   Senate   52 Republicans
17 Democrats
5 Liberals

House   134 Republicans
104 Democrats
5 Liberals

Election of 1872
(Chapter 5)

PRESIDENTIAL AND VICE-PRESIDENTIAL CANDIDATES

Republican   Ulysses S. Grant, Illinois
Henry Wilson, Massachusetts

Democrat   Charles O'Conor, New York
John Quincy Adams, Massachusetts

Liberal Republican Horace Greeley, New York
B. Gratz Brown, Missouri

Prohibitionist   James Black, Pennsylvania
John Russell, Michigan

Labor Reform   David Davis, Illinois
Joel Parker, New Jersey

ELECTION STATISTICS

Popular vote   Grant   3,597,132
Greeley   2,834,125
O'Conor   29,489
Black   5,508

Electoral vote Horace Greeley died on November 29, 1872, before the meeting of the electoral college. Votes were split then, among many candidates.

Grant 286

All others 66

(Greeley's votes went to Thomas A. Hendricks, 42; B. Gratz Brown, 18; Charles J. Jenkins, 2; David Davis, 1.)

States carried (In 1872 there were 37 states in the Union and voting.)

Grant: Maine, New Hampshire, Vermont, Massachusetts, Rhode Island, Connecticut, New York, New Jersey, Pennsylvania, Delaware, Virginia, West Virginia, Iowa, Nebraska, Kansas, Nevada, California, Oregon, North Carolina, South Carolina, Florida, Alabama, Mississippi, Louisiana, Arkansas, Ohio, Michigan, Indiana, Illinois, Wisconsin, Minnesota

Greeley: Georgia, Texas, Missouri, Tennessee, Kentucky, Maryland

43rd Congress Senate 49 Republicans
19 Democrats
5 Liberal Republicans

House 194 Republicans
92 Democrats
14 Liberal Republicans

Election of 1874

44th Congress Senate 45 Republicans
29 Democrats
2 Liberals

House 109 Republicans
169 Democrats
14 Liberals

Election of 1876
(Chapter 6)

PRESIDENTIAL AND VICE-PRESIDENTIAL CANDIDATES

Republican Rutherford B. Hayes, Ohio
       William A. Wheeler, New York

Democrat   Samuel J. Tilden, New York
       Thomas A. Hendricks, Indiana

Prohibition   Green Clay Smith, Kentucky
       G. T. Stewart, Ohio

Greenback
(Ind. Nationalist
 Party)   Peter Cooper, New York
       Samuel F. Cary, Ohio

American National James B. Walker, Illinois
       Donald Kirkpatrick, New York

ELECTION STATISTICS

Popular vote	Hayes	4,036,298
	Tilden	4,300,590
	Smith	9,522
	Cooper	81,737
	Walker	2,636
Electoral vote	Hayes	185
	Tilden	184

States carried (There were 38 states voting in the election.)
Hayes: Maine, New Hampshire, Vermont, Massachusetts, Rhode Island, Pennsylvania, South Carolina, Florida, Louisiana, Ohio, Michigan, Illinois, Wisconsin, Minnesota, Iowa, Nebraska, Kansas, Colorado, Nevada, California, Oregon

Tilden: Connecticut, New York, New Jersey, Delaware, Maryland, Virginia, West Virginia, North Carolina, Georgia,

Alabama, Mississippi, Texas, Arkansas, Missouri, Tennessee, Kentucky, Indiana

45th Congress	Senate	39 Republicans
		1 Independent
		36 Democrats
	House	140 Republicans
		153 Democrats

Election of 1878

46th Congress	Senate	33 Republicans
		42 Democrats
		1 Independent
	House	130 Republicans
		149 Democrats
		14 Nationalists

Election of 1880
(Chapter 7)

PRESIDENTIAL AND VICE-PRESIDENTIAL CANDIDATES

Republican   James A. Garfield, Ohio
                      Chester A. Arthur, New York

Democrat   Winfield S. Hancock, Pennsylvania
                      William H. English, Indiana

Prohibitionist   Neal Dow, Maine
                      A. M. Thompson, Ohio

Greenback   James B. Weaver, Iowa
                      B. J. Chambers, Texas

American National   John W. Phelps, Vermont
                      Samuel C. Pomeroy, Kansas

ELECTION STATISTICS

Popular Vote   Garfield   4,454,416
               Hancock   4,444,952
               Weaver   308,578
               Dow   10,305
               Phelps   700

Electoral vote   Garfield   214
               Hancock   155

States carried (There were 38 states voting in the election.)

Garfield: Maine, New Hampshire, Vermont, Massachusetts, Rhode Island, Connecticut, New York, Pennsylvania, Ohio, Michigan, Indiana, Illinois, Wisconsin, Minnesota, Iowa, Nebraska, Kansas, Colorado, Oregon, 1 vote from California

Hancock: California (5), New Jersey, Delaware, Maryland, Virginia, West Virginia, North Carolina, South Carolina, Georgia, Florida, Alabama, Mississippi, Louisiana, Texas, Arkansas, Missouri, Tennessee, Kentucky, Nevada

47th Congress Senate   37 Republicans
                        37 Democrats
                        1 other

               House   147 Republicans
                        135 Democrats
                        11 others

Election of 1882

48th Congress Senate   38 Republicans
                        36 Democrats
                        2 Readjusters

               House   118 Republicans
                        197 Democrats
                        1 Nationalist
                        5 Readjusters
                        4 Independents

Election of 1884
(Chapter 8)

PRESIDENTIAL AND VICE-PRESIDENTIAL CANDIDATES

Republican

James G. Blaine, Maine
John Logan, Illinois

Democrat

Grover Cleveland, New York
Thomas A. Hendricks, Indiana

Anti-Monopoly

General Benjamin F. Butler,
  Massachusetts
General Alanson M. West,
  Mississippi

Greenback (National)

Benjamin Butler, Massachusetts
Alanson M. West, Mississippi

Prohibition Home Protection

John St. John, Kansas
William Daniel, Maryland

American Prohibition National

Samuel P. Pomeroy, Kansas
John A. Conant, Connecticut

Equal (or Women's) Rights

Mrs. Belva A. Lockwood,
  District of Columbia
Marietta L. Stow, California

ELECTION STATISTICS

Popular vote	Cleveland	4,874,986
	Blaine	4,851,981
	Butler	175,370
	St. John	150,369

Electoral vote	Cleveland	219
	Blaine	182

States carried   (There were 38 states voting in the election.)

Cleveland: Connecticut, New York, New Jersey, Delaware, Maryland, Virginia, West Virginia, North Carolina, South Carolina, Georgia, Florida, Alabama, Mississippi, Louisiana, Texas, Arkansas, Missouri, Tennessee, Kentucky, Indiana

Blaine: Maine, New Hampshire, Vermont, Massachusetts, Rhode Island, Pennsylvania, Ohio, Michigan, Illinois, Wisconsin, Minnesota, Iowa, Nebraska, Kansas, Colorado, Nevada, California, Oregon

49th Congress   Senate   43 Republicans
      34 Democrats

      House   140 Republicans
      183 Democrats
      2 Nationalists

Election of 1886

50th Congress   Senate   39 Republicans
      37 Democrats

      House   152 Republicans
      169 Democrats
      2 Labor
      2 Independent

Election of 1888
(Chapter 9)

PRESIDENTIAL AND VICE-PRESIDENTIAL CANDIDATES

Republican   Benjamin Harrison, Ohio
      Levi P. Morton, New York

Democrat   Grover Cleveland, New York
      Allen G. Thurman, Ohio

Union Labor   Anson J. Streeter, Illinois
Samuel Evans, Texas

Prohibition   Clinton B. Fisk, New Jersey
John A. Brooks, Missouri

United Labor   Robert H. Cowdrey, Illinois
W. H. T. Wakefield, Kansas

American   James Langdon Curtis, New York
James R. Greer, Tennessee

Equal Rights   Mrs. Belva A. Lockwood, District of Columbia
Alfred H. Love, Pennsylvania

ELECTION STATISTICS

Popular vote

Harrison	5,439,835
Cleveland	5,540,309
Streeter	146,935
Fisk	249,506
Cowdrey	2,818
Curtis	1,600

Electoral vote

Harrison	233
Cleveland	168

States carried   (There were 38 states voting in the election.)

Harrison: California, Colorado, Illinois, Indiana, Iowa, Kansas, Maine, Massachusetts, Michigan, Minnesota, Nebraska, Nevada, New Hampshire, New York, Ohio, Oregon, Pennsylvania, Rhode Island, Vermont, Wisconsin

Cleveland: Alabama, Arkansas, Connecticut, Delaware, Florida, Georgia, Kentucky, Louisiana, Maryland, Mississippi, Missouri, New Jersey, North Carolina, South Carolina, Tennessee, Texas, Virginia, West Virginia

51st Congress   Senate   39 Republicans
37 Democrats

House   166 Republicans
159 Democrats

Election of 1890

52nd Congress	Senate	47 Republicans
		39 Democrats
		2 Populists
	House	88 Republicans
		235 Democrats
		9 Populists

Election of 1892
(Chapter 10)

PRESIDENTIAL AND VICE-PRESIDENTIAL CANDIDATES

Republican	Benjamin Harrison, Ohio
	Whitelaw Reid, New York
Democrat	Grover Cleveland, New York
	Adlai E. Stevenson, Illinois
Populists	James B. Weaver, Iowa
	James G. Field, Virginia
Prohibition	John Bidwell, California
	J. B. Cranfill, Texas
Socialist Labor	Simon Wing, Massachusetts
	Charles H. Matchett, New York

ELECTION STATISTICS

Popular vote	Harrison	5,176,108
	Cleveland	5,556,918
	Weaver	1,041,028
	Bidwell	264,133
	Wing	21,164

Electoral vote Cleveland   277
                 Harrison   145
                 Weaver   22

States carried (There were 44 states voting in the election.)

Cleveland: Alabama, Arkansas, California, Connecticut, Delaware, Florida, Georgia, Illinois, Indiana, Kentucky, Louisiana, Maryland, Michigan (5), Mississippi, Missouri, New Jersey, New York, North Carolina, 1 from North Dakota, 1 from Ohio, South Carolina, Tennessee, Texas, Virginia, West Virginia, Wisconsin

Harrison: 1 from California, Iowa, Maine, Massachusetts, Michigan (9), Minnesota, Montana, Nebraska, New Hampshire, Ohio (22), 1 from North Dakota, 3 from Oregon, Pennsylvania, Rhode Island, South Dakota, Vermont, Washington, Wyoming

Weaver: Colorado, Idaho, Kansas, Nevada, 1 from North Dakota, 1 from Oregon

53rd Congress Senate   38 Republicans
                           44 Democrats
                            3 Populists

                 House   127 Republicans
                          218 Democrats
                           11 Populists

Election of 1894

54th Congress Senate   43 Republicans
                           39 Democrats
                            6 Populists

                 House   244 Republicans
                          105 Democrats
                            6 Populists
                            1 Silver

Election of 1896
(Chapter 11)

PRESIDENTIAL AND VICE-PRESIDENTIAL CANDIDATES

Republican	William McKinley, Ohio Garrett A. Hobart, New Jersey
Democrat	William Jennings Bryan, Nebraska Arthur Sewall, Maine
Prohibition	Joshua Levering, Maryland Hale Johnson, Illinois
National (Prohibition)	Charles E. Bentley, Nebraska James E. Southgate, North Carolina
Socialist Labor	Charles H. Matchett, New York Matthew Maguire, New Jersey
Populist	William Jennings Bryan, Nebraska Thomas E. Watson, Georgia
National Democratic Party	John M. Palmer, Illinois Simon B. Buckner, Kentucky
National Silver	William Jennings Bryan, Nebraska Arthur Sewall, Maine

ELECTION STATISTICS

Popular vote	McKinley	7,104,779
	Bryan	6,502,925
	Palmer	133,148
	Levering	132,007
	Bentley	13,969
	Matchett	36,274
Electoral vote	McKinley	271
	Bryan	176

States carried (There were 45 states voting in the election.)

McKinley: California (8), Connecticut, Delaware, Illinois, Indiana, Iowa, Kentucky (12), Maine, Maryland, Massachusetts, Michigan, Minnesota, New Hampshire, New Jersey, New York, North Dakota, Ohio, Oregon, Pennsylvania, Rhode Island, Vermont, West Virginia, Wisconsin

Bryan: Alabama, Arkansas, 1 from California, Colorado, Florida, Georgia, Idaho, Kansas, 1 from Kentucky, Louisiana, Mississippi, Missouri, Montana, Nebraska, Nevada, North Carolina, South Carolina, South Dakota, Tennessee, Texas, Utah, Virginia, Washington, Wyoming

55th Congress   Senate   47 Republicans
34 Democrats
5 Populists
2 Silver

House   204 Republicans
113 Democrats
11 Populists
3 Silver
26 Fusion

Election of 1898

56th Congress   Senate   53 Republicans
26 Democrats
5 Populists
2 Silver
1 Independent

House   185 Republicans
163 Democrats
7 Populists
1 Silver

Election of 1900
(Chapter 12)

PRESIDENTIAL AND VICE-PRESIDENTIAL CANDIDATES

Republican	William McKinley, Ohio Theodore Roosevelt, New York
Democrat (and *People's* *Party* and *Silver* *Republican*)	William Jennings Bryan, Nebraska Adlai Stevenson, Illinois
Social Democratic (*Socialist*)	Eugene V. Debs, Indiana Job Harriman, California
Populist (Middle-of- the-Road *People's* *Party*)	Wharton Barker, Pennsylvania Ignatius Donnelly, Minnesota
Socialist Labor	Joseph F. Malloney, Massachusetts Valentine Remmel, Pennsylvania
Prohibition	John Woolley, Illinois Henry B. Metcalf, Rhode Island
Union Reform	Seth H. Ellis, Ohio Samuel T. Nicholson, Pennsylvania
United Christian	Jonah F. R. Leonard, Iowa David H. Martin, Pennsylvania

ELECTION STATISTICS

Popular vote	McKinley	7,207,923
	Bryan	6,358,133
	Debs	87,814
	Malloney	39,739
	Woolley	208,914
	Barker	50,373
	Ellis	5,698
	Leonard	5,500

Electoral vote   McKinley   292
                   Bryan   155

States carried (There were 45 states voting in the election.)

McKinley: California, Connecticut, Delaware, Illinois, Indiana, Iowa, Kansas, Maine, Maryland, Massachusetts, Michigan, Minnesota, Nebraska, New Hampshire, New Jersey, New York, North Dakota, Ohio, Oregon, Pennsylvania, Rhode Island, South Dakota, Utah, Vermont, Washington, West Virginia, Wisconsin, Wyoming

Bryan: Alabama, Arkansas, Colorado, Florida, Georgia, Idaho, Kentucky, Louisiana, Mississippi, Missouri, Montana, Nevada, North Carolina, South Carolina, Tennessee, Texas, Virginia

57th Congress   Senate   55 Republicans
                            31 Democrats
                             4 Populists

                  House   197 Republicans
                           151 Democrats
                             9 Fusion

Election of 1902

58th Congress   Senate   57 Republicans
                            33 Democrats

                  House   208 Republicans
                          178 Democrats

Election of 1904
(Chapter 13)

PRESIDENTIAL AND VICE-PRESIDENTIAL CANDIDATES

Republican   Theodore Roosevelt, New York
                      Charles W. Fairbanks, Indiana

| *Democrat* | Alton B. Parker, New York |
| | Henry G. Davis, West Virginia |

| *Prohibition* | Silas C. Swallow, Pennsylvania |
| | George W. Carroll, Texas |

| *Socialist* | Eugene V. Debs, Indiana |
| | Benjamin Hanford, New York |

| *Socialist Labor* | Charles H. Corregan, New York |
| | William W. Cox, Illinois |

| *Populists* | Thomas E. Watson, Georgia |
| | Thomas H. Tibbles, Nebraska |

| *National Liberal* | George E. Taylor, Iowa |
| | No Vice-President |

| *Continental* | Austin H. Holcomb, Georgia |
| | A. King, Missouri |

ELECTION STATISTICS

Popular vote	Roosevelt	7,623,486
	Parker	5,077,911
	Watson	117,183
	Debs	402,283
	Swallow	258,536
	Corregan	31,249
	Holcomb	1,000

| *Electoral vote* | Roosevelt | 336 |
| | Parker | 140 |

States carried (There were 45 states voting in the election.)

Roosevelt: California, Colorado, Connecticut, Delaware, Idaho, Illinois, Indiana, Iowa, Kansas, Maine, 1 from Maryland, Massachusetts, Michigan, Minnesota, Missouri, Montana, Nebraska, Nevada, New Hampshire, New Jersey, New York, North Dakota, Ohio, Oregon, Pennsylvania, Rhode Island, South Dakota, Utah, Vermont, Washington, West Virginia, Wisconsin, Wyoming

Parker: Alabama, Arkansas, Florida, Georgia, Kentucky, Louisiana, Maryland (7), Mississippi, North Carolina, South Carolina, Tennessee, Texas, Virginia

59th Congress Senate 57 Republicans
33 Democrats

House 250 Republicans
136 Democrats

Election of 1906

60th Congress Senate 61 Republicans
31 Democrats

House 222 Republicans
164 Democrats

Election of 1908
(Chapter 14)

PRESIDENTIAL AND VICE-PRESIDENTIAL CANDIDATES

Republican William Howard Taft, Ohio
James S. Sherman, New York

Democrat William Jennings Bryan, Nebraska
John W. Kern, Indiana

Prohibition Eugene W. Chafin, Illinois
Aaron S. Watkins, Ohio

Independence Thomas L. Hisgen, Massachusetts
John Temple Graves, Georgia

Socialist Eugene V. Debs, Indiana
Benjamin Hanford, New York

Socialist Labor August Gilhaus, New York
Donald L. Munro, Virginia

Populist Thomas S. Watson, Georgia
Samuel W. Williams, Indiana

United Christian Daniel B. Turney, Illinois

ELECTION STATISTICS

Popular vote	Taft	7,678,908
	Bryan	6,409,104
	Debs	420,793
	Chafin	253,840
	Watson	29,100
	Hisgen	82,872

| *Electoral vote* | Taft | 321 |
| | Bryan | 162 |

States carried (There were 46 states voting in the election.)

Taft: California, Connecticut, Delaware, Idaho, Illinois, Indiana, Iowa, Kansas, Maine, 2 from Maryland, Massachusetts, Michigan, Minnesota, Missouri, Montana, New Hampshire, New Jersey, New York, North Dakota, Ohio, Oregon, Pennsylvania, Rhode Island, South Dakota, Utah, Vermont, Washington, West Virginia, Wisconsin, Wyoming

Bryan: Alabama, Arkansas, Colorado, Florida, Georgia, Kentucky, Louisiana, Maryland (6), Mississippi, Nebraska, Nevada, North Carolina, Oklahoma, South Carolina, Tennessee, Texas, Virginia

61st Congress	Senate	61 Republicans
		32 Democrats
	House	219 Republicans
		172 Democrats

Election of 1910

62nd Congress	Senate	51 Republicans
		41 Democrats
	House	161 Republicans
		228 Democrats
		1 Socialist

Election of 1912

(Chapter 15)

PRESIDENTIAL AND VICE-PRESIDENTIAL CANDIDATES

Republican   William Howard Taft, Ohio
              James Sherman, New York

Democrat   Woodrow Wilson, New Jersey
              Thomas R. Marshall, Indiana

Progressive Theodore Roosevelt, New York
              Hiram Johnson, California

Socialist   Eugene V. Debs, Indiana
              Emil Seidel, Wisconsin

Prohibition Eugene W. Chafin, Illinois
              Aaron S. Watkins, Ohio

Socialist Labor Arthur E. Reimer, Massachusetts
                  August Gilhaus, New York

ELECTION STATISTICS

Popular vote   Wilson   6,293,454
               Roosevelt   4,119,538
               Taft   3,484,980
               Debs   900,672
               Chafin   206,275
               Reimer   28,750

Electoral vote Wilson   435
                Roosevelt   88
                Taft   8

States carried (There were 48 states voting in the election.)

Wilson: Alabama, Arizona, Arkansas, 2 from California, Colo-
    rado, Connecticut, Delaware, Florida, Georgia, Idaho, Illinois,
    Indiana, Iowa, Kansas, Kentucky, Louisiana, Maine, Mary-
    land, Massachusetts, Mississippi, Missouri, Montana, Ne-
    braska, Nevada, New Hampshire, New Jersey, New Mexico,

New York, North Carolina, North Dakota, Ohio, Oklahoma, Oregon, Rhode Island, South Carolina, Tennessee, Texas, Virginia, West Virginia, Wisconsin, Wyoming

Roosevelt: South Dakota, Pennsylvania, California, Michigan, Minnesota, Washington

Taft: Utah, Vermont

63rd Congress   Senate   44 Republicans
51 Democrats
1 Progressive

House   127 Republicans
291 Democrats
9 Progressives
7 Progressive Republicans
1 Independent

Election of 1914

64th Congress   Senate   40 Republicans
56 Democrats

House   196 Republicans
230 Democrats
1 Progressive
1 Progressive-Protectionist
4 Independent
1 Progressive Democrat
1 Prohibitionist
1 Socialist

Election of 1916
(Chapter 16)

PRESIDENTIAL AND VICE-PRESIDENTIAL CANDIDATES

Republican   Charles Evans Hughes, New York
Charles Warren Fairbanks, Indiana

Democrat	Woodrow Wilson, New Jersey
	Thomas R. Marshall, Indiana
Prohibition	J. Frank Hanly, Indiana
	Ira D. Landrith, Massachusetts
Socialist	Allan J. Benson, New York
	George R. Kirkpatrick, New Jersey
Socialist Labor	Arthur Reimer, Massachusetts
	Caleb Harrison, Illinois
Progressive	Various candidates: Theodore Roosevelt, New York
	John M. Parker, Louisiana

(Roosevelt declined and the national committee endorsed Republican Hughes. Parker did not decline.)

ELECTION STATISTICS

Popular vote	Wilson	9,129,606
	Hughes	8,538,221
	Hanly	220,506
	Benson	585,113
	Reimer	13,403
	Various candidates	41,894
Electoral vote	Wilson	277
	Hughes	254

States carried (There were 48 states voting in the election.)

Wilson: Alabama, Arizona, California, Arkansas, Colorado, Connecticut, Florida, Georgia, Idaho, Kansas, Kentucky, Louisiana, Maryland, Mississippi, Missouri, Montana, Nebraska, Nevada, New Hampshire, New Mexico, North Carolina, North Dakota, Ohio, Oklahoma, South Carolina, Tennessee, Texas, Utah, Virginia, Washington, 1 from West Virginia, Wyoming

Hughes: Delaware, Illinois, Indiana, Iowa, Maine, Massachusetts, Michigan, Minnesota, New Jersey, New York, Oregon, Pennsylvania, Rhode Island, South Dakota, Vermont, West Virginia (7), Wisconsin

65th Congress	Senate	42 Republicans
		53 Democrats
	House	210 Republicans
		216 Democrats
		1 Progressive
		1 Independent
		1 Socialist
		1 Prohibitionist
		1 Non-Partisan
		1 other

Election of 1918

66th Congress	Senate	49 Republicans
		47 Democrats
	House	240 Republicans
		190 Democrats
		1 Prohibitionist
		2 others

Election of 1920
(Chapter 17)

PRESIDENTIAL AND VICE-PRESIDENTIAL CANDIDATES

Republican	Warren G. Harding, Ohio
	Calvin Coolidge, Massachusetts
Democrat	James M. Cox, Ohio
	Franklin D. Roosevelt, New York
Farmer Labor	Farley P. Christensen, Utah
	Max S. Hayes, Ohio
Socialist	Eugene V. Debs, Indiana
	Seymour Stedman, Illinois

Socialist Labor	William W. Cox, Missouri
	August Gilhaus, New York
Prohibition	Aaron S. Watkins, Ohio
	D. Leigh Colvin, New York
Single Tax	Robert C. Macauley, Pennsylvania
	R. G. Barnum, Ohio
American	James E. Ferguson, Texas

ELECTION STATISTICS

Popular vote	Harding	16,152,200
	James Cox	9,147,353
	Debs	919,799
	William Cox	31,715
	Ferguson	48,000
	Macauley	5,837
	Watkins	189,408
	Christensen	265,411
Electoral vote	Harding	404
	Cox	127

States carried (There were 48 states voting in the election.)

Harding: Arizona, California, Colorado, Connecticut, Delaware, Idaho, Illinois, Indiana, Iowa, Kansas, Maine, Maryland, Massachusetts, Michigan, Minnesota, Missouri, Montana, Nebraska, Nevada, New Hampshire, New Jersey, New Mexico, New York, North Dakota, Ohio, Oklahoma, Oregon, Pennsylvania, Rhode Island, South Dakota, Tennessee, Utah, Vermont, Washington, West Virginia, Wisconsin, Wyoming

Cox: Alabama, Arkansas, Florida, Georgia, Kentucky, Louisiana, Mississippi, North Carolina, South Carolina, Texas, Virginia

67th Congress	Senate	59 Republicans
		37 Democrats
	House	301 Republicans
		131 Democrats
		1 other

Election of 1922

68th Congress Senate 51 Republicans
43 Democrats
2 others

House 225 Republicans
205 Democrats
5 others

Election of 1924
(Chapter 18)

PRESIDENTIAL AND VICE-PRESIDENTIAL CANDIDATES

Republican Calvin Coolidge, Massachusetts
Charles G. Dawes, Illinois

Democrat John W. Davis, West Virginia
Charles W. Bryan, Nebraska

Prohibition Herman P. Faris, Missouri
Miss Marie C. Brehm, California

American Gilbert O. Nations, Missouri
Leander L. Pickett, Kentucky

Commonwealth Land William J. Wallace, New Jersey
J. C. Lincoln, Ohio

Socialist Labor Frank T. Johns, Oregon
Verne L. Reynolds, New York

Workers William Z. Foster, Illinois
Benjamin Gitlow, New York

Progressive   Robert La Follette, Wisconsin
                             Burton K. Wheeler, Montana

ELECTION STATISTICS

Popular vote   Coolidge   15,725,016
                  Davis   8,386,503
                  La Follette   4,822,856
                  Wallace   1,532
                  Nations   23,967
                  Foster   36,386
                  Johns   36,428
                  Faris   57,520

Electoral vote Coolidge   382
                  Davis   136
                  La Follette   13

States carried (There were 48 states voting in the election.)

Coolidge: Arizona, California, Colorado, Connecticut, Dela-
ware, Idaho, Illinois, Indiana, Iowa, Kansas, Kentucky,
Maine, Maryland, Massachusetts, Michigan, Minnesota, Mis-
souri, Montana, Nebraska, Nevada, New Hampshire, New
Jersey, New Mexico, New York, North Dakota, Ohio, Oregon,
Pennsylvania, Rhode Island, South Dakota, Utah, Vermont,
Washington, West Virginia, Wyoming

Davis: Alabama, Arkansas, Florida, Georgia, Louisiana, Mississippi, North Carolina, Oklahoma, South Carolina, Tennessee, Texas, Virginia

La Follette: Wisconsin

69th Congress Senate   56 Republicans
                           39 Democrats
                            1 other

                 House   247 Republicans
                          183 Democrats
                            4 others

Election of 1926

70th Congress   Senate   49 Republicans
                            46 Democrats
                            1 other
                 House   237 Republicans
                          195 Democrats
                            3 others

Election of 1928
(Chapter 19)

PRESIDENTIAL AND VICE-PRESIDENTIAL CANDIDATES

Republican   Herbert Hoover, California
                    Charles Curtis, Kansas

Democrat   Alfred E. Smith, New York
                    Joseph Robinson, Arkansas

Prohibition   William F. Varney, New York
                    James A. Edgerton, Virginia

Workers   William Z. Foster, Illinois
(Communist)   Benjamin Gitlow, New York

Socialist   Norman Thomas, New York
                    James H. Maurer, Pennsylvania

Socialist Labor   Verne L. Reynolds, New York
                    Jeremiah D. Crowley, New York

Farmer Labor   Frank E. Webb, California
                    Andrew B. Nordskog, California

ELECTION STATISTICS

Popular vote Hoover   21,391,381
Smith   15,016,443
Thomas   267,835
Foster   21,181
Reynolds   21,603
Varney   20,106
Webb   6,390

Electoral vote Hoover   444
Smith   87

States carried (There were 48 states voting in the election.)

Hoover: Arizona, California, Colorado, Connecticut, Delaware, Florida, Idaho, Illinois, Indiana, Iowa, Kansas, Kentucky, Maine, Maryland, Michigan, Minnesota, Missouri, Montana, Nebraska, Nevada, New Hampshire, New Jersey, New Mexico, New York, North Carolina, North Dakota, Ohio, Oklahoma, Oregon, Pennsylvania, South Dakota, Tennessee, Texas, Utah, Vermont, Virginia, Washington, West Virginia, Wisconsin, Wyoming

Smith: Alabama, Arkansas, Georgia, Louisiana, Massachusetts, Mississippi, Rhode Island, South Carolina

71st Congress Senate   56 Republicans
39 Democrats
1 other

House   267 Republicans
167 Democrats
1 other

Election of 1930

72nd Congress Senate   48 Republicans
47 Democrats
1 other

House 214 Republicans
220 Democrats
1 other

Election of 1932
(Chapter 20)

PRESIDENTIAL AND VICE-PRESIDENTIAL CANDIDATES

Republican   Herbert Hoover, California
Charles Curtis, Kansas

Democrat   Franklin D. Roosevelt, New York
John N. Garner, Texas

Socialist   Norman Thomas, New York
James H. Maurer, Pennsylvania

Communist   William Z. Foster, Illinois
James Ford, Alabama

Socialist Labor Verne L. Reynolds, New York
John W. Aiken, Massachusetts

Prohibition   William D. Upshaw, Georgia
Frank S. Reagan, Illinois

Liberty   William H. Harvey, Arkansas
Frank B. Hemenway, Washington

Farmer Labor   Jacob S. Coxey, Sr., Ohio

Jobless   The Rev. J. R. Cox, Pennsylvania
Dr. V. C. Tisdal, Oklahoma

ELECTION STATISTICS

Popular vote   Roosevelt   22,821,857
Hoover   15,761,841
Thomas   881,951
Foster   102,785
Reynolds   33,276

Upshaw	81,869
Harvey	53,425
Coxey	7,309
Cox	740

Electoral votes   Roosevelt   472
                    Hoover   59

States carried (There were 48 states voting in the election.)

Roosevelt: Alabama, Arizona, Arkansas, California, Colorado, Florida, Georgia, Idaho, Illinois, Indiana, Iowa, Kansas, Kentucky, Louisiana, Maryland, Massachusetts, Michigan, Minnesota, Mississippi, Missouri, Montana, Nebraska, Nevada, New Jersey, New Mexico, New York, North Carolina, North Dakota, Ohio, Oklahoma, Oregon, Rhode Island, South Carolina, South Dakota, Tennessee, Texas, Utah, Virginia, Washington, West Virginia, Wisconsin, Wyoming

Hoover: Connecticut, Delaware, Maine, New Hampshire, Pennsylvania, Vermont

73rd Congress   Senate   35 Republicans
                            60 Democrats
                             1 other

                  House   117 Republicans
                          310 Democrats
                            5 others

Election of 1934

74th Congress   Senate   25 Republicans
                           69 Democrats
                            1 Progressive
                            1 Farmer Labor

                  House   103 Republicans
                          319 Democrats
                            7 Progressive
                            3 Farmer Labor

Election of 1936
(Chapter 21)

PRESIDENTIAL AND VICE-PRESIDENTIAL CANDIDATES

Republican	Alfred M. Landon, Kansas Frank Knox, Illinois
Democrat	Franklin D. Roosevelt, New York John N. Garner, Texas
Union (also *National Union for Social Justice; 3rd Party; Independent*)	William Lemke, North Dakota Thomas O'Brien, Massachusetts
Socialist	Norman Thomas, New York George O. Nelson, Wisconsin
Prohibition (also endorsed by *Commonwealth*)	Daniel Leigh Colvin, New York Claude A. Watson, California
Socialist Labor (and *Industrial Labor*)	John W. Aiken, Massachusetts Emil F. Teichert, New York
Communist	Earl Browder, Kansas James Ford, Alabama
Greenback (*National*)	John Zahnd, Indiana Florence Garvin, "unknown"

ELECTION STATISTICS

Popular vote		
	Roosevelt	27,751,597
	Landon	16,679,583
	Lemke	882,479
	Aiken	12,777
	Colvin	37,847
	Browder	80,159
	Thomas	187,720

Electoral vote   Roosevelt   523
                    Landon   8

States carried (There were 48 states voting in the election.)

Roosevelt: Alabama, Arizona, Arkansas, California, Colorado, Connecticut, Delaware, Florida, Georgia, Idaho, Illinois, Indiana, Iowa, Kansas, Kentucky, Louisiana, Maryland, Massachusetts, Michigan, Minnesota, Mississippi, Missouri, Montana, Nebraska, Nevada, New Hampshire, New Jersey, New Mexico, New York, North Carolina, North Dakota, Ohio, Oklahoma, Oregon, Pennsylvania, Rhode Island, South Carolina, South Dakota, Tennessee, Texas, Utah, Virginia, Washington, West Virginia, Wisconsin, Wyoming

Landon: Maine, Vermont

75th Congress   Senate   16 Republicans
                             76 Democrats
                              1 Progressive
                              2 Farmer Labor
                              1 Independent Republican

                  House   89 Republicans
                            331 Democrats
                              8 Progressive
                              5 Farmer Labor

Election of 1938

76th Congress   Senate   23 Republicans
                             69 Democrats
                              1 Progressive
                              2 Farmer Labor
                              1 Independent

                  House   164 Republican
                            261 Democrats
                              2 Progressive
                              1 Farmer Labor
                              1 American Labor

Election of 1940
(Chapter 22)

PRESIDENTIAL AND VICE-PRESIDENTIAL CANDIDATES

Republican	Wendell Willkie, Indiana
	Charles L. McNary, Oregon
Democrat	Franklin D. Roosevelt, New York
	Henry A. Wallace, Iowa
Socialist	Norman Thomas, New York
	Maynard C. Kreuger, Illinois
Communist	Earl Browder, Kansas
	James W. Ford, Alabama
Prohibition	Roger W. Babson, Massachusetts
(National Prohibition)	Edgar V. Moorman, Illinois
Socialist Labor	John W. Aiken, Massachusetts
(and *Industrial*	Aaron M. Orange, New York
Government)	
National Greenback	John Zahnd, Indiana
	James E. Yates, Arizona

ELECTION STATISTICS

Popular vote	Roosevelt	27,244,160
	Willkie	22,305,198
	Thomas	99,557
	Babson	57,812
	Browder	46,251
Electoral vote	Roosevelt	449
	Willkie	82

States carried (There were 48 states voting in the election.)

Roosevelt: Alabama, Arizona, Arkansas, California, Connecticut, Delaware, Florida, Georgia, Idaho, Illinois, Kentucky, Louisiana, Maryland, Massachusetts, Minnesota, Mississippi, Missouri, Montana, Nevada, New Hampshire, New Jersey, New Mexico, New York, North Carolina, Ohio, Oklahoma, Oregon, Pennsylvania, Rhode Island, South Carolina, Tennessee, Texas, Utah, Virginia, Washington, West Virginia, Wisconsin, Wyoming

Willkie: Colorado, Indiana, Iowa, Kansas, Maine, Michigan, Nebraska, North Dakota, South Dakota, Vermont

77th Congress	Senate	28 Republicans
		66 Democrats
		1 Progressive
		1 Independent
	House	162 Republicans
		268 Democrats
		3 Progressive
		1 Farmer Labor
		1 American Labor

Election of 1942

78th Congress	Senate	37 Republicans
		58 Democrats
		1 Progressive
	House	208 Republicans
		218 Democrats
		2 Progressive
		1 Farmer Labor
		1 American Labor

Election of 1944
(Chapter 23)

PRESIDENTIAL AND VICE-PRESIDENTIAL CANDIDATES

Republican	Thomas E. Dewey, New York John Bricker, Ohio
Democrat	Franklin D. Roosevelt, New York Harry S. Truman, Missouri
Socialist	Norman Thomas, New York Darlington Hoopes, Pennsylvania
Socialist Labor (*Industrial* *Government*)	Edward A. Teichert, Pennsylvania Alva Albaugh, Ohio
Prohibition	Claude A. Watson, California Andrew Johnson, Kentucky
America First	Gerald L. K. Smith, Michigan Harry Romer, Ohio
Greenback	Dr. Leo C. Donnelly Frank Jeffries
Texas Regulars	Unpledged

ELECTION STATISTICS

Popular vote	Roosevelt	25,602,504
	Dewey	22,006,285
	Thomas	80,518
	Watson	74,758
	Teichert	45,336
	Unpledged	135,439
Electoral vote	Roosevelt	432
	Dewey	99

States carried (There were 48 states voting in the election.)

Roosevelt: Alabama, Arizona, Arkansas, California, Connecticut, Delaware, Florida, Georgia, Idaho, Illinois, Kentucky, Louisiana, Maryland, Massachusetts, Michigan, Minnesota, Mississippi, Missouri, Montana, Nevada, New Hampshire, New Jersey, New Mexico, New York, North Carolina, Oklahoma, Oregon, Pennsylvania, Rhode Island, South Carolina, Tennessee, Texas, Utah, Virginia, Washington, West Virginia

Dewey: Colorado, Indiana, Iowa, Kansas, Maine, Nebraska, North Dakota, Ohio, South Dakota, Vermont, Wisconsin, Wyoming

79th Congress   Senate   38 Republicans
56 Democrats
1 Progressive

House   190 Republicans
242 Democrats
1 Progressive
1 American Labor

Election of 1946

80th Congress   Senate   51 Republicans
45 Democrats

House   245 Republicans
188 Democrats
1 American Labor

Election of 1948
(Chapter 24)

PRESIDENTIAL AND VICE-PRESIDENTIAL CANDIDATES

Republican   Thomas E. Dewey, New York
Earl Warren, California

Democrat	Harry S. Truman, Missouri
	Alben W. Barkley, Kentucky
Progressive	Henry A. Wallace, Iowa
	Glen Taylor, Idaho
Dixiecrat	J. Strom Thurmond, South Carolina
(States' Rights)	Fielding L. Wright, Mississippi
Socialist	Norman Thomas, New York
	Tucker P. Smith, Michigan
Prohibition	Claude H. Watson, California
	Dale H. Learn, "unknown"
Socialist Labor	Edward A. Teichert, Pennsylvania
	Stephen Emery, New York
Socialist Workers	Farrell Dobbs, New York
	Grace Carlson, Minnesota
American Vegetarian	Dr. John Maxwell, Illinois
	Symon Gould, New York
Greenback	John G. Scott, New York
	Granville B. Leeke, "unknown"
Christian Nationalist	Gerald L. K. Smith, Oklahoma
	Harry A. Romer, Ohio

ELECTION STATISTICS

Popular vote	Truman	24,105,812
	Dewey	21,970,065
	Thurmond	1,169,063
	Wallace	1,157,172
	Thomas	139,414
	Watson	103,224
	Teichert	29,244
	Dobbs	13,613
	scattering	3,349
Electoral vote	Truman	303
	Dewey	189
	Thurmond	39

States carried (There were 48 states voting in the election.)

Truman: Arizona, Arkansas, California, Colorado, Florida, Georgia, Idaho, Illinois, Iowa, Kentucky, Massachusetts, Minnesota, Missouri, Montana, Nevada, New Mexico, North Carolina, Ohio, Oklahoma, Rhode Island, Tennessee, Texas, Utah, Virginia, Washington, West Virginia, Wisconsin, Wyoming

Dewey: Connecticut, Delaware, Indiana, Kansas, Maine, Maryland, Michigan, Nebraska, New Hampshire, New Jersey, New York, North Dakota, Oregon, Pennsylvania, South Dakota, Vermont

Thurmond: Alabama, Louisiana, Mississippi, South Carolina, 1 from Tennessee

81st Congress	Senate	42 Republicans
		54 Democrats
	House	171 Republicans
		263 Democrats
		1 American Labor

Election of 1950

82nd Congress	Senate	47 Republicans
		49 Democrats
	House	199 Republicans
		234 Democrats
		1 Independent

Election of 1952
(Chapter 25)

PRESIDENTIAL AND VICE-PRESIDENTIAL CANDIDATES

Republican   Dwight D. Eisenhower, New York
                                Richard M. Nixon, California

| Democrat | Adlai Stevenson, Illinois |
| | Richard Russell, Georgia |

| Progressive | Vincent Hallinan, California |
| | Charlotta Bass, New York |

| Prohibition | Stuart Hamblen, California |
| | Enoch A. Holtwick, Illinois |

| Socialist Labor | Eric Hass, New York |
| | Stephen Emery, New York |

| Socialist | Darlington Hoopes, Pennsylvania |
| | Samuel H. Friedman, New York |

| Socialist Workers | Farrell Dobbs, New York |
| | Myra Tanner Weiss, California |

| Poor Man's Party | Henry B. Krajewski, New Jersey |
| | Frank Jenkins, New Jersey |

| Christian Nationalist | Douglas MacArthur, New York |
| | Jack B. Tenney, California |

| Constitution | Douglas MacArthur, New York |
| | Vivien Kellems, Connecticut |

| America First | Douglas MacArthur, New York |
| | Harry Flood Byrd, Virginia |

ELECTION STATISTICS

Popular vote	Eisenhower	33,936,234
	Stevenson	27,314,992
	Hallinan	140,023
	Hamblen	72,949
	Hass	30,267
	Hoopes	20,203
	Dobbs	10,312
	Krajewski	4,203
	MacArthur	17,205
	scattered votes	4,530

| Electoral vote | Eisenhower | 442 |
| | Stevenson | 89 |

States carried (There were 48 states voting in the election.)

Eisenhower: Arizona, California, Colorado, Connecticut, Delaware, Florida, Idaho, Illinois, Indiana, Iowa, Kansas, Maine, Maryland, Massachusetts, Michigan, Minnesota, Missouri, Montana, Nebraska, Nevada, New Hampshire, New Jersey, New Mexico, New York, North Dakota, Ohio, Oklahoma, Oregon, Pennsylvania, Rhode Island, South Dakota, Tennessee, Texas, Utah, Vermont, Virginia, Washington, Wisconsin, Wyoming

Stevenson: Alabama, Arkansas, Georgia, Kentucky, Louisiana, Mississippi, North Carolina, South Carolina, West Virginia

83rd Congress	Senate	48 Republicans
		47 Democrats
		1 Independent
	House	221 Republicans
		211 Democrats
		1 Independent

Election of 1954

84th Congress	Senate	47 Republicans
		48 Democrats
		1 Independent
	House	203 Republicans
		232 Democrats

Election of 1956
(Chapter 26)

PRESIDENTIAL AND VICE-PRESIDENTIAL CANDIDATES

Republican   Dwight D. Eisenhower, Pennsylvania
                      Richard M. Nixon, California

Democrat	Adlai E. Stevenson, Illinois Estes Kefauver, Tennessee
Prohibition	Enoch A. Holtwick, Illinois Edwin M. Cooper, "unknown"
Socialist Labor	Eric Hass, New York Georgia Cozzini, Wisconsin
Socialist Workers	Farrell Dobbs, New York Myra Tanner Weiss, California
American Third Party (*Poor Man's Party*)	Henry B. Krajewski, New Jersey Anne Marie Yezo, New Jersey
Socialist	Darlington Hoopes, Pennsylvania Samuel H. Friedman, New York
States' Rights	T. Coleman Andrews, Virginia Thomas H. Werdel, California
Pioneer Party	William Langer, North Dakota Burr McCloskey, Illinois
Greenback	Fred C. Proehl, Washington
Texas Constitution	William E. Jenner, Indiana J. Bracken Lee, Utah

ELECTION STATISTICS

Popular vote		
	Eisenhower	35,590,472
	Stevenson	26,029,752
	Holtwick	41,937
	Hoopes	2,044
	Hass	44,300
	Dobbs	7,797
	Krajewski	1,829

(In addition to the above, 196,318 votes were cast in Alabama, Louisiana, Mississippi, and South Carolina for Independent and States' Rights electors not officially pledged to any candidate; 2657 votes were cast in Kentucky for a states' rights ticket pledged to Senators Harry Flood Byrd and William E. Jenner, neither of whom was a candidate there; 8,865 scattered votes were also reported in various states.)

Electoral vote   Eisenhower   457
                    Stevenson   73

States carried (There were 48 states voting in the election.)

Eisenhower: Arizona, California, Colorado, Connecticut, Delaware, Florida, Idaho, Illinois, Indiana, Iowa, Kansas, Kentucky, Louisiana, Maine, Maryland, Massachusetts, Michigan, Minnesota, Montana, Nebraska, Nevada, New Hampshire, New Jersey, New Mexico, New York, North Dakota, Ohio, Oklahoma, Oregon, Pennsylvania, Rhode Island, South Dakota, Tennessee, Texas, Utah, Vermont, Virginia, Washington, West Virginia, Wisconsin, Wyoming

Stevenson: Alabama (less 1 vote cast for independent candidate), Arkansas, Georgia, Mississippi, Missouri, North Carolina, South Carolina

85th Congress   Senate   47 Republicans
                            49 Democrats

                  House   200 Republicans
                           233 Democrats

Election of 1958

86th Congress   Senate   34 Republicans
                            64 Democrats

                  House   152 Republicans
                           282 Democrats

Index

M